Seeking the Truth from Mobile Evidence

Seeking the Truth from Mobile Evidence

Basic Fundamentals, Intermediate and Advanced Overview of Current Mobile Forensic Investigations

John Bair
(Police Detective: City of Tacoma, WA)
Part-Time Lecturer: Institute of Technology,
University of Washington-Tacoma, WA, United States

ACADEMIC PRESS

An imprint of Elsevier

Academic Press is an imprint of Elsevier
125 London Wall, London EC2Y 5AS, United Kingdom
525 B Street, Suite 1800, San Diego, CA 92101-4495, United States
50 Hampshire Street, 5th Floor, Cambridge, MA 02139, United States
The Boulevard, Langford Lane, Kidlington, Oxford OX5 1GB, United Kingdom

Notices
Knowledge and best practice in this field are constantly changing. As new research and experience broaden our understanding, changes in research methods, professional practices, or medical treatment may become necessary.

Practitioners and researchers must always rely on their own experience and knowledge in evaluating and using any information, methods, compounds, or experiments described herein. In using such information or methods they should be mindful of their own safety and the safety of others, including parties for whom they have a professional responsibility.

To the fullest extent of the law, neither the Publisher nor the authors, contributors, or editors, assume any liability for any injury and/or damage to persons or property as a matter of products liability, negligence or otherwise, or from any use or operation of any methods, products, instructions, or ideas contained in the material herein.

Library of Congress Cataloging-in-Publication Data
A catalog record for this book is available from the Library of Congress

British Library Cataloguing-in-Publication Data
A catalogue record for this book is available from the British Library

ISBN: 978-0-12-811056-0

For information on all Academic Press publications visit our website at
https://www.elsevier.com/books-and-journals

Working together
to grow libraries in
developing countries

www.elsevier.com • www.bookaid.org

Publisher: Mica Haley
Acquisition Editor: Elizabeth Brown
Editorial Project Manager: Sam W. Young
Production Project Manager: Poulouse Joseph
Designer: Victoria Pearson

Typeset by TNQ Books and Journals

Cover designed by John Bair & Lisa Taylor

This book is dedicated to the thousands of men and women in law enforcement who spend a magnitude of hours each year sifting through electronic evidence. You may be underappreciated, overlooked, and go unrecognized. The job may require locating media of innocent children or others who are being victimized, or exploited. There may be expectations on what you can and cannot locate, and a chain of command whom you struggle with for the logistics needed in your job. I truly appreciate your efforts. I dedicate this book to each of you.

Contents

Foreword

Mobile devices and the rich data associated with them have become the single most important source of evidence in virtually every type of investigation. These data commonly include the information stored on removable media and data from backups, installed applications, and the records retained by service providers. Whether the information is being relied on in a corporate environment to protect intellectual property or in civil law to resolve disputes and provide accountability or as part of a criminal investigation to determine guilt or innocence, the reason for examining mobile device evidence is the same—to find important and reliable information that can be used in proper context to help the finders of fact make important decisions.

In *Seeking the Truth from Mobile Evidence*, John Bair has carefully and thoroughly laid out important foundational concepts, troubleshooting strategies, helpful hints, and expanded analysis considerations. He has also provided suggestions and methods to help practitioners verify and test findings and build trust in the evidence and examination process. While this book is primarily directed toward law enforcement mobile device forensics practitioners, it includes valuable information for anyone who will benefit from an improved knowledge of how and why data associated with mobile devices can be acquired, analyzed, and explained.

Like me, John Bair began his nearly three-decade long career in law enforcement at a time when cell phones, tablets, personal computers, digital cameras, cloud storage, "Apps," and the Internet had not yet penetrated our lives. We wrote police reports with pencils and paper, we looked up information in books, we exchanged information by printed interoffice memos, and we made telephone calls using hardwired telephones. As the digital world began infiltrating the real world and criminals began using the same technology to gain an advantage and facilitate their crimes, John was one of the early pioneers in police work who led the way to "figure this stuff out." As a lifelong learner, John adapted his practice of criminal investigation along with his knack for problem-solving and reverse engineering to leverage mobile device technology and find important evidence. John was not willing to allow important evidence to be locked away and remain unused.

Anyone who knows John quickly realizes that mobile device forensics is not simply a part of his job—it's his passion. John is an amazingly talented, humble, and generous forensic practitioner who is quick to share his skills, knowledge, research, and experience to help anyone who is seeking the truth. He has always been on the cutting edge of the newest methods without losing sight of the basics. Just as he has done in this book, John has the rare ability to explain complex technical issues. Through the use of examples from his extensive experience, John is able to bring important and meaningful information to levels appropriate for his audience—novice to advanced. He has trained, mentored, and coached countless students of mobile forensics both inside and outside the criminal justice community.

John has written agency policies and crafted technical guidelines, and he has testified extensively in State and Federal courts as an expert witness in mobile device forensics. While some began as reluctant students, John has educated numerous police officers, detectives, prosecutors, defense attorneys, judges, academics, and product developers. As a truly legitimate and committed mobile device "forensic" practitioner, John is obsessed with finding ways to validate, verify, retest, and prove his findings before he is willing to settle on a particular method or outcome. John recognizes and teaches others that the data in themselves are of no value unless they can be trusted and the process replicated. Throughout this book, you will find references to validation and verification that are important for any practitioner for producing defendable and reliable results.

In addition to the great depth of real-world and practical experience that John brings to the subject of criminal investigation, mobile device forensics, and data analysis, he uses easily relatable stories, scenarios, and anecdotes throughout this book to explain important concepts. These examples give relevance and context that help the reader better understand the "why" and "how." I have found John's examples useful during my own efforts to craft language for affidavits in support of search warrants; when writing forensic reports; during expert testimony; and when explaining sometimes highly technical concepts to jurors, lawyers, judges, and law enforcement colleagues.

I must admit that I am an old school guy. I prefer printed books that I can hold in my hand and pages I can flip through. I also generally like the content to be in one place. That said this book uses a Companion Site where expanded content for each chapter can be viewed. John has done an excellent job adding helpful screenshots and other content that add additional value to his book. While I was initially skeptical, I think it is very well suited for books like this one and I value having the additional material.

The field of digital forensics, and in particular mobile device forensics, is dynamic and challenging. Each day brings new device models, new operating system versions, new and changing applications, greater storage capacities, new and changing methods of storage, backups, and the frustration that come with locked screens and encryption. While automated commercial forensic tools are very valuable, John emphasizes how important it is for mobile device forensic practitioners to have the ability to know what these tools are not revealing and how these tools and methods may change, not read, or misread user data. Through this book,

John Bair will prepare you for a journey to improve your own practice and he will arm you with a technical knowledge and deeper understanding of mobile device forensics.

For those in law enforcement, you know that there is no greater satisfaction than to protect the weak, get justice for the innocent, and to hold bad actors accountable. This is particularly true in cases involving child sexual exploitation. While advances in technology have brought us greater opportunities to do our jobs, technology has also brought greater threats to civilized societies as well as more opportunities for suspect anonymity, expanded jurisdictional complexities, reduced cooperation from content service providers, and an increased public distrust and scrutiny of the government. As we move forward together, it's critical that we work to proactively influence new legislation, strive to not create adverse case law, maintain and improve examiner certifications and training, and lead the way for laboratory accreditation and policies in ways that build trust and confidence in our methods and practices. John Bair has worked throughout his career to become a model for best practices, and this book is a guide to help other mobile device forensic practitioners lay down a solid foundation for the future.

Colin Fagan, CFCE, CCME
Detective Sergeant
Digital Evidence Forensic Examiner
July 2017

Preface

It was raining (again). I had traveled from a hot and dry Texas climate to an area that in the first year, I could not seem to get my toes warm. I was now closer to my family and supposedly working for a department that had less crime than El Paso. So far, I had not seen proof of it. I sat alone and sipped on coffee in a park located in an area they called the "Hilltop." The police radio was silent, as it should be for 0415 h on a Tuesday morning. It was September 1993. I had passed my probation period and sat alone in a marked police car. In the next 6 years that followed in my career, I would have no idea that I would be involved in two officer-involved shootings, the latter nearly killing me.

Out of the corner of my eye I watched a dark figure emerge from the south. Whoever he was, he was tall and had a pronounced limp. His left leg did not bend at the knee, and to travel he brought the leg around from behind him, in a small semicircle stride. My window was down, and I was parked under an overhang of a nearby building, trying to stay dry. I could hear that he was talking to himself. I continued to watch him, and as he moved closer, I could see that he was an older male in his late 50s. His conversation turned to singing. He was directly in front of where I was parked, maybe 50 ft away.

He was now under a street lamp that produced glare of reflective light off the top of a piece of metal coming from his silhouette. I could not see the item entirely, but it was sticking out from his left side. The metal was large and seemed to be even with his head. Whatever the metal was, it caught my attention, and I turned on my patrol spotlight and shined it directly at him. He jumped and stopped in his tracks, completely startled. It occurred to me that he had never seen my marked police car until that moment. Through the assistance from the spotlight illumination, I could now see why he was limping. I dumped my coffee out the window and started my patrol car.

I turned on my emergency lights as I pulled the police car closer to him. The man never moved, except to extend his arm to block his eyes from the spotlight. I exited the car and asked him to place his hands up, and onto his head. He complied. I had radioed for assistance, and after they arrived, I placed him in handcuffs. Once he was secured, I removed a large sword that was sticking down his left pant leg. It had extended up nearly another 3 ft above his waist to his head. In all, the sword was over 6 ft in length and probably weighed 20 pounds.

The rain continued to fall, and all of us were getting wet during this contact. He never spoke while I removed this item from his pants. While the instrument he was carrying was being admired by my backup officers, I asked him, "What's up with the sword you're carrying around?" He quickly replied, *"These aren't my pants."*

I no longer drive a marked police vehicle, instead an unmarked, underpowered, "detective" vehicle. My hair has turned from brown to gray. I have incurred a few injuries, a skull fracture, and one neck surgery. My oldest child has a child of her own. I no longer patrol city streets while everyone else sleeps. I have been a detective now since April 1999. During my assignment in the homicide unit I noticed gang members were carrying around devices called Nextel's. That gave me an idea to try and learn something about how they functioned and what could be stored on them.

Now our world has fully embraced technology. So too the individuals who have chosen to commit criminal acts. Understanding just a little bit about our electronic items we all carry around with us can certainly help aid in solving crimes. It's September 2017. Now, the "clients" I contact during my course of digital investigations have changed their statement from, *"These aren't my pants"* to: *"That's not my phone."*

Thank you for buying this book. My hope, like the title implies, is that it can help you locate the truth in **your** digital mobile investigations.

John Bair

Acknowledgment

I would like to thank Mike Smith who I first met at the University of Washington, Tacoma (UWT). Mike is a combat veteran, and when I met Mike, he was senior in the IT program attending my Digital Mobile Forensic (level I) course. Mike excelled during the course, as well as the next two. After his graduation, he was hired by UWT to work in their IT department. We stayed in touch, and since Mike had a great understanding of the course content, he was hired to help with the initial editing of this book. Without his help, I am not certain if this would have ever been finished on time.

Another couple of individuals who need acknowledgment also come from the academia field: Professors Robert Friedman and Bryan Goda. I called Robert in the fall of 2013 and asked if I could have a few minutes of his time to present an idea. Robert allowed me to present the concept of creating a lab that was modeled after the Marshal University in Virginia. A few months later I was presenting the first Mobile Forensics course as a beta class at the Tacoma branch of the University of Washington. Since then, Robert has moved to another university, and Professor Bryan Goda took over where Robert left off. Bryan has allowed me to introduce advanced tools, concepts, and methodologies to senior students in the IT program at the Institute of Technology. Bryan continues to invest in new toys for our classes; most importantly, he believes in what I do and treats me as an asset. I appreciate their willingness to create this program, and all the logistical support along the way.

Of course, there is my spouse that I had to neglect in some way or another over the past couple of years. Thank you for being so patient with me. Sorry the fence (and deck) was never painted, the weeds were not pulled, and the garage looks like a Sanford and Sons episode. Like many other people who write books, I would never been able to finish if you were not around to love and support me. You always provided assistance simply by listening, even when I was boring you to tears most of the time.

Then there is my Dad. He will never be able to read this book, but he was certainly alive with me as a kid when I was testing for continuity, soldering, stripped wires, and performing hundreds of other tasks related to electronics. He was the type of person who had trouble conveying such short sentences or one liners as, "I love you, thanks, and sorry." He made all seven of his kids as they were growing up work in some capacity or another. Some of us worked on a 300+ acre farm, which he had as a "hobby" while he was employed full time for Mountain Bell Telephone. (How ironic that he spliced phone lines for 44 years, and his youngest child now performs mobile forensics) I thought for years that all this man knew from life, was how to work. Embedded and tangled into all that labor; he taught me things that carry me into what I do and utterly love now. How do I thank a person who has died, but influenced me so much? The answer I guess is to *share* with others. Just like the old saying: "*It's not what you know in life, but what you share.*"

Last, are my children. At the time I wrote this book, two of you were out in the world living on your own. All of you have given me some great memories over the past 25+ years. I have learned (and continue to learn) about patience, sacrifice, and unconditional love. Thank you for (sometimes) listening to me—and also the few times when you decided not to. Hopefully all of you will remember us riding our bikes, lighting off fireworks, the back yard swimming pool(s), the camping trips that include building our Big Ass Fires (BAFs we called them), road trips to Idaho, and most of all, the laugher. I know you didn't have a choice in the matter, but thanks anyways for being great children. The three of you will always be my greatest accomplishment in this short life.

Introduction

Introduction–The Multitool

Two individuals employed in the military were having domestic issues. Partner A wanted to break up with partner B. Partner B refused to terminate their relationship and began arguing with A. Their argument turn violent and B stabbed A in the neck with a Leatherman multitool. B initially refused to allow A to seek medical treatment, and took images (with his cell phone) while he was bleeding. B informed A that after he dies, he would dismember his body, and dispose of him of various dumpsters. A couple hours later, B drops A off at the hospital. A initially does not inform hospital personnel the correct information on how his injuries occurred, and he slips into a coma. B refuses to provide law enforcement a statement about the incident. Both A and B have the first generation HTC G1 Android phones. They have pattern locks across the screen, and at the time of this investigation, there was no commercially available forensic tool that could bypass this security.

The Sex Offender

He left school at 14 years age. Soon, he was being reported as a runaway and found comfort with others who would "crash" at an abandoned house. He learned about various street drugs and how to steal Honda Civics. For a number of years, he was in and out of juvenile detention for several offenses. As he entered into his adult life, his *friends* were always younger kids, usually half his age. Many times, the friendships would lead to various games that he had invented. Most of them were inappropriate. One of the parents of a child he was "friends" with called the police about his behavior. He decides to delete the application he used to communicate with the victim, and also deletes all the incriminating images that he shared. Again, he ends up in jail. This time accused of several sexual offenses with a minor child.

The Last Argument

She was married just a few months before her death. Her husband took her life and then his own. Her phone was triaged through a forensic tool commonly used by law enforcement.

The initial investigation located two short recordings that documented arguments they had been having. She had recorded them without his knowledge, just days prior to their bodies being discovered. After the phone was triaged, the case agent reviewed the case report (media disk). He called the examiner back a few days later. "I believe there's another large file on her phone that recorded the events that took place at her death. Can you try to get it to play?" The file had initially been "looked over" and dismissed as a corrupt, unplayable sound file. Per the request of the case agent, the file was viewed with additional scrutiny. Using a hex editor, it was found that the file header and footer were missing, but the case agent may be correct; based on the size of the file, and the time and date of its creation, she probably did record her own death.

The Drug Dealer

A missing suspected drug dealer was located, murdered. His lower torso was recovered, buried, and contained inside a duffle bag. His cellular phone had absorbed his human fluids as he had decomposed over a few mouths. Local law enforcement cleaned the device and again connected it to common forensic tools to perform a data extraction. The extraction would start, and then fail. After numerous troubleshooting steps, they still could not gain entry into the device. Although they had cleaned it, the main board was still black from his bodily fluids. The device was supported by commercial forensic tools for user security bypass, but that was not the problem. They obviously needed a different technique to locate what was needed in their case, and glean insight into who may have communicated with him before his disappearance.

Truth Is Not Pretty

These summaries were just some of the small snippets from the author's experience when it comes to triaging mobile evidence. Each of them came into the laboratory with something missing—*answers*. In these examples, the author was eventually able to locate what was being requested. Some of the cases were from the author's own department, and others were from outside agencies where he provided technical assistance. There are times when finding the answer can help add another layer to the story. There are times when the answer helps the public understand a traumatic event with precise clarity. Then there are times when no one seems to give much regards to the truth. A drug dealer? A prostitute? Many in society may not admit that they feel little to no remorse when it comes to specific victims of certain types of crimes having a tragic ending to their life. Locating the *truth* within an investigation does not necessarily mean that it can be solved. There are times when investigators know exactly who the primary suspect or suspects are. Truth does not necessarily incarcerate someone.

As we hear more horrific events unfold that involve mass causalities, one of the common things we hear being asked at work, dinner parties, and family get-togethers is the *why* question. People want to know what goes through the mind of a person, and why they acted a certain way. Why did he stab his domestic partner and took images of him while he was bleeding, or why the sex offender wanted to victimize little kids, or why a man must kill his wife and himself, or why one drug dealer kills and dismembers a fellow drug dealer? These investigations, like yours, have a *why* that must be answered to society. It is incumbent on you to gain enough knowledge to get the task accomplished. If your job focuses on locating these answers from mobile evidence, this book was created to help you.

Book Layout—The Companion Site

Seeking the Truth from Mobile Evidence has been written to allow the reader to see specific steps, program interfaces, techniques, equipment, and overall forensic methods. The author wants the reader to understand the subject materials being conveyed in each chapter. As such, the publisher strives to keep production costs down. This effort has been awarded back to the consumer, and instead of a book costing over hundreds of dollars, it is a third of that cost. Why is this being conveyed to you? As you read several of the chapters, you will encounter instructions directing the reader to images stored on the (included) companion site. There will be a few chapters (Chapters 1, 3, 12, 13, 17, and 29) that do not have references to images found on the companion site. Some of the chapters will also have additional documents such as PDF files that will be contained on the companion site (https://www.elsevier.com/books-and-journals/book-companion/9780128110560). These can assist the reader with supplemental information related to the topic in the chapter they are contained in.

Readers can utilize the (above) link to navigate to the figures, and extra materials on the companion site. On the site, click on the, "Chapter Figures" under Quick Links. The affected chapters are highlighted accordingly. Simply click on the desired chapter to begin the process of downloading a zipped folder for the items listed in the narrative of that chapter. If readers elect to do so, all the materials can be downloaded prior to reading each chapter to allow quicker reference.

Initially, the author was skeptical about the use of the companion site, as it seemed to take the "flow" away from what was trying to be conveyed. But this is obviously not a novel and should be used as a reference guide for your cases. From a learning and direction point of view however, it also certainly added additional value and aided in the overall objective. The printed book has approximately 200 black-and-white images, while the eBook version has the same images in color. Students, private investigators, corporate forensic investigators, prosecutors, and judicial officers can benefit in using this book. The main target audience is law enforcement personnel. The point of view of the author is derived from an active commissioned police officer (Detective), with over 28 years of experience and hundreds of actual forensic examinations.

Fundamental Concepts

Part 1—Chapters 1–12 deal with the investigative (forensic) foundation. Readers will begin with understanding the types of mobile forensic examinations, what causes contamination, and how to properly prevent altering evidence. They continue with the legal process, an understanding of how mobile network and virtual network operators work, and suggestions on search warrant language. The cellular network, subscriber identity module, and device identifications are also explained. Part 1 concludes with how to properly triage mobile evidence that is on and off, the logical examination, troubleshooting, manual examinations, and report writing. At the end of Part 1 the reader should have a good understanding of the core elements needed for basic, mobile evidence investigations.

Intermediate Concepts

Part 2—Chapters 13–18 provide the reader with more knowledge related to the physical examination, and the various encoding types located on mobile evidence. These chapters expand on the composition of the NAND and NOR memory. They address date/time stamp epochs and integer formats. How application and MMS data may be missed by forensic tools but decoded manually. Techniques are provided on how to perform advanced validation. By the end of Part 2, readers should have an understanding on how physical encoding will appear, various time stamps and their decoding, manual decoding MMS missed by tools, decoding application data, and how to conduct and testify on advanced validation.

Advanced Concepts

Part 3—The remaining Chapters 19–30 take the reader through advanced techniques that are nondestructive, and destructive. They start by addressing Android and iPhone user enabled security. Readers will understand how to manually decode the gesture pattern and create their own SHA-1 values that they decode with a rainbow table. Several commercial exploit tools are explained that allow the user to locate user enabled passcodes on specific Android and iPhones. They are introduced to the Joint Test Action Group (JTAG) concepts, specialized tools, and specific hardware-based tools that can be used for the JTAG acquisition. This expands into popular JTAG boxes and how to use them. Chapter 21 addresses phone disassembly and focuses on repairing water-damaged phones. The last few chapters cover destructive techniques. Thermal and nonthermal concepts are explained, which include milling and "lap and polishing" techniques. The reader will understand how to perform both types of chip-off processing, as well as how to read the chip after it has been prepared, and steps on how to create a forensic image. Regular expressions are briefly introduced and numerous examples are provided. At the end of the book, the reader is exposed to eMMC reading and the In-System Programming examination.

Summary

The goal of this book is to educate readers on various steps they can employ to locate artifacts (off mobile evidence) they may have missed in the past. Years of practical examination experience on violent cases, courtroom testimony, forensic tool experience, as well work at the University of Washington's Institute of Technology, assisted in the creation of this book. During the judicial process, the author has been referred to as an "expert." The author has always been uncomfortable with the word *expert*. This implies that a person has *"authoritative knowledge"* over _____ (you fill in the blank).

Digital forensics, just like mobile phones, changes very rapidly. Just when you think you know something, *you don't*. There are several techniques, tools, and methods that the reader will be exposed to within this book. By no means does this equate to expert advice. Imagine a coworker who works with you, whom you approach from time to time, for help. For some of you, you may need to imagine someone working somewhere else, but you respect and admire whoever this person is in your mind. He/she has a couple tidbits of information on occasion that seems to assist you with your digital forensic work. There is no magic in what he/she tells you, and he/she provides suggestions you may have not thought of. Any advice he/she renders seems to complement something that already works well for you. That is how you should think of the author who wrote this book—a friendly coworker who wants to offer suggestions. Your equal who may help you catch the bad guys or assist in locating answers for your employer. He would be offended if someone called him an expert. A nerd maybe, but not an expert.

Basic, Fundamental Concepts

CHAPTER 1

Defining Cell Phone Forensics and Standards

Information in This Chapter

- Defining cell phone forensics
- Recovering
- Data
- Logical data
- File system
- Physical data
- Validating
- Standards
- National Institute of Standards and Training (NIST)

Introduction

What is *Cell Phone Forensics*? Before we begin to answer this question, let us briefly address how the general public has recently begun to learn more about this field. At the time that this book was being written, many people who may have been uninterested in mobile forensics have learned aspects about this practice by reading about how the Federal Bureau of Investigation (FBI) and Apple had conflicting views on how to recover data from a suspected terrorist's iPhone. An outside entity ultimately assisted in the case and was able to defeat user-enabled security and allow a forensic search to be conducted. There are many moving parts that are involved in that case, and it can be boiled down to the protection of user data weighing heavily in balance with due process. However, the purpose of this book is not to address those issues. During that particular period of unresolved issues between the FBI and Apple, more individuals asked the author's opinion (about the case) than during any other criminal investigation he had been involved with up to that date. Some begin understanding a few of the elements that are involved with mobile forensics. Because of the nature of the terrorism case, people would actually want to hear more details than *normal* about this field. They would express valid points from both sides of the argument. The author would normally have "light-hearted" conversations with acquaintances regarding work. Now, they were now bringing up elements that dealt directly into their constitutional rights. Oftentimes the conversation led to answering the question that was posed at the start of this chapter.

Defining Cell Phone Forensics

Cell Phone Forensics is the process of **recovering** cellular-related **data** through a forensic examination using **validated** means. To understand this, we must expand on the three key words that have been used in this definition.

Recovering

To recover data, we must first actually have an incident in which the need has arisen to obtain the specific artifacts. For law enforcement, this will generally originate from an actual crime that has occurred. In the private sector, this could be a breach of network security or a financial loss. Within the elements of the case itself, there would be a mobile device that contains potential evidence related to the crime or incident. The key element that is necessary to *recover* potential data is the legal process. The legal process and its requirements are addressed in chapters 3 and 4. Once the legal process is met, the acquisition of the device can take place. In short, the ability to begin "recovering" data is tied to obtaining the legal process.

Data

The actual artifacts that are located on mobile devices are categorized as logical and physical. Logical data is easy to understand. Within the target device, it can be viewed through the graphical user interface (GUI). For example, this may be a stored image, text message content, or a phone book contact. Vendors who sell mobile phones often invest in features that complement the user's ability to use, manage, and interact with logical data. This will include the camera, sending and receiving messages, navigational assistance, and web browsing, to name a few.

Logical data will not require special tools, programs, or training to interpret. It will usually have its own story to tell. This is what most prosecutors will want to introduce to the jury. Fig. 1.1 depicts logical data as commonly viewed through the screen of a flip phone. This is a (redacted) short message service (SMS) that simply indicates "Hello" as the content. The entire message with the date and time it was sent can logically be viewed by scrolling down within the screen. This message would be stored in a particular encoded fashion within the memory of this device. We will explain encoding in a later chapter, but for now let us understand that this message was created by the user. Without actually knowing it, this same user of the device turned on a series of bytes that in turn were encoded by the operating system (OS). These bytes then displayed on the GUI so that it could be understood by the user. All this was going on inside the phone's memory with little to no thought of how it all works.

Physical data can be defined as the composition of logical data. These are the "ingredients" that make up what the user may be viewing or *may* have once seen, as in the case where the data have been deleted. Here is an example. Pretend for a minute that you are a bad guy. You and another bad guy have conspired to murder other individuals. The murder was committed using firearms. The (two) victim's bodies were to be disposed of in a city landfill. Your coconspirator has a phone number of 12536065884. Your phone number is the same number that was used as the example in the top image in Fig. 1.1—"TO": *514-5* (redacted). You send a message about this offense to your bad guy friend, but after it is sent, you delete it. Logically no one can see the message when they look in the *"Sent"* folder of the phone. Physically, however, an examiner could locate the message if certain circumstances were present within the file system. Using the values of the physical encoding, an examiner searches for the bad guy's number, 2536065884, within the binary. The deleted message is located. Using special programs, the entire message can now be read.

At the bottom of Fig. 1.1 is an example of physical data related to this example. Later, we will explain much more about physical data, types of encoding, interpreting timestamps, and additional elements related to this example.

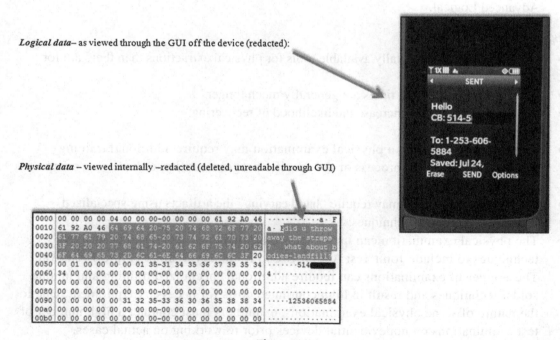

Figure 1.1
Example of logical data: short message service (SMS) sent message *"Hello"* and physical data example: deleted SMS related to homicide.

There are some things to remember about logical and physical data. Here are two lists that separate some of the main points of both data types.

Logical Data
- Data may be limited and generally do not contain deleted artifacts.
- It usually requires some form of application program interface or a specific agent to pull the requested information off the target mobile device.
- Logical data can easily be interpreted, needing no specific training or programs.
- The data is more often used in court or judicial proceedings to illustrate a theory, corroborate the incident or a particular statement, or stand alone as evidence.
- The most commonly requested logical data related to mobile forensics is SMS or multimedia message service (MMS) content, followed by images. There is of course additional logical data increasingly being sought. This will generally be based on the supported device and will include but is not limited to contacts, call history, chats, videos, web history, bookmarks, Global Positioning System artifacts, and user-installed applications.
- Some of the examples of logical data extractions that can be obtained with both open-source and commercial forensic programs include file system, Android backups, and Advanced Logical.

Physical Data
- There are less commercially available tools for physical extractions than there are for logical extractions.
- Examination processing times are generally much longer.
- Physical examinations increase the likelihood of recovering deleted data.
- The person performing a physical examination may require additional training related to the forensic process or the specific program, utility, or hardware being utilized.
- Decoding of some data may require "hand carving" the artifacts using specialized programs and search techniques.
- The physical examination can include advanced nondestructive and destructive techniques to include Joint Test Action Group Boundary Scan or chip-off removal. These types of examinations can require additional specialized training and unique solder techniques and result in high continued costs for necessary equipment. Due to the nature of some physical examinations, examiners must conduct a high number of test examinations on nonevidential devices prior to working on actual cases.

Validating

Our last key word in defining Cell Phone Forensics is the process of validation. If we were to place importance on any of the three key words in our definition, validation carries the most weight. It is often the most overlooked part of the forensic process. We will briefly discuss the aspects of validation as it pertains to our definition and expand on this in Chapter 18: Advanced Validation.

Many individuals who have attended mobile forensics training are generally excited about using their specialized equipment or practicing a technique that has been introduced to them. They quickly learn the idiosyncrasies of the program or hardware, pulling incriminating evidence off the phone used in a violent crime. Their supervisor, case agents, or prosecutors are quite pleased with the compelling results.

What may come next are the rigors of the judicial process. They are asked about their validation techniques. This may include a combination of areas to include a program, a utility, or a unique hardware solution. It may simply be the content of an SMS message or if the phone clock reflects the proper time zone, which may show as Coordinated Universal Time on the report created by the commercial forensic tool.

There are generally four ways in which data that is acquired off mobile devices during the forensic acquisition can be validated.

Visual Validation

During visual validation, the examiner is simply utilizing the GUI of the device to confirm what the tool is reporting. If we revisit our previous SMS message from our logical data example, utilize a common commercial forensic tool to pull the data, and then compare the results visually on the GUI of the phone, we have conducted a *visual* validation as pictured at the top of Fig. 1.1.

The process of conducting a **Visual Validation** can be time consuming. This will be especially true when the case involved data acquired from a smartphone. There will be times when visual confirmation is used in conjunction with another form of validation. Visual validation, should at a minimum, be conducted in nearly every case when it is possible. Later in this book the reader will discover incidents where the phone may be damaged or a destructive technique is required such as removing the memory off the main board. Visual validation may not apply in those circumstances. Fig. 1.2 is an example of visual validation. The left image is of the GUI of the phone, and the right image would be from what a logical acquisition tool would report.

GUI of screen (redacted) Logical tool report (redacted)

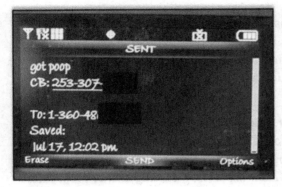 

Visual Validation

Figure 1.2
Example of visual validation.

Cross Tool

Examiners may utilize more than one forensic tool, utility, program, etc., to confirm stored data off a targeted mobile device. Some agencies or private entities may only have one or two forensic tools in their laboratories due to budgetary constraints. There may, however, be a secondary *open-source* tool that is available to support the target phone. The use of one product to confirm the findings of another is **cross tool validation**.

Our example in Fig. 1.3 provides validation from the results of one SMS entry using two free utilities: AccessData's Forensic Tool Kit (FTK) Imager and an open-source tool called *BitPim*. In this example, we can see that both products are reporting the same type of message (outbox), with the same date, time, and content of the message. Of course, the dates and times need to be manually decoded, which we will discuss in a later chapter. In this example, the content of the message regarding drugs (*got poop*) is highlighted.

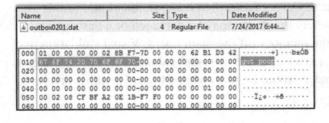 

Cross-Tool Validation

Figure 1.3
Forensic Tool Kit Imager (left) and BitPim (right) cross tool validation example.

Call Detail Records

The connecting and terminating of the service for the mobile devices in question is recorded by the wireless network provider in the form of a ***Call Detail Records*** (CDRs). CDRs are by far the most often overlooked form of validation. Most examiners locate the artifact(s) in question of the phone and they may even perform visual or cross tool validation. What may happen later during a cross-examination in court is the idea of *spoofing*. Spoofing is the process of placing specific information on a mobile device through a third party to achieve a desired outcome. It only applies to specific data, such as call records and SMS/MMS entries. It is generally designed for fun or to play a prank on the owner/user of the targeted "spoofed" phone.

The Internet provides several spoofing websites to facilitate this endeavor. Out of the hundreds of cell phone forensic examinations conducted since 2006, the author has experienced only two actual cases where spoofing was used. Both cases involved domestic relationships. One involved the custody of a minor child, with one parent creating an SMS message from her soon-to-be ex-husband where he confessed to molesting their child. This was not the case, and after many hours of investigation, it was proven that a paid spoofing service was used.

Search warrants to wireless carriers can many times confirm the parties involved in calls or message deliveries. Not all carriers maintain the SMS content by default, but the "coding" of the delivery between the parties can show on the CDR report. Many times defense may introduce how vulnerable the actual OS can be. This can be more common when an Android OS was examined, as it is open-sourced. In the same cross-examination of the forensic witness, they also may ask the examiner to discuss what spoofing is. In this line of questioning, a prepared prosecutor would ask the properly trained examiner how he/she went about validating that the artifacts were in fact not spoofed. The CDR delivery confirmation would then be introduced. Our next example is a screenshot taken from a suspect's phone. This particular phone call may not seem too important. It is, however, the first phone call the suspect made after committing a drug-related homicide. The top of Fig. 1.4 shows the actual screenshot from the call history. The box at the bottom of the image is a portion of the CDR from the wireless carrier showing the validated date and time of the call, the starting and terminating cell towers used to place the call (114 and 2403), the cell sector of the tower (4), and the to and from numbers between the parties involved in the call (redacted). The CDR validated the call stored as "RECEIVED CALLS-1" on the handset. The same phone also was used to establish times earlier in the day where the defendant was documented holding firearms. Due to the validation of correct times from the CDR matching the time in the call history, the prosecution was able to convince the jury that the images stored on the phone were in fact created the same day.

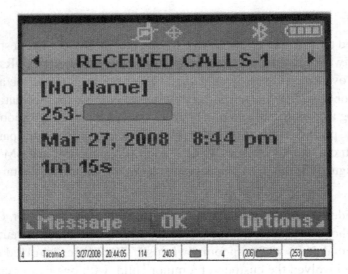

Figure 1.4
Example of logical handset stored call and call detail records for the same validated call from homicide.

We will soon understand that not all content that is used on mobile devices is recorded on a CDR. User-installed applications allow the user to connect mobile devices through wireless access. They in turn use the specifically designed application to make phone calls, chat, send and receive SMS or MMS, and conduct other forms of communications. In these cases, an examiner could use our last form of validation.

Hand Carving

Hand carving is the process by which the examiner would manually navigate into the file system and locate the artifact in its raw encoded state. This will depend on the type of acquisition that will generally be a file system pull. Not all devices support this type of examination. Hand carving can also be completed with a physical examination. The phone or forensic tool(s) may not support such an examination. Hand carving will be addressed in more detail in a later chapter. For the purposes of validating, we will use an image example.

There are many forensic tools that may miss embedded media. This can be caused by a service such as MMSs that were sent and received by two parties. The tools may not have the decoding capabilities to parse the attachment. Examiners, who obtain the file system or physical pull from the device and navigate to the suspected area, can manually carve out the media by using the file header and footers. This is just one example. Dates and times are also commonly validated by "hand carving." Fig. 1.5 is the hexadecimal encoding for an image that was missed by several different forensic tools. The figure number shows the area where the hexadecimal starting header (FF D8) and ending footer (FF D9) were saved for a Joint Photographic Group (JPG) image format. This image was part of an MMS message and dealt with a conversation regarding the author's daughter taking underwater images. Once the entire range of data is saved between the header and footer, which is shown as the highlighted hexadecimal values in Fig. 1.5, the examiner supplies the name and file extension. In this case ".jpg" is added and the carved data can be easily understood as depicted in picture contained in the upper right of Fig. 1.5.

Later in this book, the reader will be shown specific steps that outline how to locate MMSs when a forensic tool has missed them. Although hand carving can be used to validate information, it is more commonly used to locate items that a forensic tool would miss. This is usually because the item is deleted.

We have defined in detail the three key words used to define *Cell Phone Forensics* and the type of examinations. We continue in this chapter by addressing a minimum guideline that should be followed.

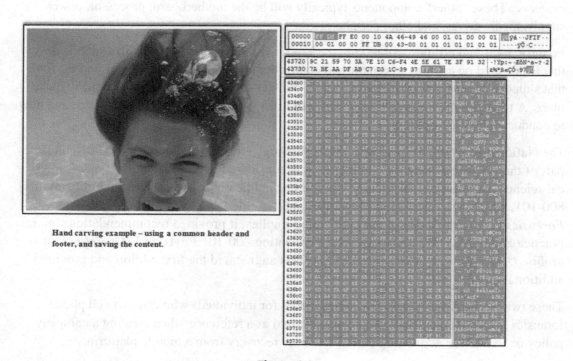

Hand carving example – using a common header and footer, and saving the content.

Figure 1.5
Header (FF D8) and footer (FF D9) located, hand carved out, and saved (multimedia message service image missed by forensic tools).

Standards

Many agencies and companies will generally have a standard operating procedure (SOP) that addresses how digital evidence is triaged. When we compare computer forensics with cell phone forensics, we will soon discover that computer evidence has for years adapted a specific accepted way in which the evidence is processed. In short, the target evidence drive is copied or "imaged" using a validated write blocker and the copy is verified by a before and after hash result. This confirms to the examiner that the image that was created is an exact duplicate of the original evidence. This copy is what will be examined using forensic tools, indexing, file carvers, and other common computer forensic methodologies. The actual evidence drive once copied is no longer used and is typically retained as evidence.

Most mobile examinations are not processed in the same fashion. This is not because someone decided it should be this way, rather it is because of the design of the phone itself. Most devices do not allow the examiner to easily remove the component that contains the OS. During a computer forensics case the examiner would locate the hard drive on the device, physically unplug it, and isolate it from the rest of the components that do not generally yield evidence. These "other" components typically will be the motherboard, processor, power supply, media drives, and other peripherals.

Forensic tools and utilities will require the examiner to physically connect to a mobile device that is powered on and has an established connection between the target device and the tool that supports the extraction. Because of this, changes to the target device will typically take place. A trained mobile forensic examiner will learn where these changes may occur and how to conduct validation techniques.

The National Institute of Standards and Technology (NIST) was founded in 1901 and is part of the US Department of Commerce; it is considered one of the nation's oldest physical science laboratories [1]. Among NIST's vast publications is their Special Publication 800-101, which was released in May 2007 and was titled *Guidelines on Cell Phone Forensics* [2]. As the name of the publication implies, it provided recommendations on the practice and in May 2014 NIST Special Publication 800-101 Revision 1, *Guidelines on Mobile Device Forensics* was released [3]. This augmented the first edition and provided additional updates.

These two publications remain the core standard for individuals who conduct cell phone forensics investigations. They should also be used as a reference when creating a company policy or an SOP on addressing digital forensics recovery from a mobile platform.

When first creating an SOP or a guide, it is important to research the requirements. If you work for a law enforcement agency, this will often include federal guidelines on the handling and storage of digital media. There are also nonprofit groups who can assist. The other element that may be needed for both corporate and criminal investigators is legal consulting. A good procedure guide will have combinations of all these items.

Chapter Summary Key Points

Cell Phone Forensics is defined using three key words: **Recovering**, **Data**, and **Validation**. To *recover* we must first have our legal process met. The *data* on the target device can be physical or logical. Physical artifacts may be more difficult to obtain, can require special tools and additional training, have longer extraction times, and are the composition of what makes up logical. Logical data is easy to understand and can "tell a story by itself." Not all phones will support a logical or physical extraction. Validating can be conducted through visual, cross tool, CDRs, and hand carving.

Those tasked with the recovery of data from mobile evidence must have an SOP, a manual, or a guide in which their methodology remains consistent. Core mobile forensic standards should be followed using publications that focus directly on the matter. These have been created by the NIST. Whether an examiner works for a private or a criminal investigation entity, he/she should also have clear instructions on chain of custody, legal guidelines, and other protocols that may need to be followed.

References

[1] NIST, Public Affairs Office – About NIST, February 25, 2015. http://www.nist.gov/public_affairs/nandyou.cfm.
[2] W. Jansen, R. Ayers, Guidelines on Cell Phone Forensics, Special Publication 800–101, Recommendations of the National Institute of Standards and Technology, May 2007.
[3] R. Ayers, S. Brothers, W. Jansen, NIST Special Publication 800-100 Revision 1, Guidelines on Mobile Device Forensics, May 2014.

CHAPTER 2

Evidence Contamination and Faraday Methods

Information in This Chapter

- Evidence contamination
- Faraday origins
- Faraday methods
- Internal settings
- Mesh
- Bags
- Boxes and tents
- Foil and cans

Introduction

For those of you who were fans of the show *Breaking Bad*, you may also be watching a character spin-off from that program. It is a recent series called *"Better Call Saul."* Saul has a brother in this series who reminds the author of an element related to mobile forensics. Of course, he takes this element to the extreme. He believes that outside signals of any kind, cause him harm. Before anyone enters his house, he makes them place their phones in an outside mailbox, and he has no electricity in his home. He wraps himself in foil blankets and lives in total darkness. This of course has some of the ingredients necessary for preventing evidence contamination. But what causes it? In most cases it comes down to two things—leaving the phone on (not doing anything about its connectivity) and the actions of the investigator.

To provide an understanding of the "investigator" part, the author goes back to cinema. *No Country For Old Men* was a movie that came out in 2007. One of the characters in the movie is played by Tommy Lee Jones. He is an older investigator on the verge of retirement. He struggles to keep up with the killer he is tracking. You may have people on your department who would have struggled with some of the same issues. For the author, it was a veteran who had no idea how to turn on a cellular phone, and sometimes his own computer. This same person later needed to recover a "powered-on" mobile phone at the scene of a double homicide. Instead of powering it down, he made a call. Imagine the examiner's surprise when the phone was later examined, and a call is recorded long after the homicide had occurred.

It is difficult to keep up with all the changes technology throws at us. You may have never seen either of these programs/shows, but they both have something in common with this chapter. One shows how to block unwanted signals, and the other conveys that we need to keep up with technology, as technology advances so must our investigations skills if we want to stay in the game.

Evidence Contamination

A few years ago, we would generally place the blame for altering or contaminating digital forensic evidence directly in the hands of the first responder. For law enforcement, this would be the first officer or investigator who physically came into contact with the device. In the corporate realm, this may be an IT person who may or may not be well versed in handling the device and has other collateral duties stacked on their plate.

The first responder will still have to properly triage the target mobile device, but the chance of altering the evidence does not end there. Let us address what causes changes, damages, or actually can *wipe* mobile evidence.

Wireless Connectivity

Picture a cellular phone's design for connectivity similar to that of a dog. Dogs by nature are constantly trying to "sniff" everything around them. Except when they are sleeping, most of the time our canine companions are requesting information about the world around them through their nostrils. When we power on our mobile devices they too are "sniffing." Only their design is seeking out a signal to complete their authentication process for service. If we have paid for communications and activated our phones (allocated), their first job is to locate service; even if we travel underground to Carlsbad Caverns, New Mexico, or to the top of Burj Khalifa in Dubai, our devices' mission is to acquire a network spectrum for their customer.

This wireless connectivity can change the data that is on the phone in few different ways:

Wipe commands that are received Over the Air (OTA) is the most damaging. In this case, the user may have installed an application on the smartphone, which allows a secondary source to wipe the phone in the event it was lost or for bad guys, they get caught. These applications are very popular and with Apple are often used to locate the device. Apple implemented this feature within the operation system of the iPhone several years ago. An example of this setting is shown in Fig. 2.1.

Find My iPhone

Apple ID   example@icloud.com

Password   required

Sign In...

Forgot Apple ID or Password?

Setup Instructions

Figure 2.1
Example of the find my iPhone application.

Apple supports remote erasing on many of their products. Instructions can be found on their website; "If your iOS device or MAC is lost or stolen, you can erase it if you set up Find My iPhone on the device before it was lost" [1]. Apple provides step-by-step instructions on how to remotely wipe the supported device with a few simple clicks.

Android has a similar process. Using the *Android Device Manager* supplied through Google, the user may under certain circumstances wipe the device. It can also send commands to *Ring* or *Lock* the operating system. An example of the sign in screen can be located on the companion site in Fig. 2.1. (It has been partially redacted.)

With regards to Android, if the device has the *Location Services* disabled on the phone, the user will encounter a notification that indicates the setting is off. It will also provide information when it was last "online." The user should be aware that this indication of when it was last online is not always a true representation of when the device was actually using the

Location Services. This setting is depicted on the companion site in Fig. 2.2. (It has been partially redacted.) The figure shows the setting being reported that it is off.

If, however, the owner or user of the phone has enabled this setting on the mobile target, they can obtain a general geographical location of where the device may be. There can be various limitations for this, and it will not always provide an exact location. Fig. 2.3 from the companion site displays an example of a device that has its Location Services enabled. Using the same Android Device Manager, we can see a general area of where this phone is located. In the example shown in Fig. 2.3 from the companion site, the actual date that the device was at this location (and queried) was April 6, 2016. The time, however, is correct.

On the device itself, if the first responder was to recover a "live," powered-on Android, and they encountered the notification example that is similar to the screenshot image from the companion site in Fig. 2.4, this means a third party has logged into the Android Device Manager and could be trying to perform a remote erase on the device. If a first responder or investigator handling the target device observes such a pop up, they must **immediately take steps to prevent the wipe process!**

These two examples are the most commonly encountered by investigators. Windows, Blackberry, and other smartphone operating platforms will also have their own settings to remotely wipe a device. Users can also install their own application on a device. Some of these can turn on the camera, record sounds, and perform other tasks remotely that could jeopardize the case if the live phone is not properly triaged.

Faraday Origins

At the beginning of this book we addressed how the reader may utilize the case experiences and "lessons learned" from the author to help them with their own cases. Several years ago the author was asked on the stand the origin of the word *Faraday*. This was an awkward moment, as the history of this word had never been researched. Instead of making up an answer, the response was that the author only knew *how* to perform a Faraday method, and that origin of the word was unknown.

The correct answer was that the origin of the word *Faraday* comes from the English scientist, Michael Faraday. He made discoveries such as electromagnetic induction, electrolysis, and diamagnetism [2].

The Faraday technique is the process of stopping, interrupting, or circumventing any wireless signal from reaching its intended target. This word is used as a verb, adverb, or noun. An examiner could have "Faradayed" the phone, or could be in the process of "Faradaying." In a report this may be explained as, *"The Samsung SCH i535 was charged in the forensics lab, applied with a Faraday technique and powered on."*

Besides the wireless network itself, phones can also have Bluetooth, or model specific settings that can also cause unwanted changes. The use of a specific Faraday technique would also apply to these scenarios.

Model Specific Capacities

The other way wireless network can cause changes to the target phone is through the phone's built-in capabilities to store information. This is usually missed calls, which are also referred to a call history.

Spilled Milk

Missed Calls

Mr. Badguy who associates with a certain street gang, decides to go one morning and get his wife a gallon of milk. He walks through the neighborhood and makes his purchase at a convenience store nearly six blocks from their home. While making his way back home through the streets, he encounters a rival gang member. The two of them are not happy to see each other. To show their unpleasantness for one another, the rival gang member shoots and kills Mr. Badguy.

Police arrive and set up a crime scene. Meanwhile, Mr. Badguy has a pay-as-you-go phone that is powered on and being clinched in his dead hand, and a gallon of milk which is now broken open, spilled on the opposite side of him. The rival gang members actually knew each other and were once childhood friends before deciding to join opposing street teams. The rival gang member had tried to call Mr. Badguy several times before running into him and shooting him over a prior drug related issue. These calls were initially stored in Mr. Badguy's phone as missed calls. On this particular model phone it can only store 20 missed calls. Meanwhile his wife is getting impatient, and wants her milk that he has promised to retrieve. She begins calling him. She calls all day until the phone finally goes dead. The phone number that was once stored as a missed call from the rival gang member has now been pushed out of the memory, replaced by 20 calls from Mr. Badguy's wife. Because the rival gang member did not let his missed calls to Mr. Badguy go to voice mail, the number is not registered by Call Detail Records from his phone, and thus the police now have no record of the missed calls prior to his death. The sent calls obviously are on the shooter's phone, which no one initially knows is part of this equation.

Many individuals who are involved in ongoing criminal endeavors prefer to utilize cheap, pay-as-you-go phones. These have a slang term called *Burner Phones*. The term comes from the fact that their wireless number may get *burned*, i.e., turned over to law enforcement or other individuals when it is used to contact another party. To avoid the possibility of being tracked back to the phone, they dispose of it and replace it with another cheap "Burner Phone."

Other Forms of Contamination

Wireless connection will always be the number one way in which a phone can be altered or in some cases, wiped entirely. There are other forms of contamination as well as scenarios in which they may occur. Here are some of the most common ones and some possible remedies.

Cooperative Witness

Many people with very good intentions can contaminate stored evidence. This is commonly a third party who may have video recorded an incident or is not directly involved but has compelling evidence such as a text message stored on their phone. If the device is examined by a law enforcement investigator, and given back to the witness, the defense team may be granted permission to conduct their own forensic examination of the phone as well. Some jurisdictions will copy the evidence and inform the witness not to "delete" the entry until the case goes to trial. There are a number of factors that can change the original evidence by the time the case is presented. It is recommended that if the crime is severe in nature, the witness phone is retained as evidence and not returned until after the trial. At a minimum, a prosecutor should be consulted before any mobile device is released. There have been cases when the witness or victim's phone was not supported by a particular version of a forensic tool at the time of the incident, and the phone was held and examined with limited results. Later, when the case was being prepared for trial, a newer version of the forensic tool supported recovery of additional artifacts on the same phone. It is not uncommon for a suspect to take a plea when faced with the compelling discovery of this new evidence.

Contamination by Officers, Investigators, and Crime Scene Technicians

First responders, investigators, and crime scene technicians can unknowingly alter, destroy, or facilitate additional problems with mobile evidence. Nearly 2 years ago, a senior homicide detective with over 40 years of police experience was attempting to turn off a cellular phone at the scene of a homicide. Instead, he sent a call to a relative that was stored as a speed dial entry. This party did not answer. The call went to voice mail and recorded his conversion with another investigator on how to turn off the "*Damned Thing*!" This family member was quite good natured about the voice mail and was aware of the proclivities that led to the murder of their family member.

Investigators who are tasked with crime scene or incident response, should be aware that they will commonly encounter digital mobile evidence. They need to have a working knowledge of how most devices work. It is important to also understand the pros and cons of pulling the battery on devices that support battery removal. Triaging devices that are on or off is covered in Chapter 8. Having a "field kit" with Faraday materials will also help. We will cover suggested types of materials in the following sections.

User Installed Applications or User Settings

When live devices are collected, it may be difficult to determine what exactly is going on inside the file system of the target. This is especially true if it is a smartphone. The end user could have installed a particular application that executes a command based on a set time, setting, a change in the screen, or even rotation of the device. Some phones may even appear to be off when in fact they are in a stand-by mode setting. User installed applications will often execute even if the phone is properly Faradayed. The setting has nothing to do with wireless connectivity. There is no real solution to prevent a user application from executing its preloaded function command on a live phone. One suggestion is to power off the phone, but this has its own problems and will be discussed in Chapter 8.

The Environment

The environment the device was recovered in can play an integral part in how the phone gets contaminated. The common sources can be water, snow, and heat. A severely cracked screen can quickly lead to main board damage if the phone was lying in a street, exposed to rain. Most phones that do not have a cracked screen can hold up for several hours in that scenario, but a few cracks in the screen, can accelerate deterioration to the vital areas where user data is stored. As bacteria from the moisture has a chance to grow, different levels of fungus begin to cause changes to the internal components of the device. These will generally have three different types of color. The color is based on time and bacteria levels. White is the least damaging, and once the device is properly cleaned, there is a high probability of functionality. The next color is green. Green fungus can generally be cleaned, but in some cases will cause irreparable damage to components. The last fungus color is black. When an internal component has black fungus present, the actual area has damage or erosion in nearly every case. If we go back to the companion site, Fig. 2.5, it provides an image from a severely cracked screen of an iPhone 5C. The user had covered the damage with Scotch Tape and continued to use the device with the cracked screen for several months after the damage. The arrows in this figure from left to right depict green fungus (left), white fungus (near top), and black fungus (right arrow) on the Molex connections. There is also brown oxidation that can be seen.

After the black fungus was cleaned off the Molex area, Fig. 2.6 (companion site) it shows the irreversible damage done to the contact pins. Even though this appears to be catastrophic, the device was still functional after it was properly cleaned and the screen replaced.

Sometimes, phones will need to be disassembled when they have been exposed to or submerged in water or other fluids. At present, the author has examined devices that have been exposed to toilets, snow, salt, and freshwater. A recently examined phone was exposed to the bodily fluids of a decomposing body. The human fluids over a several month period, had seeped into the main board of the phone. As grotesque as this may sound, this should serve as a reminder that phones can be exposed to any type of moisture. It will be the forensic examiners' responsibility to try and clean and dry the device in order to acquire user data.

For years people have believed that placing a wet phone in a bag of rice would dry it out and make it operational again. This technique may have worked, but it was only because the moisture exposure was not severe, and does not mean that the rice removed moisture from deep inside the phone. As mentioned earlier, moisture has some degree of bacteria. In some cases, moisture will have more bacteria than another, such as water from a pond that is stagnant.

Most new phones have specialized circuitry inside their batteries that will detect excess charging or shorts. This prevents the battery from damaging the phone. Most water-exposed devices will most likely need a new battery, which is the least of the overall problem that the examiner will need to deal with.

Examiners must ensure that they completely disassemble the phone and clean and inspect all parts. The parts must be dried and in some cases, heat dried with specialty ovens used for electronic parts. Compressed air is not usually recommended as it can "push" residue moisture into small component parts including chips located on the main board. This can lead to additional problems. This type of specialty work will be explained in more detail in Chapter 21.

Faraday Methods
Internal Settings

The first recommended Faraday method is the use of the phone's internal setting to stop the network from communicating with the phone. This has many names, but the most common is "Airplane Mode." Some are called *Flight Mode, Turn All Connections Off,* or *Standalone Mode.* Some phones use symbols of an airplane. Fig. 2.2 is an example of these internal settings on several different models of mobile devices.

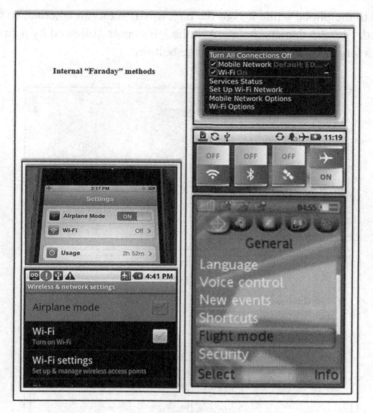

Figure 2.2
Internal Faraday settings of several devices.

Faraday Mesh

Faraday mesh allows the examiner or first responder a quick and easy way to block the signal to the device. The mesh can be reused, washed, and the user can still see the condition of the screen through the mesh. With smartphones using touch screens, it can be problematic, as the material is made of metal and interacts when it comes in contact with the phone, and that causes erratic behaviors. It will take a few seconds for the signal to stop reaching the phone, and in some cases may require more than one sheet if the signal is strong.

Faraday Bags

There are several vendors who offer Faraday bags. The issue with Faraday bags is that they prevent the user from being allowed to see the screen of the phone. When a data or charging cable is attached to the phone while it is in the bag, it will act as an antenna, so the cable must also be Faradayed. Fig. 2.3 depicts the mesh in the left corner, followed by a small bag to the upper right, and a large *Paraben* brand bag at the bottom.

Figure 2.3
Faraday mesh and bag examples.

Faraday Boxes and Tents

Some agencies will utilize a Faraday box or tent. These are not practical for field use, unless the agency or business is capable of using them in a mobile command unit such as a converted RV. Fig. 2.4 is a depiction of the Faraday box, which is also called a *Stronghold Box*. The examiner would place the mobile device inside the box. It has a power strip and internal lights. Using Faraday mesh gloves that are built into the unit, the user could reach inside and manipulate the device as needed. There is a viewing window on the lid.

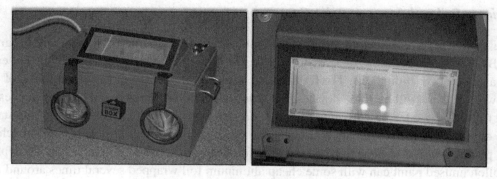

Figure 2.4
Example of a stronghold box.

Fig. 2.5 is an example of a Faraday tent. The unit pictured is actually sold by Faradaytents.com. Faraday tents have preconfigured tent packages that are based on customer's most common needs [3]. Faraday tents can come in various sizes and can also be custom made to fit a particular work area. Most are portable, but some may actually be permanently built to suit the needs of the customer or particular space requirements.

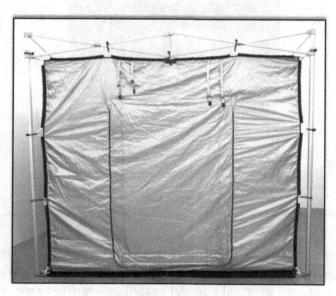

Figure 2.5
Example of a Faraday tent sold by Faradaytents.com.

Aluminum Foil and Arson or Paint Cans

The last types of Faraday techniques that we will discuss are aluminum foil and paint (or arson can). Both of these methods are a very cost-effective way to Faraday a mobile device, but each will have their own limitations. The foil must be wrapped around the device a minimum of three wraps. There will be some devices that require additional wraps based on the thickness of the foil being used. A downsize to foil is that it prevents the examiner from seeing the status of the device. Like the previously addressed Faraday bags, if a power or data cable is attached to the phone, it will also need to be wrapped in foil as it will act as an antenna. Fig. 2.6 depicts a 1-gallon unused paint can with some cheap aluminum foil wrapped several times around a smartphone.

Figure 2.6
Example of a paint can and foil being used to Faraday phones.

As we conclude our Faraday methods, it is very important that whenever a particular method of Faradaying is chosen, the practitioner has validated his/her method(s). What this means is no one should ever wait until an actual criminal or civil case arrives to use one of these methods for the first time. Each must be tested, and issues that may limit the functionality should be properly documented. For example, Verizon Wireless serviced phones have a stronger signal in certain geographical areas. They require two, sometimes three sheets of mesh to interrupt the signal. This may be true in your area, or it may be that *Paint* or *Arson* cans, does not block an iPhone 6 on the Sprint network etc.

Chapter Summary Key Points

The number one way in which mobile evidence can be contaminated is through continued connection to the wireless carrier. This can include OTA commands that remotely wipe the target device. Although many times it may be unintentional, officers, investigators, crime scene technicians, and witnesses can all contribute to altering evidence. User installed applications can be preset within the operating system and can execute various commands that may also change the data.

The word *Faraday* is named after the late 19th-century British scientist. The process of stopping, interrupting, or circumventing any wireless signal from reaching its intended target is the meaning of Faraday. There are several Faraday methods that may be employed. The most common is an internal "built-in" method typically called *Airplane Mode*. Other methods include mesh, bags, boxes, tents, paint or arson cans, and aluminum foil. If foil is to be used to Faraday a phone, it must be wrapped a minimum of three times. Regardless of which Faraday method is used, it must be validated prior to use on an actual investigation.

References

[1] Apple, iCloud: Erase Your Device, March 25, 2016. https://support.apple.com/kb/PH2701?locale=en_US.
[2] L. Pearce Williams, Encyclopedia Britannica, Michael Faraday February 17, 2016. http://www.britannica.com/biography/Michael-Faraday.
[3] EDEC Digital Forensics, Tent Packages, 2014. http://www.faradaytents.com/tent-packages/index.html.

CHAPTER 3

The Legal Process—Part 1

Information in This Chapter

- The legal process
- Mobile network operators
- Mobile virtual network operators
- Determining who services the target number

Introduction—Chapter Disclosure

In the last chapter we defined *Cell Phone Forensics*. Three main words contributed to the definition, the first being *recovering*. For criminal investigations, it is required that the examiner obtain a form of legal authority to begin the "recovery" process. Not all businesses or jurisdictions will follow the exact same legal suggestions that this chapter may suggest, recommend, or imply. The author is providing best practices that combine insights from past and present case experience, testimony, and training. In this chapter we will cover some recent case laws that also deal with *nexus*. The author is *not* an attorney and will address such subject matter from the forensic examiner point of view. This may in turn help some of you clarify the linkage of the crime to the technical aspects of the target device(s) when drafting your own search warrants. Furthermore, it is highly recommended that readers consult with their own legal advisers before adapting any recommendation(s) contained in this book.

The Legal Process

One of the aspects of cell phone forensics that consistently surprise university students are the elements of the legal process that must be met before examining the mobile device. Their thought process can sometimes be influenced by what they see on television or in the media. Many believe that law enforcement can basically search anything they come into contact with. After taking a few of the required classes and participating in laboratory scenarios that involve legal concepts, there are some students who become frustrated by how restricted law enforcement is when it comes to searching mobile devices. We will discuss the three main types of searches. These will typically apply to criminal investigations.

Consent to Search

The US Supreme Court recognized that a warrantless search is reasonable and falls under the Fourth Amendment under certain *circumstances*. They are listed as a search incident to an arrest, officer or public safety, a fleeing suspect, booking a suspect into jail, inventory, border searches, individuals under parole or probation, and finally **consent**.

Merriam-Webster defines the word *CONSENT* as: "1: to give assent or approval: AGREE <consent to being tested> 2: archaic: to be in concord in opinion or sentiment" [1].

There is also a legal definition, which Merriam-Webster provides as: "compliance in or approval of what is done or proposed by another; specifically: the voluntary agreement or acquiescence by a person of age or with requisite mental capacity who is not under duress or coercion and usually who has knowledge or understanding..." [2].

Such legal definition does not always properly answer the question of *how* investigators would conduct a search where consent of a mobile device is present. Certainly, we can understand that the person must enter into a voluntary agreement. At your own jurisdiction or company, this agreement may be written, verbal, or both. Merriam-Webster may provide their own legal definition, but we need additional elements that have also been recognized by the US Supreme Court, which involve revocation.

The owner or user is allowed to revoke the consent. So how does one go about stopping such a search if you work in a forensic laboratory and the owner/user is not there to revoke consent?

Also, how does the owner communicate with the forensics examiner to stop the search if the subject phone is their only means to contact the examiner? Some agencies have modified their internal process to address the searching of digital devices.

These issues are addressed on the "Consent to Search without a Warrant" form used by a Puget Sound police agency. The standard form allows the examiner to place additional information to address these issues. An example of this language is as follows:

> I, the said owner and user of the _____ {insert make & model} fully under-
> stand that the search of the device listed will take place in a forensic lab or facility out of my
> view. I, the said owner and user also understand that I may revoke the consent at any time by
> calling the following number and informing _____ {insert
> examiner's name and phone number} that I wish to revoke the search. I will also utilize the
> following means to facilitate in making such a call if I choose to revoke. {List the means by
> which the owner/user of said device will use to complete a call to revoke if necessary} ____
> _____
> _____
> ____.

The last section of this form, added language to the consent form requires the investigators to document the *means* in which the user or owner will revoke consent are important to clearly articulate. For instance, the owner may have agreed to come to your location for an interview and subsequent search of his/her mobile phone. He/she is aware of the forensic search that may take over an hour to acquire the data and has agreed to wait. You would want to supply him/her with the ability to make such a call. This may be a landline, or another investigator waiting with him/her who has a cell phone. Whatever the situation, it is important that the consent to search form documents this. It may be asked about later in court or at a hearing: "what access did the owner or users have to facilitate contacting the forensic examiner?" This may, in some cases, be a neighbor or another family member with a cell phone if the device was left at the forensic laboratory and the owner decides to pick it up the following day.

Other Issues With Consent to Search

In Chapter 2 we briefly discussed different forms of contamination that can take place on a mobile device that contains potential evidence. Under the *Cooperative Witness* section, issues with returning evidence back to witnesses are explained. This issue also pertains to this section as well. When it has been decided that consent will be used to acquire data from a mobile device, the examiner or those in charge of the overall investigation should be aware of potential problems when the device is returned back to the owner or user. As previously mentioned, this can cause issues later during the judicial process. These are questions that should be posed to those with legal authority over your case. This may be a deputy prosecutor or civil attorney. It may rest with your immediate supervisor. Whoever this person or persons may be, they must be aware of some of the implications that may go along with returning the item after consent to search was granted.

Exigent Circumstances

Again, we go back to the Fourth Amendment of the US Constitution. For exigent circumstances to be utilized there must be emergency conditions. Emergency conditions can be defined from case laws: "Those circumstances that would cause a reasonable person to believe that entry (or other relevant prompt action) was necessary to prevent physical harm to the officers or other persons, the destruction of relevant evidence, the escape of a suspect, or some other consequence improperly frustrating legitimate law enforcement efforts" [3].

This type of search will generally only apply to law enforcement. With mobile evidence, most incidents will involve two aspects of exigent: the destruction of evidence and preventing harm to persons. Many courts have linked one part of exigency to the "emergency doctrine," which has also been referred to as the "emergency exception" to the warrant requirement.

We do not have the ability to provide the numerous case examples here in this chapter. But as a simple example, if we responded to a child who was just kidnapped and the phone was dropped by the suspect, entering the phone for information to recover the child and prevent harm or death would be an exigent circumstance where a warrant would not be required. Of course, the semantics to the case would likely be argued later. In particular, there is usually a strong focus by the courts with regard to the *timing* of the search. It would be addressed if the investigator could have had time to procure a warrant or if such delay would have further exposed the child to harm. Also, when does exigency end? One local Puget Sound police department will generally have investigators act on information obtained through exigent means and at the same time simultaneously have additional investigators begin the process of obtaining a search warrant (if applicable).

The Commission Assistance for Law Enforcement Act (CALEA) outlines that wireless providers can only supply information to law enforcement up to 48 hours based on a single incident related to exigent. After that period, the target agency must obtain additional legal process, which is generally a search warrant.

Search Warrant

Notwithstanding exigency, most legal advisers will inform investigators that the search warrant is the preferred legal method to search for stored data or for other artifacts related to a mobile device. Civil entities may use a subpoena or "Civil Subpoena." Many of the suggestions with regard to search warrants that are referenced in this chapter can carry over to preparing a subpoena. In almost every case, investigators will be limited in what type of information can be obtained through a Subpoena versus a Search Warrant.

For those readers who currently have created search warrants and executed them during your current or past law enforcement career, you may have encountered the need to update a particular warrant. This will be especially prevalent when it comes to mobile-related evidence. Of the three legal processes that have been discussed, the search warrant is the most dynamic. It will continue to be affected by local, state, and federal rulings. The nature of digital evidence listed on the warrant only complicates matters. The next chapter (part 2) should be used to augment the legal process, in particular the search warrant. Chapter 4 will provide suggestions on the actual language.

Mobile Network Operators

Telecom market research provides a number of paid resources related to mobile network operators (MNOs). Through their related service from the MNO Directory, they sell worldwide listings of network operators published in geographical or global directories. Using search engines such as Google, they provide a short summary of 798 mobile networks in their 2013 dataset of the global wireless industry [4]. What is an MNO? Why would an investigator need to know about MNOs?

An MNO is a wireless cellular company that maintains, services, and manages *all* aspects of the business that are necessary to provide wireless service to the customer. This means it owns its own towers and related equipment, which help facilitate in connecting and terminating service. MNOs within the United States have grown over the past few years. There are still four main ones that provide the majority of service. These are Verizon, AT&T, T-Mobile, and Sprint.

Mobile Virtual Network Operators

On February 20, 2015, a research article conducted by GSMA Intelligence titled "The global MNVO footprint: a changing environment" reported there is almost 1000 MVNOs in operation worldwide in 2014 [5].

A mobile virtual network operator (MVNO) is a wireless company that does not maintain its own infrastructure. MVNOs will build relationships with MNOs. This will be based on the type of communication the device utilizes, such as Code Division Multiple Access or Global System for Mobile Communication. In many cases the actual manufacturer of the cellular handset may create a specific version of a device that will only work on authentication provided by an MVNO company. The phone may look exactly the same as a phone used by an MNO, but in some cases the model number will usually have a letter after it, which identifies it as such. MVNOs will work out internal logistics with the target MNOs that need specific service. The service will be based on the phone's features, such as simple calling and texting to smarter phone-related services such as web browsing and Global Positioning Services. Based on the agreement, the consumer purchases the MVNO phone and service and activates the device. The MNO, in turn, allows the service, which many refer to as what the MVNO is "riding" on. An example would be "MetroPCS is riding on T-Mobile." Fig. 3.1 is an illustration of the MVNO and MNO correlation, with the larger tower in the middle representing the MNO. This figure is by no means an exhausted list, and the list of MVNOs by comparison of the MNOs just in the United States far out numbers the few MNOs.

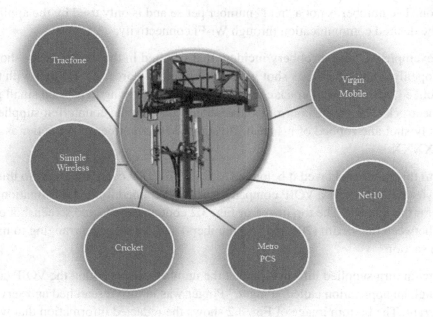

Figure 3.1
Correlations between a mobile network operator and mobile virtual network operator.

An investigator who is tasked with obtaining information from a target number needs to understand that in some cases, more than one warrant or subpoena may be required if the number is serviced by an MVNO. When these businesses respond to the legal process sent to them, MVNOs are at times including the call detail record of the MNO they receive service from, while others are not and will refer the investigator to the legal department for the MNO that provided the service. The MVNO would in some cases only provide subscriber information or a screenshot showing the authentication of services. This information provided may be limited, and the unique terminology they use will be discussed in a later chapter.

Determining Target Number

Once the number has been determined, there are steps that can be used to ascertain who is providing the service for the number and validation as to where the legal paperwork can be served. There are online services that can help point the investigator in the right direction. Also, law enforcement can request a free account that can be used to look up the number. Both types will be addressed later in this chapter. First, investigators should be aware that not all target numbers will be serviced by an actual wireless carrier.

Application Numbers

Users are increasingly using applications to facilitate in calling, texting, chatting, and other forms of communications. One of the most popular is Voice Over Internet Protocol (VOIP). VOIP companies will sell spectrum to businesses that in turn will use the spectrum to service an application. The number is not a "real" number per se and is only used by the application to execute the desired communication through Wi-Fi connectivity.

In the next example we have a robbery incident that resulted in the victim being shot. The victim openly admitted he was shot while trying to buy narcotics. He met with the seller and noticed that instead of crack cocaine, the seller was trying to pass on small pieces of broken sheetrock. The victim confronted the seller regarding the counterfeit supplies and was ultimately shot and robbed of his cash. He supplied the number of the seller as 1-425-429-XXXX.

Research into this number showed it belonged to *BANDWIDTH.com*. A warrant to this company reviewed that it was a VOIP company that only retained limited information on the call history for the number. The top image of Fig. 3.2 contains a redacted screenshot of the call history between the victim (206 and 253 numbers) and the suspect arranging to meet for the drug transaction.

This company in turn supplied information that the number was receiving the VOIP call service through an application called "Pinger." Pinger was in turn researched and served with a search warrant. The bottom image of Fig. 3.2 shows the redacted information that was captured by Pinger via warrant service.

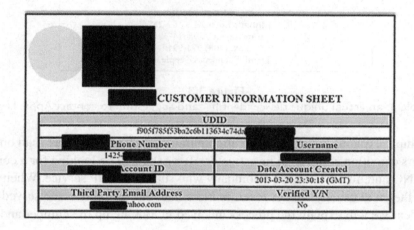

fromAddress	toAddress	startTimeUTC	endTimeUTC	durationSeconds
1425	5508	2013-03-21 20:52:29	2013-03-21 20:52:36	7
1206	1425	2013-03-23 02:20:05	2013-03-23 02:20:09	4
1206	1425	2013-03-23 02:20:26	2013-03-23 02:20:32	6
RESTRICTED	1425	2013-03-23 02:21:53	2013-03-23 02:22:22	29
1425	1206	2013-03-24 02:39:19	2013-03-24 02:39:54	35
1425	1253	2013-03-24 04:45:41	2013-03-24 04:46:17	36
1425	1253	2013-03-24 04:53:54	2013-03-24 04:54:00	6
1425	1253	2013-03-24 04:55:30	2013-03-24 04:55:36	6

BANDWIDTH.com Call History

CUSTOMER INFORMATION SHEET

UDID	
f905f785f53ba2c6b113634c74da	

Phone Number	Username
1425-	

Account ID	Date Account Created
	2013-03-20 23:30:18 (GMT)

Third Party Email Address	Verified Y/N
ahoo.com	No

Pinger information

Figure 3.2

Top image: Reflects call history recorded by BANDWIDTH.com. Bottom image: Reflects information retained by Pinger with regard to the target Voice Over Internet Protocol number.

Nearly all the fields retained by Pinger were fictitious, except one, the field that displays the UDID. UDID stands for *Unique Device Identifier*. This is a series of 40 numbers and letters, which specifically identify an Apple product. They are used on iPods or iPhones. The UDID is calculated using either 59 or 60 characters that combine a SHA1 hash of the text string. The text string can be derived from a specific combination of values of the serial number, exclusive chip ID, International Mobile Equipment Identifier, WiFi MAC address, and Bluetooth MAC address.

This value is retained by applications that utilize Apple products. iTunes being the primary program will generally retain valid credit card information that must be supplied for a user to purchase applications through the iTunes Store. Through the validation download process, the UDID is retained and linked to the application. Fig. 3.3 is the redacted screenshot supplied by Pinger, which links the UDID and number to the VOIP service. A third and final search warrant to Apple using the UDID value revealed the actual suspect who was contacted and interviewed. He confessed that he "accidentally shot the victim" during the drug sale.

Figure 3.3
Example of an actual unique device identifier and suggestion to contact Apple Legal.

This first example explains how user application numbers may require more than one warrant. These numbers can often confuse an investigator. He or she will be looking for a common MNO or MVNO and, in turn, locates a company who supplies VOIP service. When these are encountered, they will usually always result in more than one business being served with legal paperwork. Next we will explain the process involved in looking up the number and confirming who is servicing it.

Fonefinder.net

A free online service that is available is from a website called *Fonefinder.net*. This site can provide information on who may be serving the number. When using a site such as Fonefinder.net, it is important to understand the definition of wireless local number portability (WLNP) and how it factors into looking for who is servicing the target number.

WLNP allows a consumer the ability to change service providers within the same local area and maintain the same number. They can even switch from one carrier to another that is within the same general area. Consumers can, in some cases, move a landline to a wireless phone [6].

When a phone's origin is researched, the number may have been ported to another carrier, and the source being used to reveal who it may be assigned to may or may not reflect the most current wireless carrier providing services. At the time of this writing, the phone number 253-606-5884 was currently assigned to Verizon Wireless. The number, when it was first issued, was serviced through Nextel. Nextel was, in the past, serviced by Sprint. If we use Fonefinder.net to look up the number, it still shows that it is assigned to Sprint.

Many times, however, the "telephone company" that Fonefinder.net indicates the number is assigned to will, in fact, be accurate. If we look back at our number that was used in the robbery and shooting case, and determined to be a Pinger application number, it properly comes back as Bandwidth.com.

Zetx

Another alternative that is available to law enforcement is a free phone lookup service from Zetx. Their website is located at https://phonelookup.zetx.com/, and they require contact information and a valid email address. They often have courses on cellular investigations. Unlike other free services, they can also be reached by email or telephone. Once your contact information has been confirmed, they send the information they have on your target number.

Carrierlookup.com

This site is free for the general public to use. It appears based on the home page that there may be a limitation to how many target phone numbers can be researched within a site visit. The site is fairly straightforward to use, and it will generally indicate if the number has been ported or not.

Number Portability Administration Center

There is another free service that can be used to determine who a number is ported to. This service is only provided to law enforcement. The Number Portability Administration Center (NPAC) allows confirmed agencies' access to research the target number(s). Once the account is set up, the agency is provided a PIN number that is entered to allow access to a voice automated system. The system will inform the caller if the number has been ported, supplying the wireless carrier information and their law enforcement contact information. If, however, the automated prompt determines that the number has not been ported, the system does not inform who the current carrier of service may be. It will be up to the examiner to conduct additional research. This is especially true if either Fonefinder.net or NPAC is able to reveal to whom the number is properly ported to. In that case, actual phone contact with the major MNOs will be warranted. The investigator would in turn inquire if the number is being serviced by them. No matter if you use a free service, or NPAC indicates who the carrier may be, phone confirmation is highly recommended if these two methods are being used. The confirmation is completed through Search.org.

Search.org is a free site that can be used to look up not only wireless carrier contact information but also other businesses such as our previously mentioned company that provided VOIP service for the Pinger application and Internet Service Providers (ISP). Search.org is partially funded by a grant from the Bureau of Justice Assistance and the Office of Juvenile Justice and Delinquency Prevention, Office of Justice Programs, and the US Department of Justice [7].

Within the Search.org site, the investigator would navigate to the *Resources* tab at the top of the home page. Hovering over this area will in turn generate another pop-up window. This window will indicate *ISP List* as a choice. When this is selected, a drop-down bar will show and allow the user to select the appropriate business by alphabetical listing. Some targets will have more than one area within the business showing in the *ISP Quick Search* selection.

The business that has been selected will have specific phone numbers, directions, and prerecorded prompts to follow. These are not always up-to-date. The last step would be to call the law enforcement contact number and confirm that their fax, address listed, and other information are correct for the warrant that you intend to serve them.

Search.org can also serve as a great resource site for additional information and training. On their website, there is a *Quick Access ISP Information* (at the bottom). The Quick Access ISP Information allows specific law enforcement (LE) guides, policies, or handbooks to be sent to the requestor. When the *REQUEST DOCUMENT(S)* is selected, another pop-up window will display with required fields used to confirm that the requestor is law enforcement. Other businesses that are not displayed in the Quick Access ISP Information section may have similar investigative guides that may assist law enforcement. These are found by navigating into the specific targeted business and reading how to obtain such information.

Chapter Summary Key Points

It is important to understand that each business or law enforcement agency must consult with their own legal adviser and the information provided in this chapter may not always apply to your investigative scenario.

Exigent, consent to search, and search warrant are the three main types of legal processes. Investigators must generally fulfill at least one before searching mobile devices or related evidential data. Exigent has a direct correlation to emergency aid. Consent to search may require further documentation as to where the forensic examination takes place and how to revoke consent.

MNOs and MVNOs must be understood when creating a search warrant for a target number as it may require two warrants. There are only a few MNOs within the United States but numerous MVNOs.

Fonefinder.net, Zetx, Phonenumberlookup.com, and NPAC may be used to help determine which wireless carrier may be servicing a target number. Two of these services will require the investigator to be a law enforcement officer.

If you plan to draft a warrant or subpoena for your target number, the first step in the process is to understand if you are working with a number from an MNO, MVNO, or application number. The second step is to contact the legal representative and confirm that the target number actually belongs to them.

Chapter 4 continues to expand on the legal process. It provides suggestions on drafting the search warrant and covers unique legal requests such as destructive orders for chip-off examinations.

References

[1] Merriam-Webster, Consent, Verb, 2016. http://www.merriam-webster.com/dictionary/consent.
[2] Merriam-Webster, Consent, Noun, Legal Definition of CONSENT 2016. http://www.merriam-webster.com/dictionary/consent.
[3] United States v. McConney, 728 F.2d 1195, 1199 (9th Cir.), Cert. Denied, 469 U.S. 824, 1984.
[4] The MNO Directory – Tracking Networks since 2006, 2016. https://www.google.com/?gws_rd=ssl#q=mnodirectory.com+MNO+directory.
[5] GSMA Intelligence – the Global MVNO Footprint: A Changing Environment, February 20, 2015. https://gsmaintelligence.com/research/2015/02/the-global-mvno-footprint-a-changing-environment/490/.
[6] Wireless Local Number Portability (WLNP), November 19, 2015. https://www.fcc.gov/general/wireless-local-number-portability-wlnp.
[7] Search.org – about Us, 2016. http://www.search.org/.

The Legal Process—Part 2

Information in This Chapter

- Search warrant language
- Target language
- Phonescoop.com
- Call Detail Records (CDRs)
- Subscriber
- Destructive court orders

Search Warrant Language

This section provides suggestions on locating appropriate language and addresses the nexus between the incident and the technology of the target. Most of you will have years of experience with drafting and executing subpoenas and warrants. For those of you with little to no experience, this section does not necessarily help to articulate your probable cause.

Target Language (Device)

Describing the device that you want to search within the search warrant should be kept very simple. For law enforcement personnel, this can be as easy as listing the color and general description (example—white iPhone). Most agencies will utilize an evidence "marker" to label the device. This can also be used in the description. What you do not want to do is go inside the device, or remove the battery just to obtain an serial number, IMEI or MEID value. There are some vendors who offer service to assist in identification of phones without actually *looking* inside them. Simply *peeking* inside a phone for identification purposes may, in many courts across the United States, be viewed as a search.

One such tool is called *UFED Phone Detective*. UFED stands for Universal Forensic Extraction Device. This acronym is synonymous with Cellebrite. It will be very common for users of Cellebrite's main acquisition tool to call it UFED or Cellebrite. Cellebrite offers this program for users who have a paid and active account. This program allows the user to search for the phone using a variety of choices. These include phone type, vendor, body, camera location, button location, display type, miscellaneous, quick filter, and measurements.

41

Another method that can be used to help describe a phone for the search warrant (and is free) is from a website called Phonescoop.com. This site allows the visitor to search for the phone by manufacturer name. The site provides a blank search box, which can be used to access images of a particular phone they have on file by manufacturer. Fig. 4.1 depicts the results when the word "Samsung" was used in the search. Users would select the image that is the closest to what they believe is their target evidence. This will in most cases bring up more images of the phone, to include side and back views. This further helps validate that they have the correct phone. Investigators may need to cross-reference the nickname of the phone to the actual model number if they desire to list the model number in the warrant. Phonescoop.com will also list features and characteristics about the phone. They generally include which carriers service a particular device.

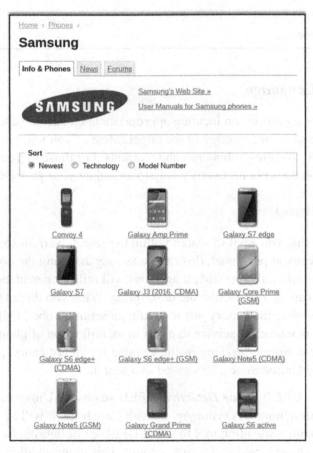

Figure 4.1
Example of searching for "Samsung" in Phonescoop.com.

If we had an iPhone that was seized as evidence, we would simply search for "iPhone" in the upper left corner of the home page on Phonescoop.com. We would select the image that corresponds to the various front, back, and side images. Once Phonescoop informed us of the carrier that services the device we are looking at as evidence, we could use Google to determine the exact model number. Many of the iPhones will have the model number printed on the back lower part of the phone. It can be difficult to see. This information would be put into our warrant.

Fig. 4.2 is an example of how the device might be described with the warrant or subpoena once the model number is determined.

```
44  affiant verily believes that above evidence is concealed in or
45  about a particular house or place, to wit:
46
47   1 each - White in color iPhone 4 model A1349 located at the Tacoma
48  Police Department - 3701 S. Pine Street Tacoma, WA 98409.
49
```

Figure 4.2
Example of an iPhone (actual model number) being inserted into the warrant.

Our next example in Fig. 4.3 documents the search warrant language and involves details about the stored data itself. This example includes authorization for almost everything on this iPhone 4 from a homicide investigation. What should be noted is that the phone does not have a subscriber identity module (SIM) card, nor does it have removable media commonly found in many phones. These should be listed if your phone supports them and you have established probable cause to conduct a forensic search of them. Apple devices have two partitions, and the iPhone 4 is supported by physical extraction that would allow the examiner to search in both. Notice the wording, *proprietary data to include deleted data*. This would cover the secondary partition.

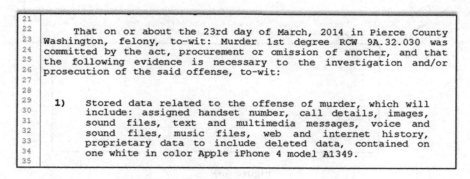

```
21
22      That on or about the 23rd day of March, 2014 in Pierce County
23  Washington, felony, to-wit: Murder 1st degree RCW 9A.32.030 was
24  committed by the act, procurement or omission of another, and that
25  the following evidence is necessary to the investigation and/or
26  prosecution of the said offense, to-wit:
27
28
29   1)    Stored data related to the offense of murder, which will
30         include: assigned handset number, call details, images,
31         sound files, text and multimedia messages, voice and
32         sound files, music files, web and internet history,
33         proprietary data to include deleted data, contained on
34         one white in color Apple iPhone 4 model A1349.
35
```

Figure 4.3
Example of potential and capable stored data on the iPhone 4.

Next, the author will provide an example that would help tie together the elements of the case and the technology of the same phone. We only included what we are authorized by the nexus to search. You are investigating a homicide. The case has revealed the suspect sent images of himself to the victim an hour before she was murdered. A forensic search of her LG (Android) phone located potential images with metadata from an iPhone 4. The images have Geo-tagged data, which show an approximate location of where they were captured. Based on this information, you now want to prepare a search warrant from this nexus and search his iPhone 4, model A1349.

Using Phonescoop, you research the features and determine the phone is equipped with the ability to Geo-tag images and video. You then limit what you want to search for based on the facts established thus far. At the top of Fig. 4.4 we see the features (from Phonescoop) that support the metadata and Geo-tagging ability you encountered when searching the victim's phone. At the bottom of Fig. 4.4 we see how we change what artifacts we are looking for. This would be an example of validating the technology (ability) to the nexus of the case.

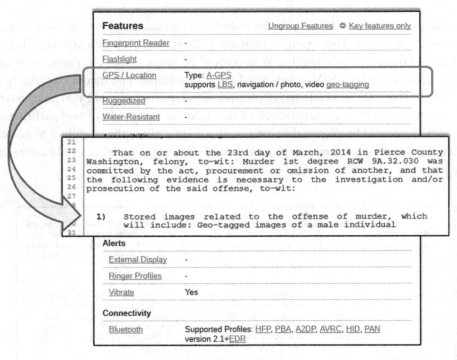

Figure 4.4
Confirmation of technology features to the nexus of the incident.

Nexus—A Hot Topic

There have been a number of national events that have triggered tighter scrutiny on the search of mobile evidence. For the author, two cases recently affected Judicial Officers' decisions on granting warrants within Pierce County, Washington. These are *State v. Besola* [1] and *State v. Keodara* [2]. We will briefly discuss State v. Keodara as it relates to cell phone searches.

State v. Keodara, Washington Court of Appeals, Division I, addressed the particularity requirement of the Fourth Amendment. Presented in that case was a juvenile who was arrested on an unrelated incident from a vehicle; a backpack was inside the vehicle, which, in turn, contained a cell phone. A warrant to search the cell phone was obtained by officers investigating the incident. The facts presented in the warrant for probable cause addressed the common practice and habits of gang members in general terms. It addressed photographing and texting in relation to firearms and drugs. The defendant was later charged with a gang-related shooting, and evidence from the search of the cell phone was introduced at that trial. The appeals court held that the evidence linking Keodara's use of his phone to any illicit activity within the affidavit was found to be insufficient under the Fourth Amendment.

Investigators in many jurisdictions within Washington State are now performing more than one search warrant on mobile evidence related to an incident. The warrant would no longer be broad in nature, suggesting common practice, habits, street activities, etc., unless it was actually part of the investigation (nexus) elements.

A Third Time Is a Charm

Staying Within Legal Authority

Three suspects were arrested for armed robbery within Puget Sound. Their vehicle was held for a search warrant and three mobile devices could be seen inside sitting on the passenger seat from outside the vehicle.

The vehicle was linked to several robberies, and thefts. During the thefts, phones had been taken that belonged to various victims. It was unknown who owned the phones or if they were from fruits of other (unknown) criminal incidents. The first warrant on these devices was to establish information related to the owners of the devices, and related to the theft investigations. Once inside the file system, images of firearms could be seen along with potential "selfies" of the owner. The search was stopped and another warrant for the offense of robbery was executed. The second warrant included images of all three defendants, firearms used in previous robbery incidents, and other elements of the robberies. In all, three different warrants were executed due to different artifacts being encountered through the authority of each warrant. The third and last warrant was for child pornography.

Regarding the search warrant language for the device and area to search, we must be able to properly describe the item to be searched and also should include areas to search that have a nexus between our incident and the phone's specific features.

Figs. 4.5 and 4.6 are examples of the case nexus and the phone's technology ability. This example is a search warrant from a child death investigation by abuse.

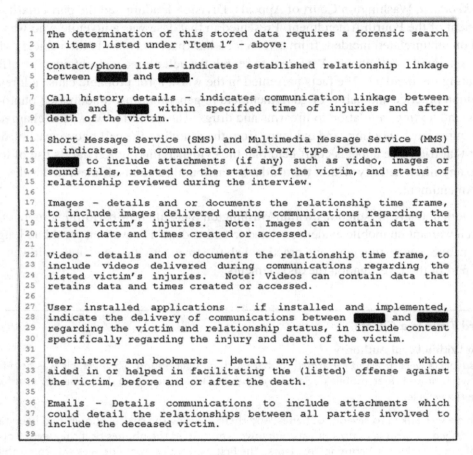

Figure 4.5
Nexus example part 1.

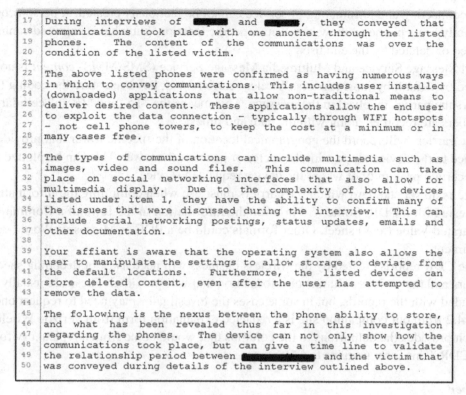

Figure 4.6
Nexus example part 2.

Call Detail Records

Investigators may also need to request data from the Call Detail Records (CDRs). This language will describe the equipment, protocols, antennas, switching locations, physical locations of the equipment, and other proprietary specific items as needed to facilitate in service. There will also be the need to include a date range, which is tied directly back to the incident. Fig. 4.1 on the companion site is an example of the type of language required by several different wireless carriers rolled into one paragraph. This example is for several Verizon target numbers. The example contains acronyms specially requested from Verizon's legal department. It is suggested that if it is the reader's first time executing a CDR warrant, contact them directly or obtain their Law Enforcement guide for assistance.

There are some general things to understand about the CDR aspect of the warrant.

1. CDR information will generally always be accurate, and unlike the Subscriber details, is not reliant on information supplied by the user, such as in cases of pay-as-you-go phones.

2. The connecting and terminating of service cannot be factiously created. A person could certainly use a phone to show it was at a specific location, but what is captured cannot be altered or deleted by the end user.
3. Short Message Service and Multimedia Message Service (SMS/MMS) *content* is not stored by default by most carriers. Wireless carriers will, however, store the coding that shows the parties involved in the message. This means the "To" and "From" cellular numbers are recorded along with the date and times.
4. Some carriers will record the geographical location of the specific tower that provided the service to the device along with the sector or panel of the tower. This can be plotted to give certain proximity of where the device requested service.
5. There is no set standard which the carriers must use when compiling the information requested for a CDR. Some will provide the information in the form of a Comma Separated Value (.csv) sheet. Other formats could be a PDF or Microsoft Word document.
6. Some CDR reports created by the wireless business will need a *key* or decoding sheet to understand the various columns of information that was provided. These are usually included with the records, but in some cases the investigator may need to request one. Fig. 4.2 from our companion site is a redacted explanation form from Verizon Wireless, which provides the definitions to the columns that would come from a typical.csv formatted CDR. This form pertains to SMS.

Subscriber

The information that is related to the person or persons who are responsible for paying the bill is part of what defines the *Subscriber*. This information pertains to the account that was created to provide the services for the wireless handset. There can be multiple handsets if the account has combined users. As such, this information will contain other information unrelated to the elements listed in the CDR. One way to keep the differences straight between the CDR and the Subscriber is to think of the Subscriber as the "*who*" and "*what*" of your warrant. Who opened the account? Who can access the bill? Who can use the features that were paid for? What services are offered? What data is stored by the provider? What are the credentials to access voice mail and other user accounts?

Just like the device itself that constantly changes from one model release to another, the examiner must find a way to stay on top of describing the subscriber language. An analogy that goes along with this is to understand playing the lottery. If you purchase a ticket, you have a *chance* (although many times it is small) at winning. If you *never* purchase a ticket, you, of course, have no chance to win. When requesting the Subscriber information, we are in some ways playing the lottery. In most investigations we do not know exactly what services the user has set up with the carrier. If your investigation is like most, the account specifics are not generally given much if any, consideration.

When drafting language pertinent to the wireless carrier it helps to know the terminology for specific features that are being used to describe service with a particular vendor. These are easy to research, and the investigator can find them by visiting the target business website. For instance, you are investigating a number that has been confirmed through a phone call to Search.org as belonging to AT&T. Your probable cause and nexus allows you to retrieve cloud-based data, which could include contacts, images, SMS, and other details. You want to create the Subscriber information on your warrant to reflect what AT&T offers for this type of storage. The information gleaned from the investigators in your case do not clearly show if the suspect is using cloud services, but you nonetheless have the right, through probable cause to search for it. The correct verbiage may be obtained from visiting their site.

When describing our target AT&T number with regard to the Subscriber, we would use the latest information researched from their site. It is not uncommon to use a standard "boiler plate" terminology when drafting warrants. There is nothing wrong with that approach as long as there is an attempt to update sections with current catch phrases or descriptions being used by the service provider in question. Verizon uses *Verizon Cloud*.

This Was Not My Phone

Account Comments

Another item to include within the Subscriber area of the search warrant pertains to "Account Comments." There was a particular defendant who wanted to portray to the jury that his life was not as the State had represented him. His shirt collar and neck tie covered a particular incriminating gang tattoo, and he denied that he was involved in gangs or affiliated with them altogether. His hair had been cut, and he sat up straight during testimony, with a look of grave concern on his face. The defendant had introduced testimony which was confirmed through the questioning of other witnesses, that the phone had been purchased by someone else, and that he was not the actual owner of the device.

These were excellent questions posed by the defense counsel. However, 4 minutes before a text message was sent to another codefendant regarding elements related to the shooting, the defendant had called the wireless carrier. This call was to dispute elements in the subscriber's last monthly bill. The defendant was required to supply several layers of security questions to identify him and access the account. The account was not actually in his name, but he had been authorized as a person who could have full access. He discussed that he wanted credit applied to the bill with regard to a string of recently dropped calls. The calls were actually to and from the codefendant! All this was typed into the *Account Comments* section by the representative, which was revealed by "playing the lottery" and requesting the Account Comments. The defense stipulated to the comments and did not want the actual operator called to the stand to validate she had created the comments. After the conviction the jury spoke about the case and advised that the Account Comments clearly convinced them who sent the message about the shooting.

In the companion site, Fig. 4.3 is an example of Subscriber language that would include account comments, voicemail passwords, and the specific language provided in the wireless carrier's website (highlighted in yellow). This example is for a Verizon target number and includes the date range.

Destructive Court Orders

At this early stage in the book, there has been no mention of the advanced techniques that may be applied to obtain stored mobile evidence. Since we are addressing the legal component of searching, this chapter will also include the destructive court order. If you wish to understand the destructive technique first, feel free to skip ahead and read on. Remember to revisit this area if necessary. Again, this is the author's own experience and preference with his legal counsel. Your actual mileage may vary.

Nondestructive—Always the First Choice

In most instances, examiners will use a commercial or open-source tool to obtain what is necessary in their specific case. The commercial forensic tools are applied to 90%–95% of all criminal cases. When phones come into laboratories for processing, every attempt is made to get to the stored user data by not damaging the phone. Many law enforcement laboratories across the world have no choice in this matter; if they obtain an evidential phone that has been damaged, is unsupported, or locked, they simply cannot process the phone because they do not have specialized tools or training. Even when laboratories do have the ability to conduct advanced destructive techniques, they should first exhaust all other means before resorting to manually pulling the memory from the main board. Due to the risks involved with destructive processing, it should never be the examiner's first choice in mobile forensics.

Typical Work Flow

The advanced technique that needs to be utilized for the experienced mobile forensic examiner will always depend on what is encountered and supported on the target phone. For example, if the device is an Android, and the user has enabled a gesture pattern, attempts would be made to defeat the security utilizing commercially available tools first. One item that is often overlooked with Androids, is if the user enabled the USB Debugging setting. This is off by default. But, if the user did enabled it, and also set security such as a PIN, gesture, or other model or application specific setting, then the forensic tool can most likely get into it. Basically, you must still try to connect your forensic tool to the supported device—because you have no way of telling if it is enabled or not. If you do not try, and it is enabled, you could have save yourself a lot of time by trying another technique. Do not assume that because there is security, the internal settings are also blocking communications.

There are several popular commercial forensic tools that support a number of phones in which they can bypass the security. The tools utilize special cables and steps such as the download mode, *ODIN*, and *Fastboot* depending on the make of phone. Generally speaking, advanced forensic techniques will include methods that do not employ conventional commercial tools. They may also use tools that may take advantage of acquiring phones' physical file (.bin) through their own developer modes.

When devices are not supported by commercially available forensic tools for security bypass, the next step would be to determine if there is a repair or programming tool that might defeat the security. This is generally some form of a flasher box. These will be discussed later in this book. Some allow the user to defeat the security of select model phones. If this option does not encompass the target phone, the examiner would begin to look for a possible JTAG solution.

JTAG options are not available for all phones. Furthermore, many phones will not have the points or Test Access Ports (TAPs) mapped out for the forensic process to take place. There will be times when TAPs are present and there is no documentation of how they communicate with the target. For instance, the Motorola XT912 does not have JTAG TAPs on the main board and therefore could not be accessed using flasher boxes that support JTAG extraction. The next approach would be an In-System-Programming (ISP) examination. Not all phones support ISP. ISP is addressed in the final chapter of this book.

The chip-off option is the last resort, and the examiner must research if the processor is supported with the adaptors that are in the laboratory. There will be times that the adaptor needs to be purchased, as there are a number of sizes and configurations. If this is the only way to acquire the data, there may be legal processes that need to be followed first. There are many newer chips that can be encrypted, even if the user has not enabled encryption through the GUI of the phone. These, of course, would not benefit from a chip-off examination, as the pulled data would be useless.

Court Order (Pierce County, WA)

Within Pierce County, the policy with regard to the destructive "chip-off" examination is to consult with a prosecutor when charges have been brought against a defendant or charges *may be brought* as a result of the examination. In those cases, if the destructive examination is to proceed, the prosecutor must obtain a court order. This allows defense to object to any aspect of the destructive process. Many times the court order is allowed only if the process is video recorded by the examiner. The court may also order that defense or their expert(s) is present during the process. All other examinations that are not destructive in nature do not require a court order; however, they generally require some form of legal process as discussed during our previous chapter (*Search warrant/Exigent/Consent*).

If the case is a "*who done it*?" and no one has been identified as committing the offense in question, then there is no expectation of privacy and a court order is generally not needed. This may also apply if the victim is deceased, such as a victim from a homicide or other felony crime. As a general rule, it is still advisable to consult with any legal adviser if there may be a question as to pending charges.

Language Used in the Hearing

Deputy prosecutors will generally be the people who will argue the merits behind the reason why the court order is necessary. In almost every case, a search warrant was already granted on the devices in question and the examiner encounters a phone that fits into the categories previously outlined. This means he/she began the process of searching the phone based on the nexus granted in the warrant and has encountered one of the previously explained problems that stopped his/her search. The prosecutor must be able to explain the next (destructive) process to the court. Present at the hearing will be a Judicial Officer (judge) and the defense attorney for the defendant(s). Here are examples of suggestions that would help explain the process. The evidence referenced would be listed on the order itself via IMEI or MEID values that were previously obtained via the previous legal process (as shown in the court order example that precedes this):

> The above mentioned items are currently in a forensic state that either has user enabled security, damages or artifacts are **not** supported for parsing using commercially available forensic, non-destructive methods. The forensic analysis of the phone(s) involves a destructive process in which the physical memory is removed from the main boards of the phone, cleaned and the binary memory parsed using a supported memory adaptor. This process destroys the phone and may involve the use of heat to extract the chip off the seated area on the board.
>
> Due to the process of introducing high temperatures and actual contact cleaning with the Ball Grid Array (BGA), it has risks to the memory and can render it unreadable, and even destroy the chip entirely. This process is similar to DNA samples that get consumed in order for the DNA profile to be complied.
>
> This destructive forensic process if successful will allow defense to utilize the same cleaned memory chip and duplicate the parsing process from that part of the forensic exam forward.
>
> Due to the police lab being a secured facility, defense is not granted access to personally watch this process–however the lab utilizes a digital microscope camera and standard micro photography to document the entire destructive exam.

Of significant importance is the prosecutor's ability to fully explain what the chip-off process involves and that defense will be given a copy of the video and images of the examination. Within Pierce County, it is strongly suggested that prosecutors attend training related to the destructive forensic examination and are provided copies of suggested wording as outlined in the previous paragraphs.

As mentioned in the language example, if the chip removal is a success, defense would be allowed to take the same chip and use tools to duplicate the forensic process. By having the state (prosecution) address the court regarding the potential risks, defense would typically not be able to argue that the data that was destroyed purposely by the state. There have been cases that when a defendant was aware that his/her phone was going to be examined using a destructive technique, he/she voluntarily agreed to the process. The defendant's cooperation may have been, in part, due to the risk of destroying the incriminating data that was on the phone. Once defense was given a copy of the examination, the defendant pled based on the findings. This type of tactic is common, as mobile devices are increasingly found to holding compelling evidence that only the defendant is aware of. They rely on the belief that it cannot be accessed with security measures enabled.

Example of an Order

The order itself will generally not contain the lengthy previous wording that a prosecuting attorney will use to argue the merits of the case. The order should be relatively short in nature and list the evidential items as well as the procedure and any special instructions. Fig. 4.4 in the companion site provides an actual destructive chip-off order (redacted).

Chapter Summary Key Points

Investigators must be able to articulate within the warrant the specific features and characteristics of their evidence. Provided in this chapter are two examples of utilities that are available. One commercial type is offered by Cellebrite. UFED Phone Detective can assist in properly identifying a mobile device without searching inside of it or taking it apart. A free site called Phonescoop.com can also provide assistance with identification and researching specific features of the device when linking the nexus elements in the narrative of the search warrant.

Account Service Comments by the vendor, can be an excellent source of documented information that links individuals back to use and activity on the number in question. The search warrant will require the investigators to stay current with specific language. The terms necessary to the successful retrieval of evidential data, require investigators to be resourceful and vigilant. This may include contacting the wireless legal department, downloading a user manual, and conducting online research. Fig. 4.7 is a quick reference table where investigators can go to obtain the specific language that is contained in the search warrant.

Device (cell phone) language	Subscriber language	Call Detail Records (CDR)
Phonescoop.com	Carrier (legal department)	Carrier (legal department)
Manufacturer site	Carrier's web site	Tower type
Device manual	Search.org	

Locating Specific Language for Search Warrants

Figure 4.7
Quick Reference Table for search warrant language.

Destructive court orders can help in investigations by disclosing to counsel the reason for the order, prior to the issue being brought up during trial. Prosecutors who draft and present the order to judicial officers should understand the process involved and how to articulate it. The actual order that is presented to the court may not require all the details of the process, but the judge and defense counsel need to fully understand the process, and the prosecutor should be able to answer any question that may be posed. If the concept of the destructive court order is still confusing regarding the process involved, keep reading, as this book explains both thermal and nonthermal chip-off examinations.

References

[1] 337 P. 3d 325 – Wash: Supreme Court, 1st Dept, State v. Besola, 2014.
[2] No. 70518-1-I – Wash. Ct. App, State v. Keodara, November 2, 2015.

The Cellular Network

Information in This Chapter

This chapter provides a number of terms used to describe the major cellular communication types and components used in the *Cellular Network*.

Introduction to the Cellular Network

If we look at the recent history of mobile phones and the networks that support them, we will find that there are two main communication *protocol* types. In this chapter we will provide a very basic overview on each of them as well as a couple of others that may be encountered, depending on where you work within the world. It is important for a beginner in cell phone examinations to understand the basic network functionality and how that will fit in with the target handset. The characteristics of the wireless network will, in most cases, always augment the forensic examination. As the examiner becomes more experienced with extracting data, the core information regarding the specific communication protocols will become clearer. The numerous terms that are used to describe the *Cellular Network* may, at first, seem a bit overwhelming. To help with this, when we explain a term we will, in some cases, provide on a *"Q & A"* section directly afterward. Fig. 5.1 provides a simple illustration that shows the correlation between the device, the network, and the cloud. All three locations "play in the evidence sandbox" together.

Seeking the Truth from Mobile Evidence. http://dx.doi.org/10.1016/B978-0-12-811056-0.00005-4
55

Figure 5.1
Simple illustrations showing our locations for evidence.

Code Division Multiple Access

Let us pretend for the moment that you work for a business that requires you to travel and meet with other executives throughout the world. Each business from around the globe works in teams of two. One person from each executive team arrives to the meeting before his/her respective partner. There are 10 different countries represented, with 20 people totally attending the meeting. Each one begins speaking his/her own native language and cannot understand anyone else in the room. An hour goes by and the other member of each team arrives. At this point all 20 executives are present, and each team of two is speaking to their partner. The entire room communicates at once; to an outsider it all sounds like gibberish, but each team of two from their own country completely understands what is being said.

This basic analogy can be used to help in understanding the way in which Code Division Multiple Access (CDMA) works. CDMA uses *Analog to Digital Conversation*. The transmission frequency is set up to vary according to a defined pattern. This "pattern" must be captured by a receiver that has the same program pattern. There are trillions of these patterns possible that makes cloning nearly impossible. CDMA uses various frequency ranges from 700 to 2500 megahertz (MHz), depending on the location and the actual device that supports specific ranges. The ranges are typically referred to as *bands* such as triband and quad-band.

Q) **Why would knowing if a device is CDMA be important?**

A) If a phone is properly identified as a CDMA-serviced device, examiners should understand that *some* basic CDMA model phones **will not** contain other items such as a subscriber identity module (SIM). Years ago, all an examiner needed to check for was the presence of a SIM card near the battery or other location. *No SIM = CDMA* phone. With the 4G network, this has changed and will be explained in the upcoming pages. Also, confirming the network type can help in determining the Form Factor. Mobile device Form Factor identification is sometimes needed for search warrants and specific examination techniques to follow.

Global Systems for Mobile Communications and Time Division Multiple Access

Using the executive teams from our previous example, let us pretend there are no language barriers to understand each other, but to talk back to the group our conversation has to be timed. All the group members are divided into specific number of teams. The teams have their own intervals assigned in which they can communicate. The communication between the entire group only works if the conversations from each team are divided into unique "slot" periods of time. Each person gets to talk exactly when his/her allotted time slot opens up.

GSM is based on *Time Division Multiple Access* (TDMA). You speak and the information is transformed into digital data and is set out and in turn given a specific time slot. The receiver (whom you communicate with) has to have the same time slot information to get the digital information complied back on their end properly. There are some experts who boil down the two main technology types not as GSM and CDMA but as TDMA and CDMA, as TDMA is actually the *transmission technique* used by GSM.

GSM, like the CDMA protocol, has its own set of frequencies by which it can function. These are from 850 to 2100 Mhz, and also similar to CDMA, phones can be dual band or triband. GSM is much older than the CDMA technology and began in Europe. GSM devices use SIMs.

Q) **Why would knowing if a device works on a GSM network be important?**

A) Unlike CDMA, *all* GSM devices will need a SIM card to authenticate and work on their assigned network. Some CDMA phone will need a SIM card, but with GSM there is no choice and the SIM must be present for the phone to obtain service from the wireless company. Just like CDMA, determining the network type will help to identify the Form Factor. Of course in the case of 9-1-1 calling, a GSM phone does not actually need a SIM to work, or network allocation for that matter (paid service).

Integrated Digital Enhanced Network

Using cellular telephone and trunked radio technology, Motorola developed the Integrated Digital Enhanced Network—*iDEN*. Within the United States, iDEN was phased out but is still used in other countries. This was known as "push-to-talk" and operated on 25 kilohertz (kHz) channels. It was not continuous and used speech compression and TDMA, resulting in a two-way radio broadcast that worked like the old "walkie-talkies."

Q) **Why would an examiner need to know about iDEN, especially if it has been phased out in the United States?**

A) iDEN devices may still be encountered during search warrants or evidence collection. iDEN devices will use a SIM card, and in the United States they are not a GSM-serviced device. Because the SIM is present, examiners must distinguish the iDEN handset from the GSM device. A company called Nextel provided service for iDEN handsets. Nextel was owned by Sprint Spectrum and used CDMA communications.

Long-Term Evolution

As phones developed over time the need to transfer data at faster rates also grew. A standard called *Long-Term Evolution* (LTE) was created. Many also refer to LTE as 4G LTE, as the number *4* would signify the fourth generation of speed. Third Generation Partnership Project (3GPP) created the specifications for LTE. Within the North American region, which encompassed the United States and Canada, 5GAmericas.org indicated in an April 2016 report that there were 69 operators offering LTE and 7 LTE-Advanced within these two countries [1]. The International Telecommunication Union (ITU) is a United Nations agency that sets standards internationally for telecommunications. The ITU states, "We allocate global radio spectrum and satellite orbits, develop the technical standards that ensure networks and technologies seamlessly interconnect, and strive to improve access to ICTs to underserved communities worldwide" [2]. This means the device is supposed to meet a specific standard imposed by ITU to be labeled 4G.

The following term is from 3GPP.org and was used to describe LTE-Advanced:

> *In LTE-Advanced focus is on higher capacity: The driving force to further develop LTE towards LTE–Advanced - LTE Release10 was to provide higher bitrates in a cost efficient way and, at the same time, completely fulfil the requirements set by ITU for IMT Advanced, also referred to as 4G.*

- *Increased peak data rate, DL 3 Gbps, UL 1.5 Gbps*
- *Higher spectral efficiency, from a maximum of 16 bps/Hz in R8 to 30 bps/Hz in R10*
- *Increased number of simultaneously active subscribers*
- *Improved performance at cell edges, e.g. for DL 2 × 2 MIMO at least 2.40 bps/Hz/cell.*

The main new functionalities introduced in LTE-Advanced are Carrier Aggregation (CA), enhanced use of multi-antenna techniques and support for Relay Nodes (RN) [3].

Most new smartphones will support standard LTE. When an examiner has navigated to internal settings within the phone, he/she may encounter specific areas that indicate the phone is LTE enabled or equipped. By the time you have read this book, this may have also changed.

The generation of speed will continue to advance and evolve. In February 2016, *GSM Association* produced a paper titled "Unlocking Commercial Opportunities From 4G Evolution to 5G." The following is an excerpt:

5G refers to fifth generation mobile technology. It offers enormous potential for both consumers and industry and in addition to being considerably faster than existing technologies, 5G holds the promise of applications with high social and economic value, leading to a 'hyper-connected society.'

It is different to previous generational steps such as 3G and 4G which have typically focused on a faster data-rate and lower latency radio technology in that 5G is being defined more as an ecosystem. A new 5G radio interface will be required to be defined to meet the requirements of some of the higher-speed, lower-latency use cases. However, the 5G ecosystem will provide multi-access connectivity that can make opportunistic use of LTE-Advanced, Wi-Fi and LPWA technologies such as Narrowband-IoT. Many of the technical advancements required to fulfil the 5G vision already form part of the network innovations being undertaken by operators today. For example, in technologies such as NFV, SDN, HetNets and Low Power and Low Throughput networks [4].

Q) **Why would an examiner need to have a basic understanding of the specific generation technology the target device supports?**

A) The answer is tied into our previous explanation that involved CDMA and GSM devices. Currently, mobile phones that support 4G or LTE will contain a SIM card. This card will vary in size, which we will discuss later in this chapter. For now, it is important to understand that if the phone is a CDMA device, it will have a SIM to assist in delivering and authenticating the LTE service. Also, specific features (and subsequent terms) used to describe those features were in the past reserved for GSM phones. Due to LTE-related services, these terms and artifacts will now also apply to CDMA handsets. Each of these terms will also be addressed in this chapter. For now, understand that they are being encountered on CDMA smartphones as the IMEI

(International Mobile Equipment Identity), ICCID (Integrated Circuit Card Identifier), and IMSI (International Mobile Subscriber Identity). Each can contain specific, unique, evidential values that we will explain.

Fig. 5.1 on the companion site is an example of the internal display of *LTE* from a CDMA phone. This Samsung SM-G900V is serviced by Verizon (CDMA) and, under the *Settings—About Phone—Status*, shows the "Mobile network type" as LTE.

My Phone Can't Do That... *(Ugh! Wrong!)*

Long-Term Evolution Settings
During a trial that involved a case with a registered sex offender, numerous screenshots were obtained from a phone, which had been forensically examined and indicated various specific, unique attributes that identified the device. These included the phone number, ICCID, IMSI, and many other terms we have yet to discuss. Among the screenshots was an image that indicated "Mobile network type LTE."

The case involved downloading specific *Hashed* images that had *Known File Filters* previously recognized as child pornography. The defendant's attorney was claiming that the particular model phone was not capable of receiving such images, and that the defendant was only using the phone for simple text and calling. The court was allowed to hear testimony regarding LTE function as well as Wi-Fi settings. This helped establish basic foundation regarding the wireless source that may have been used in facilitating the download.

International Mobile Equipment Identity

The IMEI is a unique number that identifies the *handset*. IMEI values are usually 15 digits in length, which are actually made up of 14 digits with a check digit included. There is also an IMEISV. The "SV" stands for software version. An IMEISV is the standard IMEI with additional values at the end, which correspond to the IMEI software version. This will typically result in a total of 16 digits. If the wireless device is stolen, an IMEI can be reported to the wireless carrier who in turn can flag or "blacklist" the device from service.

Depending on the age of the phone, the IMEI may also include a Final Assembly Code value within the IMEI sting. An investigator would read the IMEI from left to right; part of the number would represent specific values based on the structure design from 3GPP. The first series of numbers (left to right) are related to the Type Allocation Code. This value alone can identify a make, model, and possibly the version of the phone.

Fig. 5.2 is an example of the format that has been used for several years on IMEI numbers.

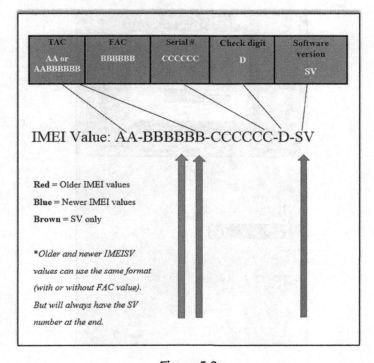

Figure 5.2

IMEI (International Mobile Equipment Identity) and IMEISV (IMEI software version) values broken down. *FAC*, Final Assembly Code; *SV*, software version; *TAC*, Type Allocation Code.

Fig. 5.2 from our companion site displays both the IMEI and IMEISV values of an active Samsung Galaxy 5 that is serviced by Verizon. The IMEI has been redacted, but this is an example of how an LTE CDMA phone will have this value within the settings of the phone.

If a device that has a removable battery and is a GSM or CDMA LTE/4G serviced phone that is encountered, the IMEI will generally be affixed to the label. Many new phones will not have removable batteries, and the setting will be inside the phone as shown in Fig. 5.2 on the companion site.

The top image of Fig. 5.3 shows the same IMEI value on the label of the Samsung Galaxy 5 as the internal value shown directly below. Note that the IMEISV is not included on the label.

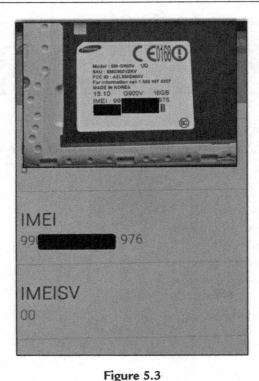

Figure 5.3
Example of label IMEI (International Mobile Equipment Identity) and internal IMEI values of Code Division Multiple Access Long-Term Evolution (CDMA LTE) phone.

Q) **Why should an investigator understand what an IMEI value is used for?**

A) IMEI values are linked to the device. This value will show up in many automated forensic tools when compiling a final report. Besides having a basic understanding of what an IMEI value is, there may be instances where the IMEI needs to be checked to determine if the device is stolen. Besides using the wireless carrier to assist, there are free online sites that can check the IMEI. Such sites include *Numberingplans.com*, *IMEIdata.net*, and *IMEI.info*, just to name a few.

Mobile Equipment Identifier

The Mobile Equipment Identifier (MEID) value is used globally to identify CDMA devices. Several years back, this value was called an *Electronic Serial Number* (ESN), but the ESN format was changed to conform closer to the MEID standard. Both the MEID and IMEI are many times referred to as the ESN for a CDMA and GSM device. MEID values are 15 hex digits in length. From left to right they contain a region code, a manufacturer code, and a serial number and end with a check digit. A June 2005 3GPP2 report outlines the MEID number format [5].

Most CDMA devices that are simple, "nonsmartphones" will only have an MEID. To confuse matters, some CDMA smartphones will have an MEID and an IMEI. The CDMA MEID may be displayed in an *MEID DEC* or *MEID HEX* format.

Q) **Why would it be important for investigators to understand the definition MEID?**
A) If a phone has an MEID, it will be a CDMA device. If the device has an IMEI, a closer examination may be required to determine if the equipment is actually a CDMA phone with LTE service.

Subscriber Identity Module

Chapter 6 is devoted entirely to explain the SIM and the file system artifacts that may be located. For now, we will provide some basic information on the SIM. *SIM* stands for: *Subscriber Identification Module*. Most people when talking about a phone that is equipped with a SIM, will indicate that the device contains a "*SIM card*." A SIM (card) is actually a small integrated chip. The chip works like a small computer. SIMs have specific network information stored on them, which helps the device receive specific services the subscriber has paid for. Two items of importance, which are stored on the SIM and are discussed in this chapter are: the IMSI and the ICCID. As previously addressed, SIMs are always used on a GSM phone and will also be found in CDMA LTE devices.

International Mobile Subscriber Identity

Just like the IMEI value which is linked directly to the mobile device, the IMSI value is linked to the SIM card. This can be used to identify the subscriber. The network needs this value to allow service to the device. Not all SIM cards will contain the IMSI. Some CDMA phones that are LTE equipped may store this value on the handset. Also, some pay-as-you-go devices store the IMSI on the SIM card as long as the user has not run out of "credits." There are also specific (rare) model phones that will not contain the IMSI on the SIM even though the device is GSM. In all other cases with a GSM device, the IMSI value will be stored on the SIM. Many forensic examiners who have examined phones for years have yet to run into a GSM device that does not contain the IMSI on the SIM. The author, however, has, and although it is uncommon, it can occur.

Just like the IMEI, the IMSI had specific numbers within the digits, which represent certain values. This value will usually be 15 digits depending on the country.

This fixed number will be comprised of a 3-digit Mobile Country Code, a 3-digit Mobile Network Code, and a Mobile Station Identification Number, that is, 9 digits.

Q) **Why would an examiner need to understand the purpose of the IMSI?**

A) Many GSM devices allow a user to move the SIM from phone to phone. In this instance, the IMEI would change, but the IMSI value stays the same. As mentioned in this chapter, the IMSI is linked to the subscriber. Obtaining this value in some instances may help in that endeavor. There would be specific (legal) conditions that would need to be met, and on a pay-as-you-go device it may not show an actual "named" individual. Lastly, the IMSI value can be used to create a forensic SIM card. A forensic SIM is used to network isolate the device and in some cases allow entry into a locked handset. Forensic SIM card creation is addressed in the next chapter.

Integrated Circuit Card Identifier

The ICCID value can be 19 or 20 characters and is stored on the SIM card. Think of this as a unique value, that is, the "serial number" to the SIM card. Each of the digits contained with the ICCID will have specific meaning and include a check digit. It is common for the ICCID value to be printed on the outside of the SIM card. Fig. 5.3 on the companion site shows a SIM card from T-Mobile. The T-Mobile symbol has been redacted off the card, but the original ICCID value can easily be viewed if the SIM is removed from the phone.

The ICCID number (from left to right) is comprised of the *ISO 7812 Major Industry Identifier*, which will be 89, followed by the *Country Code*, then the *Issuer Identifier*, account number (a.k.a.: serial number), and a check digit. Only the *Major Industry Identifier* is a fixed two-digit value. The others can be from 1 to 4 digits, excluding the account number.

Q) **Why should an examiner need to understand what an ICCID value is?**

A) This value only comes from the SIM card. Like the IMSI, it stays with the SIM even in instances where phones have the SIM card switched out. Also, there may be times when a SIM card has been security locked by the user. In those instances, the ICCID can still be read, even though the IMSI value remains unreadable due to security. By using the ICCID value, the examiner can apply an advanced technique and derive the IMSI from the ICCID value. This can then be used to create a forensic SIM clone and enter the locked phone.

Mobile Identification Number, Mobile Directory Number, and Preferred Roaming List

The Mobile Directory Number (MDN; also called Mobile Dialing Number) is the actual number that is used to call the handset on a wireless network. The Mobile Identification Number (MIN) is a derivate of the IMSI and is used to identify the *device* on the network. The MIN may also be referred to as the Mobile Subscription Identification Number. The MIN value is used to identify a *Mobile Station* (MS). The MS is explained below.

Q) **Why would an examiner need to understand a MIN and an MDN?**

A) These two values can oftentimes be confused with the actual number that was being used by the owner/operator of the phone. Not all devices will internally name the phone number as the MDN and some devices will not show a value present for a MIN. Fig. 5.4 from the companion site is again a redacted example from the Samsung Galaxy 5 (CDMA LTE). This shows the MDN being labeled by the OS as "*My phone number.*" Directly below the number is displayed the MIN. Note the image also depicts the "PRL version," which stands for *Preferred Roaming List* (PRL). The short version of what the PRL does is that it is a database associated with CDMA devices to assist the device with service, especially when out of the home area.

How a Call Is Routed Through a Global System for Mobile Communications Network

This section addresses key areas of a GSM network. This includes the MS, Mobile Equipment (ME), and Mobile Station International Subscriber Directory Number (MSISDN). To save time, we will only include how routing of calls take place on a GSM network. We will exclude the Q & A until each part of the phone call process is explained. We will also exclude how data transfer. We start with the MS.

Mobile Station

The MS is the device that is placing the call. This would be a cellular phone and the SIM card. The handset and in some cases the SIM card would also contain the MSISDN. The handset and SIM are called ME or User Equipment (UE) and are the components of the MS. This is where the call would start.

Base Transceiver Station

The Base Transceiver Station (BTS) will handle the initial protocols coming from the MS. Once a user presses "send" to call to "Mom" in the phone book, the call goes directly to the BTS. One of the biggest components of the BTS is the cellular antenna. Many people believe the antenna is actually the BTS, but, in fact, that is just one of the items from the BTS. Additional equipment at the BTS level would be the power trans-ceivers, amplifiers, combiner, multiplexer, alarm extension system, and other necessary components.

BTS components are usually housed inside of a rack. It looks similar to a large server and will usually have a backup power system in case of power failure. In some parts of the United

States, this is the small building directly at the foot of the cellular tower that will be behind a security fence.

Base Station Controller

The Base Station Controller (BSC) will handle the radio resources for one or more of the BTSs. It acts as a "manager" and performs radio channel setup, frequency hopping, and handoffs. One of its main managerial duties is to handle traffic signal issues. If a device had a signal from the BTS that was not strong enough, the BSC would pass it to another site that is capable of covering the signal. The BSC works between the BTS and the next component, the Mobile Switching Center (MSC). Up close, the BSC looks similar to the BTS and is housed in a rack that would have a cooling and appropriate backup contingency.

MSC, Home Location Registry (HLR), Visitor Location Registry (VLR), Temporary Mobile Subscriber Identity (TMSI), Equipment Identity Registry (EIR), Authentication Center (AuC), and Public Switched Telephone Network (PSTN).

Mobile Switching Center

The MSC's primary duty is routing voice calls, SMS, and other services and to include calls that need to go outside of the network. Calls outside the network are routed by the MSC to the PSTN. There are variants to the MSC, which have specific roles. These include the Gateway MSC, Visited MSC, and Anchor MSC. Think of the MSC as a "router."

Home Location Registry

The function of the HLR is connected directly with the MSC. There is one HLR that will be associated to one IMSI. The main permanent data that are stored by the HLR pertain to subscriber services that have been paid for, and the current location of the subscriber. The HLR will also include the MSISDN.

Visitor Location Registry

Unlike the HLR, which will be only one, the VLR can be one per MSC. The VLR is a database that stores information on where the target subscriber is roaming within the MSC area. The main job of the VLR is to keep the MSC from having to make inquiries to the HLR for subscriber information. The VLR stores less information than the HLR.

Temporary Mobile Subscriber Identity

In direct correlation with the VLR is the TMSI. The function of the TMSI is similar to the IMSI. As the phone travels, it is granted service by the VLR. The TMSI is randomly assigned by the VLR. This value changes often and is used for security. There will be numerous TMSI values over the life of the mobile device, but the IMSI value stays the same.

Equipment Identity Registry

Another subfunction of the MSC is the EIR. The EIR maintains a database of the IMEI or MEID that is allowed service on a network. EIRs maintain white-, gray-, and black-listed phones. White means the phone is allowed service, gray means the device is under observation, and black means the device is stolen or lost. EIR databases can be specific for the network they are maintained on. This means a stolen phone that has been black listed in one country may work on another country's network as the EIR list would be different. Fig. 5.4 provides a simple illustration on the EIR databases.

Figure 5.4
Illustration of the Equipment Identity Registry databases.

Authentication Center

The main purpose of the AuC is to validate that the device requesting service on the wireless network is "ok" to receive the said service. The SIM card is assigned its own authentication key (K_i). There is a matching key within the AuC. To prevent fraud, cloning, and other security-related issues, the K_i remains unavailable to the owner of the phone. When a subscriber requests a signal on an allocated phone, this key is randomly generated, and encryption takes place between the device and the network. If these keys fail to match one another, the device is denied service.

Public Switched Telephone Network

The last component we will discuss within the Cellular Network is the PSTN. The PSTN would be utilized to route a call that is requesting service out of the network, such as a mobile to landline phone call. Local cellular to cellular calls do not use the PSTN. The PSTN years ago was all analog and was the core ingredient to making a dial-up phone call. The PSTN has evolved and in most places is all digital. It connects itself with standard telephone lines, cellular networks, microwave, fiber optic cables, and communication satellites. The PSTN would utilize the MSC to help in facilitating the request.

Q) **Why is it important for an examiner to understand how a call is routed through the cellular network?**

A) At the very beginning of this chapter we discussed that evidence may reside on the device, the network provider, or the cloud. By addressing *how* the call is made through the network, one can better understand the processes involving how data are stored in each specific location. This will also help in the judicial process if an examiner is questioned. Also when obtaining stored information through a legal process such as a search warrant, some of the terms discussed in this chapter may be used by the wireless carrier. As we continue through this book and into the intermediate and advanced techniques, these core fundamental explanations of the cellular network will have additional clarity. Specific recoverable artifacts, encoding and decoding will also tie back to the cellular network.

The definitions that began with the MS and ended with PSTN are in the same sequential order as to how a call would be routed through a GSM network. To bring all this together, and provide additional understanding, Fig. 5.5 represents a cellular to cellular call, and Fig. 5.6 depicts a cellular to landline call.

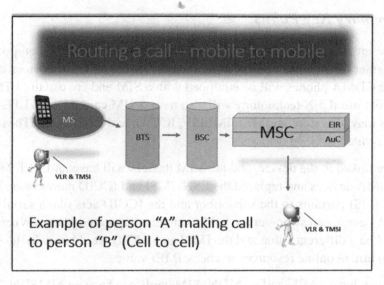

Figure 5.5
Illustration of Global Systems for Mobile Communications: cellular to cellular phone call. *AuC*,
Authentication Center; *BSC*, Base Station Controller; *BTS*, Base Transceiver Station; *EIR*, Equipment
Identity Registry; *MS*, Mobile Station; *MSC*, Mobile Switching Center; *TMSI*, Temporary Mobile
Subscriber Identity; *VLR*, Visitor Location Registry.

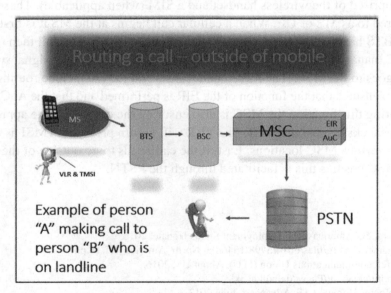

Figure 5.6
Illustration of a Global Systems for Mobile Communications: cellular device to landline. *AuC*,
Authentication Center; *BSC*, Base Station Controller; *BTS*, Base Transceiver Station; *EIR*, Equipment
Identity Registry; *MS*, Mobile Station; *MSC*, Mobile Switching Center; *PSTN*, Public Switched
Telephone Network; *TMSI*, Temporary Mobile Subscriber Identity; *VLR*, Visitor Location Registry.

Chapter Summary Key Points

Devices that use either CDMA or GSM communication protocol may be equipped with a SIM. It is important for forensic examiners to understand that all GSM devices contain a SIM, but only certain CDMA phones will be equipped with a SIM and are usually LTE supported. Older devices that use iDEN technology will also have a SIM card present. LTE-equipped CDMA devices may also store an IMEI, IMEISV, ICCID, and IMSI value. These values are no longer only limited to GSM devices.

IMEI values are linked to the device, and all GSM devices will have an IMEI. MEID values are used for CDMA devices and replaced the ESN. IMSI and ICCID numbers are linked to the SIM card. The IMSI pertains to the subscriber and the ICCID acts like a serial number for the SIM card. A person can swap out the SIM to another supported phone. When that occurs, the IMEI would be a different value and the IMSI and ICCID would remain the same. An investigator can utilize online resources to check IMEI values.

Some devices may have a MIN and an MDN. SIM cards can have an MSISDN. The MDN and MSISDN would be the number assigned to the phone that is used to facilitate in calling and sending SMS. CDMA phones may also have a PRL, which is a database to assist with service out of the home area.

The MS is comprised of the wireless handset and a SIM (when applicable). These components are referred to as ME or UE. When a cellular call begins at the MS it is first routed to the BTS. The BTS has several components to include the antenna. The call then travels to the BSC. The BSC manages the call, handing it off as needed to appropriate signal strength sites. Next, the call goes to the MSC. The MSC conducts several jobs to include routing SMS/MMS and calls. It also ensures that the function of the EIR is performed and that the AuC is being conducted. During this function the MSC is also ensuring the device has the appropriate VLR by performing checks against the HLR. The VLR will in turn provide a TMSI as the device travels through various MSC locations. Last, if the call needs to go outside of the cellular network, the MSC ensures this is facilitated through the PSTN.

References

[1] 4GAmericas.org, 5G Americas LTE Deployment Status Update, 2016.
    http://www.4gamericas.org/files/6014/5998/1546/03_North_America_4.1.16.pdf.
[2] International Telecommunications Union (ITU), About US, 2016.
    http://www.itu.int/en/about/Pages/default.aspx.
[3] 3GPP, Technologies Home – LTE-Advanced, June 2013.
    http://www.3gpp.org/technologies/keywords-acronyms/97-lte-advanced.
[4] GSMA.com, Unlocking Commercial Opportunities from 4G Evolution to 5G, February 2016.
    http://www.gsma.com/network2020/technology/understanding-5g/.
[5] 3GPP, 3GPP2 S.R0048-A Version 4.0, June 23, 2005.
    http://www.3gpp2.org/Public_html/specs/S.R0048-A_v4.0_050630.pdf.

CHAPTER 6

Subscriber Identity Module

Information in This Chapter

- SIM sizes
- Evolution of SIM cards
- Internal makeup
- The SIM file system
- Elementary Files (EFs) that may contain evidence
- EF_ICCID, EF_IMSI, EF_FPLMN, EF_LOCI, EF_ADN, EF_LND
- EF_MSISDN
- The EF_SMS, message status flag, FF values
- SIM security and forensic SIM cloning

Introduction

We are back at pretending you are working the streets of a major metropolitan city and have arrested an individual involved in a shooting incident. You transport the suspect to a local detention facility where he is to be processed for booking. He is asked to open his mouth and stick out his tongue. The corrections officer notices a white object wedged in the side of his mouth. He is asked to spit the item out, but he refuses. The correction officer fears that the white object is narcotics and struggles with the suspect, pulling his mouth open. Several other correction officers join in, and an intense struggle ensues. The suspect is able to swallow the object and is escorted to a local hospital where his stomach is pumped. Inside a large cylinder that is used to hold the contents of his stomach rests his partially digested lunch, orange juice, and a small, white, flat wafer. The item is cleaned with saline solution and discovered to not be narcotics, but a SIM card. The nurse asks you, *"What exactly could be so important about this tiny object that caused him to swallow it?"*

SIM Sizes

In our introduction the suspect had swallowed a common size SIM card that was used in his simple, pay-as-you-go flip phone. Stored on the SIM, was some compelling information regarding the shooting he was involved in. SIM cards have, over the last years, changed their sizes to accommodate the phones that use them. This is especially true with 4G (LTE) phones, regardless if the phone is GSM or CDMA. As SIM card sizes decreased, it was the amount of board materials on the outside of the actual IC chip, that become smaller. A SIM card is often referred to as a smart card, and the term Universal Integrated Circuit Card (UICC) is commonly used to describe a SIM. The function of the UICC is contained on a SIM and specifically pertains to security and protection of user data. The UICC was at one time thought of as a new generation SIM card that would be used on 3G and 4G networks. Think of a SIM card as a computer tower. It has a case, and inside the case is a processor, memory, and storage. The UICC could then be thought of as the main board that brings the function of everything together. In this example the UICC would be compatible with nearly all networks.

To better understand the various sizes, or *Form Factor* (FF), we will reference the International Organization for Standardization (ISO) and International Electrotechnical Commission (IEC) characteristics for the first two sizes. This is commonly referred to as ISO/IEC, especially, ISO/IEC 7810:2003, ID-1, and ID-000.

- Full-size SIM (1FF) is the size of a credit card. The area of the integrated circuit, however, is very close to the size used today. This card is no longer used in mobile devices.
- Mini-SIM (2FF) is, today, still the most common SIM card size being recovered as evidence. This SIM size would be used in most phones that do not use LTE service, but it does not mean it is only found in those types of phones. There are vendors who still utilize this size SIM and offer LTE plans. Large vendors who offer smart-phone service such as Apple and Samsung have elected to go with smaller SIM sizes.

As we address the next two SIM sizes, we move to different reference materials to explain their characteristics: the European Telecommunications Standard Institute, Test Specifications (ETSI TS 102 221) V9.0.0 and V11.0.0.

- Micro-SIM (3FF) size was very popular in GSM phones such as the iPhone 4 models. Again, the materials around the circuit are reduced, which in some cases allowed a smaller-sized SIM to fit into smaller phones. This is a common size for LTE phones.
- Nano-SIM (4FF) is currently being used in newer LTE phones. Nearly all the outside board materials of the SIM are removed, and only the chip remains.

The last SIM format we will address has been recognized by the Joint Electron Device Engineering Council (JEDEC) Design Guide 4.8 SON-8 and ETSI TS 102 383 V12.0.0.

- eSIM (Embedded SIM) is commonly referred to as an *Embedded UICC*. As the name implies, the SIM is not-removable and stays with the device. Many vendors are using eSIM devices to interact with the existing mobile devices. Samsung's Gear S2 was reported in February 2016 as one of the first certified eSIM devices that let the user choose carriers [1].

In 2016 Apple's iPad Pro was released with an eSIM and a standard SIM slot. They call it *"Apple SIM"* [2]. Fig. 6.1 depicts the evolution of SIM cards.

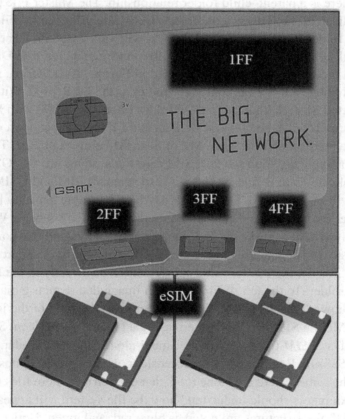

Figure 6.1
Evolution of SIM cards, from first Form Factor to embedded.

Internal Makeup

The SIM contains several components associated with the integrated circuit chip. Read-only memory (ROM) contains the firmware, the operation system (OS), and applications that are needed. The random access memory (RAM) is also used for the OS as well as functionality for the applications. The electronically erasable programmable read-only memory (EEPROM) holds user data such as phone book entries, dialing numbers, and other network-related information.

The SIM File System

The file system of the SIM is made up of three components. Its structure is similar to Windows in that there is a parent–child folder relationship. The Master File (MF) is the root directory. The Dedicated File (DF) is a file folder. Lastly, the Elementary File (EF) contains the data inside the folder. The number of EF folders will vary based on what the SIM supports. There will be SIM cards that work on different frequencies. The Digital Cellular System (DCS) is a radio frequency first established in Europe, Asia, Africa, and other countries for GSM phones. It is commonly referred to as the DCS 1800. Within the file system of a supported SIM, there may be a DF folder titled DCS 1800 with EF files structured under it. There may also be other DF folders and EF files that support other frequencies or Telecom standards under the same MF of the SIM being examined. Two other common DF folders typically found in 2FF SIM card file systems are DF_GSM and DF_Telecom. To complicate matters further, there is also standard SIM and USIM cards. Most SIM cards today will be from the USIM standard, which has more capacity in some EF locations, has better encryption, and can handle more applications at once. When reading data from the file system of a SIM card, it is important to understand that some values may repeat themselves as the EF value may pertain to a DF structure for standard GSM and DCS 1800, for example. Lastly, the ICCID value can be contained directly in the MF, without being inside a DF folder. To the left of Fig. 6.2 is an image that depicts a diagram of the SIM file system, showing the MF, DF, and EF structure. To the right of the image is an actual read of a T-Mobile SIM card file system using a tool called *SIMcon*. SIMcon was purchased by Paraben's *SIM Card Seizure* as a stand-alone SIM card reader. It is included in Paraben's *Device Seizure*. Regardless of the forensic tool an examiner chooses, the SIM file system will look the same. There are some tools that can retrieve more files than others, but the point here is examiners should understand how the file system will appear. The three different types of DF file structures are noted as blue, red, and green. Notice how the DF_GSM and DF_DCS1800 both have an EF_IMSI folder, as well as several other identical EF folders.

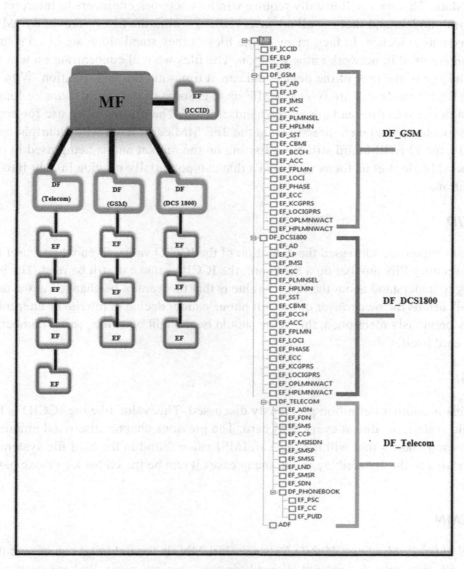

Figure 6.2
MF (Master File), DF (Dedicated File), and EF (Elementary File) areas of the SIM file system.

Where Is My Evidence?

Many of the items stored in the file system of a target SIM card will contain network protocol data. This data will usually require wireless network engineers to interpret. It is important to understand that not all artifacts located within the file system of a SIM card will be used as evidence. In fact, many of the files as they stand alone are of no significance and are used in network authentication. The files we will concentrate on will yield unique linkage to the user of the device and can at times aid the investigation. With newer 4G or LTE SIM cards that are typically 3FF or 4FF, some of the artifacts are no longer stored on the SIM but instead are on the handset itself. The examples we use for potential evidence locations are taken directly from the 2FF SIM card. Even with smartphone popularity, the 2FF SIM card still has a footing on the market and is being used in other phones worldwide. Let us focus on the EFs that can potentially provide insight into an investigation.

EF_ICCID

In our last chapter we addressed the definition of the ICCID value. Even when a user has placed a security PIN number on a SIM card, the ICCID value can still be read. The important thing to understand about the ICCID value is that this cannot be changed at the user level. This means the owner/user of the cell phone cannot decide to rewrite or alter this value. As previously mentioned, this value should be thought of as the "serial number" to the SIM card itself.

EF_IMSI

Again, this is another definition previously discussed. This value like the ICCID is found on the file system on almost every SIM card. The previous chapter discussed unique situations and phones that will not have an IMSI value found in the SIM file system. The IMSI pertains to the subscriber, and in many cases it can be traced back to those paying for service.

EF_FPLMN

The *Forbidden Public Land Mobile Network* (FPLMN) is the field that can be populated with specific networks that are not allowed service. This can generally happen in two ways. One, the carrier prepopulates the FPLMN when it is initially allocated for network service. The second way, this handset is "seen" by another network but is not allowed service. An example would be a device near a foreign border such as the United States and Canada. If the device was serviced by AT&T within the United States, but came close enough to another GSM network in Canada, the foreign network information may show in this EF location, as it was attempting service but was denied. The EF_FPLMN values do not populate when the device is serviced within its own country code and it is near other devices from the same country code (T-Mobile serviced near AT&T or a similar country example).

EF_LOCI

This area can contain a number of values that will need additional legal process to interpret. The first value is the Location Area Identity (LAI) area code. Within each area of the Public Land Mobile Network (PLMN) is a value called the LAI. The LAI can be utilized internationally for determining the location of the subscriber. The actual LAI area code value that is stored within the EF_LOCI will usually be in hexadecimal. The next value below this will be the LAI network code. The network code will be in standard digits and may show the name of the carrier or country of service next to the digits. The LAI area code and LAI network code are both "looked" at by the Mobile Station (MS) during authentication. The MS will notice the device moving through the network and will provide additional values as needed. The values are documented within the EF_LOCI and include a Temporary Mobile Subscriber Identity (TMSI) timestamp and TMSI value. The TMSI was discussed in our previous chapter and is lined to the Visitor Location Registry (VLR). Using all the values from our EL_LOCI, an investigator may be able to determine an approximate location on where the device was last powered down.

EF_ADN

Abbreviated Dialing Numbers (ADNs) are commonly referred to as "phone-book" entries or simply "contacts." These values would be generated by the user/owner of the device. SIM cards that still use the ADN feature (mainly 2FF) only have 250 available slots. The slots must fill up all the way to 250 before deleted slots are written back into. This means if you had a brand new supported SIM card and you stored phone numbers for "Mom," "Dad," and "Work" and then deleted the *Mom* entry, your next available location would write to slot 4, not slot 1 where *Mom* was originally stored.

EF_LND

Last Number Dialed (LND) pertains to an area within the file system of a SIM card that stored the 10 recent calls. Like many other variables, this may or may not truly reflect the number that was last dialed.

9-1-1 Calls

A Last Phone Call

Several years back a victim was fatality wounded in a shooting incident. His friend drove him around a popular Puget Sound city that he was unfamiliar with looking for a hospital for medical aid. Using a GSM phone, he dialed 9-1-1 and informed the dispatcher of the medical emergency and requested directions to a hospital. The dispatcher asked the driver to pull the vehicle over and wait for an ambulance. The driver refused, and he continued to request instructions. He eventually arrived at the hospital where his friend succumbed to his wounds.

The driver and the deceased victim had been involved in the shooting, and the driver was later changed with shooting at a third party who was later identified. There were several phones recovered in the vehicle the driver had transported the victim in. All were examined after a search warrant was executed on the vehicle. The EF_LND did not indicate the last number dialed as 9-1-1. It was later determined the driver had used an unallocated (no-service) old phone to make the call to dispatch as he did not want to reveal his own cellular number.

Any phone that has a charge can complete a phone call to 9-1-1 if it can be "seen" by a nearby tower. The SIM does not even need to be present if the device is a GSM handset. The phone number in this case was derived from the last values of the IMEI and was given this temporary number by the network only to make the emergency call. This number was what the dispatcher could see on her screen as the incoming number. A forensic examination of this area therefore did not show any 9-1-1 entry where past calls would normally show. Because of the design of the phone for emergency calling, the 9-1-1 call also did not reside within the call history on the GUI as an outgoing call. Investigators believed the driver was being deceptive, as all the numbers showing as assigned phone numbers did not match what the dispatcher was reporting.

His story was eventually collaborated by examining the IMEI values on all the phones in the vehicle and locating the device. Besides dialing 9-1-1, all other (nonsmart) phones that support the EF_LND within the SIM file system should populate this field accordingly.

Fig. 6.3 is one image that contains multiple screenshots from a SIM file system. This represents examples of the EF locations we have addressed thus far: *EF_ICCID*, *EF_IMSI*, *EF_PLMN*, *EF_LOCI*, *EF_ADN*, and *EF_LND*. The EF area is highlighted in blue to the left, with the corresponding values to the right. To allow examples from each area, the entire ADN (Phonebook) was not included.

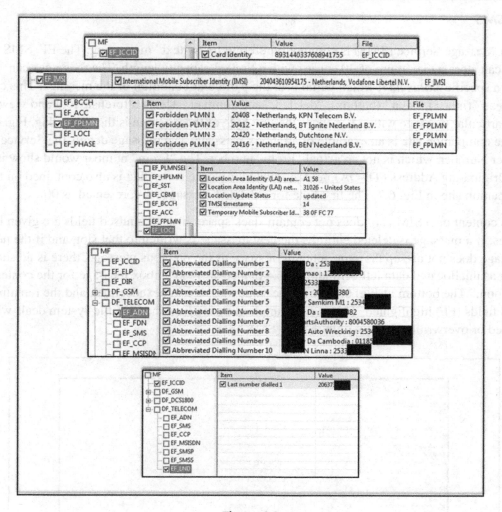

Figure 6.3
Examples of SIM File System Elementary File (EF) areas that can contain evidential data.

EF_MSISDN

We have discussed this EF value in our last chapter. The Mobile Station International Subscriber Directory Number (MSISDN) value, followed by SMS content, is one of the most requested stored artifacts from the SIM card. Some SIM cards may have more than one MSISDN, and others will not have this value present within this EF location. It is not a mandatory field and will be up to the wireless provider whether it is supplied on the SIM. Many LTE (4G) smartphones in the 3FF and 4FF size commonly will not show the MSISDN value on the SIM. On the companion site, Fig. 6.1 represents two examples of MSISDN values. The upper part is the standard MSISDN with the number "1" after the abbreviation (*Msisdn1*). The lower part of the image is an MSISDN value where the user has stored his name as "Armando."

EF_SMS

Short Message Service (SMS) is commonly referred to as "text" messaging. The EF_SMS field can store a maximum of 30 entries with a limited capacity length. The messages can have a specific *status flag*, which pertains to the particular condition of the message. This can be "read" (inbox), "sent" (outbox), "deleted," and "unread." Using a forensic tool and viewing the particular message within hex view, the first byte of the message is the status flag. Fig. 6.2 on the companion site is an example of an inbox message. The message details the Service Center Number, which is not an actual "From" number. The "From" number would show in the Originating Address (TP-OA) field. A deleted message status flag is also contained on the companion site in Fig. 6.3. The first byte for a deleted message is represented as 00.

SMS content on a SIM card does not contain slack space. Instead, unused fields are given FF values. If a message is deleted entirely, the new message is written to that slot, and if the new message does not use up the same amount of space as the previous message, there is no such thing as unallocated data left behind. Fig. 6.4 depicts a "read" inbox message for the content of "soon." The bottom of Fig. 6.4 shows the same message in hexadecimal, and the remaining SMS fields (FF) highlighted. This is an example showing how the SIM file system deals with unused or overwritten fields within the EF_SMS area.

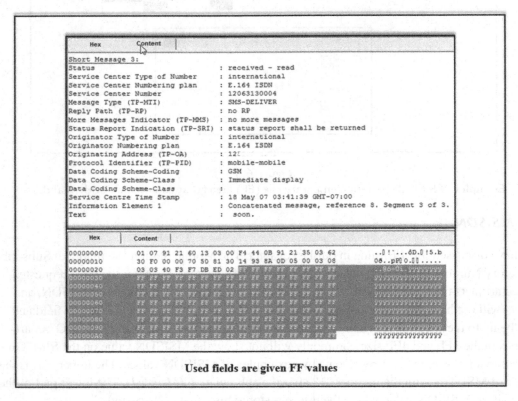

Figure 6.4
No slack space in SMS fields: unused areas are FF (Form Factor) written.

Multimedia Messages (MMSs) are also not contained on the SIM card. There may be times when the SIM EF_SMS field or a related SMS field shows specific values that an MMS message was sent or received. The actual media content, however, will not be on a SIM, as it is physically not capable of storing the media.

SIM Security

SIM cards can be protected by the user by assigning a Personal Identification Number (PIN). The carrier can also assign a default PIN when the SIM or phone containing the SIM is first purchased. Most PIN numbers are 4 digits but can be 8. The user who is attempting to enter a locked SIM will usually have only three attempts. Some carriers allow 10 attempts on a user PIN. Once the attempts are negatively exhausted, the user must enter a Person Unlocking Key (PUK). (This is also referred to as a Personal Unblocking Key.)

The PUK value is set by the manufacturer. For an investigator to obtain a PUK, a legal request must be submitted to the carrier. Most wireless carriers will retain the PUK as long as the target number associated with the SIM is still allocated for service. This means if you are investigating a cold case and it is several years old and the handset is locked with a SIM PIN, chances are the PUK is no longer available. There are 10 attempts with the PUK value. After entering 10 PUKs incorrectly the SIM is permanently locked. If the PUK value is entered correctly, the user is allowed at that point to create a new PIN number. This resets the PIN count back to three attempts. PUK management must be accomplished through specialized utilities or at the wireless network store. Fig. 6.4 on the companion site contains an image of an unlocked and locked SIM file system. The utility (SIMcon) used in these screenshots allows PUK management. The top of Fig. 6.4 (companion site) shows SIM as unlocked, while the bottom of the image shows the locked SIM.

Also, SIM cards can have a PIN1 and PIN2. PIN1 is used strictly for SIM security. The PIN value can be a default number such as 0000, 1234, or the last four digits of the assigned number. In most cases, the SIM security PIN is not enabled when the phone is sold and the user must set it. This typically takes place through the GUI of the phone.

When PIN2 is unlocked, it allows access to store additional data to the SIM card. This is usually the EF_ADN (Contacts/Phonebook) area. Some carriers have this ability and others do not. It is not standardized. There are other carriers who do not have a PIN2 feature but still allow storage to take place to the ADN fields.

Fig. 6.5 has a new SIM card from T-Mobile depicted at the top of the image. The ICCID is showing the "SIM Card Number," which is depicted with a box around it. At the top of this card is the "*PUK Code: 22202106.*" Most people would simply punch out the SIM from this holder, install it in their phone, and then disregard this card, which contains the PUK. At the bottom of Fig. 4.4 is a new AT&T card. This particular card does not display the PUK value on the card but instead has the value within the program used by the wireless vendor. Fig. 6.6 depicts PUK1 and PUK2 values for the AT&T SIM as shown in Fig. 6.5.

Figure 6.5
Examples of SIM cards issues with and without Personal Unlocking Key (PUK) values.

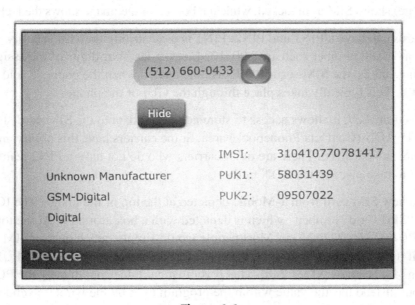

Figure 6.6
PUK1 (Personal Unlocking Key) and PUK2 values stored by the wireless carrier (AT&T SIM card in Fig. 6.5).

Forensic SIM Cloning

The process of creating a SIM card that can be placed in the evidence phone to bypass SIM security and network isolate the device is referred to as *Forensic SIM Cloning*.

What is important to realize is that we are not creating an exact copy of the SIM and all its various file system directories, as this would be illegal, not to mention very difficult to do. What we are doing is "tricking" the phone into believing that the original SIM is being inserted back into the phone. An examiner should never place a foreign SIM card into a phone that is recovered and missing the SIM. Nor should an unlocked SIM card be placed into a phone when the original SIM is security enabled with a PIN. Doing so will change original values on the target phone. When we create a SIM clone, we are reading the ICCID and IMSI values of the target phone and writing them to a blank card. The forensic card is designed for the specific tool that has this SIM cloning feature. These two values allow the phone to see the card as if it was the original evidential SIM. Since the Forensic SIM cloned card does not have any network protocol information on it, the phone is isolated from cellular connectivity.

SIM cards that have a user enabled PIN will still allow the examiner to read the ICCID value. The IMSI, however, will be locked inside the file system if the PIN is enabled. With the ICCID value an examiner can make a "test" SIM. This process uses values that mimic the original SIM values and allow the examiner to access the locked handset when the SIM has security. There is also an advanced technique that takes the ICCID value and derives the IMSI value.

The process of Forensic SIM Cloning can be completed in three ways.

1. Read an unlocked SIM card from the target phone using a forensic tool that has the SIM cloning feature, and then write those validated values (ICCID/IMSI) to a sterilized card designed for that utility. Most vendors will sell a series of blank SIM cards for this purpose. The cards can be used repeatedly.
2. Manually enter the ICCID and IMSI to the GUI of the forensic tool and write these values to a sterilized card designed for the program being used. This method would require the examiner to obtain the ICCID and IMSI for the target phone through a legal process or obtain a physical acquisition and extract the values from the physical file.
3. Create a "test SIM." There would be two reasons to use this method. (1) The user/owner of the target mobile device has enabled SIM security and an examiner is prompted to enter the SIM PIN to access the device. (2) The SIM card is missing entirely.

Years back, the process of creating a Forensic SIM involved a number of steps. The utility was only made for SIM cloning purposes. The blank card had to be manually sterilized first. Once the target SIM was read, the examiner had to create a HASH value of the original

ICCID and IMSI. The target card was removed, the sterilized (blank) card inserted, and then the stored ICCID and IMSI were written to the card. A final HASH was completed on the Forensic SIM card and if the HASH values match, the card was placed into the target phone.

The tool also allowed the examiner to manually write the ICCID and IMSI onto the blank card. Vendors did not have the option of the "test SIM" for locked SIM cards. Using forensic software, examiners had to manually create the IMSI using the ICCID, as the ICCID can still be accessed on locked SIM cards.

Chapter Summary Key Points

SIM cards can be found in three common sizes: 2FF, 3FF, and 4FF. The most commonly found size encountered is 2FF. Nearly all 4FF SIM cards would be utilized for 4G or LTE devices. There may also be devices that have eSIMs, which are embedded, not-removable SIMs.

The SIM file system may contain specific areas that can benefit an investigation. Not all SIMs will have these values present. They include the *EF_ICCID*, *EF_IMSI*, *EF_PLMN*, *EF_LOCI*, *EF_ADN*, *EF_LND*, *EF_MSISDN*, and *EF_SMS*. The two most requested areas for evidential data are EF_MSISDN (assigned number) and EF_SMS (text messages) locations. The SIM has its own memory and operating system. The file system of a SIM has an MF, DFs, and an EF. The EF area will be the location where potential evidence will be located. There may be different DF areas that correspond to a particular frequency that the SIM supports. Data may repeat within these DF locations. One common repeated value is the IMSI.

Each of the EF locations can yield specific information. EF_ICCID is viewed as the serial number to the SIM. EF_IMSI can be linked to the subscriber. EF_PLMN can indicate networks that services were forbidden. EF_LOCI may review where the device was last powered down. EF_ADN can indicate contacts or the associated that the user has stored as phone book entries. EF_LND can hold numbers the user has dialed recently. EF_MSISDN when present can reveal the assigned phone number used by the handset the SIM was inserted into. EF_SMS can reveal text messages in different message statuses such as "read" (inbox), "sent" (outbox), "deleted," and "unread." SMS messages do not have slack space and unused areas are written with "FF" values. MMS message media does not reside on SIM cards.

SIM cards may have user enabled security. Generally after three failed attempts the SIM will require a PUK value. The PUK value is set by the manufacturer and can reside on the original issued SIM holder or can be maintained on the account. A PUK can be entered 10 times incorrectly before it permanently disabled the SIM. A correct PUK value allows the user to create a new PIN number and resets the PIN security attempts. PIN and PUK management can be accomplished through specialized tools or at the wireless carrier.

Creating a Forensic SIM clone is completed for several reasons. First, its network isolates the device. Second, it allows a method of entry into the handset when the user has enabled the SIM PIN security, and last, it provides a "test SIM" for phones that are located with the SIM missing.

The process of creating the Forensic SIM is conducted in three ways. First, the original ICCID and IMSI values from the unlocked target SIM are used on a sterilized SIM card. Second, the investigator obtains the ICCID and IMSI through secondary means such as legal process or a physical examination. Those values are then manually written to a sterilized SIM card. Last, a "test SIM" is created to mimic the original SIM ICCID and IMSI values.

References

[1] The Verge.com, eSIM Wearable Smartwatch, Samsung Gear S2, February 18, 2016. http://www.theverge.com/2016/2/18/11044624/esim-wearable-smartwatch-samsung-gear-s2.
[2] Apple.com, iPad, Apple-SIM, 2016. http://www.apple.com/ipad/apple-sim/.

CHAPTER 7

Device Identification

Information in This Chapter

- Handset communication types
- GSM and CDMA
- Visual identification
- The form factors
- Common operating systems
- Steps for identification
- Removable storage

Introduction

This chapter builds upon what has been addressed up to this point. Here is a review: First, when we have an incident that involves the need to forensically examine a mobile target, we must first consider how to prevent contamination (Chapter 2). Then, we must make certain that our legal demand is met through exigent, search warrant, or consent to search means (Chapters 3 and 4). By understanding the cellular network (Chapter 5), we also understand where our evidence may be located, whether it is on the mobile equipment or contained within the file system of the subscriber identity module (SIM; Chapter 6). Now we take this baseline knowledge and use it to identify *exactly* what kind of device needs to be examined. Device identification is a key element to *triaging* devices, which is covered in an upcoming chapter.

Handset Communication Types

The two main handset communication types that have been outlined are GSM and CDMA. With the high number of mobile virtual network operators (MVNOs), this can prove to be harder to distinguish. Many MVNO companies will produce devices that work on GSM and CDMA technologies. This can be an issue when trying to locate the communication type solely on if the device was made by the MVNO company. For instance, Tracfone sells GSM and CDMA cell phones. If an investigator is trying to determine the model of the Tracfone that is "powered-on" at the scene of a homicide, he/she may have things to consider first.

Issues such as Faraday, crime scene processing, DNA processing, and latent processing, all play into an investigator even *touching* the device. Also, the legal demand must be met. But if we take the same device, and instead of the Tracfone symbol depicted on the lid, it now reads "Verizon," does this help us in determining the communication type? The answer is *"Yes!"* Verizon is CDMA. When devices are not an MVNO-serviced handset and are instead serviced by major US carriers, identifying the communication type becomes much easier. By first identifying the communication type, it can help establish if the device may or may not have a SIM card or, in some cases, a microSD card present. Let us go over some common handset communication types for devices located in the United States that are MNOs.

Mobile Network Operator—Top 8

According to a March 2016 report from Fierce Wireless, the top 8 US wireless carriers in quarter 4 of 2015 were listed as (1) Verizon, (2) AT&T, (3) T-Mobile USA, (4) Sprint, (5) US Cellular, (6) C Spire, (7) Shentel, and (8) nTelos [1]. By understanding that these types of MNO devices are the most common for a particular country, an investigator will have an idea of what will be encountered most often. You may be reading this book and conducting investigations in other regions; if so perform your own research and determine the top MNOs for your jurisdiction. After you establish a list, break the MNOs into two groups: CDMA and GSM.

Mobile Network Operator—CDMA Communication Types

If we look exclusively at the major MNO companies (within the United States) when it comes to our first step in identifying a device, we can provide answers to the communication type. Verizon, Sprint, US Cellular, C Spire, and nTelos are CDMA (MNO) devices. If the device has one of these names affixed to the outside housing, it will be a CDMA communication type. This also means if the device is not serviced for 4G or LTE, it will *not* contain a SIM card. The presence of a SIM card without entering the device can be hard to determine on some newer CDMA (LTE) devices. The good news is that if you as an investigator can see a carrier name affixed to the device, you can, in many cases, determine the communication type. This is primarily true with MNO companies, regardless of the region of the world your investigations take place in.

Mobile Network Operator—GSM Communication Types

Going back to our 2014 top 8 carriers, we are left with AT&T and T-Mobile USA. These two MNO companies will communicate through GSM. A mobile device that has either of these names affixed to the outside was designed to need a SIM card to communicate through the wireless network. With 4G (LTE) phones, the examiner does not need to determine if the phone *should* have a SIM as in some cases with CDMA devices. All GSM-serviced phones require a SIM. AT&T and T-Mobile will be two of the easiest recognizable, US serviced MNO carriers that contain SIM cards.

Mobile Virtual Network Operator—GSM or CDMA Communication?

A mobile device that is serviced by an MVNO can be the most challenging communication type to determine. In addition, MNO companies also have their own direct pay-as-you-go phones. There is also the "Bring Your Own Device" (BYOD) feature on MVNO companies. This means, for example, if the phone is a Verizon network *unlocked* phone and it is LTE, the customer could place an LTE MVNO SIM card in the device and obtain service. BYOD devices have become popular for consumers who may have fulfilled their 2-year service commitment on one carrier, and wish to keep the phone and move it to a qualified MVNO network. BYOD devices also apply to consumers who purchase an "unlocked" phone. Not all phones qualify as a BYOD, and they generally must be network unlocked and share the same type of communication (GSM or CDMA). In later chapters we will discuss network unlocking through the use of specialized equipment.

Chapter 3 referenced the number of MVNOs worldwide from a 2015 report as nearly 1000 [2]. Due to that fact, the chance of encountering a handset that is serviced by an MVNO is much more likely. However, this can vary by region and is affected based on sales. There are many sources that can assist in determining if a target MVNO phone is using CDMA or GSM. The first way is to locate any company name on the device. The problem with this is many MVNO service phones will not list the company on the housing. They simply show the manufacturer such as Samsung, LG, and Alcatel. The second issue is that some MVNOs have devices that are sold to work on either CDMA or GSM, while other MVNOs strictly provide service for only one communication type. Using several 2015 and 2016 news articles from *BestMVNO* [3–6], we provide some popular MVNO companies that use various MNO networks in the United States. It is important to understand that this list does not exhaust all the MVNO companies throughout the United States. Also, by the time you read this, some of these companies may have been sold and acquired by other networks. Acquisitions are very common, especially with virtual networks. All MNOs also offer their own pay-as-you-go plan that sometimes falls into an MVNO category.

Some 2016 MVNOs using AT&T:
- Airvoice
- Black Wireless
- Consumer Cellular
- Cricket
- Defense Mobile
- EasyGo
- H_2O Wireless
- Jolt
- Net10

- Red Pocket Mobile
- Pure TalkUSA
- Straight Talk

Some 2016 MVNOs using Sprint:
- Boost
- ChitChat Mobile
- EcoMobile
- Espanol Mobile
- Freedompop
- Good 2Go Mobile
- Ideal Mobile
- Kajeet
- Net10
- Project Fi
- RingPlus
- Pix Wireless
- Red Pocket Mobile
- Scratch Wireless
- Straight Talk
- TextNow
- Tello
- Ting
- Touch Mobile
- TPO Wireless
- Zing PCS

Some 2016 MVNOs using T-Mobile:
- GoSmart Mobile
- EcoMobile
- LycaMobile
- MetroPCS
- Nextplus GO
- Net10
- Project Fi
- Red Pocket Mobile
- Simple Mobile
- Straight Talk
- Telcel America
- Ting
- TPO Wireless
- Ultra Mobile

- Univision Mobile
- US Mobile
- UVA Mobile
- Walmart Family Mobile
- Zip SIM

Some 2016 MVNOs using Verizon:

- Affinity Cellular
- Bluegreen Mobile
- Defense Mobile
- EcoMobile
- Envie Mobile
- Net10
- Page Plus Cellular
- Red Pocket Mobile
- ROK Mobile
- Selectel Wireless
- Straight Talk
- Total Wireless

TracFone, the largest MVNO footprint

As you may see by these lists, some MVNOs allow service on all four of the major MNOs, Net10 and Straight Talk being the two largest. These two companies are actually names that fall under America Movil, which is a Mexico telecommunications company that also owns TracFone Wireless, Inc. Included on all of these MVNO lists are TracFone devices. Although TracFone ended the 2015 quarter by losing 58,000 subscribers, it still holds the number one MVNO spot for the United States with 25.7 million subscribers reported in the same year [7]. TracFone devices can communicate on CDMA and GSM networks. Besides the AT&T, T-Mobile, Sprint, Verizon, and US Cellular, other major US MNOs can also service TracFone. Because of this large MVNO footprint that this company has, investigators who encounter a TracFone device may have the greatest difficulty determining the communication type. This will be especially true with LTE smartphones. Also, TracFone offers BYOD service. This will mean that investigators who encounter devices that have names affixed on them from MNOs such as AT&T, and T-Mobile may actually be serviced in some qualifying cases by TracFone. Confused? Don't be. Determining the communication type is just one of the many ways to identify the device. Also remember when we are addressing *identifying a device*, it is assumed that the investigator has not obtained his/her legal process and is trying to ascertain what he/ she has encountered without entering or disassembling the device. On the flip side of this, if you do have grounds to search or disassemble mobile evidence, much of what is targeted in this chapter will not be necessary, as you can simply locate the model number or other unique identifying values.

The Form Factors

Besides the communication type, determining the style of the phone can help in device identification. This will be the design of a particular phone, which is commonly referred to as the *Form Factor*.

Bar

The *Bar* Form Factor is the most common style of phones worldwide. This will also be referred to as "*CandyBar*," "*Brick*," or "*Block*." The device can contain a visible keyboard or be composed of an entire screen. There are no moving parts, besides the various buttons. Older style Bar phones may also have a movable (pull-up) antenna. Examples of current popular Bar Form Factor phones would be the Samsung Galaxy series Androids and all of the Apple iPhones through 8. Fig. 7.1 depicts examples of the Bar Form Factor phone. Note: The carrier names and logos have been redacted for legal reasons, in all the upcoming Form Factor examples.

Figure 7.1
Bar Form Factor phone examples (Samsung Galaxy and iPhone).

Clamshell and Side Clamshell

Another popular name for this phone is the *Flip* phone. The Clamshell phone can be recognized by the fact that it hinges between the screen and the keyboard. The user opens the phone to speak and access the keyboard on most models and then shuts the phone when it is not in use. Some Clamshell phones will have a secondary screen with limited controls or appearance when the device is closed. The hinge may be positioned vertically or horizontally. Fig. 7.2 shows examples of the Clamshell (top) and Side Clamshell (bottom).

Figure 7.2
Clamshell and Side Clamshell Form Factor examples.

Slider and Side Slider

A Slider phone has a design where the phone would be used in the vertical position. The screen and various controls attached to the screen are affixed to another bottom layer, which when pushed upward, positions one piece of the phone above and another portion below. Generally, the lower half exposes other buttons, usually a keyboard. The standard Slider also allows the user to access the phone when the lower portion is not slid open. Controls may be limited when the phone is accessed in the closed position. Slide style phones are generally thicker than Bar phones, which allow both sets of parts to sit on one another. The Side Slider works exactly the same way, except the phone is accessed horizontally instead of vertically. Fig. 7.3 is an example of standard Slider (top) with Side Sliders (bottom).

Figure 7.3
Standard Slider and Side Slider example.

Swivel

Our next Form Factor is called the Swivel. These types of phones will allow the two halves of the phone to pivot out and will be held in place on one end. Like the Slider design, the phone will have one-part screen and the other half is usually the keyboard. The design also allows some specific functionality when the phone is closed, such as playing music or viewing incoming messages or calls. Fig. 7.4 is an example of the Swivel Form Factor.

Figure 7.4
The Swivel Form Factor.

Tablet

The Tablet Form Factor has had an increase in consumer use over the past few years. Many of these devices can perform functions similar to a computer and are frequently used to conduct face-to-face conversations. Some models will contain SIM cards and can be used to communicate, search the web, and provide nearly all the services of a smaller size phone. Tablet Form Factor has found its use in retail sales where it is commonly used to perform merchant transactions with customers. Some businesses will also set up tablets to allow customers to view menus, play games, and, in some cases of luxury cars, contain the owner's manual.

In early 2016, Hyundai automakers released an augmented reality owner's manual. *"It runs on a smartphone or tablet (both Android and iOS), and uses the in-built camera to recognize different components in the car (under the hood, in the trunk, and inside the cabin). It then overlays labels explaining what you're seeing, with tutorials you can use to show you how to check your oil and so on"* [8].

Common Operating Systems

When consumers purchase mobile devices, they will not always get to choose which operating system that they want on a particular phone. This decision is usually between the vendor who makes the phone and the company that produces the OS. Oftentimes the OS will be embedded with specific games, applications, and other targeted software that is exclusive to that carrier, make/model phone, and the version of the OS. Also, wireless vendors will in some cases only allow a specific make and model phone to work on their network. One such vendor just a few years back was Apple and AT&T. Apple had an exclusive agreement with AT&T, and if you wanted an Apple iPhone, you needed to purchase it from an AT&T store. Now, all the carriers, to include many MVNOs, offer service for the iPhone. There are still vendors who allow only specific devices to access their networks. Verizon and the Motorola Droid line are recent examples. Determining the OS can assist with identifying the device. With smartphones, this can be an easier task than with simple pay-as-you-go or less "feature-rich" devices. Let us discuss the common OSs based on figures from International Data Corporation's (IDC) 2015 quarter 2 statistics. Since 2012 have shown sales being dominated by *Android*, then *iOS*, which is next followed by *Windows*, then *BlackBerry OS*, and the last are *"Others"* [9].

Windows Operating System

Windows phones will generally have some form of a symbol affixed to them that identifies them as such. Unless the phone has been internally modified (very rare), it will, in almost every case, be the same OS that is being used for the device. Also, Nokia at one time, sold its mobile phone division to Microsoft, and as such, most of the current Nokia smartphones will have Windows Operating Systems. Windows will place their trademarked, four panel (offset) window logo at the bottom of their devices, centered. This can greatly assist in device identi-fication, as most new Nokia devices will be a Lumia with a specific model number following the Lumia name. Be aware that Nokia is not the only vendor that will have Windows OSs. Vendors such as HTC, Samsung, Huawei, LG, ZTE, and several others support Windows OS on specific models.

Blackberry Operating System

Blackberry devices were at one time a number one selling phone. They are not as prevalent as they once were and still have a footing with some government and corporate entities. They recently offer the customer the choice of the Android OS within their product line. Blackberry devices like Windows phones will be easy to recognize and have their own distinct logo. Unlike other vendors such as LG and Samsung, Blackberry has only phones that are made by their company.

iOS

Like Blackberry phones, Apple devices will have their own operation system. If an Apple device is encountered, such as an iPhone, iPad, or iPod Touch, it will have some specific version of its necessary OS. Both Blackberry and Apple produce their own hardware. As such, investigators will only encounter iOS on Apple devices. Recently a scaled-down version of the iOS was placed into select automobiles and labeled, "*Apple CarPlay*." According to Apple, it is available in more than 100 models and works with the iPhone 5 through 6s [10]. By the time you are reading this, these same automobiles will support the latest version of the iPhone.

Android

Android OS can be found on many different mobile devices. This can also include tablets and other hybrid style devices that utilize a stylus. Android devices that are powered off can be difficult in determining if they actually utilize the Android OS. Many phones that have this OS will have no specific logo on the outside or back cover. They can also be confused with Windows devices and in some cases appear exactly like specific phones that come in both OS versions. As we have previously mentioned, HTC, Samsung, Huawei, LG, and ZTE can have Windows as the OS. This will also hold true with Android. As the current sales leader, statistically, Android devices are more likely to be encountered. This may or may not apply to the region you work in, as specific geographic areas or corporations may not support this strong footing with Android.

Other Operating Systems

Many devices that are pay-as-you-go (nonsmartphone) will have their own proprietary OS. This is especially true with cheap Clamshell and Bar phones. The phones will devote an area for their own OS, and it will have limited storage, features, and capabilities. These types of phones are preferred by individuals who may have committed crimes and know they are wanted by law enforcement. Such phones allow them easy access to communicate with the logistical benefits of a low cost, no contract commitment, and easy disposal and replacement. Binary Runtime Environment for Wireless (BREW) is one of the more popular pseudo operating systems found on these "nonsmartphones." The current version is actually called BREW MP. MP stands for mobile platform. Years back, Qualcomm, a major mobile chip developer, created this application platform primarily for CDMA devices. BREW MP allowed a standard for these handsets to develop an OS that works in C or C++ using a software development kit [11]. There will be some conflicting information on whether or not BREW or BREW MP is a true OS, but many sites will refer to it as such. As an example, Fig. 7.5 is from the developer section of Verizon wireless. It depicts the *Overview* and *Highlights* of one of the LG Cosmos 3. Notice what is listed as the OS under the *Highlights* field.

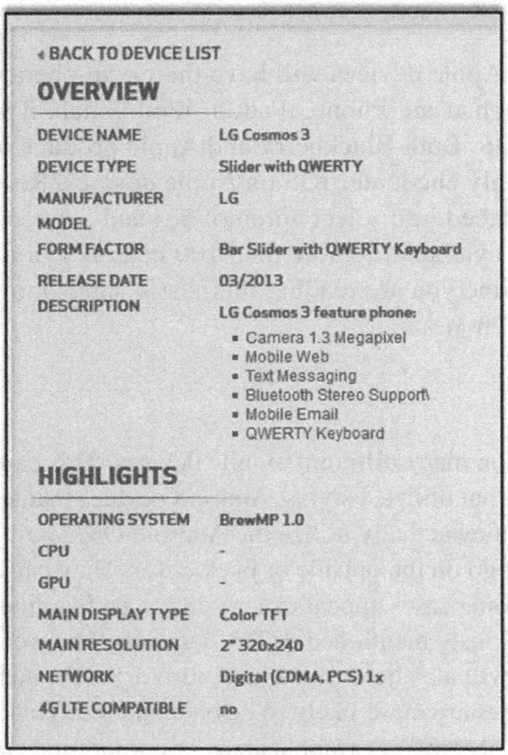

Figure 7.5
BREW MP (Binary Runtime Environment for Wireless mobile platform) operating system example
(pay-as-you-go Verizon).

Now that we have some basic knowledge on what can help us with identifying mobile devices, let us provide specific steps that can be of assistance. These are free resources that will require Internet access. This may or may not be an issue for a first responder, as some jurisdictions may not have the ability to conduct online inquiries. Other cases may involve situations where there is no cellular or Wi-Fi signal or the incident is in a remote location. This may require the investigator to contact dispatch via landline who can, in turn, conduct these steps.

Steps for Device Identification (Free)

(When you *have not yet established legal authority to search*)

Using the online companion guide, additional images are provided for each of these steps.

1. With the device in front of you, visit phonescoop.com. Enter the ***make*** of the target device you are attempting to identify in the search box, which, at the time this book was

written, was in the upper left corner. (See Fig. 7.1 contained within the online companion guide.)

2. The make of the phone (such as Samsung or Nokia) will provide search results from the companies with links that can be clicked on. The examiner can choose to sort the results based on newest release, technology type, or model number. This will allow viewing the devices via thumbnail images. For instance, if you are trying to identify a Nokia, and it also shows "Verizon" affixed on the phone, you could click on "Technology," which would sort the devices and only show the Windows-based CDMA phone as model Lumia 735. (See example Figs. 7.2–7.4 contained within the online companion guide.)

3. Use each side of the available images of *phonescoop* to help identify your device. Some models will have multiple pictures, and some may only depict the front and back. Many of the new smartphones of phonescoop will also have high-resolution images of various close-ups of specific models. (See example Fig. 7.5 contained within the online companion guide.)

4. Phonescoop commonly refers to phones by their nicknames. Examiners may need to conduct online searches for the actual model number using the nickname. One example of this is the Samsung Galaxy. Samsung has created several different models that utilize the "Galaxy" name. Phonescoop may indicate that the name is too common and additional specification is necessary—see Fig. 7.6 contained within the online companion guide. This includes cellular phones as well as Samsung's *"Note"* line and tablets of various sizes. However, if a phone was encountered that indicated Samsung Galaxy III on the back cover, along with the Verizon logo, this could easily be narrowed down through an online search as model SCH-I535.

Removable Storage

There may be times, when attempting to identify a device, that it becomes necessary to determine if it has removable storage. This does not necessarily mean that the device must have a storage card present; it simply means that we are trying to establish if the phone supports such storage. Some models that are one version apart from one another could be identified simply by determining this capability. Be aware there may be legal issues with conducting such identification. Many phones will have the removable storage slot (or port) under the battery and thus will require the examiner to "look" within that specific area. The US courts may deem such an inquiry as a "search" and later the results may be suppressed. Other phones, however, will have the slot on one side of the phone, which will, in most cases, be in plain view. The most common type of current storage is the microSD card. The "SD" stands for Secure Digital. The card is 11.0 mm × 15.0 mm and varies in storage capacities. Many Android devices will store media (images, video, sound files) to the microSD card by default, unless the user changes the internal settings. Fig. 7.6 depicts the front and back of a microSD card along with an example phone showing a side cover to access the card.

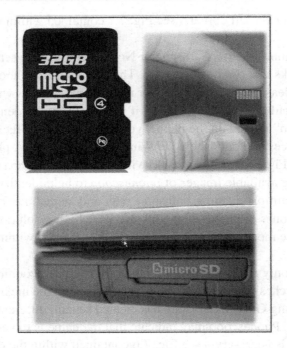

Figure 7.6
MicroSD front and back with supported phone showing access cover.

Chapter Summary Key Points

In attempting to identify mobile evidence, examiners can look to see if the device has a logo, which may depict if it is serviced by an MVNO or MNO. Devices that indicate MNO carriers serviced by GSM will always need to utilize a SIM card for network service. CDMA devices may or may not have a SIM and will be dependent on if they are LTE capable.

Many MVNO devices are capable of working on both CDMA and GSM networks. One of the largest within the US market is Tracfone. These phones may need additional research into determining what network they function on and ultimately what their exact model number is.

The five major Form Factors are *Bar*, *Clamshell*, *Slider*, *Swivel*, and *Tablet*. Determining the form factor can assist in identification. The Bar Form Factor is the most prominent style phone worldwide. Along with the Form Factor, the type of OS that the device uses can also aid in identification. There are multiple OSs that are offered; however, only three manufacturers commonly utilize their own brand trademarked symbol on the case of the mobile device. These are Windows, Blackberry, and newer Apple phones. Blackberry typically will have its own proprietary OS but recently also included the option of the Android OS. Apple devices will utilize a version of iOS, and last, many different manufacturers will offer Android OS.

Without actually powering on the target evidence, Android devices may, at times, pose the greatest difficulty in determining the version of the Android OS the device is currently using.

Phonescoop.com is an online (free) resource, which can help in identifying specific devices when all that is known is the make (manufacturer). The site allows devices to be searched based on when it was released (Newest), communication type (Technology—GSM/CDMA), or model number. Examiners can use the available images of this site to compare the front, side, and back against their target evidence. Phonescoop.com also allows the name of the phone to be used as a means to look up the phone. The examiner, however, may need to be more specific in some cases such as the Samsung Galaxy line.

Locating the visible microSD port or port cover may also aid in establishing the identity of the device. There will be manufacturers who distinguish two similar model phones by offering one with the microSD feature. Also, many Android devices store media by default to the microSD card.

In summary, the combination of establishing the network communication type (GSM/CDMA), Form Factor, OS type, and availability of removable media can all be used to help positively identify mobile evidence when the legal process has not been met. Each can be used separately or in combination to assist investigators in fully understanding what model they are faced with that may yield information in their case.

References

[1] Fierce Wireless, Topics – Service Provider Strategies, March 1, 2016. http://www.fiercewireless.com/special-reports/how-verizon-att-t-mobile-sprint-and-more-stacked-q4-2015-top-8-carriers.
[2] GSMA Intelligence – The Global MVNO Footprint: A Changing Environment, February 20, 2015. https://gsmaintelligence.com/research/2015/02/the-global-mvno-footprint-a-changing-environment/490/.
[3] BestMVNO.com, ATT MVNO Cell Phone Plans Compared, March 23, 2016. https://bestmvno.com/att-mvnos/.
[4] BestMVNO.com, Sprint MVNO's, April 17, 2016. https://bestmvno.com/sprint-mvnos/.
[5] BestMVNO.com, T-Mobile MVNO's, January 2015. https://bestmvno.com/t-mobile-mvnos/.
[6] BestMVNO.com, Verizon MVNO Cell Phone Plans Compared, March 2015. https://bestmvno.com/verizon-mvnos/.
[7] Twice.com, TracFone Lost 58K Subscribers Last Quarter, February 10, 2016. http://www.twice.com/news/smartphones/tracfone-lost-58k-subscribers-last-quarter/60411.
[8] ArsTechnica.com, Hyundai's Augmented Reality Manual: A Simple but Extremely Good Idea, January 10, 2016. http://arstechnica.com/cars/2016/01/hyundais-augmented-reality-manual-a-simple-but-extremely-good-idea/.
[9] International Data Corporation, Smartphone OS Market Share, 2015 Q2, August 2015. http://www.idc.com/prodserv/smartphone-os-market-share.jsp.
[10] Apple.com, iOS CarPlay Available Models, 2016. http://www.apple.com/ios/carplay/available-models/.
[11] Brewmp.com, About BREW MP – SDK, October 07, 2011. https://developer.brewmp.com/content/about-brew-mp-sdk.

CHAPTER 8

Triaging Mobile Evidence

Information in This Chapter

- List steps involved with processing mobile evidence that is powered "on"
- List steps involved with processing mobile evidence that is powered "off"
- Extraction and tool validation steps
- Phone security—devices powered on
- Forensic intake form

Introduction

As we continue with our fundamental core chapters, we must address how to handle mobile evidence that is located in a specific *"power state."* Many examiners tasked with mobile and computer forensics will receive evidence days after the incident took place. As such, the items will be powered off or the battery will be completely discharged. Other investigators may have collateral duties, and be part of other investigative teams who may get called to a scene that contains possible mobile evidence. Regardless of which role you have, it is important to understand that the initial steps regarding how the evidence is handled can have an impact on the recovery of stored artifacts.

Bloody Phone

Faraday or Swab?

The dispatcher put out a priority call with an alert tone, *"Shooting, 13th and M Street. Possible victim has crashed into a parked car at that location."* Patrol units began driving to the location with lights and sirens. While in route, dispatch provided additional information that this incident may have been a drug exchange per a witness in a neighboring home.

Officers arrive and locate the victim who is slumped over the wheel, deceased with an apparent gunshot wound to the head. The victim his holding a cellular phone, and the device is powered on and ringing. The device is also covered in blood. The investigation team is immediately called to the scene. Several officers have conducted door-to-door canvassing, and it is determined that two other suspects had approached the driver side of the vehicle. The driver held a mobile phone to his ear, words were exchanged and then gun fire broke out. Next to the victim's left hand is a wad of 20-dollar bills.

Seeking the Truth from Mobile Evidence. http://dx.doi.org/10.1016/B978-0-12-811056-0.00008-X

The victim's phone is photographed as it sits on his lap. Wearing latex gloves, the detective removed it from the vehicle, swabbed it, and biomedically decontaminated it. It is, at that time, Faradayed and placed on a 12-V cigarette charger, which is part of a field kit in the responding detective's unmarked vehicle.

All of the answers to the incident are soon found to be stored on the phone. Based on the number the victim had called to set up the drug buy, the suspect is tracked via his cell phone to a nearby home. In this case the blood that was swabbed off the phone belonged to the victim, and the case was ultimately solved.

What if the blood had not been the victim's, and the stored user data on the phone did not reveal the suspects responsible for his death? Proper triaging could still assist in identifying those responsible, and Faradaying a phone may at times not always be the **most logical** first step.

Devices Powered On
Sleep Mode?

Before we specifically provide steps for triaging mobile evidence, let us first understand that many manufacturers allow the phone's operating system to go into a "stand-by" or "sleep" mode. Basically, in most cases, the screen will go dark and appear that the device is actually powered off. Similar to moving a mouse attached to a computer, the phone can be "awakened" by touching one of the buttons. If the phone is in a stand-by or sleep state, the Graphical User Interface (GUI) will light up and display. The investigator who is tasked with recovery must make certain that he/she is not dealing with devices that appear to be powered off but are in fact "on" waiting for user interface.

Legal Issues

A second clarification that should be noted, is where we stand legally. In criminal cases, most law enforcement entities who are responding to *in progress* or *just occurred* incidents may *not* have the right to fully search the device. They do have the right to prevent destruction or altering of evidence, which should be a priority next to officer safety and scene security. This chapter cannot address all the legal issues that may be encountered. In most cases, officers will have a legal right to be at the scene of some criminal incident and must perform various tasks. The initial steps with devices that are powered "on" or "off" do not require a search warrant. Before carrying out these steps, make certain you consult with your own legal department. There should also be a standard operating procedure (SOP) in place if your jurisdiction (or business) is tasked with triaging mobile evidence. Within the SOP it should contain elements that address the legal issues that must be met before searching the evidence in question.

Steps—"On" Devices

1. **Identify what you have.** In the last chapter we focused on device identification. Along with determining what make and model you may be presented with, there is also the need to *identify* if additional forensic work needs to be completed. As in our initial homicide story, this may include processing what is contained on the outside of the evidence. It is because of the dynamics of case work we must always try to determine exactly what it is that needs to be addressed in a particular order. Many mobile forensic training vendors will advise that Faradaying the device is the first priority with a live phone. This is true, but what may trump this step is the need to conduct preliminary samples of evidence that can be altered. Network contamination prevention is still important, but the first responder steps may be different based on the needs of the case. If we go back to our initial homicide that involved the suspect crashing his vehicle, what changes would take place if it was raining and the victim was lying on the ground with blood on the outside of the phone? We would *identify* that we have a live powered-on cell phone that has blood on it, which may be washed away. To add to this, the phone may be damaged if it is left laying there exposed to moisture. We would in turn expedite our processing, or possibly try and cover the area until resources could arrive. Here are some things to consider with the upcoming, "identifying what you have" step.

    a. Does the device contain latent prints, blood, DNA, or other substances that may be change, altered, or contaminated if not immediately addressed?

    b. Does pulling the battery or shutting down the device pose a risk of a user enabled SIM lock PIN or other security being enabled?

    c. Are you following an SOP that addresses triaging mobile evidence located powered on? Does the SOP utilize aspects of *NIST* or other established guidelines?

With regard to an SOP, have a plan on how you or other investigators can conduct field research on a "live" mobile device. Besides the free, online Phonescoop.com site we mentioned in a previous chapter, there is a paid utility called Phone Detective. Cellebrite includes this program with its yearly renewal. This can be installed as an application on most smartphones that could be used directly at the scene.

2. **Isolate network, Wi-Fi, and Bluetooth.** This is one of the most important steps involved with a device that is powered on. Most of the time, this particular step is always going to be the first tactic employed on your evidence. As a reminder, here are the different ways in which network isolation can take place:

    a. *Airplane mode or similar internal setting, to include internal settings for Wi-Fi and Bluetooth.* Remember, go directly to these settings only. Without proper legal authority you do not have the right to search through the phone. The owner or user of the phone has an expectation of privacy in the other areas of the phone's file system. The bottom line, know exactly what you are doing and the steps to get to the signal settings, and do not navigate beyond them.

b. *Signal blocking mesh or bags.* Faraday mesh or bags may be reused. Mesh can be semitransparent but can present issues for touch screens. These are absolutely necessary with mobile devices that do not have an internal setting to shut off the signal (airplane mode, etc.). Depending on the type of forensic work being done, the likelihood of encountering these devices can be high. Many individuals who are involved with criminal endeavors use cheap disposable phones. The OS on these devices is not "feature rich" and can at times have no internal means to stop the signal from being received.

c. *Foil or paint cans.* Depending on the logistics involved with collection, you may or may not have the financial means to afford mesh or bags. Basic, aluminum foil can be used and reused. If you do use aluminum foil, the device needs to be wrapped a *minimum of three wraps*. The use of paint cans (with lids) can also be effective. If you choose to use these methods, make certain you test and validate the effectiveness before employing them on an actual piece of live evidence.

3. **Obtain legal process.** In Chapters 3 and 4, we discussed the three types of searches that are involved in most criminal cases. In civil cases, an employee would most likely have signed an agreement or other legal document allowing access by the employer or designee to the device. The point of this is to make sure you have a legal right to enter and look at what is on the device.

4. **Perform extraction.** The purpose of this book is not to promote one particular forensic tool over another. What is important to understand is that you utilize the tools and utilities you have been trained on and have validated. This includes physical extraction. Physical processing techniques are covered in upcoming chapters, and during your case work you should attempt to obtain a physical extraction on any device that legally supports it. This is followed up with a logical examination. In some scenarios that are extremely time sensitive (missing child, etc.), a case agent may request only specific items. We will expand on the protocols involved in the logical examination, but for now understand when the timing of the extraction should take place.

5. **Validate findings.** Many students who attend mobile forensics training often overlook the fact that what they have extracted from a device must *ALWAYS* be validated. It is imperative that we do not take the "word" of a vendor selling a particular tool who may insist that their product performs as advertised. Furthermore, people can "spoof" things like text messages. The complexity and time needed for validation seems to be common reasons why some examiners fail to perform this step. They often argue that they do not have a separate tool or utility to cross-validate. This may be a valid point, but the simplest form of validation is often overlooked. Here are some steps for validating your extraction findings:

a. *Use the GUI (visual).* You connect your phone via USB cable to tool "A." Tool "A" obtains 250 call history entries, 687 text messages, and 32 images. Using the phone's GUI, you visually validate these entries. Visual validation is easy and only costs the examiner his/her time.

b. *Obtain a Call Detail Record (CDR).* If the phone utilized normal cell phone towers to communicate, obtain the CDR. Many cases have argued about specific dates and times on the actual phone. These dates and times can be confirmed through the CDR results. This can also help with confirming or denying the content of SMS. Although most carriers do not retain the actual text content, they will retain the delivery results, meaning "to" and "from" numbers with a code showing it was SMS. CDR results are part of the forensic process and recommended when your device used towers to connect and terminate service.

c. *Cross-validate.* If you have the ability to utilize two or more different tools to obtain the stored data, this can confirm each of the product's results. This in combination with visual validation can certainly ensure that the tools are getting what you can *see*. Using product "A" to confirm product "B" cross validates both.

d. *Hand Carving.* Manually locating artifacts may or may not always be an option. If you have the training, time, and tools, you can use this method to confirm what a tool or utility was able to acquire through the automated process. If you have the ability to obtain the file system (or physical dump), you will often be able to use free utilities to manually locate times, dates, and content. By doing this, you will be able to articulate in court that you manually located the same artifact that tool "A" was able to pull. Hand Carving is also used to locate artifacts missed by tools and explored in greater detail in following chapters.

6. **Report.** Document what you locate. The reporting process is what will later be attacked in court. This must contain many of the items listed above. The legal portion of the report process is the number one target defense that will go after. It is often addressed at various hearings by defense counsel hoping to suppress it before jury selection has even begun. Defense counsel does not want to talk about the incriminating text message, image, or video that implicates their client; they want to battle the legal process and keep the stored artifact(s) from the jury or judicial officer. It is imperative to establish a sound reporting process that will accurately convey your findings. With "live" devices, the report must clearly articulate what was done to preserve the evidence. The content of the report itself will be covered in a later chapter.

To reiterate, it is important for the person tasked with collection to make sure he/she preserve what is on the device as best as he/she can. Live devices are not only touching something wirelessly; they are also eating up the battery. Have a plan for phones with a low battery charge. Many agencies have charging adaptors, and once the device is isolated from the signal, it is kept on and placed on a charger until the legal requirements have been met. The best rule of thumb with powered-on evidence: **if it is** "ON" **keep it** "ON" **but isolate it**. Of course, one would only apply these techniques to devices that have been involved in a serious felony offense. Most agencies could not justify nor do they have the departmental resources to employ all these steps for the theft of a candy bar for a 10-year-old suspect who dropped his/her powered on Android when he/she fled.

Suggested Items for a "Field-Kit"

First responders should have resources that they carry with them. These are commonly referred to as a *field kit*. Although most of these tools would be applied to devices that are powered on, the digital camera would generally be needed for all of the encountered scenarios. At a minimum, try and have the following available in the field. Remember this list is what is needed as a minimum; you can always add additional items to each of these categories, such as Faraday mesh to the aluminum foil:

1. Assorted charging cables, to include 12-V vehicle type. Currently, the most common cables for most newer phones would be the Apple Lightning, Apple 30 pin, USB micro, and USB mini. Fig. 8.1 depicts each of these cables.
2. Aluminum foil. This is by far the most cost-effective item that should be contained in the field kit. A roll of generic foil should be less than $3.00. It can be reused. Remember to

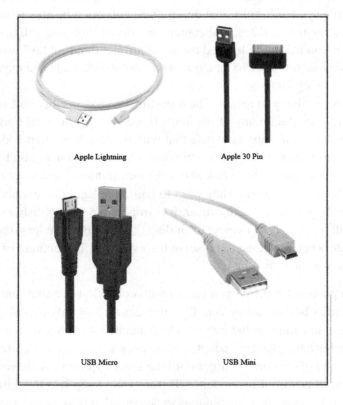

Figure 8.1
Examples of Apple Lightning, Apple 30 Pin, USB Micro, and USB Mini charging cables.

wrap devices a minimum of three wraps. In some cases, for larger phones or tablets, the item may need to be wrapped more than three times.

3. Cheap digital camera. A digital camera can assist with documenting settings or assist in indicating the state the evidence was located in prior to network isolation or additional processing. The important thing about the camera, is that the user must be able to operate it without delay. This means if your agency or business can afford a full frame digital camera that sells for thousands of dollars, you need to know how to work it. Many times agencies purchase cameras for this purpose, that need a training course on how to operate them. The suggestion here is to use something that needs minimal work to operate. It should be at a minimum of 5 megapixels and have a microcapability or micro/macro lens. An internal flash is also useful.

4. USB external battery packs. These can be very useful when 12-V adaptors are not available or your vehicle may be several feet away. They must be periodically charged and if left for extended periods of time in the field kit, they will discharge. These are often useful when collecting the device that is powered on and the phone is indicating that it is about to go dead. Fig. 8.2 contains some examples of USB external battery packs. The brand names have been redacted.

Figure 8.2
Examples of USB external battery packs.

Devices Powered Off

There is a general rule regarding mobile evidence that is powered off. *If the phone is off, keep it off.* Unless circumstances are exigent or other unusual situations are involved, the phone should not be turned on until ready to do so. This means you must be able to take steps to isolate the device and in some cases charge the battery just to power it on. If you are not trained in forensically processing mobile evidence, the item, in most cases, is best left powered down. The following are the general steps in processing devices that are collected in the "powered-off" mode:

Steps—"Off" Devices

1. **Identify what you have.** This is similar to the steps involved with a live device. The main difference is that because the phone is powered off, you have additional time to conduct your research. Do not be in a hurry (unless the case dictates). Use this time to find out if the device is equipped with removable media and/or a SIM. Find out everything you can about the device. This information will also help you with the legal process, and if a subpoena or warrant is required, you can list everything that is a possible location for evidence. Also, you can determine if anyone else in the forensic community has experience searching this type of device. If you are new to mobile forensics, or have a device that is new to the market, forums and other forensic blogs can contain a wealth of information on proper tools, techniques, or other prudent directions. Identify what tool(s), utilities, or methods are needed for processing. If possible, take images of the device before going any further.

2. **Obtain legal process.** Again, you must meet the legal requirement to search for stored data. As mentioned before, one of the three requirements will need to be met before you can start the processing.

3. **Process removable media and SIM first.** Photograph all the components to your device(s). If so equipped, this will include the SIM and microSD card. These will also need to be removed from the device and processed independently of the handset. Many forensic tools do not thoroughly pull data from the SIM and microSD while they are housed in the phone. Others can do a partial pull. It is important that you process these without the influence of the phone. Also, the microSD uses a **File Allocation Table** format and can be imaged using conventional computer forensic techniques. This means it uses a validated write blocker to image the content. SIM cards are write protected and do not have this issue. Failure to use a write blocker on the microSD (or other types of removable media) can result in changes being made to the media. Fig. 8.3 details a popular USB write blocker sold by Cellebrite, which allows various types of removable media to be connected.

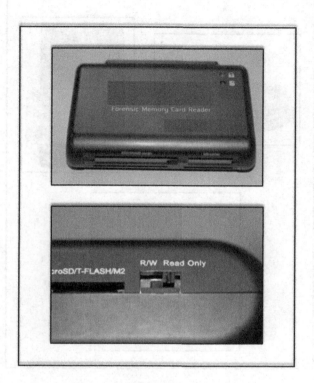

Figure 8.3
USB hardware write blocker used for microSD cards.

4. **Charge the battery.** If the battery is removable use a universal "probe" style charger, charge it outside of the phone. If the battery is not removable or does not properly charge with a universal battery charger, take care when charging through the charging port off the phone. Devices such as Apple and Blackberry can be turned on once they reach enough of a charge to trigger the boot process. If this happens the device can again touch the network or other wireless exchanges (Wi-Fi, Bluetooth). If you are charging these types of devices, use a wall charger instead of a charger that charges through a computer's USB port. This keeps the device from syncing with the computer and making changes. Also, take steps to provide a Faraday means to the phone. This ensures that if it is powered on at least it is being properly isolated from the network. Fig. 8.4 outlines a few different universal cell phone battery chargers.

Figure 8.4
Examples of Universal Cell Phone Battery Chargers.

5. **If GSM, consider creating a forensic SIM.** If you have researched the device and determined that it is a GSM phone and the SIM card is present, a network isolation technique available through forensic tools, is to create a forensic SIM. This obtains the ICCID and IMSI value off the target evidence and utilizes a sterilized writable blank SIM to copy the values onto. The forensic SIM is then placed into the suspect phone. These two values allow the OS to believe it is seeing the original SIM, thus keeping stored data in place but causing network isolation. The forensic SIM does not have the rest of the required network data for the device to get service. This method was almost always used on devices that were GSM and powered off. Now many phones have internal settings that can be enabled and this step is not necessary. Remember that many of the cheaper phones on the market, especially pay-as-you-go devices, may not have an internal setting that allows the signal to be disabled. This is why it is so important to conduct research on your device. User manuals will show if the device is equipped with

a SIM. If it is GSM, you can begin the process of creating a forensic SIM to ensure network isolation when you are ready to begin processing with your forensic tools.

6. **Perform extraction.** Once the battery is charged and the processing of the SIM and microSD has concluded, place these items back into the phone and begin the extraction process. If the device is GSM and does not have an internal signal stop setting (airplane mode or similar), consider the forensic SIM and/or additional Faraday steps. The steps involved with the extraction should include physical if supported and you have proper training for such examinations. Once the extraction is completed, power off the device.

7. **Validate findings.** Follow the same validation methods for a live device.

8. **Report.** The documentation will be the same as what is outlined for reporting under a live device.

Locked Devices Powered On

The two largest types of phone being sold worldwide are Android and iPhone. As such, the most popular forms of security are gesture (pattern) and 4–6 digit numeric. Fig. 8.5 displays both.

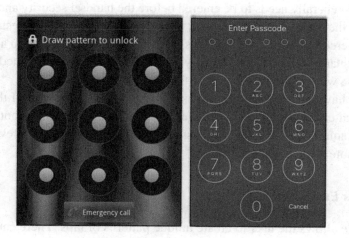

Figure 8.5
Android Gesture Pattern and iPhone 6 Digit PIN.

Most users will enable their devices with some form of security. This can include simple or complex pass codes, gesture patterns, fingerprint recognition, facial recognition, and many others. Some of these are explained in more detail below. Also phones may have more than one form of security enabled. The user can also install third-party applications that add additional layers of protection. Most first responders are not forensic technicians and are usually not carrying around utilities and specialized tools that can defeat or bypass a user lock. Here are some suggestions when dealing with powered-on mobile evidence that has user enabled security.

1. If possible, ask the owner for the credentials. This step is often forgotten. If the owner is also the suspect in a criminal investigation this may, at times, warrant Miranda warnings. There have also been times when a spouse or family member revealed the password and the information was then contained in a search warrant to access the device. If your suspect or owner is cooperating, disable the user enable security before collecting the device. There have been numerous investigations where the suspect started out cooperative, and changed their mind. A seasoned investigator had the suspect disable the security before they had a "change of heart." This allowed a full exam on a phone that normally was protected by encryption when the user applied a six-digit PIN number.

2. If you have the capability to bypass the security, Faraday the device, keep it charged, obtain your legal process, and then access the necessary information. At this point it will be a case-to-case decision if you are going to keep the device powered on. One thing to remember with a device that is powered on and only shows security for the handset: powering it down then later back on may enable a SIM PIN, which is much more difficult to bypass. The SIM PIN generally needs to be entered before the handset security and, in many cases, displays after the phone restarts. You may not even know that the SIM security was enabled until it is powered back on. There are pros and cons with powering down a security enabled device. It is usually weighed against the type of incident being investigated and if there is access to those who are trained to bypass the specific user lock.

3. If you do not have the technical resources to bypass security, power off the device and remove the battery if possible. Your biggest concern is now network contamination. Since the security cannot be defeated, you must preserve the evidence and prevent altering or potential remote wiping from occurring.

Additional Types Embedded Security

LG's Knock Code allows the user to create unique patterns of taps. There can be more than 80,000 Knock Code Combinations possible [1]. On the companion site, Fig. 8.1 is an image of how the knock patterns can be enabled on specific supported phones.

Face Unlock was introduced with Android's Ice Cream Sandwich. It was soon proven to be very unsecure and users could even hold up a picture of the face that created the security to bypass it. Later Jelly Bean improved on Face Unlock, which created the need for blinking to be validated when creating the facial security. Face Unlock is still not as popular as other forms of security as it takes much longer for users to unlock their phones. Fig. 8.2 on the companion site depicts the Face Unlock interface from an Android. Apple has recently introduced a better form of facial recognition. Time will tell just how many people use this feature, and if there's any issues with long time usage.

Fingerprint readers. Motorola was one of the first vendors to offer a fingerprint sensor on some of their smartphones. Apple, HTC, Samsung, LG, and others soon followed. Many vendors used fingerprint swiping, not just fingerprint recognition. Also, some allow fingerprint security along with security PIN numbers.

Forensic Processing Triage Forms

One of the items that can be of assistance to the actual individuals who will be performing the data recovery from mobile evidence is a forensic processing triage form. These can clarify many of the questions the examiner may have as the phone eventually finds its way to the laboratory. Between the times the incident took place, when the phone was recovered, and when it was actually processed can be days, weeks, or even months apart. In many jurisdictions, the forensic laboratory may not be close to the actual agency that is performing the investigation. The need to have a clear understanding of what is wanted is often overlooked or not actually brought up until the processing is about to begin. Getting the correct answers at that point may unnecessarily delay the process and could actually affect how many days are left to serve the legal process. These forms are easy to create and **should not be created by administrators or others who are not actually performing the forensic examination**. Here are a few suggestions to include when creating a triage form:

1. *Requestor (case agent):* This is the person (or people) who are in charge of the case. This may or may not be the person who is delivering the phone to the laboratory or who seized the phone for processing. This also may not be the person who obtained the legal process to search the device.
2. *Type of search:* As previously addressed, this will be a search warrant, consent to search, or exigent situation. In some civil cases this may be labeled "internal" or "administrative."
3. *Case number:* This can be the criminal investigative (dispatched call) number or an internally assigned number.
4. *Type of Incident:* The type of crime(s) should be indicated as this may help the examiner locate specific artifacts in question.
5. *Make:* This may or may not be something that can be easily documented during recovery. Most vendors will usually display the manufacturer's name clearly on the outside of the target device.
6. *Model:* Again, the model may be something that cannot be revealed without an actual search of the phone. Devices such as Apple iPhone have the model number listed on the back of the phone in small print.
7. *Carrier:* Many phones also display the carrier on the outside of the phone. This can be important later when a phone is designed for a wireless carrier, but the SIM that was located inserted into the SIM port was from a different carrier.
8. *User enabled password/PIN/SIM PIN:* Depending on if the phone was recovered in a powered on or off state, this information may not be known. There will also be times

when the owner/user of the phone is cooperating with the investigation. This is a good time to inquire what the security values are to "get into" the phone.

9. *User/owner name:* This can help with identifying who may have used or corresponded with the device. The owner or user could be a suspect, witness, or other party not directly involved with the investigation, but the handset could have information useful to the case. Some jurisdictions find it useful not to indicate "*Suspect name*" but rather call this, "User/owner" instead.

10. *Unique data requests (keywords, dates, etc.)*: This area should contain information that may not be automatically parsed out using a forensic utility. In investigations such as gang-related crimes, monikers, and specific names given to street sets could be useful. Also, there may be specific vernaculars used by the players in the case.

Fig. 8.6 is an example of a mobile forensic processing form. This particular document contains all of the above fields and would accompany the device into the laboratory. Copies of any legal forms would also be attached.

Figure 8.6
Example of a mobile forensic process form.

Chapter Summary Key Points

Both powered "on" and "off" devices will require the need to research the device. With devices that are off, this will allow, in most cases, additional time to conduct the necessary examination steps. Remember, your case will dictate if other forensic processing such as DNA, latent recovery, swabbing, or other services are needed before network isolation or other processing steps begin.

Devices that are powered on will need to be isolated from the network. In most cases, the phone should be left on if the seriousness of the investigation warrants it; turning off a phone could enable other security such as a SIM PIN lock. To aid with the collection of mobile evidence, and aid in the first initial steps with triaging, it is recommended that first responders have access to "field kits," which should include aluminum foil, charging cables, portable power blocks, and a cheap digital camera at a minimum.

Both the powered "on" and "off" devices will also require legal process, extraction, validation, and report writing. In both situations, validation should be performed in every case. Forms of validation can be visual, CDR, cross-validation, and Hand Carving. All tools, utilities, or programs used should be validated prior to working on an actual case.

Live devices that have user enabled security should be powered off (and batteries pulled if supported), if investigators do not have the means to defeat the security. There can be other forms of security besides the user enabled gesture pattern or PIN.

A mobile forensics processing form should be created to assist the examiner performing the data extraction. Such items to include on the form you create, would be the requestor's name, type of search, case number, type of incident, date of intake, make, model, carrier, user enabled security credentials, user or owner's name, and unique data requests typically not automatically parsed by forensic tools.

Last, triaging mobile evidence will, at times, also rely on those involved to "think outside the box." Although we have listed steps for specific power states, it does not mean that this chapter can provide exact suggestions for unusual situations one may encounter. Being flexible, adaptable, and resourceful will not only go far with how mobile evidence is handled, it will also come in handy when a phone has been thrown in a lake, burned, or broken into pieces. Like many aspects involved with this job, it is the examiner's willingness to adapt to what he/she may be faced with that affects the entire methodology involved with mobile forensics.

Reference

[1] LG.com, Mobile-Phones/Knockcode, 2016. http://www.lg.com/us/mobile-phones/knockcode#video.

CHAPTER 9

The Logical Examination

Information in This Chapter

- Computer forensics and mobile forensics
- Write blocking
- Connection interfaces
- Agent/client
- Logical protocols
- Attention Terminal (AT) commands
- Port Monitoring

Introduction—A "Logical" Home

In this chapter we will explain in more detail important aspects of the logical acquisition. Let us begin by thinking of the logical examination using the analogy of a house. A home may contain various rooms. If we wanted to locate the stove and refrigerator we would travel to the kitchen. To discover a bed and dresser, we move to a bedroom. The room we enter, yields the appropriate fixtures for that area in the dwelling. If we compare this to the business of the logical examination, we are telling a "tool" to go to a specific "area" (room) and report back to us what is there. The logical tool can only "report" what it is programmed to "see." It is not going to show us how the stove is made or include the entire bedroom with the other components. For example, we know that if we travel into a particular home we have a journal that is in our master bed room. The journal contains names and phone numbers of all our friends and family members. The master bed room is upstairs, all the way down the hall, to the right. The journal is contained in a large dresser, inside the top drawer, to the left, under our shirts. If this home was a cellular phone, we could use a program that supported finding the contacts, and it would go directly to the necessary location and find the entries we have stored in the file system. The logical tool, however, could only get data that is formatted in the correct format. It may only be able to get specific entries in our journal, say A–Z entries, but not the pictures next to them. A file system logical examination would get more, maybe the entire container (dresser) or "journal" that contains the entries we stored. A logical examination would never be able to get the entire house that contains everything. It certainly could not obtain the pages from our journal we ripped out and are waiting inside a recycle bin stored in the garage. The entire house and trash would be the analogy of what a physical acquisition would yield.

This chapter does not support one logical tool over another, as the business of mobile forensics will always require more than one tool, technique, or program. We will also discuss the ways communication occurs, the changes to the file system that may take place, and ways in which to understand and validate what a logical forensic tool does to our evidence.

Computer Forensics and Mobile Forensics

Although we previously defined *Mobile Forensics*, it is important to also understand the major differences between the disciplines of computer and mobile extractions. When computer forensics first began, there was no set standard, but, over the past years, one general standard is used. After a legal process was met on a target computer, the drive that contained the operating system was "imaged" and a bit-by-bit extraction verification was used, called a hash result. The copied image was then used to perform additional searches, and depending on the forensic program, deleted artifacts could be located. We will not address the processing of RAM on a "live" computer, which is a unique process typically conducted at the scene. Instead, we are comparing the mobile forensic examination to that of the computer hard drive(s). Computers for years have used hard drives to store the operating system and other user-related files.

Mobile devices by their design, do not allow the examiner the ability to simply remove the drive that contains the evidence. Destructive techniques such as "chip removal" are, in fact, very similar to imaging a computer drive. The various tools needed can become expensive, which may limit some agencies from conducting this type of examination. The other issue is the advanced training needed for such an extraction. Above all, most investigative cases do not need such an intrusive style approach. The case agent may be requesting a series of text messages, images, call history, or other data. In the case of logical artifacts, if the device is not enabled with a user lock or damaged, the evidence needed can be viewed directly through the Graphical user interface (GUI). Even without forensic software, pictures of the evidence could be taken from the screen as a last resort.

Write Blocking

During the process of conducting computer forensics, the actual drive is connected to a hardware or software write blocker. This prevents any changes on the evidence itself and ensures that the drive is in the same condition after imaging takes place. During a logical examination, to include a file system examination, the specific software must communicate with the target. If a write blocker utility was used, this communication cannot take place. The way the tool "speaks" with the phone is called a *communication protocol*. Each phone can have a different type of protocol that may be needed for the data in question to be read by the commercial, or open-source tool.

Connection Interfaces

Before the specific logical protocol can take place, the utility being used needs to connect to the evidence. This can be accomplished in several different ways, most of which are hardware based through a specific cable. Others can be wireless. Here is a list of some of connection types:

* *Serial* to *serial*—Proprietary serial connection to mobile device, connected to serial communication port on computer. Typically, would require a serial driver for the cable to properly work. This was one of the first forms of logical acquisition methods, and is not commonly used today. Many of the early Palm devices required direct serial connection.
* *Serial* to *USB*—Similar to serial to serial. This type of connection allowed devices still using a serial style connection to connect to computers that were equipped with USB. One end of the cable would have a specific serial cradle or serial adaptor for the mobile device, and the other end would have a USB male. This type of connection is also not commonly used today.
* *Proprietary cable* to *RJ45*—This style of connection is usually make and model specific and will generally require a serial driver. It is commonly used for a physical pull but can also be used to acquire logical data of specific model phones.
* *Proprietary cable* to *USB*—Requires a unique cable that would connect through a data port on the device, under the battery, or other locations. Some models are even connected through the audio connection or unique diagnostic contacts that may also be used for physical pulls. Mini-USB, Micro-USB, Apple 30 Pin, and Apple Lighting would be examples of current types of common proprietary cables that could be used on different models of the same manufacturer.
* *IrDA*—Infrared Data Association usually works with a "line-of-sight" data transfer. The range is usually around 1 m, using low power with transfer speeds from 2.4 kilobits per second to 1 gigabit per second.
* *Bluetooth*—This transfer type exchanges data by utilizing specific UHF (Ultra High Frequency). Operating within ranges of 2400 MHz, the connection can transfer data distances up to 100 m. The connection typically "pairs" with the mobile device and the transfer program or utility. There are many versions of Bluetooth, and each version increases the range, speed, power consumption, and other features. In June 2016, Bluetooth v5 was announced as the next release, coming in the late 2016 to early 2017 [1].

Agent or Client

A few years back, forensic software companies developed specific programs that an examiner would allow to be installed on the target phone. These applications would target the supported operating system and mimic specific communication protocols that are commonly afforded to other applications running on the same system. These programs are commonly called an "agent" or "client." The program that is installed on the target phone is only for a logical pull of specific data. The connection between the forensic tool and the phone must first be established using one of the previously mentioned connection types. Because the *agent/client* needs access to install itself on the OS, the phone generally cannot be locked. Also, specific internal settings and application "trusts" must be allowed. Fig. 9.1 shows a pop-up window that will display on the target phone when connection communication begins. The investigator must allow this communication to take place by selecting "Trust."

Figure 9.1
Example of the "Trust This Computer" confirmation screen.

In the case of Android devices, a logical acquisition using this technique must have the internal Android Debug Bridge (ADB) setting enabled. In some cases, the phone would need to have the developer mode "turned on" to actually be granted access to the ADB debugging setting. Fig. 9.2 depicts the common internal developer settings on an Android phone. This also shows the warning when the ADB debugging is enabled. By default, this setting is off.

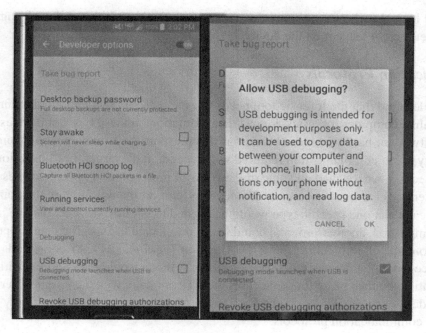

Figure 9.2
Android developer settings with Android Debug Bridge (ADB) debugging warning (after enabling).

The ADB setting also applies to many of the commercially available tools used to pull a physical extraction. Understand that for the supported logical agent/client to install itself on the target phone, specific settings must be enabled. Also, the specific vendor will support different types of logical data on the target phone. This often means that one tool will acquire a group of logical data while another tool may be needed to obtain additional data.

When examiners are using a logical tool, the interface of the particular program will indicate what it supports for that specific phone. For example, Susteen Secure View may only support SMS, Contact, and Call history for a simple LG flip phone. The GUI of the forensic software would allow the examiner to select or deselect these fields. There is no preset rule that governs whether or not a phone is supported on what it has stored. It is strictly up to the vendor on what they decide to support.

Once we have enabled the required settings or allowed the "trust" setting to take place between the utility and the mobile device, the agent or client will begin installing and executing. As previously mentioned, this installs a specific program to the phone and begins copying the supported data back to the forensic tool. There are settings within each of these commercial logical tools that, in some cases, can allow the examiner to delete the agent/client after the operation or leave it on the device.

Communication Protocols

We now understand that the forensic tool needs to establish communication with our mobile devices. Unlike computer forensics, logical data extraction on these types of devices cannot utilize a software or hardware write blocker as this prevents the communication from occurring. The "type" of communication required will depend on the target. In Connection Interfaces section, we touched on some of the types of protocols that specific cables or wireless interfaces require. Also, many devices may support the use of more than one protocol. This means that one specific type would be needed to get the phone to "listen," and after this is accomplished, another protocol could be used to locate the specific data supported. One common type of communication is the *Attention Terminal* (AT). AT commands are often used to place the target device into a specific *mode*. A mode would then allow additional communications to take place. In some cases the AT command would continue after the desired mode is enabled. We will come back to the AT protocols. Let us first supply a list of some other communication protocols:

- Sync ML (Synchronization Markup Language)
- OBEX (Object Exchange)
- OBEX File Transfer Protocol (OBEXFTP)
- OBEX Object Push (OBEXOBJECTPUSH)
- IRMC (Infrared Mobile Communications)
- IRDA (Infrared Data Association)
- FBUS (Fast Bus)
- MBUS (Message Bus)
- MTP (Media Transfer Protocol)
- PTP (Picture Transfer Protocol)
- Object-C
- AFC (Apple File Communication Protocol)
- MPT (Motorola Phone Tools)

This is not a conclusive list of every communication protocol that would be utilized on a mobile device. Many devices will also communicate through the USB Mass Storage, which is primary utilized for media.

Attention Terminal Commands

There are many commercially available mobile forensic programs available to the examiner. It is important to understand the very basic way in which many of these tools communicate with the device. First, let us understand a little history regarding these commands.

The AT command was used to communicate with modems. Many GSM and CDMA devices can be "seen" within the Windows environment as a modem. If a supported device has the appropriate drivers installed, Device Manager may list the phone under the Modem settings. The device may also show under a Serial Port, and in some cases both. Fig. 9.3 shows a Motorola device showing in Device Manager.

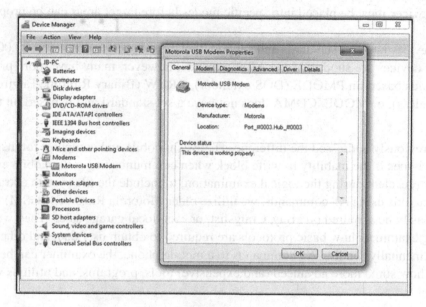

Figure 9.3
Device Manager indicating a Motorola device connected to Windows as a Modem.

Within the third Generation Partnership Project (3GPP) V.3.13.0 Technical Specification released in 1999, a number of AT commands as well as recommendations for controlling Mobile Termination (MT) functions are specified. These are related to GSM and UMTS (Universal Mobile Telecommunication System) [2]. The commands listed within this technical document are not the only ones available to mobile devices. Many manufacturers have similar documents that outline commands for their device models. Vendors such as Motorola, Nokia, Kyocera, and many others offer documents online, which specify their own AT commands.

Here are some very basic rules related to AT commands. We will show readers how to set up a phone within Windows and send specific commands to obtain SMS and stored phone book contacts.

- Commands will begin with "AT" or "at."
- "A/" can be utilized to repeat a previous command.
- Commands can be given in uppercase or lowercase.

- Users can backspace over an error and rewrite the entry.
- All commands must be executed with the *ENTER* key.
- AT commands will be followed by +, $, or # symbols.
- =? provides the required parameters of the command and will show the user what is supported.
- ? will dump the supported registry.
- Some devices must be placed into specific modes before target areas can be properly read.
- GSM devices have set standards and support Technical Specifications (TS) 27.007.
- CDMA devices are supported via AT commands; however, many have more proprietary commands based on PMODE (DOS extender), BREW (Binary Runtime Environment for Wireless), or MODE. CDMA does not have a set standard and is based on the TS 27.007.

When we previously addressed the differences between mobile and computer forensics, one of the main issues is the inability to write block when communicating with mobile evidence. This is very prevalent during the logical examination, to include the file system extraction. To help illustrate this using AT commands, we utilize older Motorola Razor V3 (GSM) devices. These can easily be acquired on eBay, Craigslist, or even local garage sales. They work great for teaching examiners how basic protocols are required to obtain user data and other information. By manually sending AT commands to a mobile phone, the examiner can better understand how some more advanced (and expensive) tools, programs, and utilities work at the low level.

This example uses Windows 7. Windows XP and previous releases had a program called HyperTerminal embedded in the OS. Since newer versions of Windows exclude HyperTerminal, users must obtain two main files to use it. These can easily be found through online searching. They are also contained on the companion site, under Chapter 9 in a folder titled "HyperTerminal files." To prevent any issues with HyperTerminal, keep these files within the same folder. The files needed are called *hypertrm.exe* and *hypertrm. dll*. There are other programs besides HyperTerminal that allow AT commands to be executed on supported target phones. Since Windows is still the most common OS used, this technique may be easier for many to replicate and does not require a command shell. We use a GSM Motorola V3 Razor from T-Mobile or AT&T in working condition. It must power on. It does not need network allocation (service). It should contain a SIM card, as some AT commands pull from the SIM. Before using it on a host PC, users may need to download the Motorola driver execution file. This installs several drivers for many different Motorola products, older legacy, and new smartphones. It is not necessary to try and locate the old drivers just for the Razor; the standard Motorola.exe (driver) install for Windows will work for this phone. Once the drivers are installed, charge and power on the phone. Connect the Motorola Razor to Windows using a standard mini-USB cable. Check to make certain there are no driver issues within Device Manager. Correct if any issues are noted. Look under the Modem tab within Device Manager. Make a note which *Com Port* is indicated as the connection to the phone modem, as you will need to know this information when connecting through the HyperTerminal. Users should see the Motorola phone listed. If the device in not listed, check internal settings within the phone (if supported) and ensure the Modem setting within the phone is enabled. There will be some phones that need to have the setting "Fax" enabled. Sometimes, simply disconnecting and reconnecting the USB cable corrects the problem.

1. The next step is to set up HyperTerminal. This must be done each time a user wants to send commands to a new phone. In the next chapter we will address troubleshooting and an option called *Query Modem*. This feature can confirm that Windows is properly communicating with the target phone. Contained on the companion site is a PDF with step-by-step instructions (with images) on how to set up HyperTerminal. It is labeled "HT_setup." Here are the overall steps:

    a. Launch the HyperTerminal "exe" file. Users will be prompted with the "***Open File—Security Warning***" screen. Select ***Run.***

    b. The ***Default Telnet Program?*** window will present itself the first time the program is launched. To prevent this from popping up each time, check the box next to "***Don't ask me this question again***" and either select *Yes* or *No*. (Selecting this either way has no effect on this exercise)

    c. The next window is the "***Connection Description***," which requests the user to enter a name and choose an icon for the connection. Select ***Cancel.***

    d. At this point, there should be no additional pop-up windows: only the terminal screen that shows *File, Edit, View, Call, Transfer,* and *Help* are at the top. Users must click on the ***File*** setting, which will reveal: *New Connection, Open, Save, Save As, Page Setup, Print, Properties,* and *Exit* from a drop-down menu. Select ***Properties.***

    e. After selecting Properties, another Window titled "***New Connection Properties***" will be presented to the user. There are two tab choices: ***Connect To*** and ***Settings.*** Under the *Connect To* setting, users must use the drop-down arrow next to the "***Connect using:***" option. This setting allows users to manually select which Com Port they want HyperTerminal to communicate with. This selection must be the same Com Port you noted your Motorola (modem) was connected to after connecting it to Windows. After the correct Com Port is selected go to the ***Settings*** tab. Under the "*Function, arrow, and ctrl keys act as*" select "***Windows keys.***" Next, select the ***ASCII Setup*** button. Make certain all boxes are checked within *ASCII Sending* and *ASCII Receiving.* Leave the *Line delay* and *Character delay* set to the default 0 ms. Click *OK* once these settings are enabled. The terminal is now set up to send commands to the Motorola V3 Razor.

Common Attention Terminal Commands

CDMA devices, many times, will respond to AT commands that are from the GSM standard. The make of the phone can also require specific commands that are only used with that device. Refer to online resources related to CDMA AT commands. The device used in this example is a Motorola GSM phone. Users should be aware that most of the below-listed commands will work on the phones mentioned (V3 T-Mobile or AT&T); however, some devices will report errors with certain requests. Motorola devices will also need to be placed into a mode to access specific inquiries such as phone book and text. The mode needed is addressed in the next few pages.

Here is a shortcut of commands from the various sources located online. Most of these are GSM AT commands, but many will work on CDMA phones. Try commands with and without the letter "C": attempt to send some of these commands to the Motorola through the HyperTerminal. Remember, all of the commands listed in this chapter begin with *AT* or *at*.

+CGMI (manufacturer of phone)
+CGMM (model identification)
+CGSN (IMEI or MEID or ESN of device)
+CGMR (software revision)
+CIMI (IMSI value)
+CNUM= (subscriber phone number)
+CPAS (provides a code for the activity of the phone)
+CCLK? (displays the time and date value)
+ICCID= (ICCID of the SIM)
+CBC? (battery condition)
+CLAC (lists all the supported AT commands (some are mode commands))

Besides these listed commands, the user can also call the stored phone book entries as well as the SMS. On this particular model phone, for this information to be displayed through the HyperTerminal, the phone must first be placed into a specific mode.

Modes

Some phones require a mode to allow access to a location in the file system or for a tool to read or write data to other areas of the file system. When users first turn on the phones used in this exercise, the device is in *MODE 0*. Mode 0 is the standard AT command mode. This phone and many others will respond to several types of AT commands. To get to the SMS content and in many cases the phone book entries, Motorola devices may require MODE 2. *MODE=2* sets up the phone to receive the commands. For those readers who may have served in the military, think of the MODE command as a preparatory command. It is telling the device, "*Hey, I need something in this location—standby and I will tell you what it is!*" If users do not first inform the file system what it is they are looking for, the command to retrieve specific information fails to execute. The second part of this analogy is the *command of execution*. If soldiers are standing at attention in formation and the drill sergeant yells "*Left*…(pause)…*Face!*" our preparatory command would be "Left" and the command of execution would be "Face." Mode 2 is our preparatory command. It places the file system in a specific state to allow access to complete the rest of the request. In the next few pages we will explain the commands that can be thought of as the "command of execution" using this analogy.

Once the phone is in this mode, *Echo typed characters locally* must be turned off under the Properties tab in HyperTerminal (**File—Properties—Settings—ASCII Setup**). Failure to uncheck this setting will result in double commands being placed in the terminal screen. Send the following command to the Motorola through HyperTerminal: *AT+MODE=2*. The response from the phone should be "OK." Within HyperTerminal users may see "*+MBAN: Copyright 2000-2002 Motorola, Inc.*" after the "OK."

While the phone is in Mode 2, users have two formats to list the text (SMS) messages. These are *TEXT* and *PDU* mode. PDU stands for *Protocol Data Unit* and is a 7-bit GSM encoding format that will require an interpreter to decode. Users must send a command to the phone for it to list the TEXT mode. These commands are as follows:

> **+CMGF=?** (will indicate which modes the phone supports and the replies will be 1, 2, or both). Depending on what is supported, the next command will be as follows: **+CMGF=0** (for PDU mode) and **+CMGF=1** (for TEXT mode). Text mode will be used in this exercise. You are welcome to try PDU mode, but we will not provide steps for decoding the string during this chapter. Once you send this command with a 0 or 1, the phone will reply *OK*, which sets it up to receive the next command to the phone.

If you are in TEXT mode first (command +CMGF=1), you can list what type of available supported parameters are featured for the device. The command is as follows with the possible supported replies: **+CMGL=?**

> "REC UNREAD"—these are received unread messages
> "REC READ"—messages that have been received and read
> "STO UNSENT"—stored unsent messages
> "STO SENT"—stored sent messages
> "ALL"—lists all the above types of messages

If you are in PDU mode first (command +CMGF=0) you can also list what type of available supported parameters are featured for the device. The command is the same: **+CMGL=?** with the following possible supported replies:

> 0—received unread messages
> 1—received read messages
> 2—stored unsent messages
> 3—stored sent messages
> 4—all types of messages

Some Motorola devices also allow a command to list all the messages at once. You must be in Mode 2, turn off Echo, send the type of messages you wish to read, +CMGF=1 for TEXT or 0 for PDU, and then send **+MMGL**. If the phone supports it, all of the stored SMS messages will list using the +MMGL command.

Phone Book Entry Commands

To read stored phone book entries, you must switch the phone into reading the proper location. **+CPBS** switches the handset to the SIM or handset (Mobile Equipment, *ME*) to the location. **+CPBS?** will provide a list of current supported Call History and Phone book locations. These will be coded as the following if the device supports it:

"AD"—abbreviated dialing numbers
"BC"—own business card
"DC"—ME dialed calls
"HP"—hierarchical phone book
"EN"—SIM/ME number for emergency
"MV"—ME voice activated dialing list
"FD"—SIM fixed dialing numbers (ADNs)
"MC"—ME unanswered (missed) call list
"ME"—ME phone book
"ON"—SIM/ME assigned number (MSISDN)
"OW"—own telephone number
"RC"—ME received call list
"SM"—SIM phone book
"TA"—TA data card phone book (old analog devices)
"MD"—last number redial memory
"LD"—SIM last number redial memory (LND)
"MT"—combined SIM and ME phone book

The command **+CPBR=?** will list the parameters needed to receive data of **+CPBS**. Fig. 9.4 indicates that a command of *at+cpbr=?* was sent to the phone, which resulted in a reply showing the parameters of the phone book location and potential entries (1–1250). 1250 is the capability and the lowest storage is the number 1. The command *at+cpbr=1* would result in the data in entry #1 within that container location. Users must place a space between the equal sign and the number entry they are requesting. If users wish to display all of the entries stored in the phone book at once, they must first determine the range of storage. For instance, a command of at+cpbr=? was sent to the phone. The phone responds through HyperTerminal with the following: **+CPBR: (1-1250),40,18**.

The (1–1250) figure represents the format and maximum number of stored entries that can be on the device. The number 1 represents where the first entry would be stored, listed under 1. The other numbers can be used to indicate how many entries are on the device, although this may not show used entries that have been deleted. The 40 would indicate how many slots were used and the 18 represents how many entries are stored. Because some entries may have been deleted, these two other numbers may or may not be accurate. Users should focus more on the number within the parenthesis as they can send another command with that range to display the stored entries. The following command will list all logical stored entries within that range.

The command in this example would be: *at+cpbr=1,1250*.

If this command yields a high number of stored entries, and they scroll across the terminal screen very fast, or continues to a new screen, the user can specify a range that only displays those entries using *at+cpbr=1,200* and would yield the first 200 entries, or a single entry can also be sent using *at+cpbr=1*.

Figs. 9.4–9.6 are examples of AT commands sent to a Motorola V3 Razor using the HyperTerminal. Fig. 9.5 shows positive replies using the commands *at+gmm* (model number), *at+cnum* (assigned phone number), and *at+cimi* (IMSI). Fig. 9.4 depicts the Razor being placed into MODE 2. A command to request the number of phone book contacts the phone is capable of storing is sent: *at+cpbr=?* The reply is 1250. The next command is *at+cpbr=1,1250* to show all the contacts stored within that range. Fig. 9.4 shows the first four entries that start with +CPBR: 1. These have been redacted. Fig. 9.6 shows the last eight entries in this range (again, redacted). Notice how the count jumps from 13 to 37. The entries between these ranges have been deleted and are not viewable using AT commands.

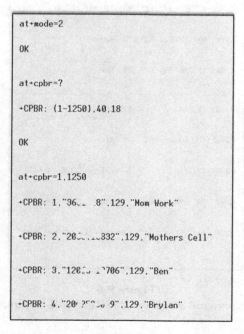

Figure 9.4
AT commands *at+gmm*, *at+cnum*, and *at+cimi* example.

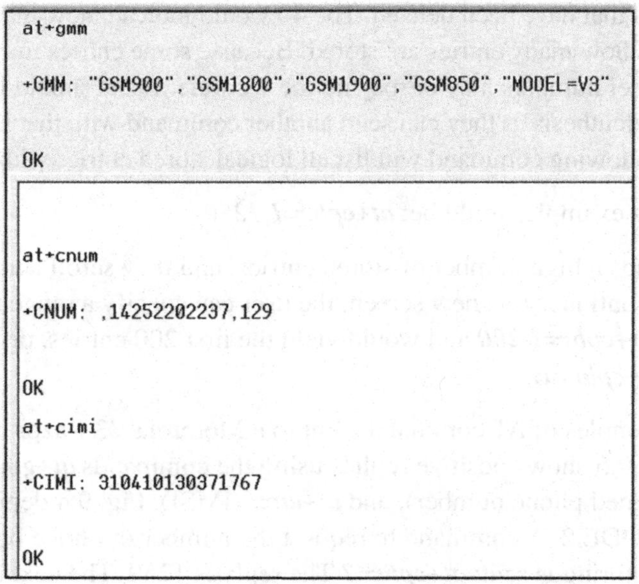

```
at+gmm

+GMM: "GSM900","GSM1800","GSM1900","GSM850","MODEL=V3"


OK


at+cnum

+CNUM: ,14252202237,129


OK
at+cimi

+CIMI: 310410130371767


OK
```

Figure 9.5
AT commands *at+mode=2*, *at+cpbr=?*, and *at+cpbr=1,1250* example.

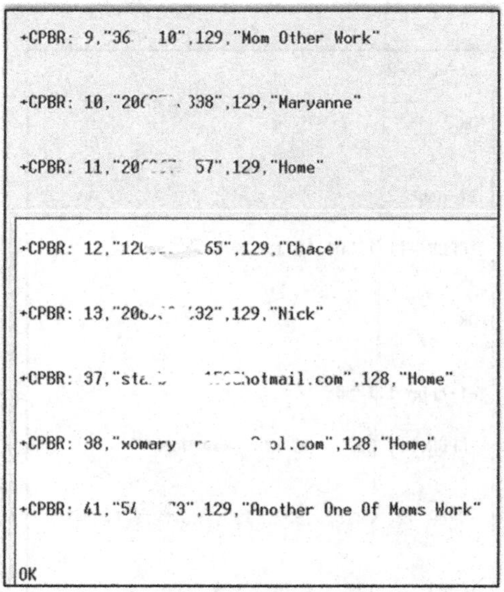

```
+CPBR: 9,"36   10",129,"Mom Other Work"

+CPBR: 10,"20(    338",129,"Maryanne"

+CPBR: 11,"20     57",129,"Home"

+CPBR: 12,"12L     65",129,"Chace"

+CPBR: 13,"20b     32",129,"Nick"

+CPBR: 37,"sta      otmail.com",128,"Home"

+CPBR: 38,"xomary        ol.com",128,"Home"

+CPBR: 41,"5(     3",129,"Another One Of Moms Work"

OK
```

Figure 9.6
AT command *at+cpbr=1,1250* example continued.

Using the same phone, the previously addressed commands were sent to the device to show the stored SMS. These examples are contained within the companion site, Figs. 9.1–9.3. Fig. 9.1 (companion site) represents the Razor phone being placed into *MODE 2*. The command *at+cmgf=?* provides a response from the phone indicating that it supports (0) PDU and (1) TEXT. Below this, in Fig. 9.1 (companion site), is the next command *at+cmgf=1* and the phone replies "*OK.*" At the bottom of Fig. 9.1 (companion site) we see the command *at+cmgl=?*, which provides us with a list of the type of SMS messages the phone is capable of storing. *REC UNREAD*, *REC READ*, *STO UNSENT*, *STO SENT*, and *ALL* are the replies. The "REC" stands for received and "STO" stands for stored. Fig. 9.2 (companion site) continues the commands with the *at+cmgl=ALL*. The phone provides three "REC READ" messages (some redacted). Fig. 9.3 (companion site) shows the command of *at+mmgl*, which is the same as the previous command (*at+cmgl=ALL*). Why would we send the same type of command when the results reported are the same? The main reason is that not all phones will provide a response under a particular command. Some may not support one (replying an error) but another command will elicit a reply.

Once you have completed reading either your phone book or text entries you must place the phone back to mode 0. This is accomplished with *AT+MODE=0*. Some phones can also be placed back to normal mode using the command *ATZ*. Once the phone is back to normal mode 0, users must recheck the *Echo typed characters locally* box under **File—Properties—Settings—ASCII Setup.** The keyboard will not work within the terminal until this setting is enabled.

In summary regarding AT commands, Motorola V3 Razor (GSM) handsets can be communicated with using HyperTerminal. Within this terminal, the phone can receive many commands in normal mode 0. Mode 2 is required to obtain phone book and stored SMS fields. Conducting a simple exercise using these basic commands can help the examiner explain during the judicial process what may take place with basic logical commands. It also helps illustrate how forensic tools work and how write blockers would interfere with this necessary communication. Here is a brief summary when using HyperTerminal to locate SMS or stored contacts on Motorola V3 Razor (GSM) devices.

1. Place device in *Mode 2*.
2. Uncheck *Echo*.
3. Send preparatory command to the area desired.
4. Send command (view desired stored data).
5. If requesting text, send desired text-type command (TEXT or PDU).
6. Send command (view desired stored data).
7. Place back in *Mode 0*.
8. Recheck *Echo*.

Port Monitoring

Readers may be wondering why a chapter devoted to logical tools does not actually show steps on how to use a specific (logical) tool. There are many vendors throughout the world who have excellent programs devoted to the business of extracting data from mobile evidence. While it is tempting to show how the author may have specific preferences with some of these tools, it is more important for the reader to understand the principles of how they work, and what may be going on with the phone when they are connected. Later, in a chapter, we will show readers an advanced validation technique. This will indicate changes to the file system, as well as changes that take place to binary areas, simply by using a tool to extract data from a device. For now, we will conclude this chapter by addressing a technique called Port Monitoring.

NIST's Guidelines on Cell Phone Forensics Special Publication 800-101 briefly addresses the use of Port Monitoring [3]. Port Monitoring can allow a user to view information as it is being sent to and from a device that is connected to a computer. This can be useful in understanding what is being read (or written) to the device. As NIST addresses, it is very useful when using nontraditional "forensic" programs. These devices may have the ability to "write" data to the target phone. This does not necessarily equate to the program being "bad" or unuseful. As examiners conduct mobile forensic work over a period of time, they will realize that open-source or manufacturer-specific programs may be required to fulfill case requirements. Utilizing a USB monitoring tool will allow them to understand what is going on when specific buttons are clicked on to extract data. It is very easy to get into the grove of "push-button" forensics. Vendors are making the extraction business much easier, targeting their products with straightforward steps and numbered cables for specific phones. Those who use these products may have no idea how the communication takes place. It is extremely important to be able to provide a basic explanation on how their programs work during a judicial process.

The following example elaborates on using a product from HHD Software and our Motorola V3 Razor (GSM). There are other commercial monitoring tools available. At the time of this writing, HHD allows full trial versions of their software. Here is an overview of the steps. Be aware that these are not step-by-step procedures; users must read additional instructions found on the HHD help menu if they encounter problems.

1. Install the HHD USB Monitor software. This process will require the host PC to reboot. *Note:* Rebooting is a required step during the install. Power on the Motorola Razor and plug the device into the host PC, which has the monitoring software installed.
2. In the menu of the HHD program use the *View—Tool Windows—Devices* to show all the peripherals attached to your target PC. This will show in a Window on the left side of the GUI of the HHD software. Fig. 9.7 depicts devices plugged in to show this example. In this

screenshot, our Motorola Razor shows under the Modem tab as Susteen USB Cable #6. On the PC used for this example, a forensic tool called Secure View for Forensics is installed. This is produced by Susteen. It is common for this program to rename the make of the plugged-in target phone to reflect its own company name. If you are following this example with no other programs installed, your device should show as a Motorola under the Modem tab.

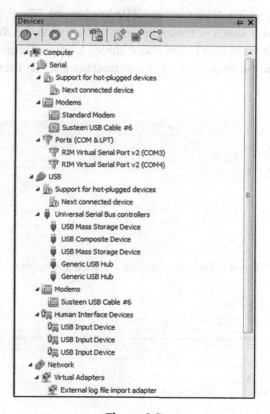

Figure 9.7
HHD USB monitoring program indicating devices plugged into the host PC.

3. Users can double-click on the item they want to monitor. In this case, it is the Motorola Razor showing under the Modem tab. HHD will pop up a window requesting the user to select a **Session Confirmation (Session Type).** For this example, choose "One packet a line" (separated by 0D—AT commands, NMEA, etc.). The next window will allow users to choose "**Available processing**" Visualizers. This will be up to the user's own preferences, and some Visualizers are easier to understand or only show specific types of information. For this exercise using the Razor, choose **Raw Data View** and **Data View** then select **Apply**.

4. While HHD is still open, launch HyperTerminal and connect to the Razor. Send the command *at* followed by *at+gmm*. Make certain the "OK" reply comes from the phone. If "Error" is reported, troubleshoot accordingly. If successful commands are sent and received, go back to HHD and view the two Visualizers (Data View and Request View). Users will see a color-coded scheme that represents what is "***Read***" and "***Write***" (written) to the phone. Fig. 9.8 shows the HyperTerminal commands at the top of the image. Below this is the *Data View*, which depicts what HHD has logged. Fig. 9.9 is again the image of the HyperTerminal commands at the top and at the bottom is the *Raw Data View*. Based on the commands that were sent to the phone through HyperTerminal, users can easily identify what was sent (written) and what was read back to the user. This can be saved as a log if needed.

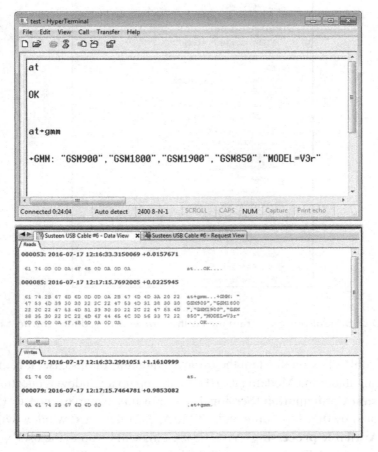

Figure 9.8
HyperTerminal commands (Top); Data View HHD logged data (Bottom).

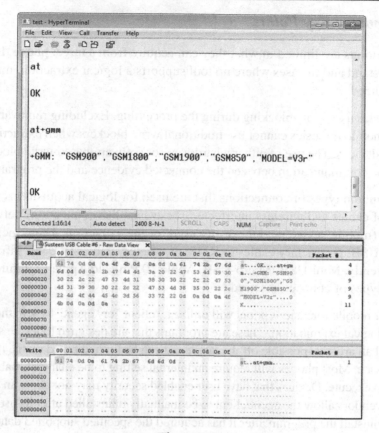

Figure 9.9
HyperTerminal commands (Top); Raw Data View HHD logged data (Bottom).

There is much more to the HHD software than what is listed here in this simple exercise. Users should be aware when using HHD on a commercial program or an open-source tool, the commands sent to the phone will be more detailed and much longer than these simple commands sent through HyperTerminal. These requests can change bits and bytes at the binary level, and we will address this during the Advanced Validation chapter. In Chapter 8, Triaging Mobile Evidence, we discussed the importance of not charging certain phones using the USB ports on a PC. Using a USB monitoring tool, an examiner can further illustrate the importance of this processing step, allowing him/her to see visually the changes that may take place to the target evidence without the knowledge of the examiner. USB monitoring is a very useful tool to help show the activities of devices plugged into a host PC. There are many devices that do not need any interface from the user: simply plugging the item into the PC begins the process of creating changes. Port Monitoring helps with the validation process and understand the various protocols used for mobile forensics.

Chapter Summary Key Points

Logical examinations are limited in what they can acquire from a target phone. Logical data is easy to understand and in cases where no tool supports a logical extraction, manual screen-shots can be utilized.

Computer forensics uses write blocking during the processing. Excluding removable microSD media, logical mobile forensics cannot use traditional write blockers when extracting specific data off mobile devices. The use of either a hardware- or software-based write blocker would interfere with the communication between the connected evidence and the program or tool used.

Some of the common types of connections that are used for logical acquisitions involve various forms of cables and wireless interfaces. These establish connections between the target evidence (mobile device) and the utility used for the extraction. These include serial to serial, serial to USB, proprietary cables to RJ45, proprietary cables to USB, Infrared, and Bluetooth. Currently, Mini-USB, Micro-USB, Apple 30 Pin, and Apple Lightning are the most common types of connections used.

It is common for mobile forensic vendors will utilize a "client" or "agent" to help the program facilitate in the logical examination. These are programs that are designed to locate specific data. They do not pull all artifacts possible off the target and can be limited based on the make and model of the device. Most phones will require an internal setting to be enabled/disabled for the agent or client to execute. Devices that have user enabled security may not allow an agent or client to work. Some vendors allow the agent/client to be manually uninstalled after its use. Others will automatically uninstall the program after it has acquired the specified supported data.

Mobile devices will require specific communication protocols to acquire what is needed as evidence. In the case of logical examinations, there can be several. Some include Sync ML, OBEX, OBEXFTP, OBEXOBJECTPUSH, IRMC, IRDA, FBUS, MBUS, MTP, PTP, Object-C, AFC, and MPT. AT commands are also still commonly used.

Users can validate how AT command protocols work by utilizing a test Motorola V3 (GSM) Razor and connecting through HyperTerminal. This allows the user to view stored contacts and SMS entries. Many phones to include the Motorola V3 Razor will require a specific MODE (MODE 2) to be set. This allows access to other parts of the file system that could not be accessed in a standard AT mode. AT commands are often used to place the target device into a specific state so that other forms of communications can take place. Some basic AT commands include +CGMI (manufacturer of phone), +CGMM (model identification), +CGSN (IMEI or MEID or ESN of device), +CGMR (software revision), +CIMI (IMSI value), +CNUM= (subscriber phone number), +CPAS (provides a code for the activity of the phone), +CCLK? (displays the time and date value), +ICCID= (ICCID of the SIM), +CBC? (battery condition), and +CLAC (lists all the supported AT commands—some are mode commands).

The use of Port Monitoring programs allows the examiner to visually see what data is being *read* and *written* to a target device. Users who are new to Port Monitoring can utilize a test phone such as the Motorola V3 Razor and HyperTerminal to send basic AT commands to the device. This will in turn allow various visualizers to record the session. More advanced forensic programs can also be recorded during their acquisition. By studying these sessions, examiners can better articulate the process during judicial questioning. They can also validate the functions of open-source and other nonforensic programs.

As we have addressed in this chapter, the logical examination has several components that must be understood by the forensic examiner. Forensic vendors often miss addressing the core fundamentals on the *functionality* of the logical pull. Instead, they focus on *what* they may find when we used their product(s). In the sea of logical products that are capable of acquiring contacts, call history, SMS, images, MMS, and much more, it is incumbent that those who send the commands to the phone have a basic understanding of how it all works.

References

[1] Bluetooth.com, News/Press Releases, June 2016. https://www.bluetooth.com/news/pressreleases/2016/06/16/-bluetooth5-quadruples-rangedoubles-speedincreases-data-broadcasting-capacity-by-800.
[2] 3rd Generation Partnership Project; Technical Specification Group Terminals; AT Command Set for User Equipment (UE), 1999. 3GPP27007_V3.13.0.pdf.
[3] NIST Guidelines on Cell Phone Forensics Special Publication 800–101, May 2007. http://www.crime-scene-investigator.net/GuidelinesCellPhoneForensics.pdf.

CHAPTER 10

Troubleshooting Logical Examinations

Information in This Chapter

- History and problems
- Truck and Trailer analogy
- Device Manager
- Modem and Serial Ports
- Advanced tab
- Diagnostics tab
- Using log files
- General troubleshooting steps

Introduction

In January 2006, a homicide investigation was conducted in a town located in the Puget Sound region of Washington State. Months before this incident, one of the investigators had attended a basic (5-day) mobile forensics class. After successfully completing the course, this same individual also convinced his agency to purchase their first mobile forensics tool, which cost just over $1200. The program included a metal box with several cables that could connect to various phones. Since the investigator had attended some form of mobile forensics training, it was expected of him to extract all the necessary information from the mobile evidence to help solve the crime. To his agency, he was the closest thing they had and an "expert" even though he had never examined a phone, and only attended one course. However, the investigator could not get the forensic program to even "see" the target evidence. To expedite getting the information to the case agent, he ended up using a camera and documenting the artifacts. This took several days to complete. His supervisor could not understand why the tool could not simply "pull" what it advertised that it supported. Confidence in the examiner's abilities and in the tool's ability was certainly momentarily lost. When time finally permitted it, the investigator began to understand a necessary step involved with mobile forensics. After several years and thousands of examinations, this step never ends, and in many cases with new phones, operating system upgrades, and various forms of user security, it always seem to come back. This, of course, is the ability to execute fundamental troubleshooting.

History of Common Problems

Mobile examiners, regardless of experience, will tell you that the extraction process is never smooth, and troubleshooting issues can be different from one phone to the next. In computer forensics, the examiner is working with a copied, validated image file and will not usually encounter problems that are out of the ordinary. In every controlled classroom setting that teaches mobile forensics, the attendee learning a specific course of instruction will oftentimes encounter various extraction-related problems. In a training perspective, this in many ways is good, as this is what will take place in the "real world" during actual cases. This chapter only addresses the issues that are commonly encountered during the logical or file system extraction.

In the world of smartphones there are a number of different issues, and they can be make and model specific. Advanced techniques that deal with things such as Factory Reset Protection, Team Win Recovery Project, CF Auto Root (Chainfire), ODIN, Netcat, and other specific tools or advanced techniques are not addressed in this chapter. These typically deal with accessing a physical pull, or getting past a locked device or locked boot loader. New examiners must first understand some of the common logical problems that can be encountered and how to deal with them. These basic steps can come in handy even when the examiner conducts more complex examinations. Regardless of how much training one may receive, as well as the case experience, the need to conduct troubleshooting of some sort cannot be overlooked.

There are a number of reasons why the extraction process can be problematic, and the following checklist is in no way a complete representation of all the causes but merely a short list of situations that happen most often. These are in no particular order.

- **Forensic program issues and driver installation**. The forensics program is not installed completely or it lacks required drivers. In cases where the specific program is installed correctly, a new phone may reveal a problem that was not encountered before. Many of the older programs will run only on a Windows OS, and some Apple-related forensic software will only function in an iOS machine.
- **Internal settings on the device**. The phone has an internal setting that needs to be specifically "set up" for the tool to communicate with the phone. Next to user installed security, this is one of the most common problems. Some of these examples were mentioned in previous chapters and include enabling USB debugging and setting the phone to "modem" or "fax." Others include manufacturer-related settings such as enabling Samsung PC Studio and Nokia PC Suite. iOS devices must "trust" the connection between the tool and the phone. Androids can have a number of settings besides the debugging. These can include changing from *Charging*, *MTP*, or *Mass Storage Device* depending on what the forensic tool may advise within its interface.
- **Defective Cable or Data Port**. The physical cables can wear out with repeated use, and phones may also have loose or damaged data ports. The data port on the phone may also work if the cable is manipulated to a certain position to allow the transfer to take place.

The examiner will see the device actually break connection through Windows and then reconnect when the phone cable is moved.

- **The phone is partially charged**. Phones should be charged at least 50% before beginning the acquisition. Large-capacity smartphones may even require fully charging, given the time involved in the examination process. Many of the larger-capacity phones may begin the process of acquiring the data, only to fail after several minutes or hours of pulling data. One of the main causes may be the battery or lack of charging during the pull. Some phones are enabled with a specific setting or download state that may prevent charging while the phone is processing. The cable in those scenarios is only used to transfer data.

- **High port numbers assigned to the device**. This chapter will cover this particular problem, but devices generally prefer to communicate on lower available ports. Over time the port number will grow, even when a device is no longer being utilized by the Windows environment. This is called "phantom ports."

- **Device environment is locked by the carrier**. Phones can have internal system locks such as the Subsidy Lock Codes and Master Subsidy Locks. These are set by the manufacturer and can sometimes prevent a forensic tool from communicating with the target phone file system.

- **User enabled security**. This has quickly become the most commonly encountered problem. A mobile forensic laboratory can have thousands of dollars' worth of equipment and highly trained personnel, but if the user has enabled security on the device, it may very well limit the access. Many new phones encrypt files when the user has enabled a simple four- or six-digit passcode. Even with advanced chip-off, ISP, or JTAG techniques (when the file system has data encryption enabled), the final pull has little to no evidential value.

- **Environmental factors or damaged devices**. Phones exposed to snow, water, fire, or other destructive forces can be irreparable. On the other hand, phones that fail to power on or have broken screens can, with proper attention, be brought back to "life" and data acquisition completed. For example, it is common to replace a severely damaged screen on an Android and in turn access the USB debugging setting to allow the forensic program to locate potential stored user evidence. Damaged USB data ports can also be replaced, which in turn can prevent hours of unnecessary hand documentation through screenshots.

Truck and Trailer Analogy

Figure 10.1
Analogy of the "Truck and Trailer."

Fig. 10.1 represents an image of a semitrailer and attached trailer. We can use this as a troubleshooting analogy that may assist with isolating an acquisition problem. Anyone who has ever connected a "pull behind" trailer to a vehicle can appreciate this. For the author it is a pickup truck and boat trailer. The process involves the tongue and safety chains connected to the source truck, as well as plugging in the 7-way connector. After this was connected we would check the trailer lights, ensuring all of the necessary lights worked properly.

Fig. 10.2 is an example of the 7-way connector and all the various required wires that need to be connected to the trailer.

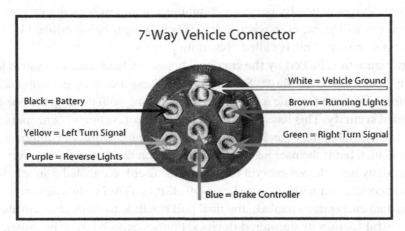

Figure 10.2
7-Way vehicle connector.

Let us say the 7-way cable is connected to our truck and we get absolutely no lights on the boat trailer to respond. Now, take this scenario and apply it to the problems we may encounter when attempting to acquire data in a Windows environment to a mobile phone, and allow it to guide us through the troubleshooting process step-by-step.

Let us go back to the boat trailer light problem. Where should we start? Let us start with the truck itself (Windows). We can see the truck lights work properly as well and so do the turn signal and brake lights. Obviously, Windows too must be able to function properly with no other driver-related issues present in Device Manager (DM). Try and eliminate preexisting problems beforehand. If we are dealing with the truck, we would start with the fuse box and determine if any of the required fuses are already burned out. When we look at the PC that is going to be used to extract our evidence, we must think of our fuse box as DM. From this location we can conduct simple analysis and, in some cases, perform diagnostic testing. When a PC is running properly, most users are not going to have yellow question or exclamation marks in their DM by default. Think of these yellow notices as burned-out fuses on our truck. We must correct this source first before moving on to another troubleshooting step. Some *fuses* will be an easy fix and others may require additional resources to correct the issues. Fig. 10.3 is an example of a problem showing within DM that represents this analogy of a burned fuse.

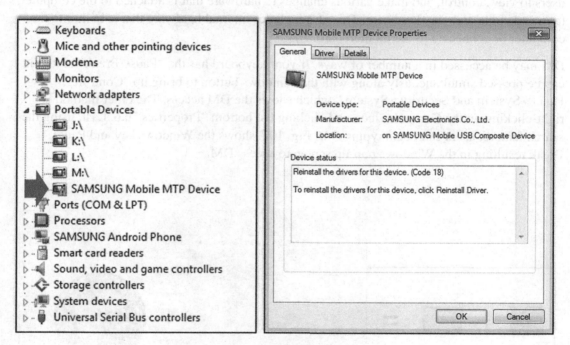

Figure 10.3
Example of problem showing in Device Manager (Analogy of burnt fuse—Truck and Trailer).

When we encounter communication problems between Windows and the cell phone, we must begin a systematic process of elimination. As we mentioned, it first starts with Windows. Before we can begin looking at the program, we must ensure that it was properly installed with all the necessary drivers. Does the USB port respond to other devices, or is the port itself having problems? Is the data cable working correctly? Does the same cable work on another phone or another USB device that is not mobile related? Is the phone itself blocking commands due to an internal setting? Slowly we can begin a process of getting each step of the problem eliminated. Let us keep this Truck and Trailer analogy in mind and move on to some of the issues you as an examiner can look at as possible sources of your problem.

Device Manager

Many of you may already be familiar with **DM**. DM was introduced with Windows 95 and later added to Windows 2000 [1]. This control panel option within Microsoft Windows allows users to view, control, and make various changes to hardware that is attached to the computer, to include plug and play hardware. This also includes internal hardware that is built into the computer or connected to the motherboard.

DM may be accessed in a number of ways. If your keyboard has the "Pause/Break" button it can be pressed simultaneously along with the Windows button to bring up "Control Panel > System and Security > System," which shows the DM access. The other method is right-clicking on the Computer Icon and clicking the bottom "Properties" tab. Last, using the search feature, users can begin typing *DM*. Fig. 10.4 shows the Windows key and Pause Break resulting in the Windows pop-up screen to access DM.

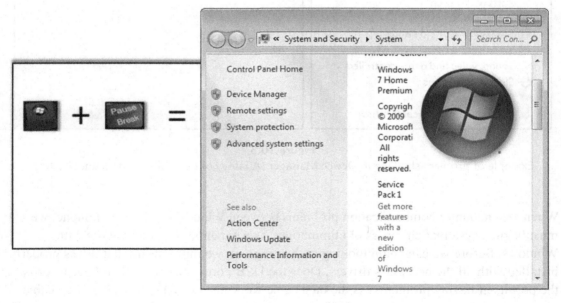

Figure 10.4
Windows key + Pause/Break key = Access to Device Manager example.

Most phones will need to be powered on and have proper internal settings enabled for Windows to "see" them. Also, within DM, some phones can show up under the Modem tab and the Ports tab. Many devices when plugged into a PC with proper drivers installed will show within DM under the Modems section as well as the Ports (COM and LPT). The specific forensic program will use the setting it needs to communicate directly with the device.

When a phone shows as a modem, the examiner can conduct some additional diagnostic inquiries. In this case, we can double-click on the associated Modem tab, which will bring up some additional tabs we can use for troubleshooting. Using the ***Diagnostics*** tab we can conduct a ***Query Modem***, which sends a series of AT commands to the phone. If the result is a success, the *Command* and *Response* fields will populate as such, showing the AT command used and the result sent back to Windows from the phone. Users can utilize the ***Logging— Append to Log—View log*** to show a complete listing of the commands. Fig. 10.5 shows these various steps. This feature of Query Modem only works when the phone shows in DM as a Modem. It is not available if the device shows up under the Ports (COM and LPT) section.

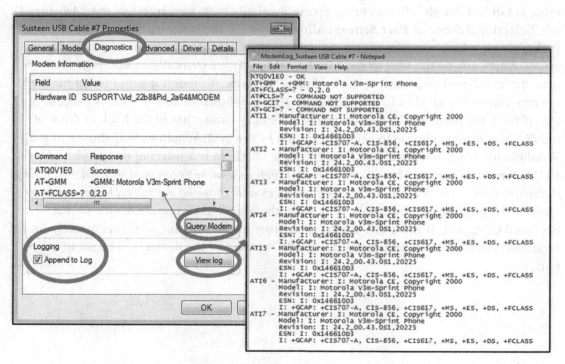

Figure 10.5
Available tabs under the Modem settings. Query Modem example.

When we get a positive response back from a Query Modem, this is informing us that Windows and the device are properly communicating. If we go back to our Truck and Trailer analogy this would equate to the hardness on the back of the truck testing positive when we check for brake lights, signals, and other necessary power. We could now move on to trouble-shooting the utility (trailer) to see why the specific forensic tool cannot communicate with the phone.

If users click on the "Modem" tab (as depicted in Fig. 10.5), this will indicate which COM port has been assigned by Windows for the device. Most of the tools and utilities that install in a Windows environment work best at lower COM port numbers. As a machine is gradually used over time, and the operator or other individuals plug various peripherals into the USB ports (or main board), these COM port numbers can get higher and higher—even when previous devices have been unplugged and are no longer being used.

Advanced Tab (Device Manager)

Another way ports can be reassigned is through manual direction. If we go back to our modem tab and double-click to bring up our available tabs, we can select the "**Advanced**" tab. Selecting **Advanced Port Settings** allows us to see the entire number of COM ports. It also shows which ones are in use. To the right of COM Port Number is a drop-down arrow, which allows the user to see which COM ports are currently in use. Fig. 10.6 provides numbered steps next to each of these settings. Although it is not recommended, devices can be assigned to lower Com ports that are shown as active. This is especially true if there are no other devices plugged into empty Com ports in the back or front of the PC. When users choose to select an *(in use)* Com port, Windows will show a pop-up Window titled "Communications Port Properties." There is a warning that reads: *"This COM name is being used by another device (such as another com port or modem). Using duplicate names can lead to inaccessible devices and changed settings. Do you want to continue?"* Ignoring these settings will allow the user to reassign the device to that occupied Com port. If there is a conflict and other devices do not perform correctly or act erratically, another Com port can be manually selected or the device can be set to a free port.

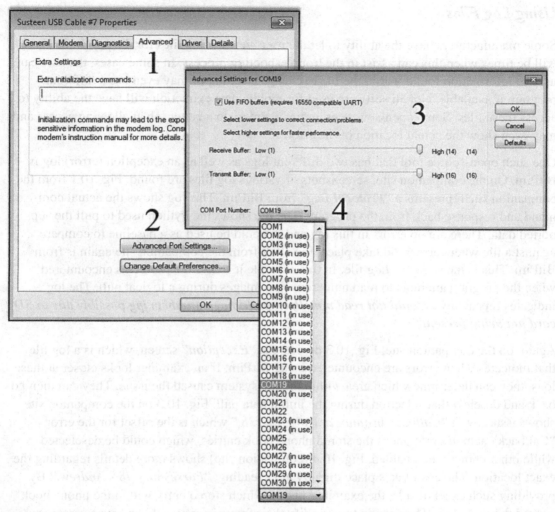

Figure 10.6
Using the Advanced tab—Advanced Port Settings to manually assign a Com port.

Another option is to utilize a utility that can reclaim the "phantom" unused Com ports. At the time of this writing Cell Phone Detectives offers a product called *CPD PortScrubber*. This product was originally distributed by Mobile Forensics Incorporated, which changed their name to *Cellphonedetectives.com*. This product can scan the target PC for Com ports that are no longer in use. It removes them and allows Windows' access to lower Com port numbers for future peripherals plugged into the machine. The Com ports that are being used at the time of the scan go unchanged.

Using Log Files

Some manufacturers have the ability to let the user view the log files for the program. There will be times when this can assist in the troubleshooting process. In some cases, the user can use the information found within the file to change a setting or may even use a different program if available. Not all software used for mobile data extraction will have the ability to access these files. Some open-source programs seem to do a better job at allowing access and may even show the actual location of the error.

One such open-source tool that has two different logs as well as an exception (error) log is BitPim. On the companion site, screenshots of various log files are found. Fig. 10.1 from the companion site represents a "*Protocol Log*" from BitPim. This log shows the actual command and response back from the program. The file shows the Python used to pull the supported data. There are no errors in this log and it would be used as a baseline to compare against a file where errors did take place. Fig. 10.2 from the companion site again is from BitPim. This is the standard *Log* file. In this example it shows the problems encountered when the program attempts to read numerous .jpg images during a logical pull. The log indicates repeatedly, "*Could not read mmcl/my_pix/(image number).jpg possibly due to SD card not being present.*"

Again, on the companion site, Fig. 10.3 depicts the "*Exception*" screen, which is a log file that indicates when errors are encountered using BitPim. If an examiner looks closer at these logs, they can determine which area within the file system caused the issue. They can then go back and deselect that selection during the initial data pull. Fig. 10.3 on the companion site shows issues with "*Callback instance at 0x088CA738*," which is the offset for the error. "Callback" actually references the stored phone book entries, which could be deselected while other choices are enabled. Fig. 10.4 (companion site) shows more details regarding the exact location. The error takes place directly after reading, "*Parse entry 48 – Andrew*." By providing such exact details, the examiner knows which stored entry within the phone book caused the problems. They can in turn modify their forensic approach, and even screenshot that one entry if all else fails.

Another popular forensic tool is Cellebrite Physical Analyzer (PA). Within the program GUI is a setting called *Trace window*. This allows a display area (within the program) to view a log of the actions performed during a session of decoding by PA and plug-ins. By studying any log file or similar decoding interface, it can help save additional time in locating and rectifying the problem(s).

General Troubleshooting Steps

When examiners encounter a situation where a particular phone is supported for logical extraction and problems arise, there are some standard (general) troubleshooting steps that can be followed to help illuminate the acquisition problem(s). In most cases, these steps should help correct the issue. Be mindful that these steps are intended for forensic tools, utilities, programs, or methodologies where a phone and a target extraction device (any listed) are actually supported.

1. Remove the battery and reinsert. Does the battery have 50% or more charge? Does the acquisition begin and after several minutes or hours fail? Consider replacing the battery with a known "good" battery that holds a charge. Many of the older phones may have water-exposed batteries. There are color-coded stickers on some batteries that reveal if moisture has been in contact with it. If the stickers indicate moisture, it is a good practice to replace them with a new battery—if acquisitions start but do not finish.
2. Unplug and replug the cable. Do you see any activity in DM that changes if the cable is wiggled or moved? If so, replace. Have you used the cable successfully before? Are you using a cheaper cable, especially Apple Lightning? The Apple Lightning cable contains a small chip. Cheaper, China-made cables can be very problematic. Consider using an original Apple cable on their devices to avoid issues. Is the USB port on the device itself loose or problematic? Again, move the cable to see if anything changes in the Windows machine or attached tools. If the USB port is damaged, consider fixing it or having it fixed. It may be worth the effort if the device happens to be a smart device with several gigabytes of potential evidence.
3. Does DM reflect any issues with drivers? Correct all these before attempting to use a forensic program. Some mobile phones may require updated drivers. If previous drivers were installed and worked, users can manually locate these drivers following these steps:
    a. Open DM and locate the device that needs driver roll back to a previous version. Double-click on the device. This will bring up various tabs to choose from, select: "*Driver*" then select "*Update Driver.*"
    b. Windows will pop up a screen that asks the user, "*How do you want to search for the driver software?*" There will be two choices: "*Search automatically for updated driver software*" and "*Browse my computer for driver software.*" Select *Browse my computer for driver software.* Note: This only works when the driver(s) has been installed previously and initially worked. If this selection requires the user to manually locate the actual peripheral, then the previous driver is not being recognized.
    c. Once the Browse my computer for driver software is selected the next window will allow the user to either "*Browse for driver software on your computer*" or "*Let me pick from a list of device drivers on my computer.*" Select, *Let me pick from a list of device drivers on my computer.*
    d. Select from the list a previous driver or related choice and see if this resolves the issue.

On the companion site, Figs. 10.5–10.7 show an example of a Smart card within DM where these steps were followed and a different profile (driver) choice was selected. Many vendors will provide a numbered version for the driver. Older drivers will have a lower (version) number.

Chapter Summary Key Points

It is very common for mobile forensic programs as well as other open-source or proprietary software to be problematic. Unlike computer forensic programs, which usually stay the same, mobile examiners are forced to use a number of tools. This can lead to a number of issues during the extraction process. Some of the problems can be the forensic program itself, driver installation, internal settings, defective data cables, defective data port on the phone, inadequate charge of the battery, high Com port numbers on the forensic PC, carrier locks, and user enabled security. User enabled security recently has been the most encountered problem. Examiners must try and use a systematic approach to troubleshooting. Using the analogy of the Truck and Trailer, the specific problem can be broken down into smaller workable issues.

Using Windows DM, a user can glean useful information that may indicate the stage of the problem. This can help determine if the problem lies between communications taking place between Windows and the *attached device,* or the forensic utility and the *attached device.* The examiner can utilize the Advanced Tab within DM to reassign Com ports to lower numbers. There is also a commercial tool that can be used to reclaim lost ports. Using the Diagnostic tab they can conduct "Query Modem" on phones that reside as Modems. Previous drivers that once worked can be managed and "rolled back" and reassigned to the attached device.

The use of program log files can greatly assist in locating a specific acquisition problem. Some open-source tools such as BitPim also allow Protocol logging, which may indicate additional details to the offset. BitPim also logs its Exception Errors. These logs will show specifically what type of data selection caused the problem. Other vendors offer logs that show if a plug-in is decoded correctly.

There are "overall" general troubleshooting steps that should be attempted when examiners encounter errors. These are (1) remove the battery and reinsert, (2) unplug and replug in the data cable, and (3) correct any DM issues.

New mobile devices are emerging on the market each day. Many of these products will require specialized tools, training, unique techniques, and time to obtain evidence stored by their owners or users. Some vendors can charge over $10,000 for a single piece of mobile extraction equipment. The device may even support thousands of different model phones, tablets, SIM, and microSD cards. Most manufacturers will provide step-by-step instruction, allowing the entire process to be clearly understood. Within the "process" will be various problems that must be overcome. Because there can be so many different issues, vendors provide little to no steps on how to overcome these problems. The examiner may have an arsenal of the latest and greatest forensic "toys," and even have financial resources to keep up with new gadgets as they emerge. They will soon realize no matter how great or expensive their "Swiss-army-knife" laboratory may be, it is the ability to fix an acquisition problem that is oftentimes priceless.

Reference

[1] Device Manager, 2016. http://www.webopedia.com/TERM/D/device_manager.html.

CHAPTER 11

Manual Examinations

Information in This Chapter

- History
- Reasons for the manual examination
- Hardware tools
- Software tools
- Alternatives: digital camera, Word, and CutePDF

History

Readers who may have been involved in digital investigations when cellular phones first emerged may have found themselves using the "thumb-jockey" method of documentation. Using a piece of paper, pen, or pencil, and lots of time, they went through the phone writing down contacts and call history. Soon, SMS-supported devices emerged, and this required even more documentation time. During these early days of cell phone technology, there were no commercially available tools that would assist in acquiring user data of the first-generation cell phones. The phones also required proprietary charging cables or, in many cases, a cradle or charging stand designed for the specific model phone. As features increased, early vendors emerged with technology that allowed the consumer to transfer contacts and images. During this time there were little to no forensic vendors who were addressing this issue for investigations. On the consumer side, one popular vendor that was founded in 1992 in Southern California was Susteen Incorporated, who offered a product in 1992 called Data Pilot [1]. Data Pilot transfer kits came with various proprietary cables for various phones that were popular sellers at that time. On the companion site, Fig. 11.1 shows an overview of this kit.

The kits were limited as to what could be transferred and were primarily designed for individuals who were looking for a way to transfer personal information onto a new phone or add/remove ringtones, images, and contacts.

For the investigator, during these early years they would rely almost entirely on manual documentation. Fast-forward to our present day. Android, Apple, Blackberry, and Windows rule the market. Everyone is familiar with Cloud storage. Large commercial vendors target private and law enforcement investigations. Names such as Cellebrite, Micro Systemation, Oxygen, Susteen, Parabeen, AccessData, Blackbag, Final Data, and Encase are just a few that have made products directly for cell phone extractions. More phones are supported forensically than ever before. Regardless of how many tools a laboratory may have, we will address how the manual examination still has its place in the mobile forensic process.

Reasons for the Manual Examination
Completely Unsupported Phone and Locked USB Ports

There will be target devices that do not allow the transfer to take place, between the forensic utility and the mobile evidence. This seems to increase if the phone is a simple pay-as-you-go model. One of the reasons behind this is for revenue. By restricting the device, the manufacturer forces the customer to pay for ringtones, screen backgrounds, and other features over the air. The main board is designed to only allow charging to take place through the USB port. There are vendors who work out specific arrangements with mobile virtual network operators (MVNOs) and create a model phone that may only be "locked down" through the USB port because it is serviced by the MVNO. It is not uncommon for the model number to have a letter or number identifier that distinguishes it from the mobile network operator (MNO) counterpart. The MNO model may even have the USB ports open, which allows forensic tools to acquire the data.

Fig. 11.1 depicts a label affixed to a Samsung model SCH-R355C (redacted). The name given to this device is a "Freeform" or "Link" (depending on the carrier). The device pictured in Fig. 11.1 was serviced by Tracfone (MVNO). This is an example of an unsupported (at the time of this writing) mobile device. Often these phones may be supported if the model number is from a standard wireless carrier serviced by an MNO.

Figure 11.1
MVNO model (label) of an unsupported phone.

Another way the carrier may restrict the ability to pull logical data off the phone is through a Service Provider Lock or Master Subsidy Lock (SPL/MSL). Although many larger forensic vendors have written code into their tools to obtain the SPL or MSL, some open-source tools such as BitPim may not allow the phone to be read within specific areas of the file system when the phone has a carrier lock enabled. There are many online vendors who offer services for "unlocking" mobile phones. Using specialized equipment, the phone can be internally changed to allow it to receive service on a different wireless carrier. This generally would apply to phones that communicate via CDMA to CDMA or GSM to GSM networks, for example, if a consumer had an AT&T device and "unlocked" it to work on T-Mobile. In recent years most carriers "release" the phone once the owner has fulfilled his/her contractual obligation. For purposes of this chapter, understand that these locks set by the carrier can also cause issues with some programs.

Forensic Tool(s) Does Not Support Everything

During logical extractions it is very common to encounter specific forensic vendors who will only support limited artifacts on the targeted phone. In some cases, the use of more than one utility is necessary, and there will still be times when using several tools will not allow access to all the necessary logical evidence. As an example, Fig. 11.2 shows two different programs that support logical data on an LG VX 10000 (Voyager). The left image is the open-source (free) software, BitPim. To the right of BitPim is Secure View for Forensics (Susteen). Notice how these examples support "Contacts" (also referred to as PhoneBook), Call Logs (Call History), SMS (Messages), and Images (Pictures/Wallpaper). In this example none of tools support MMS acquisition. The examiner would need to locate this type of unsupported logical data and document the entries through manual examination. It is common to use screenshots to augment what is missed by commercial and open-source tools.

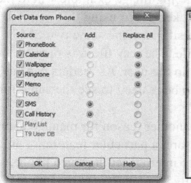 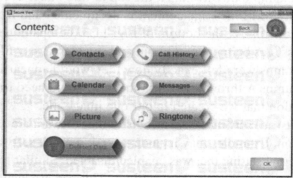

Depending on the utility used, only specific logical data is supported for extraction

Figure 11.2
Example of three logical tools on an LG VX 10,000 Voyager—not all logical data is supported.

Documentation

During the course of compiling the necessary mobile evidence, examiners will need to provide proof of specific settings, manually carved artifacts, deleted data, decoded steps, or other case-specific required items. The common types of manual "documentation" is expanded on with additional explanations, and examples:

1. **Internal settings**. Either enabled or disabled the following settings: Airplane (or similar) mode, USB debugging, fax settings, PC-Sync, data transfer mode, USB Mass Storage Mode, Media Sync Mode, Modem Mode, File Transfer, Photo Transfer, and many others. Fig. 11.2 on the companion site depicts two different types of phones with internal setting choices. The left image in Fig. 11.2 (companion site) is an example of an Android running Marshmallow (6.0). To the right would be a simple flip phone (non-Android).

2. **Locking down a file**. By creating an image file, an examiner can "lock" down a file that would normally be fully capable of being edited. Using .jpg images (or similar image file types), the examiner prevents the file from being easily changed by investigators, prosecutors, or others who would commonly need to review the documents. Common files that are easy to alter or change would be Excel (.csv), Text (.txt), and Word (.doc). Spreadsheets that are commonly saved as Comma Separated Value (.csv) are the most notorious files that get changed. This is usually because the columns that contain the data need to be moved to view the string(s) of information. When the viewer of these files makes changes to allow individual viewing, the file can inadvertently get saved with changes to the original. An option would be to create screenshots of the file, or before making a .csv (or similar file), document the parsed data within the tool, before actually creating the report. Fig. 11.3 on the companion site is an example of BitPim. At the top of this image is a .jpg image example where the entire SMS message content is documented and locked down using this method. Below this, at the bottom of Fig. 11.3 (companion site), are the same two SMS messages being exported out and saved to a .csv file. The .csv file was opened, but the columns were left exactly how they would appear to the user. As readers can see, columns A through J within the .csv would need to be resized to see the same information that we created in our one image file.

3. **Software settings**. Screenshots of the software are another reason for manual documentation. Examples may include a version of the software, a particular feature, or an internal setting that was enabled/disabled. Similar to internal settings on a phone, some programs will have these settings. This can especially be important to document if examiners are using open-source or "nonforensic" software. Just because the program or utility was not necessarily designed for forensic investigations, it does not mean it

cannot be used for those types of acquisitions. Documenting exactly *how* it was used ensures that the forensic process was followed and thus the overall mobile forensics methodology stayed the same. Fig. 11.4 on the companion site is an example from BitPim. This program allows the user to "write" information to the source phone. Internally, however, there is a specific setting that when enabled prevents data from being overwritten to the phone. This would be an important screenshot to include in the forensic report, along with a validation explanation on how this setting was tested on a nonevidential device. Fig. 11.5 on the companion site is an example of a screenshot showing a software version. The example shows BitPim and Susteen Secure View (License Information, redacted).

4. **Hand Carving/Manual Decoding**. In our last 10 chapters we covered the fundamental (basic) components involved in mobile forensic examinations. In Chapter 1 we provided an example of logically parsed data and also an example of the use of encoding to locate deleted (physical) data. As examiners become more proficient in locating physical data that is missed by commercial tools, the need to properly document the information will also grow. Hand Carving and Manual Decoding are also used to validate what a target tool may have parsed.

Hardware Tools for Manual Extractions

Unlike numerous commercial software tools that are created specifically for mobile forensics, the examiner has only a few choices when it comes to hardware tools used to manually document data of the device. Most vendors will have their own proprietary software program that is used with the hardware. The hardware used does vary significantly and thus the cost reflects this as well. Manufacturers will include digital cameras in their manual extraction kits. The camera can also be used for video. Here are examples of some of the hardware tools used for manual extractions:

- **Project-A-Phone**. This product was originally sold under the Project-A-Phone company name. In 2011, Paraben Corporation acquired Project-A-Phone [2], and as of August 2016, Paraben offers two different models: the Project-A-Phone Flex and the Project-A-Phone ICD-8000 [3]. ICD-8000 features an 8 megapixel HD video–capable camera, which allows it to connect directly to the PC. It is one of the more inexpensive solutions available. It comes with the software that allows advanced reporting, which includes hash value validation [4]. Using Project-A-Phone involves a simple desktop holder, the USB camera, and software. Fig. 11.3 is an image of Project-A-Phone ICD-8000, Project-A-Phone Flex, and the associated cases. The Flex version utilizes a more robust camera boom arm as well as a nonslip mat and can integrate with Optical Character Recognition (OCR) software.

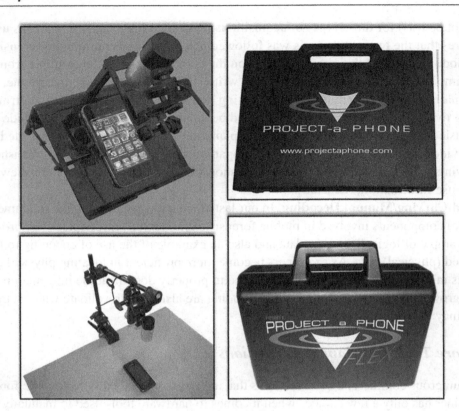

Figure 11.3
Paraben Corporation's Project-A-phone ICD-8000 and Flex.

- **Fernico ZRT**. As of August 2016, Fernico offers both the ZRT Kiosk and ZRT 3 model for manually documenting the stored information on mobile evidence. Fernico made its way to the commercial market in 2007 and is considered by many agencies the leader in hardware used for manual documentation of mobile evidence. The ZRT Kiosk is a downsized version of its bigger brother, the ZRT 3. The Kiosk is used to quickly document evidence, without the need of the other features usually utilized in a forensic processing laboratory. Fernico promotes the Kiosk product for detectives who need the information quickly and front desk officers [5].

  What stands out with Fernico products (besides its robust hardware) is the software that helps triage the manual process. This has the ability to categorize, resize/format, and label, all through an automated process. The software also has OCR abilities, but unlike Project-A-Phone, the OCR engine will extract the embedded text from a photograph and store it in a case database for searching and further analysis [6]. Fernico utilizes an optional Pelican 1520 style case, which holds the user's choice of a USB HD webcam, or Canon DSLR camera, as well as the desktop mount, foot pedal, and glare shield. They also offer an optional mounting arm to hold the camera [6]. If users choose the Canon DSLR, Fernico will use the Rebel T2 through T5 series. The T5 feature has 12.2 Megapixel CMOS Image Sensor and Canon DIGIC 4 Image Processor [6]. The foot pedal included in the kit allows the user to perform processing much faster, not to mention freeing up both hands for other tasks. Another feature of ZRT 3 is its ability to import video evidence. The frames of the video can be captured as images. Users can export the report as PDF, DOC, or HTML. Fig. 11.4 showcases some of the highlights of ZRT 3.

Figure 11.4
Fernico ZRT 3 key highlights.

- **Eclipse Screen Capture Tool**. EDEC Digital Forensics is based at Santa Barbara, California. This company was mentioned in our previous chapter that covered Faraday methods. Not only do they offer Faraday tools, but they also offer manual capturing tools and associated software. Their latest top of the line version (August 2017) is the Eclipse 3 Pro. The kit is very similar to ZRT 3, which also utilizes a Canon DSLR, OCR software, video frame extraction, hands free (foot petal) capture, Manfrotto Camera Arm and Mount, UV filters, metal base and clamps, and a rugged hard case [7]. They also offer a Webcam Kit and stand-alone software that has no camera or associated accessories. Fig. 11.5 provides a glimpse into the kit and features of the current EDEC products related to manual capture of mobile evidence.

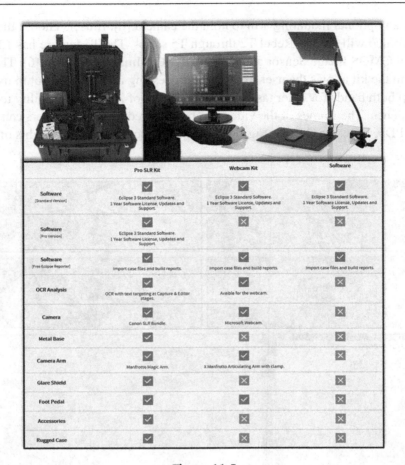

	Pro SLR Kit	Webcam Kit	Software
Software [Standard Version]	✓ Eclipse 3 Standard Software. 1 Year Software License, Updates and Support.	✓ Eclipse 3 Standard Software. 1 Year Software License, Updates and Support.	✓ Eclipse 3 Standard Software. 1 Year Software License, Updates and Support.
Software [Pro Version]	✓ Eclipse 3 Standard Software. 1 Year Software License, Updates and Support.	✗	✗
Software [Free Eclipse Reporter]	✓ Import case files and build reports.	✓ Import case files and build reports.	✓ Import case files and build reports.
OCR Analysis	✓ OCR with text targeting at Capture & Editor stages.	✓ Avaible for the webcam.	✗
Camera	✓ Canon SLR Bundle.	✓ Microsoft Webcam.	✗
Metal Base	✓	✗	✗
Camera Arm	✓ Manfrotto Magic Arm.	✓ X Manfrotto Articulating Arm with clamp.	✗
Glare Shield	✓	✗	✗
Foot Pedal	✓	✓	✗
Accessories	✓	✗	✗
Rugged Case	✓	✗	✗

Figure 11.5

EDEC Digital Forensics Eclipse Screen Capture Tool 3 with associated manual capture tools and program features.

- **Cellebrite USB camera**. Cellebrite has been a worldwide leader in mobile forensic extractions for several years. They also offer an optional USB camera that plugs into their main extraction tools. The camera can, in turn, be used with their embedded software from the specific forensic tool. This allows the user to include additional manual screen-shots into the final report or, in some cases, document an unsupported phone through the manual process. It is not necessary that examiners only use the Cellebrite-offered camera; they can utilize any USB camera such as "web-cam."

Software Solutions

Besides the need to create screenshots of what is actually on the phone itself, investigators will also encounter the need to use software-based solutions. The scenarios behind their use are typically to document an artifact, to show a particular setting being enabled or disabled, to "lock" down a file, and manually validate. Instead of submitting a Word or Excel document that could be edited and changed, the same product is submitted as a .jpg, which is much harder to edit. The market is saturated with software options. Here are a few examples:

- **ScreenHunter**. Wisdom Software is the company that produces ScreenHunter. The program is offered in both free and paid versions, currently titled Pro, Plus, and Free [7]. Unlike the embedded capturing tools typically found in newer versions of Windows, ScreenHunter allows the user additional features and control over the capture. With Windows software tools it would normally take several steps to capture, rename, and save. ScreenHunter can be set up to allow hot keys to snap the image in a particular (fixed area) screen location. The file format selections can be saved to include BMP, JPG, PDF, PNG, TIF, and GIF. Examiners can edit their images, adding items such as Captions, Watermarks, Borders, Autoscale, and Color effects. Additional features such as using multiple windows, including the mouse pointer, timer delay, web capture, freehand, recurring capture, and much more [8]. Fig. 11.6 on the companion site shows the four main internal setting areas of ScreenHunter 6.0. These are left to right, top to bottom as "From," "To," "Options," and "Tasks."

- **Snagit**. Produced by TechSmith, Snagit software allows the user to grab the entire desktop, a specific region and window or a scrolling window from any webpage or application, all with a single hotkey or click [9]. Snagit also has a dynamic editor. With these features, users can control a number of ways in which they can embed other communications or effects into the image. Such items include customized or downloaded stamps, special effects, past saved libraries, and magnification (zoom). Snagit is available in a trial download and, as of August 2016, allows the user access for 15 days to the fully equipped version. Unlike ScreenHunter, Snagit has a unique "Output Manager," which allows the user to upload the capture directly to popular sites, such as YouTube, and to Microsoft products such as Excel, Word, PowerPoint, and OneNote. Other format choices within the Output Manager include Google Drive Output and other TechSmith software. TechSmith also produces other software packages. Camtasia Studio can be used to create a video recording of all activity taking place on the desktop. It allows editing audio and video separately. Incorporating a webcam and importing existing videos, photos, and music to create unique videos is also an option [10]. The video editor is robust and allows open and closed captioning, noise removal/leveling, unlimited tracks, deleting, and splitting or stitching of clips. Fig. 11.7 on the companion site depicts some of the internal settings previously outlined from the Snagit program.

An Alternative Solution to Hardware and Software Vendors

- **Digital camera/MS Word/CutePDF**. There will be some agencies or companies that do not have the resources to purchase some of the hardware and software products outlined. There are other commercial products available, and in this chapter we address only a few. One inexpensive method is to have examiners create their own manual report or file.

- Inexpensive digital camera with macro and video capabilities. A recommendation here is a camera that is easy for anyone to use. For the author this would be a camera that his 84-year-old mother could operate! There are a number of very nice, inexpensive DSLR cameras on the market. The problem with these cameras is that if the user is new to digital photography, or does not shoot with that particular camera enough, they can take more time to learn all the necessary features. Plus, this is usually *more* than what is necessary for the task. It is much easier to have a simple "point-and-shoot" camera with minimal features than have to worry about how to use a more elaborate DSLR. The point-and-shoot camera should also have a tripod mounting ability on the bottom. Unless the examiner is experienced with DSLRs and the appropriate lens needed, generally, the point-and-shoot works best.
- Inexpensive tripod or small desktop tripod. This item helps tremendously when the examiner needs to screenshot hundreds of items such as SMS messages. It is not absolutely necessary, but does help prevent blurry images. It also does a nice job with framing each shot, ensuring each image stays the same.
- Plastic suction style or clamp-type vice. These can often be located at a hobby store. They hold the source phone at an angle that helps eliminate ambient lighting problems. Just like the small tripod, a vice can help prevent blurry images.
- Dry erase board. This is one of the most useful components in the kit. It acts as the photography slate. The examiner would use it to document the case number, date, date of laboratory intake, case agent name, phone make and model, and type of investigation. The mobile evidence will rest to the side of this information. Even when the entire phone was processed completely with forensic laboratory tools, the dry erase board would still be used to take images of the actual evidence.
- Microsoft Word (or a similar program). MS Word program allows the examiner to place the images they have taken with their digital camera into a repository that can be edited accordingly. The images can be resized, color corrected, and edited with additional shapes as needed. For manual decoding of specific hand-carved artifacts with secondary tools, the actual tool can be screenshot and placed next to the file, showing the exact way the file was decoded. The newer versions of MS Word can also allow the final product to be exported to a more secure file such as a PDF.
- CutePDF Writer with converter. This is a free program that may or may not be necessary depending on which version of MS Word is used. This allows the user to "Print" to PDF. It installs as a printer; but instead of actually printing the document, the user would select "CutePDF" from the printer choices, and once it converts the Word document, it allows the user to save the file as a PDF.

A typical manual work flow using these products would be first to capture the necessary images. Remove the media from the camera and transfer the documents to an appropriate labeled folder for each type (i.e., SMS, MMS, Call Logs, Contacts, etc.). Once this is completed, bring the images into MS Word in the same order they are shown in the GUI of the phone. For SMS this may be by date or conversation. For call history this may have been stored chronologically. Once the images are in MS Word, they can be further processed as needed. This may include minor color adjustments, cropping, or specific labeling. Once the document is created exactly how the examiner wants, it should be saved to a PDF or a similar format. This would be labeled according to the file type, such as *SMS.pdf* or *Call Logs.pdf*. Fig. 11.6 depicts images of each of these products with an approximate price shown on Internet searching. Many examiners will already have MS Word installed on their desktop or laptop machines. This will reduce the cost by approximately $120. As the image shows, the entire "kit" can be assembled for less than $300. The camera shown also has 720p video. The kit does not include a Secure Digital media card. Depending on the size, these can also be found for less the $20.

Figure 11.6

Overview of the associated (estimated) cost of creating a screen capture option.

Chapter Summary Key Points

There are a number of reasons needed to manually document evidential artifacts from mobile devices. With the growing population of pay-as-you go devices, mobile forensic examiners have increased their need for specific hardware and software tools to fulfill this task. Many of the wireless cell phone manufacturers will lock down the data transfer ability through the USB port. Other reasons for manual documentation include the ability to augment their forensic tools when the extraction was unable support all the necessary data or media. There may also be incidents when the examiner needs to show a particular setting that was enabled or disabled. Examiners may require that an editable file be "locked down" and instead submits an image of the artifacts or summary of findings. Hand Carving, decoding, and/or validating would be other tasks where manual documentation is commonly used. Lastly, the documentation of the actual evidence should always be included in every case. Examples of hardware and software vendors include Paraben's Project-A-Phone, Fernico's ZRT, EDEC Digital Forensics' Eclipse Screen Capture Tool, Cellebrite's USB Camera, TechSmith's Snagit, and Wisdom Software's ScreenHunter. There are cheaper alternatives to these commercial examples. One solution is the use of an inexpensive digital camera with video recording, a desktop tripod, suction cup style desktop vice, erasable dry board, MS Word, and CutePDF with decoder.

It will be up to the examiner to properly document all aspects of the forensic examination. It does not matter if you are a seasoned investigator who is capable of performing advanced destructive chip removal, or someone who just started at this job, you will find the task of pushing a shutter button part of the necessary duties and responsibilities in all your cases.

References

[1] Data Pilot, About Us, 2016. http://www.datapilot.com/aboutus.html.
[2] Forensicmag.com, 03.02.2011. http://www.forensicmag.com/product-release/2011/03/paraben-acquires-project-phone.
[3] Project-A-Phone, 2016. http://www.project-a-phone.com/.
[4] Project-A-Phone ICD-8000, 2016. http://www.project-a-phone.com/icd-8000.html.
[5] Fernico, 2016. http://www.fernico.com/ZRT-Kiosk.aspx.
[6] Fernico, 2016. http://www.fernico.com/ZRT3.aspx.
[7] Wisdom-soft.com, 2015. http://www.wisdom-soft.com/products/screenhunter.htm.
[8] Wisdom-soft.com, 2016. http://www.wisdom-soft.com/sh/sh_compare.htm.
[9] TechSmith.com, 2016. https://www.techsmith.com/snagit.html#snagit-features.
[10] TechSmith.com, 2016. https://www.techsmith.com/camtasia.html.

Report Writing

History—Our Forensic Wheel

Some readers may be performing forensic investigations and are quite familiar with how to create a report. The target audience who reads these documents for law enforcement is usually a prosecutor or a deputy prosecutor. In the private sector the report may be reviewed by a direct supervisor, a client who has hired you, or the business you work for. Years back, the formats for reporting did not have as many choices. In the late 1980s the author was using a manual typewriter to generate a police report. By the time basic forensic investigations were being completed on the first set of mobile (brick) phones, the technique for finalizing the report had changed to a basic Word processing program. The tools at that time were limited, and most examiners used 35 mm cameras or in some cases Polaroid pictures to document basic information that the phones were capable of storing. In our last chapter we addressed manual examinations. The manual examination is just one component—a "spoke" in our overall "wheel." The mobile forensic *wheel* contains other spokes, and all of them are necessary for us to *roll* with the proper methodology. As phone capacities and features increase, and user installed applications seem to be endless, so must the examiner increase the ability to address and validate more information. Even with the dynamic nature of these devices, there are consistent things we will always do. It is in this chapter that we provide those standard, *fundamental components* that should be contained in your report. We also want to again disclose to our readers that the suggestions on reporting are based on the author's case experience. Some of the preferences apply to his particular target audience, which typically consists of deputy prosecutors charging cases in the violent crimes unit. The author has been for years a witness to the state and has molded what is necessary is his jurisdiction. Remember to take what is needed here and consult with your own legal adviser, supervisor, or others who are familiar with what is required in your finalized document.

A Final Report Example

During NIST's Guidelines on Cell Phone Forensics, they address reporting as, "*…the process of preparing a detailed summary of all the steps taken and conclusions reached in the investigation of a case. Reporting depends on maintaining a careful record of all action and observations, describing the results of tests and examinations, and explaining the inferences drawn from the evidence. A good report relies on solid documentation, notes, photographs, and tool-generated content*" [1].

To begin this chapter, we will provide an example of a report and go back over the elements and discuss them within this chapter. The forensic report created contains a brief overall synopsis that is written as a supplemental report. This supplemental report does not contain the work product from the various tools and utilities used. For the author, those results are burned to disk. The size of the disk will vary. The contents on the media will be in subfolders. Here is how this looks:

I am currently assigned as a cell phone forensic examiner. I have received several years of specialized training in this field and hold several certifications related to the same. I also instruct local prosecutors, judges, police officers, and other professionals in the digital evidence recovery field.

On May 19, 2013 at 0238 hours I was called from home to the scene of a homicide. Upon arrival I was briefed on the incident and tasked with obtaining a search warrant for a mobile cell phone obtained from a possible suspect. The device had been removed from the pocket of the suspect by the responding officer during a "pat down" for weapons. It was sitting on the hood of the patrol car along with the other personal effects belonging to the suspect. Prior to obtaining the warrant, I noticed that the device was receiving a signal and incoming calls could be heard on the handset. Based on past training and experience, the device was placed into airplane mode to keep it from being network contaminated or altered. These settings accessed on the home screen by going to 'settings' then enabling airplane mode. No other areas of the file system were entered. Using a "field-kit" digital camera, I obtained images of the settings I enabled. The device was placed on a charger until the warrant was signed. This process took approximately two hours.

The device was photographed after the warrant was signed. Internal settings that uniquely identify the device were also noted. The cell phone was identified as a Motorola XT1060. At the time of this report our lab had a Cellebrite Universal Forensic Extraction Device (UFED), Touch model – version 3.1.2.001.

UFED was used to obtain a logical file system pull. Once this extraction was completed the results were parsed using another Cellebrite tool, Physical Analyzer (PA) version 3.9.1.

PA parsed phone book entries, call history, SMS, MMS, chat logs, images, videos, and browser history. PA was used to create a PDF report that is linkable, similar to HTML. PA has the ability to set the time zone and in this case it was set to UTC 07:00 which was validated as a match from the same entries off the phone.

PA was also used to conduct a malware scan. The results were negative. Once this aspect of the exam was completed, the device was powered off and the SIM card was removed. The SIM was also examined using UFED Touch (same version). After the acquisition was completed a PDF report was created using the PA interface. The Coordinated Universal Time (UTC) was again set to validate the time from the phone. After this was completed the SIM was placed back into the phone and the item was sealed.

Four DVD case reports and one archive disc were created. Three of the case reports were given to the case agent on May 24, 2013. The fourth case report, archive disc, and sealed phone were placed into property as evidence on May 24, 2013.

The case report DVD contained the following folders:

1. Search warrant—Scanned copy of the original search warrant converted to a PDF.
2. Overalls—Images of the actual evidence to include, front, back, internal settings and SIM card, converted to a PDF.
3. Phonescoop—Screenshots from a website called Phonescoop, which details this phone's features and other characteristics. Converted to a PDF.
4. SIM card—PDF report from PA that details some of the stored data of the SIM card file system.
5. UFED—Linkable PDF report that contains parsed data. This was created from UFED Touch acquisition and PA parsing.

The case reporting disk that is referenced above will have these folders burned to it and will usually be zipped to help with long file name issues as well as conserve space. Many media burning software programs will error when they encounter long file names that do not conform to Window OS rules. The archive disk contains everything that was used to create the case disk. This includes proprietary files from the various tools, as well as the original images from evidence before being converted to PDF.

General Questions to Answer/Include in Your Report

When examiners are creating the report, they should try and answer a standard list of general questions. Some of the answers can be contained in the narrative of the supplement, similar to the previous example. Others, such as hashing, may be contained on the additional reports from the tools that are being used and referenced. In our example the hashing results are within the summary report created by the particular tool. Some investigators may choose to speak about such things in the narrative, and others leave those findings within the tool(s) interface. Here are some questions to address within the report:

1. How did you come in contact with the device? What state was it in (on or off)? How did you or others interact with the evidence or initial seizure? Were other forms of processing such as latent print recovery, swabbing for blood, or DNA testing needed?
2. If the device was on, or later turned on, how was it isolated from signal or other forms of contamination?
3. What legal method was used to search the device?
4. What tools, utilities, or methods were employed to extract the stored data?
5. What were the versions of the tools used?
6. What type of data was acquired?
7. Explain any reporting issues and/or any anomalies.
8. How did you validate your findings?
9. Did the programs used include hashing the results?
10. What format did you create to compile the report?

Initial Contact

There is no difference between how you begin your investigation when you are employed in law enforcement or if you work for the private sector. The point is that there is a need to begin the process. A failure to clearly indicate where your initial role began can become problematic down the road when called to explain your investigation. Using the simple "*who, what, where, why*, and *how* helps with this.

"*I was <u>called</u> to the scene of a <u>homicide</u> by Sgt. Smith. A <u>powered on</u>, live mobile device was present at the scene*." In this statement the underlined words are used to explain *how* this person was contacted, for *what* purpose, and *what* state the phone was discovered in.

Here is an example of a noncriminal investigation (initial contact) with a mobile device:

> I currently <u>work for T-Mobile</u> and I'm assigned to the <u>mobile security team</u> 2. Using internal forensic tools, I was tasked with <u>identifying an unknown malware issue</u> on a series of Android phones. All of the devices were <u>powered off</u> and contained in a work order box labeled, 15-1599912.

This example provides even more details. *Who* you are (T-Mobile employee) is qualified with *what* exactly you do (mobile security team who uses internal forensic tools). *What* the problem is (malware) and the state of the devices (powered off).

This seems very obvious but let the audience who reads your report know that you were directed for a particular cause and to get a particular item of interest. You can fill in the blanks with any scenario—it makes no difference—just be detailed. This may even begin by explaining who you are. Introducing yourself, as well as your role in the investigation, and length of time in your position is a good way to begin your narrative. You may even explain what type of training you received. This may keep questions from arising that pertain to why you are qualified to perform this type of forensic work.

> *I am currently employed with Boeing and assigned as a Mobile Applications and Support Specialist. My duties include forensic processing of mobile devices. I was contacted on October 9th, 2014 to perform analysis on a Samsung SCH-i605 that had been previously been submitted through troubleshooting ticket A1234567. The item was removed from secured storage and triaging began…*

Obviously, the private sector will have their own documentation methods that are required when involved in this type of work. This may be as simple as checking off boxes, or inputting a few mandatory fields of a template that was created electronically. From our chapter that addressed the content of the search warrant, it is very clear to the criminal investigator what device they have the authority to search, and what data is allowed to be located. The point being made here is to not overlook the *"Who"* you are, *"What"* do you do, *"Where"* did you begin this process, and *"Why?"* was the specific work required.

Device State

The technical aspect of the report process will usually begin when describing the *"state"* the device was recovered in. *State* refers to if the evidence is powered on or off. You may work in a capacity where this never changes as many laboratories do not triage live devices in the field. Instead, they are forwarded to a digital forensic lab, neatly packaged in crime scene sealed bags. In almost every case, they are always powered off or completely dead. However, if you deal with live devices, this is where you begin the process of explaining why you did certain things. Let us assume your initial contact statement is already completed and now you need to explain the condition the phone was in when you received it.

> *…upon arrival at our forensic facility the device was found to be powered on. The device was therefore placed in a Faraday mesh to prevent signal contamination. It was then placed on a charger and remained secured until the date of 10-10-14 when a search warrant was granted to the officer assigned to this investigation.*

In this example we have documented *what* state the device was in, and *why* a particular step was necessary.

Documenting Other Initial Issues (DNA/Prints/Swabbing)

In Chapter 8 we addressed triaging steps with devices that are on or off. Within the same chapter, it is also explained that there may be times where evidence will require initial forensic laboratory work that involves DNA, latent recovery, swabbing, or other types of specific processing. This, of course, would need to be addressed or at least referenced as to who conducted the additional work in the final report. Based on the case that presents itself, your report may need to detail why you decided to swab a powered-on phone before placing it in Faraday mode. Or how your forensic crime scene technician collected samples of blood from the screen prior to you decontaminated the phone. If you work criminal investigations and are part of an evidence collection team, the possibilities here are endless. Fig. 12.1 depicts a phone powered off, one being Faradayed, another covered in blood, the DNA symbol, and an image of a fingerprint. This collage represents the initial state of mobile evidence and other issues that would need to be outlined in the final report.

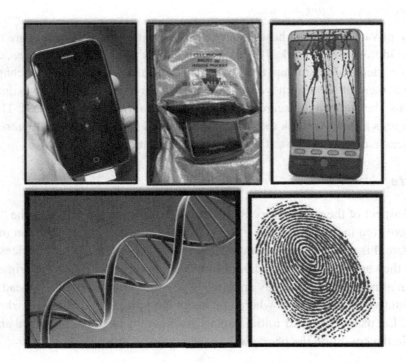

Off? On? Blood? DNA? Prints?

Figure 12.1
Collage of images that represent the initial state and other issues commonly addressed in the final report.

Specific Tools and Versions Used

This portion of the reporting process will clearly indicate which particular tool, utility, or method was used to acquire the data in question. Many of the automated forensic tools will provide a summary. The summary usually will indicate the version of the particular device that was used. In most cases the date and time of the extraction is also included. This is important because many times a newer version of the same tool will come out with a feature that was not embedded at the time of the examination. There have been cases where defense counsel has brought up the lack of a particular piece of evidence that currently (at the time of trial) is supported. The author has also had trials where the state requested time to conduct additional analysis on the defendant's phone. They would argue that new technology and techniques that were not available during the past exam, have now emerged. Generally, those types of motions would be fought by defense counsel. Sometimes, however, defense supports such work, as the findings may help exonerate their client, or help paint the picture of reasonable doubt.

Fig. 12.2 shows a summary from Secure View. This shows the Activity Map in the center, providing the audience who reads it, activity by hour, and day. This example is from an extraction involving an iPhone 5C. The final report output would list this information as well as the version of the tool.

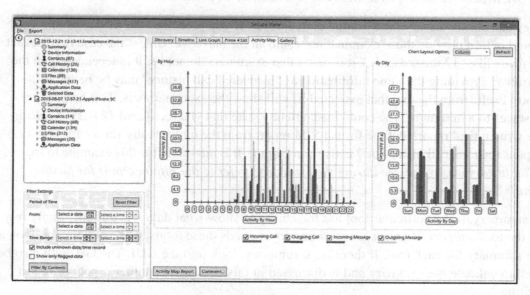

Figure 12.2
Secure View for Forensic Reporting Interface showing the Activity Map.

Some tools do not have built-in summary areas nor do they have any formal reporting process. It is important that if you used these types of tools, you document any steps to disable write blocking, or explain how you validated the data once they were pulled. For example, Chapter 11 explains how we would use a screen capture tool to document "Block writing to the phone" while using BitPim. This step should also be mentioned in the narrative during the reporting process.

Listing Parsed Data

Many of the automated forensic tools will provide an extraction summary within their own reporting interface. Understand that this summary pertains only to *that part* of the reporting process. For example, the summary on some forensic programs may not show the Micro-SD examination or the SIM examination that was completed outside of the device.

When creating an overall report that covers the entire process, it is better to indicate overall specifics than exact specifics, as the individual tools that have automated reports will list what was found. The next example involving an HTC would have had an overall statement to list the various data locations similar to this:

> *The HTC G1 was found to have stored user data on the SIM, Micro-SD, and within the handset. Reports for each of these areas can be located on the finalized media DVD.*

They can also be listed as the examination unfolds. If you processed the SIM card first you would in turn provide those examination results in the narrative. Unless the case needs exact numbers like "12 missed calls," it is better that examiners do not list it independently in the narrative. Providing the same information as "recovered call history" may be better as the report itself (from the tool that extracted it) will show the exact numbers. This helps keep mistakes to a minimum. You could inadvertently state that you recovered *12 missed calls* in the written final report, but the formal SIM report from the tool actually shows 13. Fig. 12.3 depicts the total call history of 7 calls from Bitpim. It is advisable for this example to say, *"Call history was recovered during the extraction, refer to the Bitpim report for further details."*

In summary, if the particular tool has the ability to show what data it acquired, simply rely on the tool's report. If your agency or employer needs these totals, make certain you look at the summary for each tool. If there is no summary, look into the GUI. The GUI will also be used to validate the summary and is discussed in this chapter as another aspect of report writing.

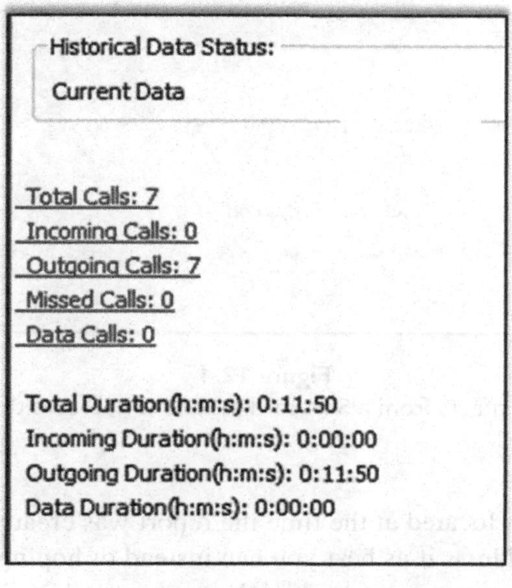

```
┌ Historical Data Status: ──────────────
│
│  Current Data
│  ──────────────────────────────────
│
│
│  Total Calls: 7
│  Incoming Calls: 0
│  Outgoing Calls: 7
│  Missed Calls: 0
│  Data Calls: 0
│
│
│  Total Duration(h:m:s): 0:11:50
│  Incoming Duration(h:m:s): 0:00:00
│  Outgoing Duration(h:m:s): 0:11:50
│  Data Duration(h:m:s): 0:00:00
└
```

Figure 12.3
Example of a call history summary from a utility.

Reporting Issues and Anomalies

It is important (if possible) that investigators create only the reports that they can explain. The example here would be a SIM utility that pulls the entire file system. Many of the folders located in the entire file system are part of network authentication and protocol and were not outlined in Chapter 6 and generally do not contain easy-to-explain evidence. Without an engineer's explanation (from the actual target network), these artifacts would be very difficult for the average mobile forensic examiner to testify about in court.

It is equally noteworthy that if you have the choice over what lands in the report, you choose what you have been trained on. Fig. 12.4 would be an example of what the author would *NOT* want to include as part of a SIM report. This example includes artifacts not addressed in Chapter 6, nor addressed in the previous training that the author had attended during his career. Readers may view this example and, because they worked with a wireless carrier, might completely understand it. For the average mobile forensic examiner, this will not be the case.

```
Ciphering Key Sequence Number: 7

HPLMN search period: 01

Broadcast Control Channels (BCCH): FF FF FF FF FF FF FF FF FF FF FF FF FF FF FF FF

Access control class: 13

SIM Phase: phase 2 - profile download required

Routing Area Identifier (RAI) network code: 310410 - United States, Cingular Wireless

Message Reference, last message sent: 194
```

Figure 12.4
Can you explain these artifacts from a SIM card report? If not leave them out of your report!

Anomalies are not always located at the time the report was created. If you do note an anomaly, it is better to address it as best you can instead of hoping it goes unnoticed. There will be times when you cannot explain the cause or origin. This still must be addressed and in some cases, by the time the case goes to trial, the answer may be revealed.

If you are new to mobile forensics you may not have enough training to understand why or when these types of inexplicable things occur during the examination process. But, if you keep conducting forensic examinations on mobile phones you will encounter them! Read that last line again and remember: "You were told so" as it may not happen quickly but it will happen.

Understand that the tools on the market created for this process are only doing what is asked of them. They are reading certain areas within the file system or memory and based on the program code, reporting back what they find. It does not necessarily mean it is wrong or right. For example, a common issue located in the report summary is the date of 1980 or 1970. This can show up in many locations. We are all aware that cell phones were not around in 1980 (or 1970) and a 1980 created, accessed, or modified date is not possible. So the 1980 date shows as the date of the phone at the time of the examination. How would you address this? One way is to look at the phone GUI and see if the date is correct. Sometimes the date is off because the phone has been without power or is no longer getting service (Faraday). It does not mean the rest of the report is invalid. The point is that there will always be a reason for various anomalies to appear. Some of you will find an answer based on your training and skill level, and others may not.

The author has found that on a certain model phones that were placed into airplane mode, the system date showed January 1, 1980. While using the same model phone that was not an actual evidence phone, the same exact issue was encountered. When the phone was not

Ringtones

#	File Name	File Size	File Date/Time	File Link
1	aimmsg.mid Path: brew/mod/4972/aimmsg.mid MD5: F853E50B9D84592BD75CD15356A4B093 SHA256: E2DDF74B A4EC753 FEDDD4F B389DBC 066F98E 5F1E1B0 03C3EB7 C8ACCE5 2C690CE	189 Bytes	01/06/80 00:00:00 (GMT)	aimmsg.mid
2	aimol.mid Path: brew/mod/4972/aimol.mid MD5: B7DBCAB3EE81F20CDBED6E5FE8882130 SHA256: 2C974469 8E091A4 0DF3DD7 F8488FC 1852EC2 73B61FF FB89AD5 61745CB 9595D55	166 Bytes	01/06/80 00:00:00 (GMT)	aimol.mid
3	aimsys.mid Path: brew/mod/4972/aimsys.mid MD5: 14C728F9FB061CDA2D30839BA4C03CDB SHA256: 0B0327DB 15C44F1 B96ACFB 6A99BBB ADD1E44 EFF2329 F358F43 7C5BF95 0D17763	153 Bytes	01/06/80 00:00:00 (GMT)	aimsys.mid
4	msnmsg.mid Path: brew/mod/4972/msnmsg.mid MD5: A199B0C0C89868D1F621D33967EF27E8 SHA256: 4C5602E0 3906337 DF9AA48 D70F3BE 8711103 267DF17 A028485 16E30C6 6FD69CC	471 Bytes	01/06/80 00:00:00 (GMT)	msnmsg.mid

Figure 12.5
Example of common 1980 dates that show in forensic reports.

in airplane mode the system date was correct, but when airplane mode was enabled, it reported the 1980 date. Also addressed was the fact that although this date being reported was incorrect, the actual evidence dates were not affected. This was further validated by pulling the file system and locating the offset using a specialized date decoding utility, and where the actual bytes of this date were being interpreted from was found. This type of anomaly is explained in upcoming chapters that address Epoch dates. A unique date and time tool (that is commercially available) can assist examiners on how a tool may read the offsets and interpret dates, is Sanderson Forensics—ReEnge. This product allows the examiner to preselect the epoch or date format, and as the user advanced the space bar (one byte at a time), the tool provides a decoded value. For now, try and review your specific tool case reports very carefully and address any issues, *even if you do not have all the answers*. By finding them before someone else who may challenge you does, you will, at the very least, not be surprised. Fig. 12.5 is a screenshot taken from a logical examination of a forensic tool. Shown in this image are .mid ringtone (sound) files from the OS of this target phone. Notice the "File Date/Time" listed as 1/06/80 00:00:00 on all these files. This is commonly encountered in case reports, especially with system files that were not created by the user. Could you explain this? You may at this point only be able to at least address that it is in the case report.

Validation

The documentation of "validation" is by far one of the single most important aspects of the reporting process. Your forensic report could be as simple as the examination of a SIM card, which may have been located loose at a crime scene. Using the forensic tools available in your laboratory, you pull the file system and locate an ICCID value, listing it within the report. Then you visually validate the same number as being stamped on the outside of the SIM card.

We have already addressed all the different types of validations that can be used. Visual validation is, by far, the most often overlooked. Fig. 12.5 is an example of this same scenario involving the ICCID value located internal and printed outside the SIM. Just remember that externally you can also find values that ***DO NOT MATCH*** the ones that are stored internally. Locating such a finding would still be considered as validating (Fig. 12.6).

Validating does not necessarily mean to confirm *correct* data or artifacts, but simply confirming the data that are presented to you. Use cross-tool validation to confirm findings. You can list that tool "A" located the following and these entries were also confirmed with tool "B." Call Detail Records can help with tower deliver entries. Be aware that dates and times on phones for these entries may be different from what the call center retains from the wireless carrier.

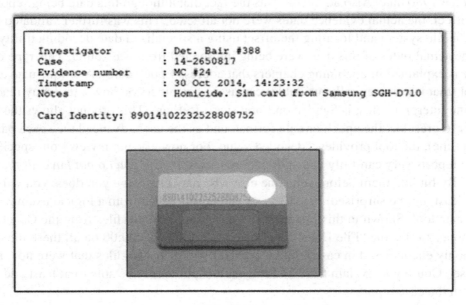

Figure 12.6
ICCID value located internally within the file system of the target SIM and also on the outside of the card itself.

Methods of Reporting

Consideration should be given to the methods in which the final reports are saved and the positive and negatives of each format. This may be what the prosecutor, supervisor, or company actually wants for the final product. The formats may also be based on the specific utility used for the examination. As you have learned some of these tools are open source or made specifically for the consumer to use, not necessarily designed as a "forensic" product. Because of this, you may have to create your own format. There will be times when using a combination of various methods works best. For example, a logical report generated by Susteen or Cellebrite relies on HTML to view the report properly. Here are just some of the more popular formats and a few of their pros and cons.

Text Reports
- Pros: Easy to create. Generally, the cost of the software is minimal, as Microsoft Word, Word Pad/Text Document, or other OS embedded text editor can be used.
- Cons: Can be quite large. Videos and other playable media cannot be viewed within the report. The user must create templates or use other features to obtain the desired effect.

HTML
- Pros: Links attachments and allows media files to play. The media (CD/DVD) can be set to "auto-play" and launch exactly what the creator wants the audience to see, such as the file index or case overview. HTML creation is relatively easy.
- Cons: Attachments must stay together. If the case is large, going back and forth to the index may become confusing. A specific player for proprietary file formats must be installed separately.

Media Disks (CD/DVD/Blu-ray)
- Pros: Makes it possible to bring all the different reporting methods together. Allows documents such as search warrants and consent forms to be viewed. Can be used to compile reports on more than one target device. Is used to provide specific information on the evidence in question. Does not require specialized equipment to view.
- Cons: Can become quite large. Usually requires the work product to be zipped then unzipped for proper burning due to long file name restrictions in Windows.

PDF
- Pros: PDF documents are harder to edit or change; this helps the integrity of the final report to remain consistent. PDF reports can now open attachments, similar to HTML. Creating a PDF document is free with various internet tools now available.
- Cons: Requires a PDF player on the host machine. Reports created with the new version may not open properly (or attachments) if the host machine is using an older PDF viewer.

Other Formats and Proprietary Readers

There are forensic tool vendors that allow free readers to be utilized on their advanced (paid) products. The readers can be used to see the acquisition (file) before it is made into a formal report with one of the previously mentioned formats. These readers must be included as an installable execution (.exe) if the audience does not already have the product on their machine. Some of the features of these types of viewers allow artifacts to be located that may or may not have been included in the final report. These programs are "read-only" and can be used without changing the source image file.

Most commercially made forensic programs will allow the examiner to choose the output—and in some cases a proprietary output as well. The point of mentioning this is if an examiner reports findings from a tool in a certain type of format, he/she must also provide a copy of the program that can open it. Cellebrite and AccessData both have viewers available for their programs, which allows a person to search, view, print, etc., without changing the original source file. One of the advantages to creating a finalized report that includes the viewer, is that the person can choose what exactly they want to print or export. For example, the examination may have 12,000 pages of PDF data that was found on an 64 GB iPhone. If the same findings included the viewer for the program, the prosecutor could created individual reports on only the fields of interest, and not the entire 12K of overall pages.

Hashing

This term can be somewhat confusing if you ever had to explain it during testimony. In simple terms, to "hash" or "hashing" involves determining a string of characters that represent an exact value to something else. The definition has arisen several times during court cases and was explained to the jury by simply defining it as a "unique serial number" usually given to a target file. This was followed up by providing an example of creating a letter to your own mother using a Word program or text program in Windows. After you finish the letter, a hashing utility was utilized to run an algorithm to give this document a specific value or in the author's own words, a unique "serial number." If, after having hashed the letter, we go back to the document and change anything, even something small like the first letter of "Mom" to a lowercase "m," and rerun the hashing tool, then the serial number (hash value) will also change, thus showing that the two documents are in fact different because of the changes we made. Hashing is used to determine authenticity, as it becomes important to show that we did not change the artifacts that contain our evidence presented during a legal process.

There are different levels of hash algorithms, and it is not necessary to know all of them. We, however, must understand that commercial forensic tools can "hash" the values of the data that is being acquired and reported. This value can be challenged during the legal proceedings. If it is included in your report, be aware of it and understand some basic reporting issues.

Hash values from two different forensic tools related to the same artifact(s) can be different.

Let us say that tool "A" compiles all of the contacts in your phone book, then in its reporting interface it numbers them starting with 001 and ends with the last contact as 100. Then it hashes the container with all these contacts and provides that value in the report. It may even provide the number system to reference the type of call history.

Tool "A" performs an MD5 & SHA1 hash on the "call history" container in its report and gives the type of calls their own sequential numbers based on the type of calls (dialed, received, missed). This particular example of tool "A" is an example of a hash value provided to the entire container that was created to show the call history in the report. If we take another tool, tool "B" that does not number the call history in this manner in its reporting container, the hash values will be different. Say for example, they number the call history 1 through 100, not 001 through 100. This may affect the hash. Many vendors have fixed this issue and supply hash value to the actual file, not their container they created for the reporting process.

It is the difference in what is being hashed not what the content actually is that may cause differences in hash values between two tools. This means that two different reports may have different hash values based on the format they compile the data into. But the content, times, and length of calls will be the same!

There are individuals who are tasked with securitizing your forensic work (such as defense counsel); they may locate these hashing discrepancies in your final reports. Simply be aware that the hash values can be different when comparing the same content from more than one tool.

Some tools will have the overall binary or zipped file system within their summary. If your actual call log is located under "Image0" and you were to take the MD5 hash value from tool "A" and compare it to the above MD5 hash values from above tool "B"; they may not match. Why? One is the overall partition that contains the call history and one is a container with the call history inside.

It is not that hash values are unimportant. It is that with mobile forensics we must understand what it is we are hashing. Realize that tools may report different hash values but the content of what they are reporting is (usually) the same. By realizing what is being hashed you can explain this if called on by someone who is questioning your work product based on different hash values of the same data.

The Archive Disk

The archive disk (CDROM, DVD, Blu-ray, etc.) should always contain all the data and proprietary files that were used to create your case report. The disk size used for the archive disk would be determined by what size is needed to hold all this information.

For example, the archive disk would contain the original scans from the search warrant: the images (.jpg' s) from the overalls, the screenshot.jpg' s from the Phonescoop website, the proprietary saved file from the SIM card utility, micro-SD image, and the entire file system or other specific files created by the program(s) used. The archive disk should be created in such a way that would allow defense to replicate your entire case report. Obviously, defense would need to obtain the same forensic program (versions) that you used. Because the archive disk contains the original source files, the media disk used to create them are usually quite larger than the case report media. In most cases the archive disk is placed into evidence and only called on if needed. The case report, however, is copied and given to the defense counsel, prosecutor, and case agent. The original folders on the archive disk would look something like this and contain the following:

- Search warrant (scans of the warrant, before PDF conversion)
- Overalls (original digital camera images in full size, before PDF conversion)
- SIM card (original HTML or proprietary tool format for the data retrieved off the SIM card, before PDF conversation)
- Micro-SD (original image file before parsing and PDF format)
- UFED (original UFED extension file and supported file system image before parsing and PDF format)
- Folders for report (contain the final folders for the case report as listed above)

Keep in mind that the exact folders listed above are just examples for that particular model phone and tools needed. Let us say that you obtained a consent form and the target device did not have a SIM or Micro-SD. Also, the forensic tool utilized was Susteen Secure View. The file folders for report would be different as well as the folders used on the archive. Here are examples for the content differences between a case report disk and an archive disk:

Case Report Disk Example Contents: (Titled "Folders for Report")		Archive Disk
(A)	Consent Form	Original scanned consent form
(B)	Overalls	Original full size images of evidence
(C)	Phonescoop	Original images from website
(D)	Susteen*	Original proprietary file from pull
		Folder with "Folders for case report"

*Folder "(D)" is just one example from a forensic tool. The actual case may need additional folders for each tool used. It may continue as (E) *BitPim* and (F) *UFED* or in the case of manual screenshots, (G) *Manual documentation*. The case report folders will vary based on the legal process used, and overall tools and programs needed to complete the entire forensic examination.

Chapter Summary Key Points

Mobile forensic examiners should be answering standard, general questions when they create their final report. Follow the: *who, what, when, where*, and *why* format. The beginning of the report lays out the initial contact, which would explain who you are and what type of work was requested to be performed on the evidence. The device state would explain if the device was powered on or off. This may also include elements that involve detailing additional processing for such things as DNA, latent print recovery, swabbing, or other necessary forensic work. With powered-on devices specific initial contamination steps such as Faraday methods would also be addressed. At this point in your report narrative you may need to explain how you proceeded with the proper legal authority before conducting the extraction(s). Next would be the need to list the tools, programs, or hardware that was used to perform the extraction and the versions of those same products. It is suggested that instead of listing exact totals within the narrative of your report, provide summaries of the parsed data. The exact totals for each field would be contained in the specific programs used and this would keep mistakes minimized.

Reporting issues and anomalies should be located prior to finalizing the report. If possible, try and determine the cause of these issues. If this is not possible, at least address the issues in the narrative; this will keep you from being surprised by them during a judicial process. Make certain that the findings from your examination are always validated. The easiest form of validation is visual. A Call Detail Record (CDR) can also assist, and even if the CDR does not contain the actual content of SMS (delivered through standard tower connection), it will show the coding that the message was delivered to or from the target evidence. Hashing is generally completed with the specific tool interface. Be aware that some tools may hash additional attributes along with the specific artifact. The examiner must articulate if necessary that the content is in fact the same, even if two tools report different hash results. Finally, the report should be zipped and burned to media that cover the overall size of what you located. This would include CDROM, DVD, Dual-Layer DVD, Blu-ray, and Dual-Layer Blu-ray. The format of the actual report will have its pros and cons. Popular formats would include PDF, HTML, and Text. Consult with those who will be reading your reports and determine what format works best with them.

The ability to create an outstanding report may take practice and, unfortunately in some cases, unintended embarrassment from testifying on your examination. There is nothing more humbling than being in front of a jury, and being called on to answer why your report did not have a documented answer to a question, or was missing a fundamental aspect. If this has happened to you, you usually remember it and hopefully make changes so that it does not happen again. It is up to each of you to "tell the story" with your report. Stories have a beginning, middle, and end. In this line of work, they are usually not a nice story to tell, and it is a great responsibility that has been bestowed upon you. The jury already knows how the story ended. They just need to know who is responsible and hopefully *why* it took place. Sometimes the person who owned the mobile device you examined has had his/her life violently taken. As his/her family, friends, and acquaintances sit on one side of the court room, they will eagerly and carefully watch, listening intently to you as you speak. It will, at that point, be the test that you created the correct narrative—one that may include *SMS, Calls, Videos,* and *Images* which document their last moments on earth.

Reference

[1] NIST, Guidelines on Cell Phone Forensics, NIST Special Publication 800-101, May 2007. http://www.crime-scene-investigator.net/GuidelinesCellPhoneForensics.pdf.

Intermediate Concepts

CHAPTER 13

Physical Acquisitions

Information in This Chapter

- Explain a "flasher box"
- Flasher box uses
- Bootloaders
- List popular makes and models
- Permanent Memory (PM)
- Early vendors
- BKForensics
- Paraben
- Motorola Flash and Backup
- CDMA Workshop
- Cellebrite physical extensions

History

Many readers can recall a TV show called Miami Vice. This TV series ran between 1984 and 1990. The main characters were vice detectives named Crocket and Tubbs. This program seemed to have at least one scene per week where someone on the show (even the bad guys) were communicating on early model cellular phones. Most of these were large Motorola "brick" style devices. During some of the episodes, they would show them hardwired in expensive sports cars. In some cases, they even carried the external battery pack as they talked on the phone. Imagine having to examine this type of digital evidence back when the technology was relatively new (and expensive). What if we needed to examine the same devices using a physical examination technique? In Chapter 1 we briefly discussed the differences between the logical and physical examinations. We revisit the physical explanation, this time from Wikipedia:

> Physical acquisition implies a bit-for-bit copy of an entire physical store (e.g. flash memory); therefore, it is the method most similar to the examination of a personal computer. A physical acquisition has the advantage of allowing deleted files and data remnants to be

examined. Physical extraction acquires information from the device by direct access to the flash memories.

Generally this is harder to achieve because the device original equipment manufacturer needs to secure against arbitrary reading of memory; therefore, a device may be locked to a certain operator. To get around this security, mobile forensics tool vendors often develop their own bootloaders, enabling the forensic tool to access the memory (and often, also to bypass user passcodes or pattern locks).

Generally, the physical extraction is split into two steps, the dumping phase and the decoding phase [1].

Many people who are employed in any capacity to perform digital forensic investigations are usually relying on a program or stand-alone utility to perform the heavy lifting. Back in the day when Miami Vice was showing on TV, the popular forensic vendors (we have today) were not around. Programs were limited, and those that could pull a physical from these early phones may or may not have been able to decode all of the artifacts needed for the investigation. As time went on, more vendors emerged to address the physical examination. Even today only a few companies have developed specific programs that can be used to decode several thousands of various phones, but they are not capable of supporting everything.

Flasher Boxes

Flasher boxes are the name given to small, model-specific metal or plastic boxes that are designed to repair or write (flash) to the memory on mobile devices. They communicate through data ports or proprietary terminals on the back of some cellular phones. Cables are attached to the target phone at one end and the other to the specific box. Another cable is routed from the box to the computer that has the software installed.

Based on the model of the device in question, a bootloader is sent to the phone, which in turn has a starting and ending offset that pulls data. In some instances, the GUI of the flasher box software allows the user to control the offset addresses. Fig. 13.1 is from the interface using the RIFF/RIFF 2 flasher boxes. The interface of this tool allows the user to specify where they want to search. They can use predetermined (set) lengths or manage the area themselves. This can also be used for JTAG and ISP examinations. The RIFF box is expanded on in upcoming chapters.

Another example is from the Z3X (Easy JTAG) box. Similar to the RIFF interface, this tool supports both JTAG and ISP extractions and allows the user to use preset configuration sizes or set the starting and ending offsets themselves. Fig. 13.2 depicts the interface settings for both JTAG and ISP examinations.

RIFF JTAG starting and ending offset choices

RIFF eMMC starting and ending offset choices

Figure 13.1
Example of flasher box (RIFF/RIFF2), which allows the user to specify the starting and ending
address of the physical search.

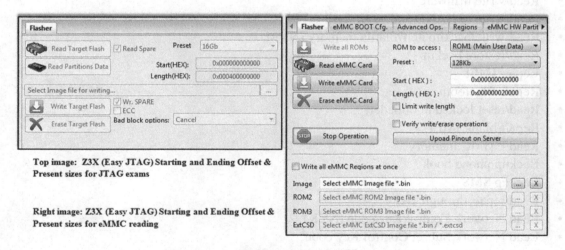

**Top image: Z3X (Easy JTAG) Starting and Ending Offset &
Present sizes for JTAG exams**

**Right image: Z3X (Easy JTAG) Starting and Ending Offset &
Present sizes for eMMC reading**

Figure 13.2
Example of the Z3X (Easy JTAG) interface, which allows the user to specify the standing and ending
address of the physical search.

Also, a number of flasher boxes sold may have the ability to communicate with the memory through the *JTAG* TAP (Joint Test Action Group Test Access Point) pinouts, which may require soldering to the contacts. The vast majority, however, do not need the user to solder to the main board to communicate with the target phone. They support pulls using standard USB cables and placing the phone into a download or service mode.

Flasher boxes typically create a file extension that is specific to the manufacturer of the box, or in some cases a standard format. For example, some of the common extensions that will be created from using flasher boxes on Samsung (NSPro) and LG (Octoplus) phones are listed:

- LG = .nvm, .dump, .nand, .bin
- Samsung = .tfs, .nfs, .cla, .bin

Some manufacturers also offer a dongle service. The dongle works the same way as the flasher box but takes away the need for the phone to connect to the box. Instead, the installed software is allowed access through the dongle that is inserted into the host machine. Cables are still used to connect to the supported phone but connect directly to the computer.

These devices are not designed for mobile forensics, but some of the *features* may be used for that purpose. They are manufactured to repair or to modify phones. Here is a list of some of the common features that flasher boxes are used for: (Note—Not all boxes are capable of every feature on this list.)

- Read/write firmware
- Read/write to NAND and NOR flash
- Read/write/backup nonvolatile memory (NVM)
- Read/restore backup
- Repair IMEI
- Repair Bluetooth
- Read/reset locked bootloader
- Repair blank IMEI
- Read EMMC memory
- Backup phone book
- Backup SMS
- Read/repair through TAP
- Read Network Control Key code (NCK)
- Read Network Subset Control Key code
- Read Service Provider Control Key code
- Read Corporate Control Key code
- Read Personalization Control Key code

One of the more popular features of the flasher box is the ability to "unlock" the device. Unlocking does not mean getting past the user security to access the GUI of the phone, although a few can include that feature. Unlocking pertains to a code set by the provider or manufacturer

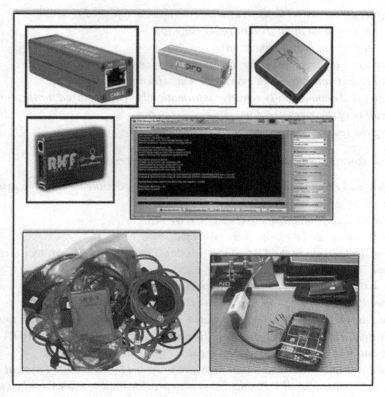

Figure 13.3
Examples of various flasher boxes, associated cables, and proprietary software.

that "locks" the device to only be used on a specific network or feature. The latter features of the abovementioned list include just some of the codes used by carriers. In this chapter we will not go over each of these codes; however, it is important understand what the "unlock" feature means as it pertains to flasher boxes. Fig. 13.3 depicts several different model flasher boxes along with an example of the proprietary cables and necessary software that must be installed.

Pros and Cons—Flasher Box Usage

In an article, John Thackray, a former British Police Detective and vice-president of GetData Forensics USA, outlines some pros and cons of using flasher boxes.

> *All tools whether used for computer or mobile forensics must be validated and checked against each other. Prior to using any tool, investigators must consider the strengths and weaknesses of that tool and how to effectively apply it to the many different situations they will encounter. Flasher boxes do have weaknesses, amongst which are:*

- *Flasher boxes are invasive.*
- *Changes to the data may occur.*

- *Some flasher boxes are technically challenging and complicated to use.*
- *Some do not create an audit trail or processing log.*
- *They do not perform hash verifications.*
- *There are many different boxes for the array of devices in the market place.*
- *Each flasher box can come with many different software interfaces.*
- *Proprietary and commercially sensitive information is often required for the correct interpretation of the extracted data.*
- *Analyzing the recovered data can be time consuming.*

Given these weaknesses, why should flasher boxes be considered at all?

- *A complete and reliable understanding of all activity is possible through the extraction and analysis of a hex dump taken from a suspect device.*
- *Truly deleted data from the handset can be retrieved.*
- *Damaged devices can be forensically examined.*
- *Data from devices where the SIM card is missing, damaged, or PIN protected can be recovered.*
- *Devices without a battery can be forensically examined.*
- *Data from PIN and other protected areas of a handset can be accessed.*
- *Analyzing the extracted data with automated processes is possible with such tools as: GetData Phone Image Carver, TagView, Hexaminer, Cell Phone Analyzer (CPA), EnCase, and FTK using EnScripts and regular expression search terms.*
- *Utilizing the mobile forensic analysis software provided by CelleBrite Physical Pro and Micro Systemation, XRY Physical may also provide quality evidence when they cannot achieve an extraction of the raw data.*
- *Flasher boxes are alternative, cost effective solutions that provide truly deleted recovery capability for organizations on limited budgets* [2].

In Chapter 18, we will show the reader how additional validation tools can be utilized to actually see the changes that take place when flasher boxes work. There are changes that take place, especially at the binary level. These changes are necessary, and are part of the communication protocols taking place; as the tool must "speak" with the target. What will be stressed is that even with these binary changes, our specific targeted artifacts (evidence) such as call history, SMS, MMS, images, and other user stored data *do not change*. Most of the commercial forensic tools that support physical acquisitions, will utilize similar mechanisms that flasher boxes employ.

Bootloaders

Many flasher boxes will utilize a specific program (or code) that allows commands to take place, referred to as bootloaders. These basically tell the hardware on the mobile device what to do. Many people use a "custom bootloader" to place specific software or a customized OS on their phone. Terms such as jailbreaking or rooting pertain to specific Apple or Android-based devices that have in essence been "unlocked." The unlocking process usually takes place through the bootloader. Vendors even sell "developer" editions of their phones, which for a specific price, allow users to customize the OS by placing what they want on the phone through customized bootloaders. In recent years, some vendors go to extremes to ensure that their bootloaders are "locked" or encrypted. There are two main reasons for this, the first being revenue. Their ability to unlock a device comes back to the subsidy. Manufacturers make more revenue when the consumer is forced to "use" their product over a targeted period. The longer they control this ability, the longer they can charge for data usage. Some vendors even place a time period on how long the device has to be assigned to their network. This even applies to pay-as-you-go model phones. The other reason, which has gained national attention, is security. Apple has made it clear that it takes user stored data very seriously. Forensic tools, flasher boxes, and other exploits that once allowed physical examinations through a bootloader process are in most cases not supported, "locked", or encrypted. Of course this also goes hand-in-hand with the hardware and software that continues to improve. One aspect that Apple has that many other vendors do not, is their ability to create hardware that works with their specific software. Android-based devices are not necessarily designed this way. Lastly, Chinese chipsets have also become very popular. These products are a much cheaper alternative for the consumer and, from their outside appearance, look exactly like their name brand counterparts. Forensically, they may require a specific bootloader to allow the physical acquisition to take place. Many forensic vendors will utilize a "read-only" bootloader. These generally do exactly that and allow access to the physical download, making little to no changes.

Current Popular Boxes

It is important to understand that no single flasher box will work with every make-and-model phone on the market. The devices are targeted for specific models, and in many cases may cover several makes of mobile devices within one box. Most of the manufactures of these boxes are from China. Software is needed to interface with the actual box, and the support and maintenance is also from the East. This can be problematic when the install does not go as planned or users encounter a virus, or root kit after the install. Some agencies are not allowed by internal policies to purchase directly from China and rely on resellers that are in the United States. Generally, a box is sold with a set of supporting cables that pertain to a number of different model phones supported. As the user makes their selection on a specific make and model phone, the GUI of the program will inform the user which cable to select. Here is a list of some of the popular boxes that are commercially available:

- RIFF/RIFF 2
- Smart-Clip
- Sigma
- Medusa/Medusa Pro
- Volcano
- Z3X/Easy JTAG

- ORT
- Advance Turbo
- GPG
- Octoplus
- NSPro
- GPG EMMC
- UFS Turbo
- BST
- Miracle
- Pegasus
- ATF
- SELG Fusion
- Spookey
- AsanSam
- NCK
- Miracle Eagle Eye
- Piranha
- SPT
- Avator (box & dongle)
- Magma
- MXBox Thunder
- Dream Box SE
- Micro Box
- Polar Box 3
- SmartSamBox
- Furious Gold Box
- Multi-Unlocker
- Vygis
- GcPro Key
- Cylclone Key
- Infinity Pro Slim
- Miracle GSM Cocktail
- McnPro

This is not an exclusive list. There are additional products that can be purchased that perform specific jobs related to repairs, unlocking, or modifications.

Early Physical Examination Vendors and Tools

Just a few years back, many of the commercially available mobile forensic companies only sold products that were capable of logical acquisitions. Paraben was one of the first companies to utilize physical pulls (based on the flasher box) through their program called Device Seizure (DS). Paraben began by supporting Nokia, which at the time was the largest manufacturer of mobile phones worldwide. This period was before iOS and Android, and DS utilized the flasher box style cables that were designed to connect to the back of specific model Nokia devices. Paraben's audience was nearly entirely law enforcement investigators who conducted both computer and mobile forensics.

At that time Nokia used a proprietary physical file system called PM (.pm). PM stood for Permanent Memory. The physical file system works with keys and subkeys. The keys are numbered within the physical file system. Examples of keys would be storage locations for the phone book, call history, images, etc. Keys are initially empty when the phone is manufactured. Once the phone is sold and activated, users would store data within these keys, thus making a subkey. Stored subkeys began their numbering at 0. Some of the stored information that is not media, may be stored in Protocol Data Unit (PDU) format. Fig. 13.4

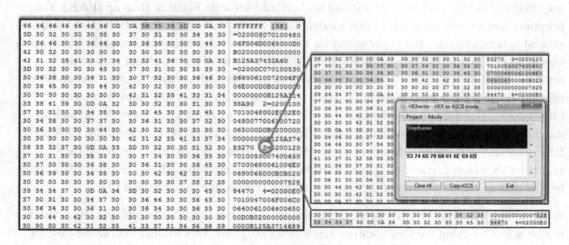

Stephanie 828-9447

Figure 13.4
PM Key 58 (Contacts) and decoded subkey 3 example.

depicts the PM file and Key 58. Key 58 is where the stored contacts would be saved by the end user. Subkey 3 is the fourth entry and in this example it has been decoded. The stored entry *Stephanie* uses standard Unicode format, or ASCII if the examiner wants to strip the zero padding.

The next example, shown in Fig. 13.5, is pulled from Key 150, which stores the SMS content. This example has the content in Unicode.

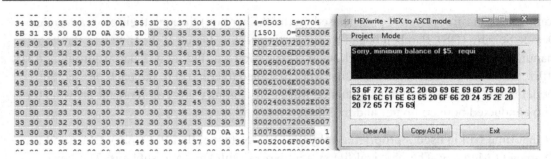

Figure 13.5
Example of an SMS message stored in key 150, subkey entry 0.

Another early vendor called BKForensics made utilities that could decode the PM file as well as other physical files from vendors such as Motorola. At the time, Motorola also had developed a popular selling product called the V3 Razor. The GSM version of the V3 could be acquired physically with a programming tool called Motorola Flash & Backup (F&B). This program also supported several other models from Motorola to include C, E, K, L, U, and several V series besides the popular selling V3. F&B was not designed for mobile forensics; it was designed as a repair/programming tool. This tool allowed the examiner to save and rewrite Code Groups (CGs). CGs were flash storage areas with specific starting and ending offsets. These areas would contain standard stored user data and could include deleted information. The user could select all the supported CG areas on a supported Moto and save the physical file as one Single Binary File (SBF). The SBF could be imported into CPA by BKForensics for decoding. Many of these Motorola phones at that time stored the user security PIN in a specific file system location. Using the Motorola SEEM feature, F&B could be directed to go to this area of the file system and remove the user enabled PIN.

When CDMA phones first emerged, examiners would constantly run into phones that could not be acquired using the free open-source BitPim program. This usually was caused by the file system being locked with a subsidy lock. If the lock was placed into an "unlocked" state, the utility, however, could download the file system and complete the examination. As logical forensic tools emerged on the market, many of them could not bypass or reveal the user enabled passcode. This meant that if the examiner did not have access to the PIN, many times the examination could not be accomplished. Later it was determined that many manufacturers placed the security and user code just a few offsets apart. This meant that a popular LG CDMA phone would have the user PIN in the same general location for most of the LG CDMA models. The same held true for Samsung. A popular tool that was used to remove the subsidy lock and/or reveal the PIN on CDMA phones was a program called CDMA Workshop. This tool could also quickly display the MEID, MIN, and phone number for the handset.

As we have explained, examiners who were tasked with recovering physical mobile data during these early years typically used a number of programming, flasher, repair, diagnostic tools, utilities, and programs to obtain proprietary physical files. During these first few years, most vendors specialized in logical decoding, and tools that could pull and decode the raw data were few and far between. The typical problem with physical examinations was not necessarily locating a hardware or software-based tool to conduct the pull; it was the ability to decode the physical pull from the proprietary utility.

MSAB and Cellebrite

If we jump from those first years of conducting physical exams using a variety of tools, to where we are today, there are two major companies who lead the way—MSAB and Cellebrite.

MSAB (Micro Systemation AB) was founded in 1984 and is considered one of the first major mobile forensic companies. They are based in Sweden and have three main products available as of September 2016—XRY, XAMN, and XEC. Many people refer to all their products simply as XRY. XRY can perform both logical and physical examinations on phones and cloud-based investigations. XAMN is used to analyze the data using a viewer or what they call "Spotlight." XEC is used as a management tool and can export the final analysis. XRY is still considered one of the best GSM forensic tools available.

Cellebrite was found in 1999. Just like XRY they have several products that can acquire, analyze, and report stored user information off mobile evidence. Unlike XRY, Cellebrite began as a wireless carrier support tool that was used to transfer contacts, images, and other user data. Cellebrite's Universal Memory Exchanger was a stand-alone phone to phone transfer unit. This meant that carriers could entice would-be buyers into new phones when one of the downsides was transferring user information to the new device they were selling. Cellebrite sold thousands of units to wireless phone companies. Cellebrite had a unique relationship with the manufacturers of mobile phones. They were allowed access to the beta versions of the devices before they were released to the market. This allowed them to correctly identify problems with data transfers and ensure that consumers, when buying the new phone, could easily integrate their old data. Cellebrite was so good at supporting phones that oftentimes law enforcement agencies would visit a wireless carrier to obtain assistance with mobile evidence, and would end up using the Cellebrite equipment. In 2007 Cellebrite began producing digital forensic products. They were labeled Universal Forensic Extraction Device (UFED). Cellebrite only sold the devices to government-specific organizations. One of Cellebrite's current decoding programs is Physical Analyzer (PA). It is currently a core tool needed in decoding physical pulls from a vast number of different source tools.

Using the principle concepts that are employed with all the various repair and programming tools, Cellebrite embedded the features into an easy-to-use interface with PA. Users can also create their own chains and plug-ins. The examiner can also work directly within a Python Shell and create customized scripts.

Cellebrite physical extractions will generally have two types of file extensions. Some of these extensions are similar to those that would be encountered when using a flasher box. It is important to understand, however, that flasher boxes and programming tools have other coding within the file that must be "cleaned up" for proper logical rebuild. The code was written to be read by the software for the flasher or programming tool, not for mobile forensic investigators. Cellebrite, on the other hand, creates physical pulls that can, in turn, be decoded using its own software, PA. PA takes the physical "dump" that Cellebrite pulled from the acquisition and rebuilds the various partitions, decoding the data based on what is supported. The physical files pulled using Cellebrite Touch or UFED 4PC may be named one of the following, with a subname but the extension generally stays as:

- .bin (Android, proprietary OS, etc.)
- .img (iOS)

Chapter Summary Key Points

Physical acquisitions allow the examiner to access additional storage areas that can be further analyzed. The physical examination can at times reveal deleted data that may have been limited by a logical pull. Tools that were designed as repair products such as the flasher box can be utilized to conduct a physical exam. Flasher boxes can be used for a number of services to include reading and writing firmware, NAND and NOR flash, NVM, IMEI, MEID, and other values. One of the primary uses of the flasher box is not for mobile forensics but to unlock the phone so it can be used on other networks. Flasher boxes have pros and cons. They are considered invasive, can make changes to data, are difficult to use, do not perform hash verifications, and are difficult to decode. However, if used correctly they allow an examiner a complete hex dump of the target evidence, access to locked devices, access to damaged devices, and the ability to analyze deleted data.

Bootloaders are often used to pull physical data from phones. Custom bootloaders can be used on phones that are not locked or encrypted by the manufacturer, and are also used on Chinese chipset phones that need forensic analysis.

There are currently several popular makes of flasher boxes on the market. Each support a specific number of makes and models of phones, but there is not one brand that covers every phone. A few are RIFF, Smart-Clip, Sigma, Medusa, Volcano, Z3X, ORT, Advance Turbo, GPG, Octoplus, NSPro, GPG EMMC, UFS Turbo, BST, Miracle, Pegasus, ATF, SELG Fusion, Spookey, AsanSam, NCK, Miracle Eagle Eye, Piranha, SPT, Avator (box & dongle),

Magma, MXBox Thunder, Dream Box SE, Micro Box, Polar Box 3, SmartSamBox, Furious Gold Box, Multi-Unlocker, Vygis, GcPro Key, Cylclone Key, Infinity Pro Slim, Miracle GSM Cocktail, and McnPro.

Some of the early commercial vendors that supported physical pulls and decoding were Paraben and BKForensics. Nokia physicals were called PM and they utilized keys and subkeys. PM files could be decoded using BKForensics CPA. CPA could also be used to decode SBFs that were created from Motorola F&B. F&B allowed the user to save specific CGs. F&B also had the ability to remove the user lock (PIN) through Motorola SEEM.

Many early model CDMA phones would not be properly read using open-source tools such as BitPim. CDMA Workshop allowed physical access to these phones. The examiner could reveal the PIN number, MEID, assigned number, and the SPC. The SPC would in turn place the phone into an unlocked state to allow the file system to then be acquired.

Soon two major vendors began creating tools to pull and decode the physical examination from mobile evidence: MSAB and Cellebrite. Cellebrite's PA can be used to decode physical pulls that were acquired from a number of sources. Two common physical file formats that Cellebrite labels their pulls are .IMG (iOS) and .BIN (Android and other phones).

We have come a long way from the early days of physical extractions that required a number of steps, as well as tools, just to decode a single phone. In this chapter, we only touched on a few of the tools that were used. In closing this chapter, it is important to understand that most of the commercial tools used today employ the basic technology used by flasher boxes and bootloaders.

References

[1] Mobile Device Forensics, Wikipedia, September 18, 2016. https://en.wikipedia.org/wiki/Mobile_device_forensics#Physical_acquisition.
[2] Flasher Boxes: Back to Basic Mobile Forensics, Forensicmag.com, July 13, 2010. http://www.forensicmag.com/product-release/2010/07/flasher-boxes-back-basics-mobile-phone-forensics.

CHAPTER 14

Physical Memory and Encoding

Information in This Chapter

- Flash memory
- NAND
- NOR
- eNAND
- iNAND
- MoviNAND
- eMCP
- eMMC
- eMLC
- Read/Write operation of NAND
- Structure of the NAND block
- Spare area of the NAND
- Error correction code, wear leveling, garbage collection
- SQLite database
- Data encoding types

History

The Toshiba corporation invented electronically erasable programmable read-only memory (EEPROM). Dr. Fujio Masuoka worked for Toshiba inventing both NOR (1984) and NAND memory (1987). The original name was erasable EEPROM but was soon changed to flash because it could erase memory cells such as the flash of a camera [1]. In 2012, Toshiba marked its 25th year anniversary on its NAND flash invention. Since 1984, Toshiba has advanced this technology with larger capacities, multilevel cell (MLC), solid-state drives, multibit per cell technology, and, in 2012, the world's largest density and smallest die size [1]. Toshiba is not the only player in the flash market. Samsung, SanDisk, Intel, Marvell, ADATA, SK Hynix, Kingston, and Micron are just of the few commonly encountered memory chips found on mobile devices.

NAND and NOR

There are differences between the NAND gate (negative-AND) and NOR gate (negative-OR). Both behave according to truth tables based on high (1) and low (0) input/outputs. Their differences are the way the cells are arranged. NOR provides them in parallel, whereas NAND is in series. The efficiency greatly increases when the cells are arranged in series.

The *functional completeness* is a property used to describe the ability of the NAND gate. When implementing a combination of NAND gates, any Boolean function can be made. On the companion site, Fig. 14.1 depicts (at the top) the NOR and NAND truth table. The bottom of Fig. 14.1 (companion site) is a short list of the pros and cons of NOR and NAND.

If a specific system directly requires booting out of flash, in turn execute code, or read latency, NOR flash would be the best for those functions. If the flash is needed for storage applications such as multimedia that would use higher density, high programming, and erase speeds, NAND would be the obvious choice. There are currently several variants to the NAND flash memory. Later we will discuss some of the common types of flash memory chips that an examiner will encounter during destructive chip-off reading. Here is a short list of different types besides the standard NAND. All of these are structured off NAND flash memory.

- eNAND
- iNAND
- MoviNAND
- MoviMCP
- eMMC
- eMCP
- MLC
- TLC
- 3D NAND

As of September 2016, another form of (NAND) memory that is being found in newer smartphones is Universal Flash Storage (UFS). eMMC (NAND) works with half duplexing, whereas UFS is full duplex. Other advantages are ultrahighspeed data rates, lower power, integrated controller, error-correcting code (ECC), wear leveling, command queuing, and improved system performance. Toshiba produces both eMMC and UFS flash memories with an integrated controller. Toshiba (and other vendors) also have 3D flash memory. Toshiba calls theirs BiCS Flash. Toshiba promotes single-layer cell NAND configurations, which by comparison with other forms of NAND is a very small part of the overall market. Toshiba calls these SLC NAND, BENAND, and Serial Interface NAND. According to the March 2016

Toshiba Flash Memory catalog, they provide the following information on additional flash memory configurations besides eMMC and UFS:

- SLC NAND

The high read/write performance and write endurance of the Toshiba SLC NAND make it a superb choice for a broad spectrum of commercial and industrial applications.
- BENAND

BENAND is a NAND flash memory that incorporates ECC logic. BENAND eliminates the need for a host processor to perform ECC, making it possible to utilize the latest 24-nm SLC NAND regardless of whether the host processor has an adequate ECC capability.
- Serial Interface NAND

Serial Interface NAND provides a commonly used six-pin Serial Peripheral Interface (SPI) for flash memory interfacing and is offered in small WSON and SOP packages [2].

Multichip Package

Many designers are combining solutions into stacks of memory. These allow various combinations to include mobile DRAM, SRAM, PRAM, NAND flash, NOR, and eMMC to be in a single packaged chip-stacking technology. Samsung has **moviMCP**. This is designed to support a wide range of multimedia applications, which is comprised of Samsung's eMMC (embedded MLC NAND and MMC controller).

Package on Package

There are also configurations that are called package on package (POP). These are quite common and they allow the processor, or coprocessor to have RAM affixed to the top. The RAM will be soldered to the processor and only utilizes the outside edge for communication to the processor. The manufacturers can vary, and many times the RAM can be a completely different manufacturer than the processor it is housed on. Some phones can also have a dedicated video card that uses its own memory. To assist with illustrating this, Fig. 14.2 of the companion site depicts components (chips) from a Motorola XT912. Notice how this particular phone utilizes two POP style configurations.

The important thing to understand is that the forensic physical extraction does not generally include data that are contained within the processor, coprocessor, RAM, ROM, or dedicated video memory, even if the phone has all of these on the main board! During a nondestructive exam, the forensic program will communicate with the processor. The processor in turn would go to the location of the request. The location of this "pull" is usually on a different chip. (In the upcoming chapter that covers destructive chip-off removal, we will discuss how to visually identify this flash memory location.) The user data partition (and other partitions) is accessed and the data are brought over; the partitions are rebuilt and decoding and parsing begins.

As an example in Fig. 14.2 (companion site), our evidential areas would be contained in partitions within the eMMC (NAND) memory. This will store the phone's specific operating system with important values such as contacts, call logs, SMS, MMS, media (images/video/sound files), chats, emails, bookmarks, Web history, application data, unallocated space, and much more.

NAND Blocks, Spare Area, Operation Rules, Wear Leveling, Garbage Collection, and the SQLite Databases

NAND Blocks

The composition of NAND memory (internally) will be with a specific fixed number of blocks, and each block will have 32 pages. Each page has 512 bytes of main data with 16 bytes of spare data. The fixed number of blocks depends on the size of the device, and will be up to the vendor. The spare area has specific functions. It is used for ECC, wear leveling, and other executions.

Pages are typically 512, 2048, 4096, or with newer devices, larger bytes in size. On the companion site, Fig. 14.3 is an example of a small block NAND page. The page size corresponds to the spare area, i.e., $512 = 16$, $2048 = 64$, $4096 = 128$.

When a user of a phone is interfacing with the device, the function of read and write is performed on a page basis. Input and output pins receive commands and address for a page to be read; there is specified delay employed in this process, and then the selected page is loaded into data and spare registries.

Another issue is a term called, "Bad Blocks." The bad block area cannot be written to nor erased. As mentioned previously, bad blocks may exist at birth (creation of NAND) or caused over time. The system is set up to address the bad blocks so that storage attempts to that specific area are not permitted. The bad block map table will hold the values of the blocks that cannot be written to. Software (SW) and hardware (HW) will consult with the map before attempting storage, thus avoiding the bad blocks entirely.

NAND Spare Area

ECC is the primary function of the spare area. Other functions also take place, to include wear leveling and functions of the SW. Part of the duty of ECC is to ensure that the data stored in the main area maintains its integrity. To do this, the ECC calculates error-correcting code for information that the block stores. That code is then written back to the spare area that applies to the block. Then, when the data is called upon, the code is checked before it goes out to ensure that it is correct. If errors do exist, corrections can be made depending on the algorithm used.

NAND Operation Rules

There are some basic operational rules that take place for NAND memory to function properly. Reading and writing to NAND takes place one page at a time and is organized into blocks. Values can only be changed from 1 to 0, not 0 to 1. A page within a block and the single cell (1 or 0) cannot be erased on its own—the entire block must be erased. Erasing a block sets all bits to 1. The delete and writing executions are subject to the control of to two algorithms that NAND flashes utilizes; which are referred to as garbage collection and wear leveling. These two functions are important to understand. Based on the stage of where the function of the algorithms are (at a given moment), deleted values can be recovered during an examination.

Wear Leveling and Garbage Collection

Flash memory employs a process that allows the entire memory to degrade evenly over time. Think of flash memory similar to a tire on a car. If the tire is over inflated, then the center of the tread wears prematurely. If there is not enough air pressure (under inflated), then the side wall area can wear out. If, however, the correct amount of air is placed into the tire, the surface of the tread shares the load evenly. This allows the tire to wear out in a consistent fashion. Since flash memory has a certain number of read, write, and erase cycles, there is a process that spreads this out, thus ensuring no area degrades faster than another. This is referred to as *wear leveling*.

To help with this, there is an additional controller over this process, which is referred to as the *flash translation level (FTL)*. The OS command(s) communicate with the FTL. The FTL in turn will prevent repeated writes to the same memory location. Therefore, the data cannot be written to areas in flash until the section is cleaned. This process sets the area to 1's. This is called *garbage collection*.

SQLite Databases

Mobile operating systems such as Blackberry, Apple, and Android utilize and store information in SQLite databases. These are SW based and found within the OS. They can be main (default) standard apps or user installed. These containers have the ability to retain deleted artifacts within their own specific location for their function. For example, sms.db is a SQLite database for SMS messages. Under certain conditions, when a user deletes an SMS entry, it will remain within this specific location and in some cases may be recovered.

What Does This All Mean?

Examiners must have some basic understanding of how flash memory can play in the role in recovering deleted artifacts. As mentioned when describing the functions of garbage collection and wear leveling, there will be times when due to FTL performance, deleted data is unavailable within the hardware area (physical memory). The other can be the SW (databases). The bottom line is that there will be instances when an examiner will locate deleted artifacts in both hardware and software areas. Also, it is not uncommon to locate data which has already been parsed and decoded, to repeat itself in more than one area of the memory. Again, the cause of this is from the performance of wear leveling. (Just remember the tire analogy)

FAT 12, 16, 32, and proprietary systems (Nokia, Motorola, BREW) will generally serve as the OS for the file system. FTL implementation communicates with these various OS's and can use both HW and SW locations for storing and accessing data. SW is the most common area in mobile devices where examiners can locate deleted information. Now that we have covered the basics of where data may reside, we must understand the various formats that may be encountered when reading physical data.

Encoding

Data may be present on physical as well as logical exams and can be recovered using encoding. This data may reside in HW physical memory or SW locations such as the previously mentioned SQLite databases. There are several different ways the information may be stored, decoded, and displayed. Here are the encoding types:

- Binary
- Hexadecimal
- Nibble
- ASCII
- Unicode
- Big and Little Endian
- Reverse Nibble
- 7-bit GSM PDU

Binary

Mobile devices, just like computers, store data at their physical level in binary form. These are bits that are either a "1" or a "0." Each represents whether the bit is on or off. The one (1) means the bit is on while zero (0) is off. Eight bits equal 1 byte.

While looking at words within the GUI of a mobile device, these first must be converted from binary to American Standard Code for Exchange (ASCII). ASCII is a set of digital characters that can be letters, numbers, or symbols. These are a standard that are used in computers and related digital devices.

Binary to Decimal

We should understand that when we convert a binary to decimal, each bit from *right to left* (total of 8 bits in a byte) has a value if it is on or off. If all the values are on, the total possible is 255.

Another way of conveying this is as follows: *Power of 128 to 1, power of 64 to 2, power of 32 to 3, power of 16 to 4, power of 8 to 5, power of 4 to 6, power of 2 to 2, power of 1 to 1.*

Binary number example: **01000110**.

Since we have 8 bits in a byte, we must look at which is turned on and which is off. We can then add those bits to get the decimal conversion (remember—we are counting from right to left).

- First bit in the example is 0=off and is not counted.
- Second bit in the example is 1 and is on. The second bit represents a value of 2.
- Third bit in the example is 1 and is on. The second bit represents a value of 4.
- Fourth bit is 0=off, no value and is not counted.
- Fifth bit is 0=off, no value and is not counted.
- Sixth bit is 0=off, no value and is not counted.
- Seventh bit is 1 and is on. The seventh bit represents a value of 64.
- Eighth bit is 0=off and is not counted.

What is our total? 2+4+64=70.

The top part of Fig. 14.1 is an example of our 8 bits (in a byte) being turned on (1). The possible decimal number when these bits are added is **255**. The bottom part in Fig. 14.1 shows our 8 bits either off (0) or on (1). Adding the appropriate bit value provides us with a decimal total of **89**.

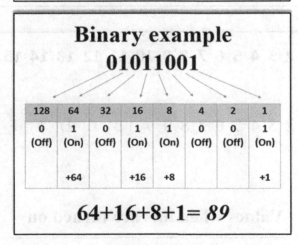

Figure 14.1

Example of all 8 bits in a byte being turned on and converted to decimal 255, and another example of some bits off and on in a byte configuration totaling 89.

As previously mentioned, binary numbers can represent letters and characters. This chapter will not cover all the ASCII values for every letter and character; however, the examiner must be aware that binary values are converted (encoded). For example, for word *F U N* (upper letters), we take the letters and an ASCII table to determine the binary numbers for each uppercase letter. On our companion site, Fig. 14.4 shows the binary value for upper and lower values of the entire alphabet along with the binary values for our word F U N.

Hexadecimal

Four (4) binary digits represent a hexadecimal. These four binary digits are known as a "nibble." Two nibbles equal a byte. This equates to eight binary digits. The two nibbles are used to represent 1 byte—using digits or characters. There is a maximum numeric value of 15 for each nibble if all bits have been turned on. When values are used in a nibble, which are over 9, a letter will be used. The top part of Fig. 14.2 shows the breakdown of each nibble. The bottom part of Fig. 14.2 depicts the values when all bits are turned on.

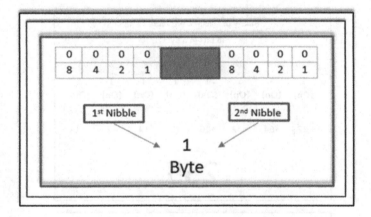

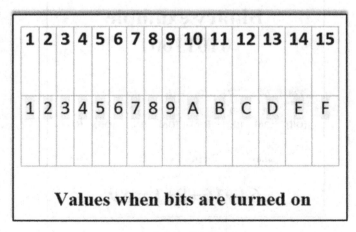

Figure 14.2
Nibble example with hexadecimal example.

If we used the word **BYTE**, we can take the first letter and show the example of the binary to decimal, then show the hexadecimal. The letter B would be 42, Y would be 59, T would be 54, and E would be 45. On the companion site, Fig. 14.5 depicts the first and second nibble breakdown of the uppercase letter B to the number 42.

The word (in uppercase) **BYTE** would show within the file system of the supported phone after encoding as **42 59 54 45**. Examiners can utilize numerous online resources to assist with ASCII to hex or decimal conversions. A few websites are listed below:

- http://www.asciitable.com/
- http://www.acii-code.com/
- http://ascii.cl/
- http://www.rapidtables.com/code/text/ascii-table.htm

ASCII

Earlier in this chapter, the definition of ASCII was provided. This was derived from telegraphic codes using 7 bits for the character and then the eighth bit for parity. ASCII tables can reflect all 256 codes (0–255). There will be 95 printable codes. There are 52 US English codes with 26 lowercase and 26 uppercase. The remaining codes represent codes from the decimal 128 decimal values. This is commonly referred to as the extended table. The most common table is the ISO 8859-1, which is also called the ISO Latin-1.

Using a free tool called **HEXwrite**, a sample of hexadecimal (hex) is converted to ASCII. By using the *Mode* setting, HEXwrite can also convert ASCII back to hex. Users must provide a space between each value when using HEXwrite.

Unicode

Languages other than English were limited to the 256 codes of ASCII. They could not fit into this limited space and developers created Unicode. This creates a two-byte number for every character, no matter what language is used. Using 16 bits (2 bytes), 65,536 characters can be defined, whereas 256 were possible with 8 bits (1 byte). The English language can fit into the ASCII space (256 characters) and only needs padding between hex values of 00 in Unicode. Fig. 12.2 shows an example at the top of HEXwrite in use, with the Mode being switched between ASCII to Hex and Hex to ASCII. At the bottom of Fig. 14.3 is an example of HEXwrite decoding Unicode data. Note: Examiners would need to use the space bar between the hexadecimal values.

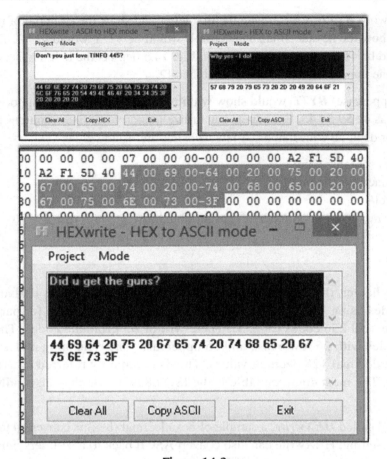

Figure 14.3
HEXwrite ASCII to hex, hex to ASCII, and Unicode decoded values.

Big Endian/Little Endian Formats

Big Endian (BE) and Little Endian (LE) are additional formats that correspond to how data can be stored. Both relate to how specified bytes are most significant in their order. Big Endian refers to the most significant byte being first, whereas Little Endian refers to the least significant byte being first. Both are read from left to right. This also holds true for Unicode.

Nibble Reversed

Mobile devices may store information in what is called *Nibble Reversed*. This means the data within the specified field is actually reversed. On mobile phones, it is not uncommon for the year of the entry to be just part of the year, and reversed. For example, if a date of SMS was 2012, the value for the year would be reversed and represented as 21. Fig. 14.4 shows, at the top, examples of Big and Little Endian. The bottom of Fig. 14.4 depicts a Nibble Reversed date and time stamp from a Samsung GSM phone.

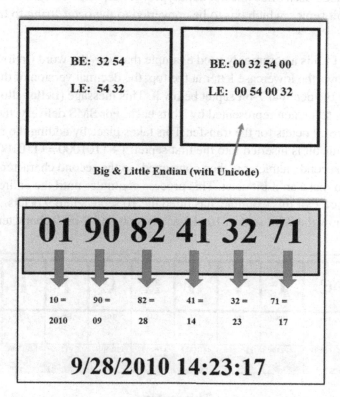

Figure 14.4

Big and Little Endian (with Unicode) examples and Reverse Nibble date and time stamp example.

7-Bit SMS PDU

Short Message Service Protocol Data Unit (SMS PDU) is a message feature that uses 7 bits per character compared to the 8 bits per character of traditional messaging. This efficiency allows 160 characters to fit into 140 bytes. This allows wireless carriers to save space using this encoding when transmitting SMS. PDU can also be referred to as packet data unit. When an SMS message is sent from one user to another, a series of sequences take place during the transmission and delivery. On the companion site, Fig. 14.6 shows the SMS transmission steps. The left side of Fig. 14.6 represents the SMS delivery. The Short Message Service Center serves as the area that delivers, converts, stores, and forwards the message(s).

7-Bit SMS Encoding and Decoding

When an SMS message is sent, encoding and decoding must take place. PDU may be used in some cases. PDU mode uses three special data types: Octet, semi-octet, and septet. 7-bit GSM PDU uses 7-bit septet, which has to be converted to the octet string to transfer through the network.

The top part of Fig. 14.5 is a commonly used example that uses the word (in lowercase) "hello-hello." The table shows the lowercase letter at the top, the decimal version of the letter in the middle, followed by the decimal 7-bit septet below it. This message (**hellohello**) consists of 10 characters, called septets when represented by 7 bits each. For SMS delivery, these septets need to be converted into 8 bit octets for the transfer. This takes place by adding the rightmost bit of the second septet. This bit is inserted into the first septet. $1 + 1101000 = 11101000$ (E8). The rightmost bit of the second character is then consumed, so the second character needs 2 bits of the third character to make an 8-bit octet. This process continues until the entire string is complete and in the case of this example, has fitted the 10 septets into 9 octets. The bottom part of Fig. 14.5 shows how the 7-bit septets 10 characters start and 8-bit 9 characters end.

h	e	l	l	o	h	e	l	l	o
104	101	108	108	111	104	101	108	108	111
1101000	1100101	1101100	1101100	1101111	1101000	1100101	1101100	1101100	1101111

7 bit septets

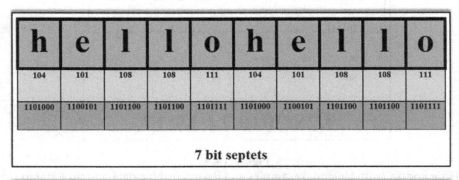

7 bit septets 10 character example start

1101000	1100101	1101100	1101100	1101111	1101000	1100101	1101100	1101100	1101111

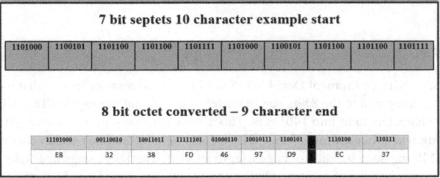

8 bit octet converted – 9 character end

11101000	00110010	10011011	11111101	01000110	10010111	1100101	1110100	110111
E8	32	38	FD	46	97	D9	EC	37

Figure 14.5
7-bit septets 10 character (top), 7-bit 10-character start with 8-bit 9-character ending.

This type of data may be present on certain phones. When it is in the encoded state and examiners are looking at messages in a hexadecimal viewer it will not be readable. This is important to understand, as a particular artifact may not be located using ASCII searches or other types of inquiries.

SMS PDU Encoding Example

Here is an example of SMS PDU encoding on a message of *"Where did you bury the body?"*

00110000910000FF1C5774595E0691D36450FE5D0789EBF23C888E2E83C46F72FE07

There are a number of free programs and online sites that can assist with PDU strings. Be aware that not all PDU is in a 7-bit format. One online site that uses a Javascript PDU converter allows the user to select the alphabet size as 7, 8, or 16. A few links to sites that can assist in decoding 7-bit SMS PDU are listed below:

- http://www.diafaan.com/sms-tutorials/gsm-modem-tutorial/online-sms-pdu-decoder/
- http://rednaxela.net/pdu.php
- http://www.smartposition.nl/resources/sms_pdu.html#PDU_CONVERTER

Chapter Summary Key Points

Mobile devices have for several years utilized two main types of flash memory—NOR and NAND. Currently, variations to NAND are the most popular. UFS, 3D NAND are currently being employed to optimize user's high storage capacities and faster read and write speeds. Some vendors will utilize an MCP or POP, which efficiently uses the processor and RAM or ROM within the same area, allowing these components to be embedded on the same chip or affixed to the top. The basic principle behind NAND memory remains the same, with NAND blocks having pages and a spare area. The page size will correspond with how much spare area is available, typically 512, 2048, or 4096 bytes in size.

Reading and writing to NAND takes place a page at a time and are organized into blocks. Values can only be changed from 1 to 0, not 0 to 1. A page within a block and the single cell (1 or 0) cannot be erased on its own, the entire block must be erased.

Flash memory is developed in such a way to allow the entire area to degrade evenly. This is referred to as *wear leveling*. The FTL prevents repeated writes to the same memory location. Data cannot be written to areas in flash until the section is cleaned. This process sets the area to 1's. This is called *garbage collection*.

The types of encoding that may be located on mobile devices are binary, hexadecimal, nibble, ASCII, Unicode, Big and Little Endian, Nibble Reverse, and 7-bit GSM PDU.

In this chapter, we exposed the reader to the various types of flash memory where data may reside. The physical pull will create such data, and automated tools will generally do a good job of decoding and parsing information. If an examiner takes the time to look at what type of encoding was decoded, they in turn can begin looking for values that the tools missed. There are very popular tools on the market that cost over $10K to purchase, with a yearly mainte- nance fee of $3000 or higher. The tool is only locating what it is programmed to find. This encoding needs to be in a "friendly" format, and not missing parts of the data. When users delete things, these values may not look so "pretty" to the forensic tools used in locating them. By using the known values that were decoded, we can begin to find other values missed by the tools. Why would values be missed? Wear leveling, garbage collection, and how SQLite databases work would be our first answer. Now that we know where it is stored and the format it may be stored in, our upcoming chapters reveal how to decode *the encoding* even further.

References

[1] Flash25Toshiba, Toshiba Timeline, September 18, 2016. http://www.flash25.toshiba.com/downloads/toshiba-timeline.pdf.
[2] Toshiba Flash Memory, Flash Memory Catalog - PDF, March 2016. http://toshiba.semicon-storage.com/us/product/memory/nand-flash.html.

CHAPTER 15

Date and Time Stamps

Information in This Chapter

- Epoch
- GMT
- UTC
- Integer
- Formats
- UNIX
- UNIX 48 bit
- UNIX decimal
- Binary coded decimal
- GSM
- Windows 64 bit
- OLE automation
- MSDOS
- BitDate
- Filetime/HTML Filetime
- AOL/GPS
- ISO 8601
- Fortran
- HFS
- Apple
- Safari plist
- Google Chrome
- Mozilla Firefox
- BlackBerry/JAVA
- Nibble Reversed (Reverse Nibble)
- Multiple format

Introduction "In the Beginning..."

There are many of us who may have or continue to have various religious beliefs or a general understanding of theology. Some may follow their own choice of publication references that address the creation of man. Regardless of your personal religious belief, or in some cases, no belief at all, there is still a starting period in history when it comes to man's starting point here on earth. If we take away religious or Darwin point of views with regards to *how* mankind arrived, we all can agree that at some point there was a period when life started. Most of us have heard of the two main common labeling periods as before Christ (BC) and anno Domini (AD), which some refer to as "after death." There is also an age system that uses Stone, Bronze, and Iron age(s). Although it is somewhat of a leap between the creation of mankind and the creation of an electronic artifact, both have similarities that began with a specific date and time. The good news is that the dates and times found in their digital encoded state will not rely on where you stand with religion—they depend entirely on math.

Using a creation period that is derived from using a precise starting day, month, year, and time (and seconds), we can decode a creation period on digital evidence. Unlike computers that have a general set of dates, mobile devices can vary with their dates and in many cases have more than one format within their specific file system. Because mobile phones also share and exchange data between more than one device, dates from other file systems can end up on systems that normally would not have such a format.

Some of you may also recall the Millennium scare. This was the 1999 date that was supposedly going to cause problems with computers who were not designed to count to 2000 or beyond. Many projected that once the computer advanced to the year 2000, chaos would ensue. The issue was referred to by a few different names—*Y2K, Y2K bug*, and *Millennium bug*. One of the basic problems was that within the programming, the 2000 date would read as 1900. Early programmers realized they could save space by dropping the 19 from the year. The other problem had to do with the leap year, again, a counting problem. This was one period in time when people who had little to no regard to programming took notice on this interesting problem. The good news is that like our theologian reference to time, the Y2K issue is also just a reference but brought up because most of us probably remember that particular computer date as being a potential catastrophic issue. Unless we deal with manually decoding dates and times, we may give much thought to computer dates and times since the Y2K issue. In the following pages we will expand on date and time stamps. They all have specific rules they follow, with origins of when things began and how they record their own format. Mankind has used various ways to record time. With electronic devices it has been pretty straightforward and will rely on how many bytes make up a particular date and time. For examples that we reference in this chapter, we used online (free) epoch decoders, BlackBag Technologies Epoch Converter, Cellebrite Physical Analyzer, and DCode as various tools for decoding.

So, to close our introduction to this chapter and begin addressing date and time stamps, let us start out by saying; *"In the beginning, man created a cell phone."*

Epoch, GMT, and UTC

The word "epoch" pertains to a specific period or origin. A specific designated *period* is used as the reference point by which a particular time in question is measured. It is often used in astronomy and geology. For cell phone forensic examiners, this *origin* plays a role on how a particular series of bits of information may be interpreted. It establishes the starting origin by counting from that point. The way the counting is conducted can vary. Some readers may be asking as to why computers just do not utilize a date, but instead rely on an epoch. The answer is math. Periods of time can be converted to a number. We all know a minute equates to 60 s. One day is 86,400 s and a week is 604,800 s. By using numbers as time and converting to an epoch, this can then be subtracted from another epoch to obtain a needed value. Most of the computer programming–related epochs will use an exact date and apply specific intervals such as milliseconds, seconds, minutes, etc. For example, UNIX dates typically originated in seconds starting since January 1, 1970. This means time that elapsed (in seconds) after January 1, 1970, at 00:00:00 GMT (Greenwich Mean Time). Simply stated, mobile device times can have epoch dates that have origins that differ from 1970, or are a specific derivative format of 1970. Because of this, the decoding of a set number of bits will have different outcomes based on the number used, and the intervals used from the date it was counted.

Many people believe that epoch (with regard to time formats) only has the definition that comes from the origin of the UNIX time (1/1/1970). In fact, UNIX time uses the name "epoch time" as another way of describing itself. This must be clarified as some decoding tools used to interpret mobile dates and times use different epoch dates that are not starting at 1/1/1970. We will try to address in this chapter the various names that may be given to time formats.

Some tools can allow the examiner to choose possible epoch periods and thus affect how the selected string gets interpreted (counted). To complicate this, the same series of bytes can have more than one interpreted date and time that may appear to be valid. We will also explain this in further detail, but for now we must define *GMT*, *UTC*, and *integer* as how it relates to our date and time formats.

GMT and UTC

GMT stands for Greenwich Mean Time. Several years ago it was also called Zulu time. GMT in some countries is still the official time zone. It is the mean solar time at the Royal Observatory in Greenwich, London. GMT was replaced by Coordinated Universal Time (UTC). UTC is a time standard, not necessarily a time zone. Both are time formats and have been accepted as meaning the same thing. There are some differences in their definitions, however. UTC adds leap seconds to address the earth's slowing rotation. Just like GMT, UTC ±00:00 would be a location in earth where a line is drawn vertically, which happens to cross Greenwich, London. It is also simply called UTC 0 or UTC zero. Similar to time zones, equally divided spacing around the globe is applied either east or west of this line, additional vertical lines are drawn, creating either a negative (−) or positive (+) correlation from the ±00:00 origin. These numbers are either ahead (+) or behind (−) by hours. The observation of daylight savings can also contribute to which UTC value is applied based on the time of year. For instance, on the west coast of the United States, UTC-7 or UTC-8 would be the correct negative time format that is applied depending on the time of year. When daylight savings is being observed, the time *zone* in America would reflect this. In the United States, from Hawaii to the east coast these would be Hawaii–Aleutian Daylight Time, Hawaii–Aleutian Standard Time, and Hawaii Standard Time followed by Alaska Daylight Time or Alaska Standard Time. Then Pacific Daylight Time (PDT) or Pacific Standard Time. Next is Mountain Daylight Time or Mountain Standard Time and finally Central Daylight Time or Central Standard Time, and Eastern Daylight Time or Eastern Standard Time. There are also US territories that are considered in the US time zones. These are Samoa Daylight Time or Samoa Standard Time and Chamorro Standard Time.

A final example of this would be to say that in Seattle, Washington, the local time is 12:59 p.m. PDT on Tuesday, October 11, 2016 or 12:59 p.m. UTC-7. If we jump 1 month ahead after Daylight Savings ends on November 6, 2016, the time would be 11:59 p.m. PST or UTC-8.

Since UTC has taken the place of GMT, many of the forensic tools will use the UTC format. In some cases, this will allow the examiner to set a specific value when it decodes known time formats. This means the final report can adjust for the correct UTC and in some cases even allow it to show the proper daylight savings adjustment if applicable. Some vendors will first read the original source and prompt the examiner if they want to adjust the UTC to the offset that they have discovered. In this chapter, having a good understanding of time zones and how it can affect a decoding tool is very important. Tools may not get all the artifacts. If examiners are manually carving for specific bytes that deal with a date, it becomes important to understand what type of format they are trying to decode. Some of the tools that will be mentioned in this and the upcoming chapters allow the user to sweep or input specific bits or bytes, then select the desired UTC to be applied. Obviously, if the incident took place in a specific geographical location, and that value is known at the time of interpretation, then correct decoding can take place. So we have addressed the epoch, UTC, GMT, and time zones. Let us continue on and explain briefly why it may be important for examiners to also have knowledge of how many integers are used in a specific time format.

Integers

When we are dealing with the decoding of potential artifacts that are believed to be date and time stamps, it will become important to understand 8-, 16-, 24-, 32-, 48-, and 64-bit integers.

Webster defines the word integer as: "*Mathematics: any number that is not a fraction or a decimal: any whole number or its negative*" [1].

If we then understand that dates and times could utilize 8, 16, 24, 32, 48, or 64 bits, we can convert this to bytes and know how many are used for a particular format. There will be times when the file system will use digits in one place and a series of bytes in another area. In reality the date is the same, but the decoding process from the tool being used is allowing the examiner to see the same artifact the same way.

As per the previous chapter that explained encoding, 1 byte = 8 bits, 2 bytes = 16 bits, 3 bytes = 24 bits, and so on. Simple multiplication of the bytes by 8. This converts to 1-, 2-, 3-, 4-, 6-, and 8-byte date and time stamps. Realize, however, that not all of the time stamps follow these integer rules. To understand this, we address several different types of date and time formats. You may or may not encounter each and every one of these during your work as a forensic examiner. There will be specific formats that seem to be used more than others. In the world of mobile phones, some may even have two, three, or more different formats within their file system—all using different integers!

Formats

This section of this chapter contains a number of possible date formats. Some can be based on an origin of the target they were designed for such as an OS, File Allocation Table, chipset manufacturers, and many other sources. This chapter will include a few examples of the actual formats as they were located within the file system.

UNIX

Many people refer to the UNIX date and time as the *C Time*, *C Date*, or *Epoch Time*. It is also called UNIX time and POSIX (Portable Operating System Interface) time. The description within C programming language would be "time_t" (without quotes). Thus, the name C Time or C Date. UNIX date formats are commonly found on computers and mobile devices. It will utilize a 32-bit integer and records the number of seconds from UTC midnight since the date of January 1, 1970. UNIX dates can be decoded based on Big and Little Endian configurations. An interesting note about the 32-bit UNIX date is that it can present a problem on January 19, 2038. Just like the Y2K issue, it is referred to as the Y2038 problem. The letter "Y" signifies year. After this 2038 date, the numbers will wrap around and be stored as a negative number. At the top of Fig. 15.1 is a screenshot from a portion of SMS from an older

LG flip phone. Using UNIX Little Endian, these 4 bytes (32 bits) convert to 3/24/2002 11:15:04 (UTC+0) using the January 1, 1970 epoch. While this value decoded correctly for this series of bytes, it is in fact not the correct date for this particular SMS message. We will revisit examples just like this one when we address other date formats that can utilize the same bytes but apply a different epoch referenced date.

UNIX 48 Bit

When looking at Android devices that contain date and time stamps, examiners will notice a string of 6 bytes that commonly utilizes the 48-bit UNIX date. As the name signifies, this date uses a 48-bit integer. The epoch is still January 1, 1970, but it records from that date in milliseconds. Fig. 15.1 also contains a file system pulled from a Motorola MB810 (Android) phone. At the bottom of Fig. 15.1 is a screenshot from a segment of 844 SMS messages that were decoded. The highlighted string of 6 bytes, with a value of UTC-7 applied would decode using the epoch of January 1, 1970 as 3/30/2013 3:24:41 a.m.

```
00 00 00 00 02 00 00 00   00 00 00 00 66 BB 06 3A
66 BB 06 3A 42 6F 6E 6A   6F 75 72 0A 62 65 72 74
72 61 6E 64 20 65 6E 71   75 65 74 65 75 72 20 61
70 70 65 6C 65 72 20 6D   6F 69 20 35 31 34 35 36
```

UNIX date example (32 bits)

```
34 33 01 3D BA D3 E3 BA   01 00 FF 02 53 68 65 6E   43 =°Óã°   ÿ Shen
20 6E 65 76 65 72 20 63   61 6C 6C 65 64 20 69 6D   never called im
2E 73 75 72 65 20 73 68   65 20 70 61 73 73 65 64   .sure she passed
20 6F 75 74 FF 00 00 01   01 3D BA D3 E3 E3 00 6C   outÿ   =°Óãã 1
```

UNIX date example (48 bits)

Figure 15.1
UNIX 32- and 48-bit date examples.

UNIX Decimal 10 and 13 Digits

Using our previous definition for a 32-bit UNIX time, which still utilizes an epoch based on January 1, 1970, this date would be represented as 10 or 13 digits. If the string has 13 digits, this represents a decoded value showing milliseconds from our same starting date. This type of date is commonly found in SQLite databases, within the schema, under columns for the date records (Note: actual column may be called something else). It is not uncommon for these to then be converted (decoded) to the previous hexadecimal 6-byte string by various forensic tools. If we look at the database first, we can see the 10- or 13-digit UNIX date. Then, if we look at the decoded value in another part of the same file system, we will see the same date/time in a 6-byte hexadecimal configuration. Fig. 15.2 depicts the 13-digit UNIX decimal date in the SQLite schema and the same date showing as 6 bytes. Then, two digits are removed from the end of the 13-digit original date and converted. The bottom image in Fig. 15.2 shows the conversion on the entire (original) string of 13 digits. Removing three of the digits only removes the millisecond conversion when values are present. The above SMS example has all zeros, and thus no milliseconds were converted.

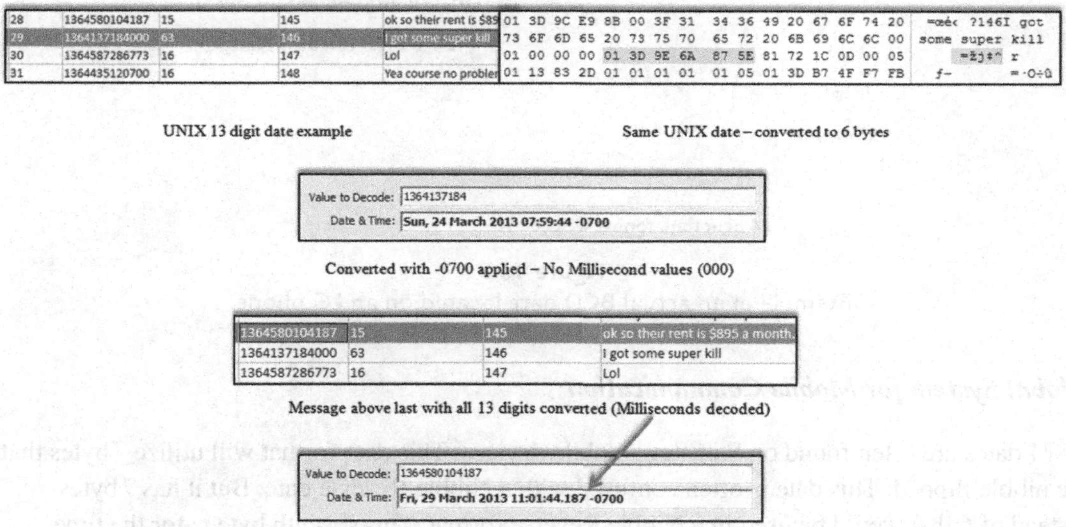

Figure 15.2
UNIX decimal 10- and 13-digit examples.

Binary Coded Decimal

This date can be found in many pay-as-you-go style devices that do not utilize a SQLite database. These styles of handsets would be commonly referred to as "nonsmartphones." Binary coded decimal (BCD) dates utilize 6 bytes to indicate the entire date string along with seconds. This date does not need specialized equipment to convert the date; however, the examiner must have baseline knowledge that the 6 bytes in question represent the date. This may or may not be difficult to see. For example, bytes represented as 14 03 23 19 36 02 with an SMS message that is viewed in hexadecimal view, may not have significant meaning. This series would be interpreted as a BCD date: 14 = year of 2014; 03 = month; 23 = day; 19 = 19th hour of the day or 7 p.m.; 36 = minutes; 02 = seconds;

decoded as 3/23/2014 7:36:02 p.m. Fig. 15.3 depicts an example of a BCD date (high-lighted), which was located on the second offset of the .dat file. Also noteworthy within this file are two other dates we will discuss in this chapter.

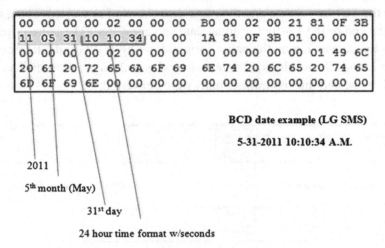

BCD date example (LG SMS)

5-31-2011 10:10:34 A.M.

2011

5th month (May)

31st day

24 hour time format w/seconds

Figure 15.3
Example of an actual BCD date located on an LG phone.

Global System for Mobile Communication

GSM dates are often found on Samsung mobile devices. This date format will utilize 7 bytes that are nibble flipped. This date is often confused with a Nibble Reverse date. But it has 7 bytes instead of 6 that would be used in a Nibble Reverse format. This seventh byte is for the time zone. It is oftentimes given the value of FF when the time zone is not applied. The time zone byte utilizes a 15-min period interval between the device local time and GMT. Here is an example of a GSM string in bytes and then broken down. This phone is a Samsung nonsmartphone. This extracted date was given a value of FF for the time zone. Applying FF instead of an actual value can be caused by a number of reasons and is not uncommon. The important thing to understand is that the 6 bytes of the 7-byte string are what matter: 7-byte located: *80 60 21 41 00 02 FF*.

These values would be nibble flipped back as follows: 08 = 2008 (year), 60 = 06 (month), 21 = 12 (day), 41 = 14 (hour), 00 = 00 (minutes), 02 = 20 (seconds), FF = time zone value (no value applied). Decoded as 6/12/2008 2:00:20 p.m. This date may have bytes within the string that are showing in hexadecimal format. The hexadecimal values would be flipped and then converted to the decimal value. For instance, if our second byte showed as C1, this would be flipped to 1C then converted to the decimal value of 28. Fig. 15.4 is from a Samsung flip phone. This shows a GSM date with the time zone byte in place. This can be decoded, however, without this value applied.

```
0A 81 35 06 95 10 83 FF   FF FF FF FF 00 11 90 20
60 41 23 02 F7 23 C8 32   9B FD 06 E5 DF 75 10 BB
6C A6 83 F2 EF BA 1C 14   5E 83 C2 74 10 1D 5D 06
C1 C3 72 7A 1E 00 00 00   00 00 00 00 00 00 00 00
```

GSM date example from an older Samsung flip phone

2-6-2009 2:32:20 PM

Converts as:

90 = 2009

20 = 2nd month

60 = 6 / 6th day of month

41 = 1400 hour (2 PM)

23 = 32 minutes

02 = 20 seconds

F7 = 7F converted is 127 (affecting time zone)

Figure 15.4
GSM date decoded from a Samsung flip phone.

There are also certain Nokia phones which utilize a similar GSM date. The year, however, will utilize 2 bytes and will be in Big or Little Endian format, and there will be no time zone byte. All other bytes (month, day, hour, minutes, and seconds) will be nibble flipped. 2 bytes for year + 1 byte for month + 1 bytes for day + 1 byte for hour + 1 byte for minute + 1 byte for seconds = 7 bytes.

Windows 64 Bit

This date format has an epoch of 12:00 a.m. January 1, 1601. The New Technology File System Master File Table is where this date is typically located. It uses 100 ns intervals from the 1601 date. The 8 bytes that would compose this date could also have a starting value that utilizes Big or Little Endian. Microsoft sometimes refers to this date as a *file time*. The string will not be affected by specific time zones or if daylight savings is in effect. It uses UTC (zero).

OLE Automation

An OLE automation date would typically be located in Windows applications, particularly the script language. There are several languages, which support automation such as C, C++, C#,

Java, Perl, and Python just to list a few. Programs that were developed using one or more of these languages may contain an OLE automation date. This date format definition was obtained directly from the Microsoft Development Network:

> *An OLE Automation date is implemented as a floating-point number whose integral component is the number of days before or after midnight, 30 December 1899, and whose fractional component represents the time on that day divided by 24. For example, midnight, 31 December 1899 is represented by 1.0; 6 A.M., 1 January 1900 is represented by 2.25; midnight, 29 December 1899 is represented by -1.0; and 6 A.M., 29 December 1899 is represented by -1.25.*

> *The base OLE Automation Date is midnight, 30 December 1899. The minimum OLE Automation date is midnight, 1 January 0100. The maximum OLE Automation Date is the same as DateTime. MaxValue, the last moment of 31 December 9999.*

> *The ToOADate method throws an OverflowException if the current instance represents a date that is later than MinValue and earlier than midnight on January 1, 0100. However, if the value of the current instance is MinValue, the method returns 0 [2].*

MSDOS (32 and 16 Bit)

Microsoft DOS and Windows File Allocation Table would utilize this 32-bit/4-byte date. What is unique to each bit is that particular parts identify the seconds, minutes, hours, days, month, and year and will have encoding for specific bits from the 32-bit time stamp. It scales at 2 s on each format. The bits would be represented as follows:

Bits 31–25 = Year
Bits 24–21 = Month
Bits 20–16 = Day
Bits 15–11 = Hour
Bits 10–5 = Minutes
Bits 4–0 = Seconds with 2 s divided by 2.

The 16-bit MSDOS records the file date as follows: Bits 0–4 signify the day of the month 1–31. Bits 5–8 signify the month. Bits 9–15 the year offset from 1980, which means if an examiner adds 1980 to this value they will have a total which equals the correct year. The 16-bit MSDOS time uses 0–4 bits for the seconds, which are divided by 2. Bits 5–10 are the minutes 0–59. Bits 11–15 represent the hours on a 24-h clock.

BitDate (Model Specific)

This date format is very similar to how the MSDOS date uses its 32-bit integer. The BitDate format, however, does not record seconds. Bits 32–20 represent the year. Bits

19–16 represent the month. Bits 15–11 represent the day. Bits 10–6 represent the hour. Bits 5–0 represent the minutes. This format can be found on specific model LG and Samsung phones.

Filetime and HTML Filetime

The other name that is used for Filetime is *File Time Formatted* or *Formatted Filetime*. This is a 32-bit integer that resides next to another 32-bit integer. It uses 100 ns since January 1, 1601. These two integers are separated by colons or periods in some cases. For example, the date of August 13, 2007 00:13:40 UTC 0 would be *CD4E55C3:01C7DD3E*.

HTML Filetime, or Filetime HTML, would utilize the same 100 ns January 1, 1601 epoch, and the 32-bit integer would be next to another 32-bit integer, separated with a colon or period. The difference between the Filetime and the HTML Filetime is the values from each integer are swapped in the HTML version.

AOL and GPS

The AOL date uses a 32-bit integer date that has an epoch using the number of seconds since January 1, 1980. This can be confused with a standard 32-bit integer UNIX date and even more confusion can be caused by interpreting the value with an epoch of seconds since January 6, 1980. This date is used for GPS dates. Let us go back to our example depicted in Fig. 15.3. That example decoded a BCD date. There are two other dates within this example. On the far right of the first offset, are the bytes of **21810F3B**. If we take the same bytes and apply our AOL-based January 1, 1980 epoch, we decode these bytes as 5/26/2011 10:10:41. If we applied the GPS epoch of January 6, 1980, the day of the month increases by 5 days to 5/31/2011 10:10:41. AOL and GPS dates are very common dates that can be located on many different model cellular phones. Because a day of the month can be decoded so close to one another, it is important that the examiner validates what date would apply. Validating what should be the baseline date can be accomplished through visual confirmation (GUI), secondary tools, looking at another parsed date and time, and using a CDR (Call Detail Record). Sometimes, the decoded secondary device also may assist (to or from phone). Fig. 15.3 also has an additional GPS/AOL date a few bytes after the BCD date. To provide more understanding, Fig. 15.5 shows (highlights) the 4 bytes from our previous example that can be decoded as AOL or GPS dates and times.

It is also interesting to note that the other systems utilize the January 6, 1980 epoch. These are *Qualcomm BREW* and *ATSC* 32-bit time stamps. January 1, 1980 epoch is also used by IBM BIOS, DOS, OS/2, FAT 12/16/32, and exFAT file systems.

```
00 00 00 00 02 00 00 00   B0 00 02 00  21 81 0F 3B
11 05 31 10 10 34 00 00   1A 81 0F 3B 01 00 00 00
00 00 00 00 02 00 00 00   00 00 00 00 00 01 49 6C
20 61 20 72 65 6A 6F 69   6E 74 20 6C 65 20 74 65
```

```
00 00 00 00 02 00 00 00   B0 00 02 00 21 81 0F 3B
11 05 31 10 10 34 00 00   1A 81 0F 3B 01 00 00 00
00 00 00 00 02 00 00 00   00 00 00 00 00 01 49 6C
```

Both highlighted values can be decoded as *AOL* (Epoch 1/1980)

Or

***GPS* (Epoch of 1/6/1980)**

Figure 15.5
Example of AOL and GPS dates.

ISO 8601

The ISO 8601 is easy to read as it is formatted in a year–month–day–hour–minutes–seconds in textual format. An example would be 2016:08:10: 19:22:05.

This type of format is often located in the EXIF metadata of media such as images and videos. It is commonly located on media created by Android devices. For instance, if the user created a video, the file named would actually contain this date format—example: 20160913_112813.mp4. The underscore separated the time down to seconds (9/13/2016 11:28:13 a.m.). The time is in a 24 h, two digit format.

Fortran

The Fortran date format will utilize a 32-bit integer that counts in *minutes* from January 1, 1970. UNIX uses seconds or milliseconds. When an examiner is interpreting the series of bytes that represents a Fortran date format, standard UNIX can decode it different as it is not applying minutes.

HFS

HFS was designed for the Macintosh file system. The time stamp uses the number of seconds since January 1, 1904 UTC 0. What may be of importance is that this does not equate to all products that may use HFS (or HFS+). Just like Windows, you may have already noticed that the OS of a particular device may have a particular date format, but the applications themselves reflect something different. Areas such as .plist files, previously mentioned SQLite databases, and EXIF metadata are examples. They may use an entirely different epoch.

Apple

There is no standard name that has been used for the file date that is typically located on many of the Apple mobile devices. iPhone, iPod, iPad, etc., will not all be based on an epoch from the HFS standard. Instead, many will utilize a 32-bit integer or in the cases of database schemas, they may utilize a 9-digit date that converts to the same format. This is similar to the 10- and 13-digit dates that equate to the 32-bit integer on Android phones. The difference here is that Apple uses an epoch of January 1, 2001, for Apple's Cocoa framework or January 1, 2000 for AppleSingle, AppleDouble, PostgreSQL, and ZigBee UTC times. Using a file system from a popular Apple iPhone, we look at an SMS message as it resides within the common sms.db container. Here, we locate the 9-digit decimal date which is depicted in the schema for this particular message about "cats" as *477988107*. This is found in the nonpartition rebuilt areas of the same .tar file as (hex) bytes *1C 7D 85 0B* representing the exact same SMS message. It can also be located as an ASCII value of *34 37 37 39 38 38 31 30 37*. Again, the ASCII type format would generally be found in a part of the file system that has not been rebuilt as a database.

Like the UNIX dates we previously explained, both the 32-bit integer and the 9-digit decimal date convert using a January 1, 2001 epoch as 2/24/2016 6:28:27 a.m. Examiners can easily convert the hexadecimal value to decimal with online converters.

Safari Plist

Property list files were developed by Apple and GNUstep. These are used to store sterilized objects. Plist files are commonly located during MAC and Apple acquisitions. Safari would utilize a date that relies on a referenced WebKit time stamp. These formats may have a 9-digit decimal between the date that would need to be decoded and another number located to the right after the decimal, which is not needed for the decoding.

Similar to the 32-bit integer date that was previously explained, this would use a January 1, 2001 UTC 0 epoch. Apple's Cocoa and WebKit would share this same epoch date. An example from the Cookies.plist for a created date would be 347160273.64099997282. 347160273 would be decoded using this epoch and would result in the date and time of 01/02/2012 01:24:33 UTC (0).

Google Chrome

Google Chrome uses an epoch of January 1, 1601 (UTC 0). This format would use 17 digits for the string that represents the date and time. Because it records down to the second, the last part of the integer will be six zeros, which are not needed by conversion tools and represent the decimal seconds.

Mozilla Firefox

Mozilla Firefox utilizes an epoch of January 1, 1970 (UTC 0). This format would use 16 digits for the string that represents the date and time. Just like the Google Chrome integer, the last six digits are not needed in the conversion, as they too represent decimal seconds.

BlackBerry/Java

There are at least three common areas (SMS/MMS/Call log) within BlackBerry file systems that will utilize a 64-bit integer (8 byte) date format. This format will use the number of milliseconds since January 1, 1970. There will be some of these dates that will need a particular byte order (Big Endian). The date is the same format as the 8-byte Java date. The calendar dates will utilize a 32-bit integer (4 bytes) format, with an epoch of January 1, 1900. The email will use a 2-byte date and 2-byte time value for both sent and received entries.

Nibble Reversed (48-Bit Integer)

In Chapter 14 we addressed Nibble Reversed artifacts that may be encountered on mobile devices. The computer language used to format Nibble Reverse artifacts is doing this because it needs the significant (or less significant) nibble in that order. The structure of this date string will be a 6-byte configuration that may look very similar to the BCD date. The bytes, however, are Nibble Reversed and begin with the year, followed by the month, day, hour, minutes, and last, seconds. Also supplied in Chapter 14 is an image example of a Samsung GSM phone. Here, we will simply supply the same numbers from that figure example:

6 bytes as read in the physical file structure: *01 90 82 41 32 71*.

01 = 10 = 2010 (year); 90 = 09 = (month); 82 = 28 (day); 41 = 14 (24 hour); 32 = 23 (minutes); 71 = 17 (seconds); 9/28/2010 14:23:17 or 2:23:17 p.m.

Multiple Formats

As we being to end this chapter, it is important to point out and clarify that it is not uncommon for devices to have different formats of dates within the file system. Most readers may think that this would usually apply to our "heavy-hitters"—the common operating systems from Apple, Android, and Windows devices that have higher capacities, use SQLite and .plist files and thus rely on the need for various epoch dates. This is simply not the case. This example is simple and does not cost much to replicate. We use BitPim and obtain the file system. We then use FTK Imager (also free) to view an SMS.dat file that represents an inbox message. This example is from an older phone, and the format is still being used on newer (nonsmart) style devices. The make and model is an LG VX8500 (Chocolate) which can be found in working condition on eBay for under $20. This one SMS message has three date and times. Two use 32-bit integers and the other uses 6 bytes. The date with the 6 bytes does not need any specialized epoch decoder to read it, and both are explained in this chapter. Take a look at Fig. 15.6. Can you see the three dates using these hints provided?

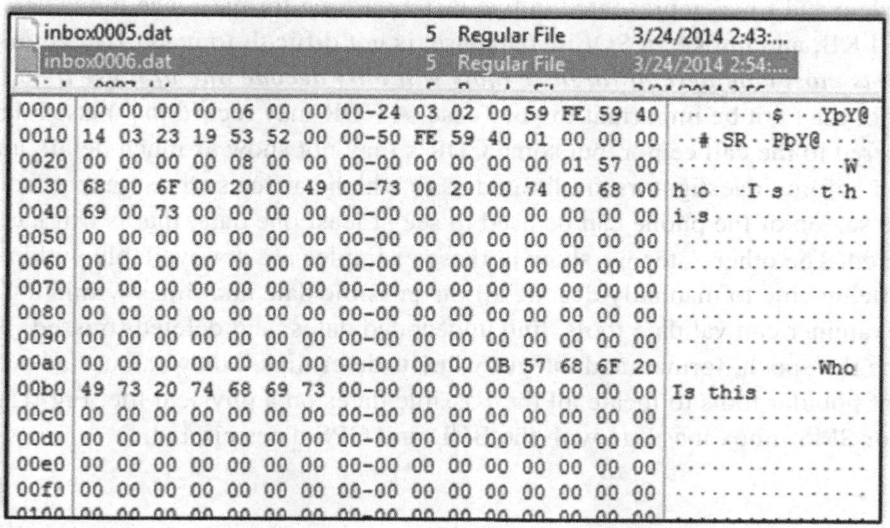

```
inbox0005.dat                    5    Regular File      3/24/2014 2:43:...
inbox0006.dat                    5    Regular File      3/24/2014 2:54:...

0000  00 00 00 00 06 00 00 00-24 03 02 00 59 FE 59 40   ·········$···YpY@
0010  14 03 23 19 53 52 00 00-50 FE 59 40 01 00 00 00   ··#·SR··PpY@····
0020  00 00 00 00 08 00 00 00-00 00 00 00 00 01 57 00   ··············W·
0030  68 00 6F 00 20 00 49 00-73 00 20 00 74 00 68 00   h·o· ·I·s· ·t·h·
0040  69 00 73 00 00 00 00 00-00 00 00 00 00 00 00 00   i·s·············
0050  00 00 00 00 00 00 00 00-00 00 00 00 00 00 00 00   ················
0060  00 00 00 00 00 00 00 00-00 00 00 00 00 00 00 00   ················
0070  00 00 00 00 00 00 00 00-00 00 00 00 00 00 00 00   ················
0080  00 00 00 00 00 00 00 00-00 00 00 00 00 00 00 00   ················
0090  00 00 00 00 00 00 00 00-00 00 00 00 00 00 00 00   ················
00a0  00 00 00 00 00 00 00 00-00 00 00 0B 57 68 6F 20   ···········Who
00b0  49 73 20 74 68 69 73 00-00 00 00 00 00 00 00 00   Is this·········
00c0  00 00 00 00 00 00 00 00-00 00 00 00 00 00 00 00   ················
00d0  00 00 00 00 00 00 00 00-00 00 00 00 00 00 00 00   ················
00e0  00 00 00 00 00 00 00 00-00 00 00 00 00 00 00 00   ················
00f0  00 00 00 00 00 00 00 00-00 00 00 00 00 00 00 00   ················
0100  00 00 00 00 00 00 00 00-00 00 00 00 00 00 00 00
```

Can you locate the 3 dates?

Figure 15.6
Inbox SMS.bit file showing different date formats.

Were you able to locate it? You should have been able to see the one date that does not need any tools to decode. It starts at the beginning of offset 0010 with the number (byte) 14. Does it help if you are told that the 14 is our year of 2014? This is the first byte for a BCD date: 14 03 23 19 53 52 or 3/23/2014 7:53:52 p.m. Now that we know this value, and we know that it was an inbox message, we have an idea what type of epoch would give us that date. Toward the end of our first offset, 4 bytes are showing as 59 FE 59 40. Because this is a 32-bit integer it could be decoded as UNIX, but that would provide an incorrect value as we are counting from 1/1/1970. (It does not manner if Big or Little Endian is used—it is still the wrong date using UNIX.) If we use an epoch of 1/6/1980 (GPS), we will get a decoded value using Little Endian of 3/23/2014 7:54 p.m. This is 1 min past our BCD date. Now on to the last date. Two bytes (depicted as 00 00) after our BCD date on offset 0010, we can see bytes 50 FE 59 40. Using our same GPS epoch, this decodes as 3/23/2014 7:53 p.m., which matches our BCD date and time. You may be asking why there are two different recorded dates showing the same minute and one showing as 1 min off. One time is the inbox time and one is the recorded time from the delivery. This means the sent/received by the call center 1 min apart. Even though this is an inbox message, we can still locate the time differences. These will not always be off, and on this same phone, other .dat SMS files show all three of these dates and times the same. What is important for this chapter is that in this simple .dat file we could clearly see three date and times represented in two different time formats. The file is very small, at just 4.71 KB, and unlike an SQLite database, is not difficult to read. *Also equally important is most commercial forensic tools will only decode one of these time formats!* This may or may not be important to your case. A CDR may record the missed date, as it was delivered to the call center, but some CDR's may not show as much detail, and as we mentioned before, investigators are limited as to which carrier's store content from an SMS. The screen of the phone can be used to see at least one date, that is if it has not been deleted. The other dates we show in these examples are not available within the GUI. By being able to manually decode all the possible date and times within a given file, the examiner can validate tools, find undecoded dates, and deleted (missed) ones as well. Once the epoch, format, and integer value is determined, they can use advanced features of popular tools to locate all the possible dates on a physical file. Fig. 15.7 depicts our SMS inbox message with the BCD and GPS dates circled.

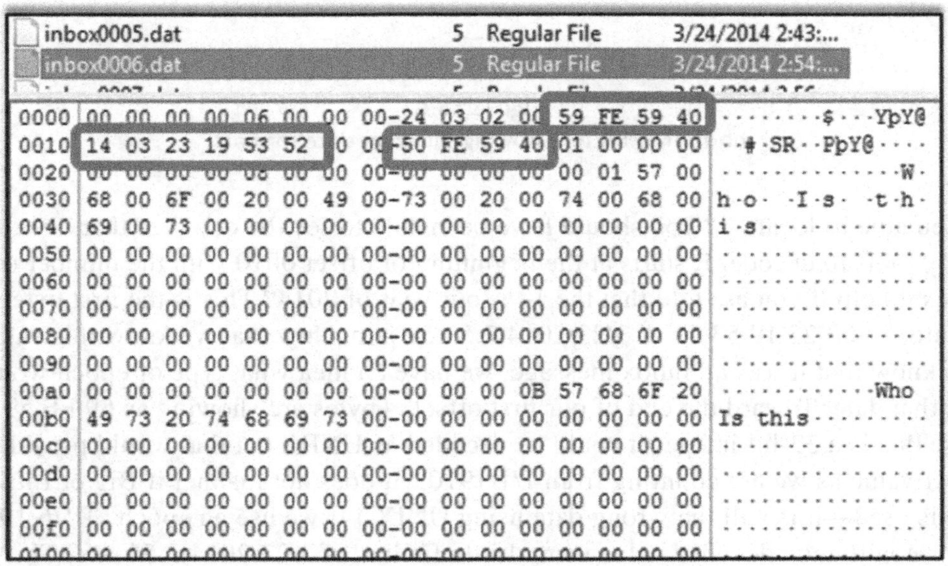

Figure 15.7
Inbox SMS.dat file with BCD and GPS dates located and circled.

Chapter Summary Key Points

This chapter does not address every date and time format that could possibly be found in the digital world. As we can see, there are many different ways in which a file system can store a date. The good news is that most forensic tools will rebuild the partitions, decode the values they support, and provide the examiner a way of at least understanding the *known* values on the mobile evidence. By using the *known* values, we can decode the *unknown* values that our tool may have missed. There are, of course, conditions that would need to be followed to allow us to see the format. Hex viewers certainly can assist, and just looking at a logical report will not allow insight into the date format. In most cases we will need a file system or physical exam.

Examiners must understand that it all begins with an origin—the epoch. This period of time will vary, and although there are names given to these formats such as AOL, GSM, GPS, BCD, BitDate, and so on, it really does not matter *what* it is named. What is important is that before decoding begins, the number of bytes needed is identified and the appropriate epoch is applied.

Also of equal importance in decoding the date is knowing which time zone to apply. In the United States, examiners must also understand if they are dealing with daylight savings. These settings alone have been a source of long arguments in court proceedings where counsel was attempting to convert artifacts in question. It is much easier to apply the correct zone when the report is being prepared, validate that it is a match, and not need to add or subtract during the judicial process.

When we are "looking" or "carving" strings of information that may be a date, it is important to know how many integers the particular format is using. Is the format being presented as a number of digits, such as is encountered in an SQLite database? What type of phone is it? Is the OS Android, Windows, Apple, or other? There may be times when we may know the OS, but the applications utilize a completely different epoch.

As an examiner looks at a date in a file system, they must understand that the manner in which they go about viewing the same bits and bytes can have a difference on their decoding. If, for instance, we were looking at the file system obtained from an Android *before* the partitions were decoded and rebuilt, the SMS would show in a hex viewer as a 48-bit integer, in a 6-byte configuration. If that same date was viewed after the supported partitions were rebuilt, and we looked at it within the database folder titled *com.android.providers.telephony > databases > mmssms.db*, the date would now reflect as a 13-digit number. Both values are in fact the same and will decode the same because of our epoch that is applied. Remember, not all applications will be parsed, but if an examiner can view the actual database, they can typically locate the values for their date. Depending on the OS, this will be a series of digits that just needs the appropriate epoch applied.

Finally, it will be very common to encounter more than one type of integer or series of bytes that correspond to a date. Simple phones that do not rely on iOS, Android, Windows, or other complex operating systems can be used to help illustrate this point. These types of phones will utilize a ".dat" file to record each individual SMS message. The folder within the file system will include draft, and in or out box. On our companion site, several screenshots from various file systems are listed as Figs. 15.1–15.5. Readers are encouraged to try and decode the values that are contained in each of these images. Hints are provided to help readers establish the various values based on the definitions supplied in this chapter. Online epoch converters, DCode, and other date and time decoders can be used.

References

[1] Merriam Webster, Merriam-webster.com, November 10, 2016.
[2] Microsoft Developer Network, System – DateTime Structure – DateTime Methods, 2016. https://msdn. microsoft.com/en-us/library/system.datetime.tooadate(v=vs.110).aspx.

CHAPTER 16

Manual Decoding MMS

Information in This Chapter

- SV Strike and Burner Breaker
- The Multimedia Message (MMS) container
- Carving attachments
- MMS containers (date and times)
- Keyword search (smil)
- Other MMS container examples
- MMS/SMS file signatures

Introduction—Lab Work

The author has a typical work day that consists of the following activities: Get up early, shower, eat, and commute to work. Go through a series of locked gates, up a flight of stairs, and finally enter a secured room with the glow of computers working on various cases.

Check the queue and the next case involves a simple, flip style phone from a robbery case. The case notes and search warrant explain that the owner may have taken pictures of stolen merchandise and sent it to friends and potential buyers. The case agent also requests to provide proof that the phone being examined was the device that created the images—as it was retrieved from the suspect's front pocket after a foot pursuit.

The model is checked against all the various tools it the forensic lab: Oxygen, Secure View, Final Data, Mobiledit, XRY, and Cellebrite. The phone is only supported logically, and some of the tools are able to obtain call details, SMS, images, and sound files. There is no tool that supports everything, and none of the tools support a physical exam. For this example, the lab does not support advanced forensic pulls through JTAG, ISP, or chip-off.

One of the tools supports the ability to obtain the file system. In the next few hours, the extraction of all the supported logical data and media takes place. It is also possible to manually manipulate the phone and see MMS messages that are related to the case. There are hundreds of them, and manual screen captures will take several days to complete. The good news is that the case agent is only looking for a specific time period. Within the output of the lab tools, it is not possible to locate any of the correspondence that was suspected by the case agent. The images, however, show potential stolen merchandise, but nothing that is mentioned within the affidavit of the search warrant. By manually opening up the file system and inspect some of the folders. Located is a folder that is labeled, "MMS." There is a file folder of potential interest. Inside it there is content that appears to be a message sent to, "Snoopy." The owner of this phone appears to have created, or received, a message that involves correspondence to this person. The content is regarding a shotgun. This happens to be mentioned in the warrant and was a unique weapon stolen in a burglary and used in the robbery.

Within the message is embedded hexadecimal content. It is difficult to locate a date and time of when it was sent or received, but it is possible to utilize the GUI to cross-reference.

Does any of this sound familiar? The vendors, who create tools that target law enforcement and corporate e-discovery, are microfocused on supporting the "big" models. Until recently, there were only a few companies that began to see the need to not only support the "burner" style phone, but also work on the ability to unlock the data port on unsupported phones.

Susteen—SV Strike and Burner Breaker

Later in this book, readers will be introduced to a few tools that work on bypassing the user-enabled security without destroying the device. This chapter is designed to show techniques to the reader with regards to MMS decoding. The first hurdle, however, can involve simply getting into the phone, or in the cases of cheap, pay-as-you-go phones, acquiring them. One company that has focused efforts in this area is Susteen. The following is directly from their website regarding their product that deals with user-enabled security:

> *The SV Strike is capable of acquiring 6 digit pincode/passcodes on the most popular phones including the new iPhone 6 and 6 plus. More than just a simple brute force "box." Created and built in the United States, this new technology gives the forensic investigator the go-to tool for breaking into iPhones and Androids. With easy to view videos and instructions, the SV Strike will replace foreign devices with questionable abilities. While hacker tools were able to break into certain phones, they were not built for law enforcement purposes. The SV Strike combined the need to access phones quickly, with need for accurate reporting features. Current phones supported include Android phones with USB OTG capability and iOS devices through 8.0. New features include pattern lock acquisitions for Android phones and advanced passcode setting to crack longer, more advanced passcodes. What sets the SV Strike apart from the competitors?*

- The only product of its kind to acquire pincodes/passcodes on both iPhones and Androids
- Forensically sound (not a simple hacker tool)
- Acquires Pincodes, Passcodes, Pattern Locks
- Uses advanced scripting to find the most commonly pincode/passcode/patterns
- Easy to use interface designed in the USA
- SV Strike uses USB cameras to store pictures of EVERY missed attempt and Final acquisition. This allows for better reporting and keeps the product forensically sound
- SV Strike has the ability to text or email the user once the software has finished its acquisition. This allows the user to simply set the software and go about other tasks.
- Built by Susteen Secure View with over 14 years of experience in mobile forensics
- Currently supports Android phones and iPhones. For "burner" and "throw-away" phones, please contact us for our new "Burner Breaker."
- Constant updates available [1]

The following information is also from Susteen, and this pertains to a tool they labeled, Burner Breaker:

THE BURNER BREAKER IS THE FIRST & ONLY PRODUCT OF ITS KIND!

BREAK INTO THOUSANDS OF "BURNER" PHONES! REOPEN COLD CASES! ACQUIRE NEW EVIDENCE TODAY! ALREADY HAVE MOBILE FORENSIC TOOLS?

Add the most advanced pincode/passcode/pattern breaking technology to your arsenal! Built in your forensic lab with onsite training. The Burner Breaker will revolutionize the mobile forensics industry. This hardware/software combination will allow law enforcement and government agencies easy access to thousands of locked phones.

Up until now, no company in the world has had the capability of breaking into "burner, pre-paid, throw-away" phones and non USB OTG Android phones. These phones can be categorized as pre-paid phones including smartphones that are non USB OTG compliant. Some examples include common Android phones found in Walmart, 7–11, Target and other distributors. Other examples would be phones found outside the US including Central and South America, Asia, Europe and most Chinese Chipset phones. In some cases, law enforcement agencies were able to use invasive JTAG dumps to get data off of locked phones. This will no longer be needed as a phones data can easily be accessed once the pincode, passcode, or patternlock has been acquired.

Due to "burner phones" having limited data port access (ie. TracFones), no pincode/ passcode breaking software was able to "talk" to the phone and break into it. This all changes with our Burner Breaker. Susteen now has the capability to break into almost any phone including Chinese Chipset phones and South American phones.

Susteen's Burner Breaker can access these phones by pinpointing the location of each number and manually pressing it. Our software can go through thousands of codes and allows access to these locked phones for the first time.

Susteen is leveraging our 18 years of cell phone expertise. Our database of thousands of phones allows us to easily program the Burner Breaker to meet each individual form factor. Every variation of screen size and phone width and height can create thousands of variations, but our engineers have created a hardware/software combination that can be easily adjusted, calibrated and improved [2].

Of course there are other vendors who have specialty tools that are designed around user-enabled bypassing, but Susteen was one of the first to market a product that targets the cheaper models. Some of you may be familiar with these devices, as you have had to take hundreds of mind numbing images to document the contents. To address our MMS content, the file system has to be obtained even though the MMS will not parse with any of our tools.

MMS Carving

Just as reminder, MMS are messages the user creates, which not only have content (similar to SMS) but also an attachment. There are three basic types of attachment, and the message can have one or all of these to qualify it as MMS.

- Video file
- Sound file
- Image file

Within the file system of the device, there will not be a standard labeling configuration when it comes to MMS storage. This will be up to the manufacturer and typically, the operating system. Since we are not addressing Windows, Android, iOS, or BlackBerry, the OS we will be dealing with is usually working off *BREW* (Binary Runtime Environment for Wireless). Smart phone style devices will house their SMS/MMS content within a application database (SQlite). These cheaper phones do not use that type of format. There will be three things that should be located when dealing with unsupported MMS. The first is the message itself. This may or may not have content. The user may have chosen not to send any comments associated with the attachment. The second is the attachment involved in the message. The last item is the date and time stamp, and "to"/"from" numbers. Understand that what we are looking for on "nonsmart" style phones will usually be in different locations, uncarved by the forensic tool we used. Let us start with some basic container information. Fig. 16.1 contains a file system from a simple flip phone. We are working with containers that are labeled MMS, SMS, and PIM. These are in different areas of the file system. Why are these important to us? SMS may provide the examiner with file signatures and phone numbers of common contacts, to include the owner of the phone. The MMS folder is obviously what we want to focus on, as our tool was unable to parse it. Last is the PIM folder. This may or may not be named "PIM" in your target file system. Whatever the name is on your evidence, the folder will contain some very useful information when dealing with MMS carving. In our example, the PIM folder has additional subfolders, one labeled "pbmyentry.dat." This can contain the phone number assigned to the target phone.

Some of you may be thinking that the GUI would show the assigned number. This may not always be the case, especially if the screen is damaged, and the phone still powers on and acquires. Also, you may have had the ability to chip-off this phone, and even though tools like Physical Analyzer (PA) were used to rebuild and parse the binary, it does not mean that PA decoded the MMS. This is very common.

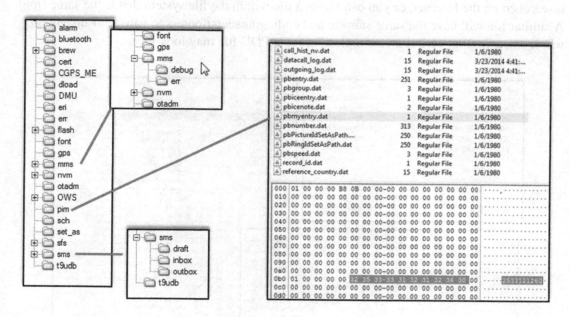

Identify folders that will help with MMS carving and the target number for the phone

Figure 16.1
Example of identifying folders with file system that will assist with MMS carving.

Within our PIM folder on this sample phone are other areas that can also assist with MMS carving. These can be the phone book entries (if your tool did not parse them). If the MMS uses a stored contact, it may be referenced within the container from one of these storage groups.

MMS or PDU

When a user created an MMS message on a "nonsmart" style phone, the phone file system will create an entry that will have a unique extension. Two common ones are MMS or PDU. Our next example shows the expansion of the "MMS" folder on this file system. The example has three files that end with the ".PDU" extension. This means that the user either sent, received, or had a combination of both types of MMS messages. In the example, the top message was clicked on with a hex viewer enabled. The information located with this .PDU file may have date and times, content, and an attachment embedded. This will need to be looked at carefully to see what was missed by the forensic tool. In the next example provided, we see information that shows a ".jpg" name, and a common header for the jpg file (FF D8). The data after this header are the information needed for the embedded image. The footer for this jpg is FF D9. If you are unfamiliar with headers and footers for files, they can easily be researched on the Internet, or you can locate a file within the file system that is the same (jpg). A similar file will have the same starting and ending headers/footers to gain your insight on where to carve. Fig. 16.2 is an example of what a .PDU file may look like.

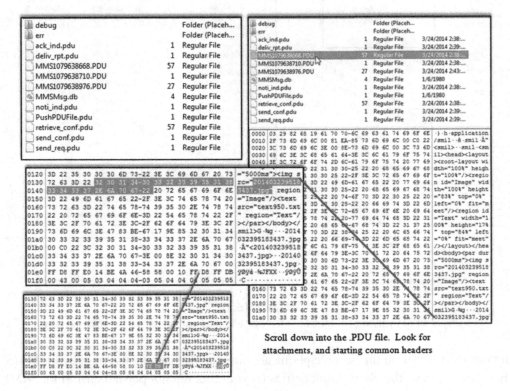

Figure 16.2

Example of opening a .PDU file and examining the potential attachments. This example shows a jpg embedded.

Search Techniques

In the example shown, we are using AccessData's FTK (Forensic Tool Kit) Imager. This program is free to use, and if we place our curser anywhere within the hex area of the .PDU file, we can select keys *Ctrl + F* to bring up the Find window. It is not uncommon for images on cellular phones to embed the thumbnail for the GUI in with the actual full size image. This means there can be two images within the information found in the .PDU file. We can search for both the headers and footers using this feature. Once all the searches have been exhausted, the FTK Imager will display a window that indicates, "String not found." Once we have the header and footer information, we can place our curser to the left of FF D8, hold down the Shift key, and locate the FF D9, and place the curser to the right of D9. This will highlight the entire area between these values. Once this is highlighted, right click, and select, "Save Selection." A window will present itself allowing you to save the data. It must be saved with the extension you are carving out—in this example, it is a .jpg extension. This is imperative that you save the file correctly. Depending on what type of file you are carving, it will not function correctly, or be viewable. Fig. 16.3 displays the Find feature and "String not found" window. Be aware of the direction being searched within the file when using this setting (up/down/wrap).

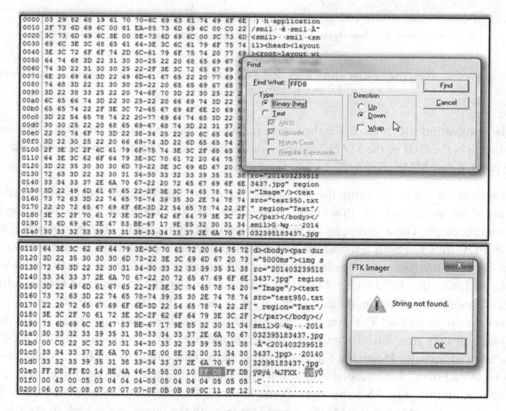

Figure 16.3

Example of using the Find tool within Forensic Tool Kit (FTK) to locate common headers and footers when embedded in the MMS files.

Fig. 16.4 depicts the saving of the highlighted area between the header and footer of this embedded .jpg file. In this example, we see only part of the overall file being highlighted; the remaining area could not be contained in a single image for the figure.

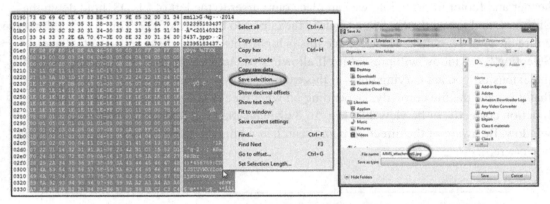

Save selection between your common header and footer. <u>Ensure you add the correct extension to whatever you name the file</u>.

Figure 16.4

Example of locating the header and footer and saving the contents with the appropriate naming configuration for the file.

On the companion site, Fig. 16.1 is the image that was embedded within this MMS message. The image is the GUI of the JTAG Manager for the RIFF box. Any guesses as to who may have created this MMS message?

We continue on with examining the .PDU file. Make sure that the files for the MMS are examined for more than one attachment. Remember, the user can embed more than one file into one message. These examples in this book are used by the author for instruction. One of the .PDU files has both a sound file and an image file embedded. How would you go about locating the sound file header and footer? The answer is to first look at the name of the extension in the .PDU string. Once this is found, look up the header (and footer) online for that sound file extension. Also, do not forget to look in the file system under other folders for the same file! The user may have used premade files from the OS to create the message. Or they may have forwarded a file from another user. Either way, there is a good possibility to actually locate the file in the file system. This can help establish where the file originated from. Just remember that not all files will originate with the target device you are examining. Fig. 16.5 shows an example of a .PDU file on this phone that has a .jpg and .mid file embedded in the MMS. It provides us with the name. If we look in the file system, these are easily located, and we can see the headers and footers to carve them out properly.

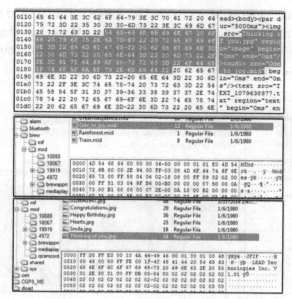

.PDU file inspection (different file then previous examples), shows the embedded .jpg and .mid files and their names. Examiners may be able to locate these files within other directories of the file system. This will reveal headers and footers for the files to allow manual carving. Even if the actual files are not found in the file system, similar types of files can be used to reference the footers and headers.

Figure 16.5

Example of an MMS file with a sound and image file embedded, which can be referenced in other parts of the file system for the header and footer information.

The .PDU file may also contain the message content. To save time, look at the top of the file first, and if it is not located there, scroll to the bottom of the file. It will usually be located after the "*.txt*" area. Remember, this rule does not apply to all phones, and message content in all cases does not necessarily follow the ".txt" extension. Ctrl+F can be used to search for *.txt*, just remember to enable the "Text" setting within the Find box. Also located at the bottom of the .PDU file is the associated number from the person who sent or received the text. Using the pim folder, we can search the databases to see if this person is listed as an entry or it is the assigned number for this phone.

Time and Date Containers

If we look at all the .PDU's used on this phone in our example, we can locate and carve out the attachments, locate the message contents, and in some cases locate at least one phone number at the bottom of the message. Where is our date and time located? Where are the "to" and "from" phone numbers? For that answer, we must locate a container that houses this information. For this model phone, the container is within the mms folder, and is labeled "MMSMsg.db." This is a very small database and is not in SQLite format. This file references all the .PDU messages that are stored on this phone. In our example, we have 3. The good news is that each .PDU MMS message has its own name, which can be used to separate each message within the database.

If we look at the first .PDU file, we see the name as MMS1079638668.PDU. This is used as the reference for the first entry. In our example, it is at the bottom of every MMS message, and the messages are separated with several offsets of zeros. See Fig. 16.6 for details, again, we are looking in the MMSMsg.db container.

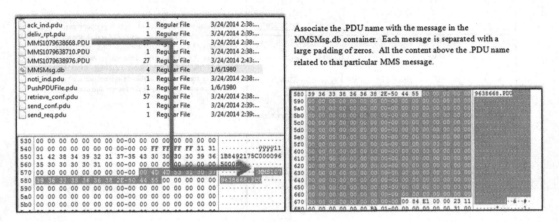

Figure 16.6
Example of where each PDU message ends and the padding that separated each message.

Once we locate the .PDU name, we scroll up from that area (again we are in the MMSMsg.db container), until we locate the numbers, date and times, and sometimes, content of the message. If it is the first message in the container, the top may be FF'ed out, like our example indicates. Here we will see phone numbers in Unicode. These can be reached from the pim container to determine who they belong to. In our example, we see an entry in this database that displays "Jb." Jb is a stored entry of a container from our pim file, which means this is a received message from Jb, to the handset. Again, examiners can use the GUI to confirm this, a CDR, or replicate this on a test phone. Just remember to check other folders in the file system for these entries. In this case, Jb was populated within the MMSMsg.db container because JB is stored as a contact. If the number was not stored as a contact, this area would be blank. Figs. 16.7 and 16.8 show the details on how the .PDU message is associated with the MMSMsg.db. It provides decoding of the entire message associated with our MMS message for MMS1079638668.PDU.

After the padding of zeros, the next PDU message is displayed, followed by the last one. Since there are only three .PDU files within the mms folder, we only have three associated files with the MMSMsg.db. There are times, however, when a user will delete an MMS message. The MMSMsg.db container may still have the associated PDU artifacts, even if this is just a logical search. The MMS-associated embedded content would need to be located with a physical search, which would require a physical acquisition. In these examples, we are strictly dealing with a logical file system acquisition and logical folder structures.

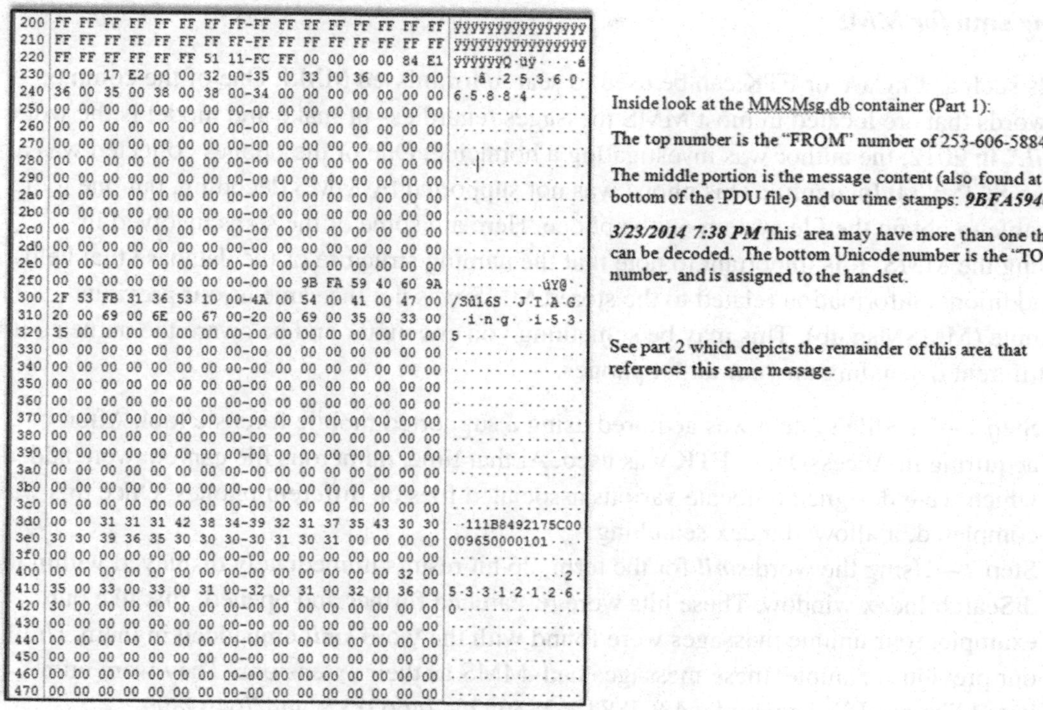

```
200 FF FF FF FF FF FF FF FF-FF FF FF FF FF FF FF FF  ÿÿÿÿÿÿÿÿÿÿÿÿÿÿÿÿ
210 FF FF FF FF FF FF FF FF-FF FF FF FF FF FF FF FF  ÿÿÿÿÿÿÿÿÿÿÿÿÿÿÿÿ
220 FF FF FF FF FF FF FF 51 11-FC FF 00 00 00 00 84 E1 ÿÿÿÿÿÿÿQ·üÿ....á
230 00 00 17 E2 00 00 32 00-35 00 33 00 36 00 30 00  ..·â..2.5.3.6.0.
240 36 00 35 00 38 00 38 00-34 00 00 00 00 00 00 00  6.5.8.8.4.......
250 00 00 00 00 00 00 00 00-00 00 00 00 00 00 00 00  ................
260 00 00 00 00 00 00 00 00-00 00 00 00 00 00 00 00  ................
270 00 00 00 00 00 00 00 00-00 00 00 00 00 00 00 00  ................
280 00 00 00 00 00 00 00 00-00 00 00 00 00 00 00 00  ......·|........
290 00 00 00 00 00 00 00 00-00 00 00 00 00 00 00 00  ................
2a0 00 00 00 00 00 00 00 00-00 00 00 00 00 00 00 00  ................
2b0 00 00 00 00 00 00 00 00-00 00 00 00 00 00 00 00  ................
2c0 00 00 00 00 00 00 00 00-00 00 00 00 00 00 00 00  ................
2d0 00 00 00 00 00 00 00 00-00 00 00 00 00 00 00 00  ................
2e0 00 00 00 00 00 00 00 00-00 00 00 00 00 00 00 00  ................
2f0 00 00 00 00 00 00 00 00-00 00 9B FA 59 40 60 9A  ..........·úY@`š
300 2F 53 FB 31 36 53 10 00-4A 00 54 00 41 00 47 00  /Sû16S..J.T.A.G.
310 20 00 69 00 6E 00 67 00-20 00 69 00 35 00 33 00  .i.n.g..i.5.3.
320 35 00 00 00 00 00 00 00-00 00 00 00 00 00 00 00  5...............
330 00 00 00 00 00 00 00 00-00 00 00 00 00 00 00 00  ................
340 00 00 00 00 00 00 00 00-00 00 00 00 00 00 00 00  ................
350 00 00 00 00 00 00 00 00-00 00 00 00 00 00 00 00  ................
360 00 00 00 00 00 00 00 00-00 00 00 00 00 00 00 00  ................
370 00 00 00 00 00 00 00 00-00 00 00 00 00 00 00 00  ................
380 00 00 00 00 00 00 00 00-00 00 00 00 00 00 00 00  ................
390 00 00 00 00 00 00 00 00-00 00 00 00 00 00 00 00  ................
3a0 00 00 00 00 00 00 00 00-00 00 00 00 00 00 00 00  ................
3b0 00 00 00 00 00 00 00 00-00 00 00 00 00 00 00 00  ................
3c0 00 00 00 00 00 00 00 00-00 00 00 00 00 00 00 00  ................
3d0 00 00 31 31 31 42 38 34-39 32 31 37 35 43 30 30  ··111B8492175C00
3e0 30 30 39 36 35 30 30 30-30 31 30 31 00 00 00 00  009650000101····
3f0 00 00 00 00 00 00 00 00-00 00 00 00 00 00 00 00  ................
400 00 00 00 00 00 00 00 00-00 00 00 00 00 00 32 00  ··············2·
410 35 00 33 00 33 00 31 00-32 00 31 00 32 00 36 00  5·3·3·1·2·1·2·6·
420 30 00 00 00 00 00 00 00-00 00 00 00 00 00 00 00  0···············
430 00 00 00 00 00 00 00 00-00 00 00 00 00 00 00 00  ................
440 00 00 00 00 00 00 00 00-00 00 00 00 00 00 00 00  ................
450 00 00 00 00 00 00 00 00-00 00 00 00 00 00 00 00  ................
460 00 00 00 00 00 00 00 00-00 00 00 00 00 00 00 00  ................
470 00 00 00 00 00 00 00 00-00 00 00 00 00 00 00 00  ................
```

Inside look at the MMSMsg.db container (Part 1):

The top number is the "FROM" number of 253-606-5884

The middle portion is the message content (also found at the bottom of the .PDU file) and our time stamps: *9BFA5940* =

3/23/2014 7:38 PM This area may have more than one that can be decoded. The bottom Unicode number is the "TO" number, and is assigned to the handset.

See part 2 which depicts the remainder of this area that references this same message.

Figure 16.7

Part 1 example of the data contained in the MMSMsg.db container and how to associate it with the pim folder.

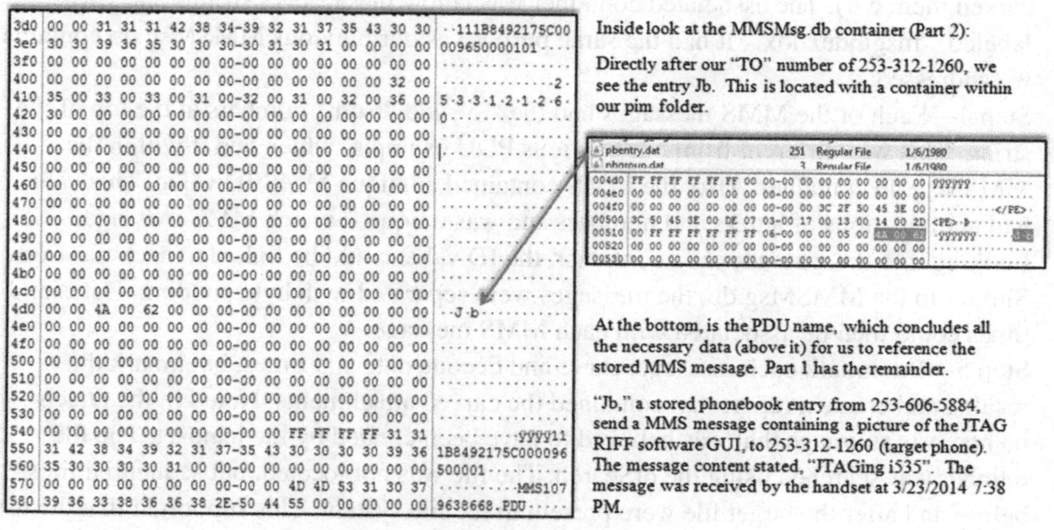

```
3d0 00 00 31 31 31 42 38 34-39 32 31 37 35 43 30 30  ··111B8492175C00
3e0 30 30 39 36 35 30 30 30-30 31 30 31 00 00 00 00  009650000101····
3f0 00 00 00 00 00 00 00 00-00 00 00 00 00 00 00 00  ................
400 00 00 00 00 00 00 00 00-00 00 00 00 00 00 32 00  ··············2·
410 35 00 33 00 33 00 31 00-32 00 31 00 32 00 36 00  5·3·3·1·2·1·2·6·
420 30 00 00 00 00 00 00 00-00 00 00 00 00 00 00 00  0···············
430 00 00 00 00 00 00 00 00-00 00 00 00 00 00 00 00  ................
440 00 00 00 00 00 00 00 00-00 00 00 00 00 00 00 00  ··|·············
450 00 00 00 00 00 00 00 00-00 00 00 00 00 00 00 00  ................
460 00 00 00 00 00 00 00 00-00 00 00 00 00 00 00 00  ................
470 00 00 00 00 00 00 00 00-00 00 00 00 00 00 00 00  ................
480 00 00 00 00 00 00 00 00-00 00 00 00 00 00 00 00  ................
490 00 00 00 00 00 00 00 00-00 00 00 00 00 00 00 00  ................
4a0 00 00 00 00 00 00 00 00-00 00 00 00 00 00 00 00  ................
4b0 00 00 00 00 00 00 00 00-00 00 00 00 00 00 00 00  ................
4c0 00 00 00 00 00 00 00 00-00 00 00 00 00 00 00 00  ................
4d0 00 00 4A 00 62 00 00 00-00 00 00 00 00 00 00 00  ··J·b···········
4e0 00 00 00 00 00 00 00 00-00 00 00 00 00 00 00 00  ................
4f0 00 00 00 00 00 00 00 00-00 00 00 00 00 00 00 00  ................
500 00 00 00 00 00 00 00 00-00 00 00 00 00 00 00 00  ................
510 00 00 00 00 00 00 00 00-00 00 00 00 00 00 00 00  ................
520 00 00 00 00 00 00 00 00-00 00 00 00 00 00 00 00  ................
530 00 00 00 00 00 00 00 00-00 00 00 00 00 00 00 00  ................
540 00 00 00 00 00 00 00 00-00 FF FF FF FF 31 31      ·········ÿÿÿÿ11
550 31 42 38 34 39 32 31 37-35 43 30 30 30 30 39 36  1B8492175C000096
560 35 30 30 30 30 31 00 00-00 00 00 00 00 00 00 00  500001··········
570 00 00 00 00 00 00 00 00-00 4D 4D 53 31 30 37      ·········MMS107
580 39 36 33 38 36 36 38 2E-50 44 55 00 00 00 00 00  9638668.PDU·····
```

Inside look at the MMSMsg.db container (Part 2):

Directly after our "TO" number of 253-312-1260, we see the entry Jb. This is located with a container within our pim folder.

```
pbentry.dat                         251   Regular File   1/6/1980
phgroup.dat                           3   Regular File   1/6/1980
004d0 FF FF FF FF FF FF 00 00-00 00 00 00 00 00 00 00  ÿÿÿÿÿÿ··········
004e0 FF FF FF FF FF FF 00 00-00 00 00 00 00 00 00 00  ÿÿÿÿÿÿ··········
004f0 00 00 00 00 00 00 00 00-00 00 3C 2F 50 45 3E 00  ··········</PE>·
00500 3C 50 45 3E 00 DE 07 03-00 17 00 13 00 14 00 2D  <PE>·Þ·········-
00510 00 FF FF FF FF FF FF 06-00 00 00 05 00 48 00 82  ·ÿÿÿÿÿÿ······H·
00520 00 00 00 00 00 00 00 00-00 00 00 00 00 00 00 00  
00530 00 00 00 00 00 00 00 00-00 00 00 00 00 00 00 00  
```

At the bottom, is the PDU name, which concludes all the necessary data (above it) for us to reference the stored MMS message. Part 1 has the remainder.

"Jb," a stored phonebook entry from 253-606-5884, send a MMS message containing a picture of the JTAG RIFF software GUI, to 253-312-1260 (target phone). The message content stated, "JTAGing i535". The message was received by the handset at 3/23/2014 7:38 PM.

Figure 16.8

Part 2 example of the remaining data from a single MMS message contained in the MMSMsg.db container.

Using smil for MMS

Tools such as EnCase or FTK can be used to search for missed MMS. One of the common keywords that are located in most MMS messages regardless of make and model is the work "*smil*." In 2012, the author was investigating a homicide. One of the phones collected was a Sanyo SCP-6760 Incognito. This phone was not supported by MMS decoding, but one tool was able to obtain the file system on the phone. Here are some of the steps involved in carving the MMS. It is important to note that the naming structure of the database that held the additional information related to the stored MMS was not the same as our previous example (MMSMsg.db). This may be something you encounter and be aware the name could be different depending on your target phones.

Step 1—The file system was acquired using a supported mobile forensic tool. After acquiring it, AccessData's FTK was used. At that time, numerous file carvers were added, which were designed to locate various associated files on different phones. Once this was completed, it allowed index searching.

Step 2—Using the word *smil* for the term, 26 hit results immediately displayed within the dtSearch Index window. These hits were researched further and opened. Just like our example, four unique messages were found with the word *smil* embedded in them. Unlike our previous example, these messages had .MMS as their extensions. They were numbered like our PDU example, 4867884, 62456525, 74662885, and 76469899.

Step 3—Using the "View in Explorer" feature, each of these messages was expanded on, which allowed the author to see where in the file system, they logically resided. This also showed the associated images for each MMS right below the numbers listed above (FTK carved them out). The associated container was below these MMS strings and was labeled, "msgindex.idx." It had the same purpose as our previous MMSMsg.db container we addressed.

Step 4—Each of the MMS messages had the "to" and "from" numbers at the top of the string. This was different from our previous PDU example, which had it within the MMSMsg.db container. Also, the MMS contained a unique MMS ID value. This value had combinations of letters and numbers and was unique for each MMS message. Looking into the msgindex.idx container, the ID value could be linked to each message. Similar to the MMSMsg.db, the messages were separated with byte padding. Dates and times could then be associated with each MMS message.

Step 5—Bookmark each message, carve and decode date and times, bookmark the results, and create a report that contained the carved attachments. Noted in the attachments, was an image that was believed to have been created by the handset. The file number was searched using the dtSearch. The file was not located, but sequential files before and after the target file were present in the file system. This supported that the user had potentially deleted the file from the phone. The file had a unique file number and the metadata showed that the others had embedded data for the Sanyo model being examined.

Since there was a time period between when the message was sent and when the phone was examined, it probably would not have been located, even with a physical exam.

The steps involved in this case utilize a combination of forensic tools designed for phones as well as computers.

Containers for MMS

The last part of this chapter deals very briefly with the naming configuration for MMS. As a reminder, this chapter deals with MMS located on nonsmart style phones. Many of these devices today have the ability to access the Internet. The next series of examples are contained on the companion site. The first is from another Sanyo. This device places the MMS entries into the file system with the *data/brew/camera/picturemail* path. Fig. 16.2 (companion site) depicts the location of these entries. So far, we have shown two different phones that have an associated database that stores the date and times for each entry. In this example, the containers for each MMS have everything that is needed, but it has to be extracted (manually carved) out.

In this example, there are many messages on this phone. Each has their own ID, which is labeled two different ways. The first is the folder name. Once the folder is clicked on, the actual MMS string also has its own name that is different than the folder. If we look at the folder first, many of them are sequential, but some jump from one number to another. This may indicate that the entries between the folders were deleted, but further validation would be needed. Fig. 16.3 (companion site) provides an example of this–showing missing folder numbers. Indicated in Fig. 16.3 are just a few, not all the missing folders present.

If the message is clicked on that is contained on each folder, the string can be read. The top of the message provides the title (if present). Scrolling down, we can read what type of message (received), and our common header for a .jpg image. Fig. 16.4 (companion site) shows an example of this information. There are two dates present. The values of 38018581 decodes as 10/15/2009 6:36 p.m. The other date is listed in plan ASCII (readable) as Thu, 15 Oct 2009 12:36:46 GMT. One has applied GMT, and the other, local time for the device. Scrolling down after the .jpg attachment, we can locate the content of the message. In this example it is quite long, and just the start of the message was included. At the bottom of the string is the file signature. For purposes of explaining SMS/MMS entries, a file signature is a unique value that the owner of the device stores on the phone after the SMS or MMS creation. This is created and saved one time by the end user. Each time the user creates and sends the message, the file signature is included –if they choose to use it. Fig. 16.5 (companion site) contains the start of the content and the user's unique file signature that is sent with each message.

This chapter could provide additional examples of MMS containers, but the point is still the same. The file system may have what you need to carve out the information in more than one location, or in the last example, it may all be within one file, and just needs to be manually extracted. Most phones will be in working order, and you will be able to view the message through the GUI. In those cases, it may be more efficient use of your time to simply create screenshots of the message(s). If you are conducting a destructive technique, or are unable to view the MMS content through the GUI for validation, it is recommended use another (working) phone for confirmation.

Chapter Summary Key Points

Not all phones will support the decoding of MMS. The investigator will need to obtain the file system at a minimum, in order to manually carve out the information. There may even be times when a physical exam was conducted and the MMS failed to parse.

One of the first steps is to get into the phone; there are several vendors who have tools for this purpose. One vendor who has addressed the need to get into locked "burner" phones is Susteen with their release of "Burner Breaker."

Once the file system is obtained, the examiner can manually search the folder structure for files related to the actual MMS, as well as ones that can identify stored contacts and the assigned number. Other files can be referenced within the file system when an examiner needs to manually carve an embedded attachment. If the file you are trying to extract is present in another location of the file system, the file header and footer can be referenced for manual carving. Online searches can also be used to help identify an embedded file. MMS files can have .PDU and .MMS extensions, or in some cases, a file that contains all of the necessary artifacts. Many phones will use a secondary database container that needs to be referenced for date and times of each message.

There may be instances where the content can be located within the MMS string by using a search for the term .txt. Other strings will have the message content near the bottom of the file container. It is common for users to store their own phrase or sentence, which is referred to as a file signature within SMS and MMS storage. This is often included in every message from that particular entry. Carving MMS is a time-consuming task. It may require the examiner to obtain a phone that is similar to the target evidence and place their own MMS on it to under-stand what they are trying to locate and decode.

References

[1] Secureview, SV Strike, 2017. http://www.secureview.us/svstrike.html.
[2] Secureview, Burner-Breaker, 2017. http://www.secureview.us/burner-breaker.html.

CHAPTER 17

Application Data

Information in This Chapter

- Applications
- Supported decoding
- SQLite (databases)
- Database naming
- Validating database content
- Virtual phone numbers
- Sanderson Forensics SQLite Forensic Browser
- Write-ahead log files (WAL)
- Journal files
- Blobs and attachments

Introduction—A Last Argument

Two people who lived in a town in Puget Sound fell in love and were married during the Spring of 2015. In August 2015, both were dead. The investigation appeared to be a murder–suicide. The family was having trouble with this conclusion and believed there was more to the investigation. They felt that due to their new "love" for one another, he would have "never" harmed her.

Their phones were examined, and there were two sound files that the victim had recorded without the knowledge of her new groom. The files were less than 2 min in length, and recorded arguments over their belongings and pending separation. The recordings took place just a few days before their bodies were discovered. The files did not have conventional file names and were instead named after the male's first name, with numbers 1 and 2 added for each file. It was obvious the files had been named by the user of the phone. Along with these files, there was a much larger file that did not have this naming structure and would not play.

A user-installed sound recording application was located on her phone. Within the schema of the application, it was found that the user had enabled a setting that allowed her to name the file before saving it. This last file was created during her last argument with her husband. It had not finalized, but did save moments before the phone went dead. The naming convention was similar to a file date that is located in Android (file system) image files. When the header and footer were compared against the files that she did finalize, necessary artifacts that would allow the file to render properly and play correctly were missing. By using the raw data located in the database of the application for the sound program, the cause of the problem was revealed, and the unfinalized sound file was eventually rebuilt to reveal the argument that led up to this unfortunate event and last moments before their deaths. The work revealed an interesting insight for the author, it was the very first case in over 27 years of police work, were an actual time of death could be precisely established. Most importantly, it allowed the family to have closure.

Your laboratory may be heavily equipped with several commercially available forensic tools. Some may be for one single purpose, such as rebuilding image files. Some may be for reading NAND or NOR flash memory, or even complex X-raying of PCB boards. No matter how lush and advanced your mobile forensic laboratory may be, you will eventually need to decode application data. This chapter addresses application evidence and provides some basic suggestions and steps that can assist in decoding the data that might be missed by commercial tools, but is waiting for you to locate them.

Applications

When the user of a computer or a mobile device installs an application, it is sometimes referred to as a **User Installed Application** (UIA). There are a tremendous amount of choices, no matter what type of mobile platform one chooses. *"By 2020, mobile apps are forecast to generate around 189 billion U.S. dollars in revenues via app stores and in-app advertising. Some of the most popular operating system-native stores are Apple's App Store, Google Play, as well as Windows Phone Store and BlackBerry App World. As of June 2016, there were 2.2 million available apps at Google Play store and two billion apps available in the Apple's App Store, the two leading app stores in the world"* [1].

The growth of user mobile application downloads has grown tremendously over the last few years. Many of the statistics that are available do not include applications that are available to the user when they "root" or "jailbreak" their phone. If those numbers were included, the "standard" or "safe" numbers that come from conservative sources would be much higher. The following information was provided by Statista, who provides statistics and studies from more than 18,000 sources [2]:

> **Number of mobile app downloads worldwide from 2009 to 2017 (in millions)**
>
> *This statistic shows a forecast for the number of mobile app downloads from 2009 to 2017. In 2009, worldwide mobile app downloads amounted to approximately 2.52 billion and are expected to reach 268.69 billion in 2017. In 2010, earnings of mobile apps providers amounted to 6.8 billion U.S. dollars.*

Mobile app downloads—additional information

With the number of mobile app downloads expected to grow in the future, app stores will also be expected to meet the demand for the number, quality, and range of apps that their customers need. As of July 2014, the number of apps available in the leading app stores was recorded for comparison. As of that month, customers could pick from Google Play's 1.3 million available apps, a figure which made it the world's leading app store. Apple's App Store was ranked second with slightly fewer, yet still impressive, 1.2 million apps.

The success of an app's appeal can be analyzed by its reach. The mobile audience reach of leading U.S. smartphone apps was measured in November 2014. The resulting ranking included YouTube, Google Play, Pandora Radio and Google Maps. However, Facebook was ranked first with a 69 percent reach among the mobile audience in the U.S. Twitter, on the other hand which is considered to be another dominant force in the social media industry, only had a 21.3 percent reach of the mobile audience.

The number of available apps and the number of people downloading may have an effect on app download rates. The average mobile app download rate per 100 users was calculated in selected countries worldwide in the second quarter of 2014. It was discovered that on average worldwide, 1.23 apps were downloaded per 100 users. India and the United Kingdom were lower than the worldwide average and the U.S. was only slightly higher at a rate of 1.25 apps downloaded per 100 users. The countries with the most impressive app rate were found in Asia. Malaysia topped the ranking with the highest app rate of 4.64 app downloads [3].

With this obvious growth with users downloading and using specific applications, the need to locate evidence within the data contained in the schema of the application also increases. As we touched on earlier, commercial forensic tools do support the decoding of many applications.

Supported Decoding—The Tip of the Iceberg

There are several commercially available programs that devote attention to decoding applications that are installed on mobile devices. Oxygen, Micro Systemation (XRY), Susteen, Paraben, AccessData, and Cellebrite are just a few that have been used over the past few years. There are two main vendors that many people feel are widely used worldwide and support the most phones: XRY and Cellebrite. If we look at one of these two main vendors that list the applications that are supported for decoding at the time of this writing, Cellebrite Version 5, December 2016, we can clearly see it only touches the "tip of the iceberg" on the overall number of applications available worldwide. Here is the list of various supported applications based upon the type of operating system (directly from Cellebrite).

Android Application Names

Aliwangwang; AntiVirus Security (AVG); Any.DO; AppLock; ASKfm; Badoo; Baidu Browser; Baido Maps; BBM; BeeTalk; BlackList; Blendr; Booking.com; Callgram messaging; ChatOn; Chatous; Chrome; CM Locker; CM Security Browser; Ctrip; Ctrip (Chinese); Desk Notes; Dolphin Browser; Dropbox; Ebuddy XMS; Endomondo; Evernote; Expedia; Facebook; Facebook Messenger; FireChat; Firefox; Flipboard; GBWhatsApp; Glide; Go SMS Pro; Google Calendar; Google Docs; Google Maps; Google Photos; Google Quick Search Box; Google Talk; Google Tasks; Google Translate; Google+; Grindr; GroupMe; Hangouts; HERE WeGo; HeyTell; Hide My Text; Hide SMS; Hike Messenger; Hot or Not; HTC Mail; Hushed; ICQ; imo; InBox; Instagram; InstaMessage; Kakao Story; Kakao Talk; Keeper; KeepSafe; Kik Messenger; LINE; LINK; LinkedIn; LOCX Applock; Mail.Ru; Mappy; me2day; Meet24; MeetMe; MeowChat; Mercury Browser; Message Locker; Messenger and Chat Lock; MobileVOIP Cheap Calls; Momo; Mr. Number; Mypeople; My Tracks; Mysms; Navfree; Nike+ Run Club; Nimbuzz; Odnoklassniki; Omegle; OneDrive; OneNote; ooVoo; Opera Mini; Opera Mobile; Outlook.com; Path; Pinterest; POF (Plenty of Fish); Pokemon Go; Puffin Web Browser; QIP Mobile; QQ; QQ Browser; Remember The Milk; Runtastic; SayHi; Scruff; Signal Private Messenger; TextSecure; Silent Phone; Skout; Skype; Snapchat; Swarm; Sygic; Tango; Taxify; Telegram Messenger; Text Free Ultra Texting; Text Me Up; TextNow; textPlus; Tiger Text; Tinder; Touch; Truecaller; Tumblr; TunnelBear; Twitter; UC Browser; uTorrent-Torrent Downloader; Vaulty; vBrowse; Verizon Messages; Viber; Vine; VIPole; VKontakte; Voker; Waze; WeChat; Weibo; WhatsApp; Whisper; Wickr; Yahoo Messenger; Yahoo Search; Yandex Browser; Yandex Maps; Yeti–Campus Stories; YouTube.

BlackBerry Application Names

BBM; Evernote; Facebook Messenger; SnapChat; Skype; Twitter; WhatsApp.

iOS Application Names

AIM; Aliwangwang; Any.DO; ASKfm; Badoo; Baidu Maps; BBM; BeeTalk; Blendr; Booking.com; ChatOn; Chatous; Chrome; Copy; Ctrip; Ctrip (Chinese); Dolphin Browser; Don't Touch This; Dropbox; Ebuddy XMS; Endomondo; Evernote; Expedia; Facebook; Facebook Messenger; Facebook Poke; Find My Friends; Find My iPhone; FireChat; Firefox; Flipboard; Foursquare; Fring; Garmin Connect; Glide; GO Chat; Google App; Google Docs; Google Drive; Google Maps; Google Tasks; Google Translate; Google+; Grindr; GroupMe; Hangouts; HeyTell; Hike Messenger; Hot or Not; Hushed; ICQ; imo; Inbox; Instagram; InstaMessage; Kakao Story; Keeper; KeepSafe; Kik Messenger; LINE;

LINK; LinkedIn; Mail.Ru; me2day; Meet24; MeetMe; MeowChat; Mercury Browser; MobileVOIP Cheap Calls; Momo; MotionX; mysms; Navitel Navigator; Nike+ Run Clug; Nimbuzz; Odnoklassniki; Omegle; OneDrive; ooVoo; Opera Mini; Path; PingChat!; Pinterest; POF (Plenty of Fish); Puffin Web Browser; QIP Mobile; QQ; QQ Browser; Remember The Milk; Runtastic; SayHi; Scruff; Silent Phone; Skout; Skype; Snapchat; SpringPad FlipNote; Spy calc; Swarm; SwiftKey; Tango; Taxify; Telegram Messenger; Text Free; Text Free Ultra Texting; Text Me!; TextNow; textPlus; Threema; Tiger Text; Tinder; TomTom; Touch; TrueCaller; Twiter; Twitterific; UC Browser; vBrowse; Viber; Vine; VKontakte; Voxer; Waze; WeChat; Weibo; WhatsApp; Wickr; Whisper; Yandex Browser; Yandex Mail; Yandex Maps; Yahoo Mail; Yahoo Messenger; Yahoo Search; Yeti–Campus Stories; Yik Yak.

Database Naming—It Does Not Always Stay Original

In this chapter, we will discuss forensic tools that are produced by Paul Sanderson of Sanderson Forensics. This chapter is not meant to explain all the necessary steps of how to use these products to decode the database. Furthermore, Cellebrite Physical Analyzer released version 6, which, at the time of this writing, had new features titled: *SQLite wizard*. The purpose of both vendors' products is to help the end user decode a database that may have been missed during the automated decoding process.

To see the potential evidence that is contained within the application databases, the examination type must be able to pull the actual container. A standard logical extraction will not get the actual database but will instead pull a predefined string of information. A physical examination (and some file system pulls) will contain the origin of where the database resides in the file system. In some cases, this may involve the use of Rooting or Shell Rooting in Androids. This allows *superuser* access to the various *data/com.* folders, thus access to the application schema contained in the databases. For Androids, the applications reside in an alphabetical order, each following the "*com.*" at the beginning of the naming structure. Fig. 17.1 depicts the partitions that would be viewable to an examiner on a chip-off examination from an Android phone. This example is not the only way to view the various databases that could be visible to the examiner. We just address UIAs, but the majority of what is contained in the file system are commonly encountered default applications based on the OS version and the carrier. For example, there may be an agreement between Verizon wireless and Audible, which is an application that allows user to listen to books through their phone. The Audible application would be preinstalled on the phone, and in some cases, the user would not be able to uninstall it without rooting the device. Fig. 17.1 expands the *userdata* partition and opens the *data* folder that contains all the available *com.* folders for preinstalled applications as well as user installed apps. Just a few of these are shown in this example.

Various partitions (chip off image – Android)

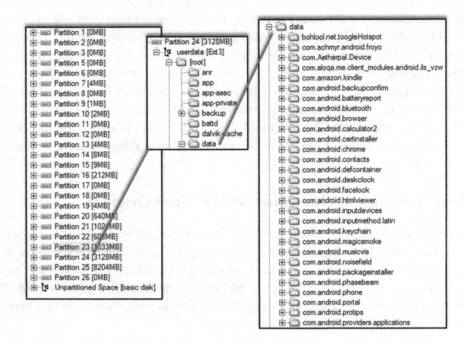

Folders that contain decoded and potential non-supported databases. Naming configurations may
be different that application name. (Additional folders continued – not shown)

Figure 17.1
Example of the *userdata* partition that contains the *data* folder and some of the available
applications.

In Apple phones, they will commonly use plist files. Many of the items of interest to an
investigation are located in the ***Applications*** and ***var–mobile*** folders. Examiners will
also encounter naming configurations with *.sqlitedb* or just *.db* after the name of the
application on the Apple device. In this chapter, all our examples use a database from an
Android. The columns used in Android or Apple OSs for the database will look very
similar, and for purposes of decoding, the steps for using the tool will remain almost
identical.

One of the first steps would be to determine the name of the database that needs to be
decoded. A word of warning here, what shows up as the name for the target application in the

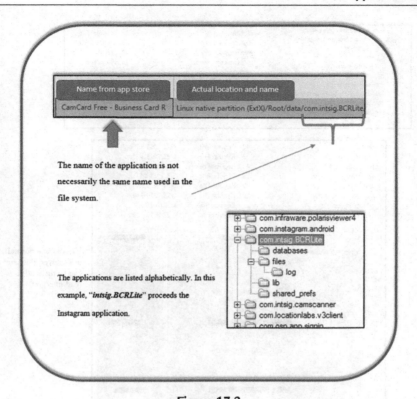

Figure 17.2

Example of the original name of the application versus the naming configuration within the file system.

Google Play Store, iTunes, or other downloading source location, may not be the same naming configuration within the file system. Users may need to look at the list of installed user applications and determine the original name of the application. Fig. 17.2 provides an example of a user-installed business card reader original app store name versus the name within the file system.

Another issue is the need to use a database viewer to better understand the structure of the information stored inside it. Fig. 17.3 is the hexadecimal view of a common ***com.android. providers.telephony***, ***mmssms.db*** container. This has been redacted, but viewing the stored information in this fashion can be difficult. Using a database viewer makes the task much easier.

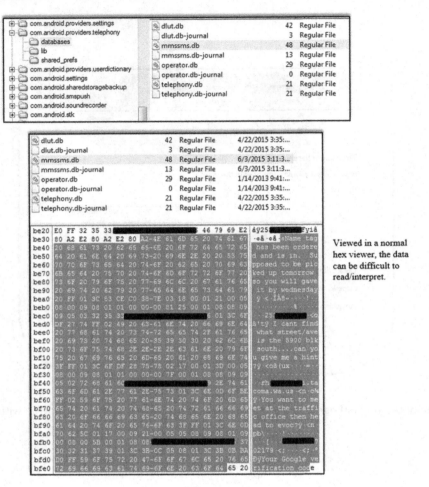

Figure 17.3
Example of viewing (redacted) database information in a Hex Viewer.

Validating Database Content

Once we have located the application, we must open the various folders and locate the potential evidence. Our next example is using an SMS application called Text Free. This is from a company called Pinger. Popular forensic tools now support decoding this application, but a few years back, they did not. Any database, supported or not supported for decoding, can be used to illustrate the example of how to validate the content.

In the case of stored SMS, an examiner would want to locate the table within the schema that depicts the stored messages. If the phone was damaged, or the physical acquisition was through a chip-off procedure, examiners may not be able to validate the content of the target application as easy. In cases where the GUI cannot be used to confirm what is in the database in question, another option is to replicate the application on the same model test device. During an investigation, there are times when the case investigator will reveal through other sources that communications did take place through the mobile devices. However, when the *known* device(s) are forensically examined, the typical SMS/MMS areas do not reveal such activities. Examiners must therefore determine if a UIA was used to facilitate the communications. If found, they may need to be decoded by hand or with secondary tools.

Locating what is of interest in your case may take a few minutes. To do this, we will need to expand each of the folders under the main root folder. This allows access to view the tables associated with the application. The tables will perform various functions and can include data related to an investigation. The problem for investigators is linking this data together in a format that makes sense and can be understood outside of the phone.

Our example in Fig. 17.4 shows how we first expanded the main folder, which revealed another folder titled "databases." The bottom image in Fig. 17.4 depicts what is contained in the *textfree* database and associated tables. Notice the *contact_addresses, contact_structured_names, contacts,* and *conversation_items*. These will not necessarily be the same if you are manually looking at a similar application, or even this same one for that matter. Each of these can be clicked on to explore how the application stores the necessary information. Under the *conversation_items*, we can see the conversation that is taking place between the owner of this phone (George Rubin), "Marie," and "Jimmy" regarding where a body is buried. Within Fig. 17.5, the example displays how examiner can scroll over and see the *sender_id, recipient_id, recipient_name,* and *timestamp*, which are displayed in UNIX.

Virtual Phone Numbers

It is important to understand that many of the applications will create their own (virtual) phone numbers that are used to identify the user. These are not wireless allocated phone numbers. They may require multiple executions of search warrants or subpoenas to determine the origin. An example of this was from an actual phone number used in a robbery investigation. The number came back to Bandwidth.com, which is a Voice-Over-Internet-Protocol company. A search warrant to Bandwidth revealed the number is assigned by Pinger. A

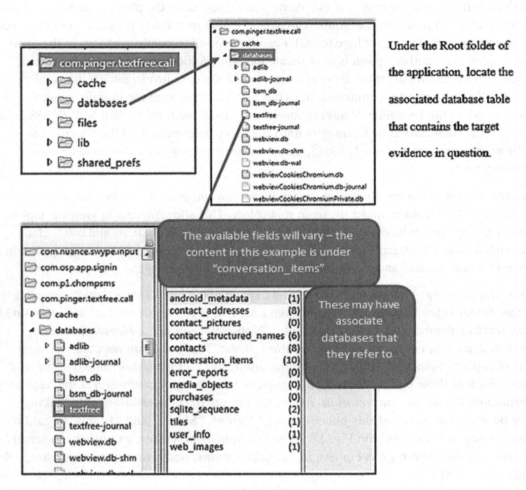

Under the Root folder of the application, locate the associated database table that contains the target evidence in question.

Figure 17.4
An example of locating the table containing the SMS content.

warrant to Pinger revealed the iPhone's Unique Device Identifier that was used to download the application from iTunes to the target device. A warrant to Apple revealed the actual person linked to the iTunes account.

This is just one example of how a database may look. Others can have more elaborate schemas to include blobs that link to stored images, URLs, and other associated data.

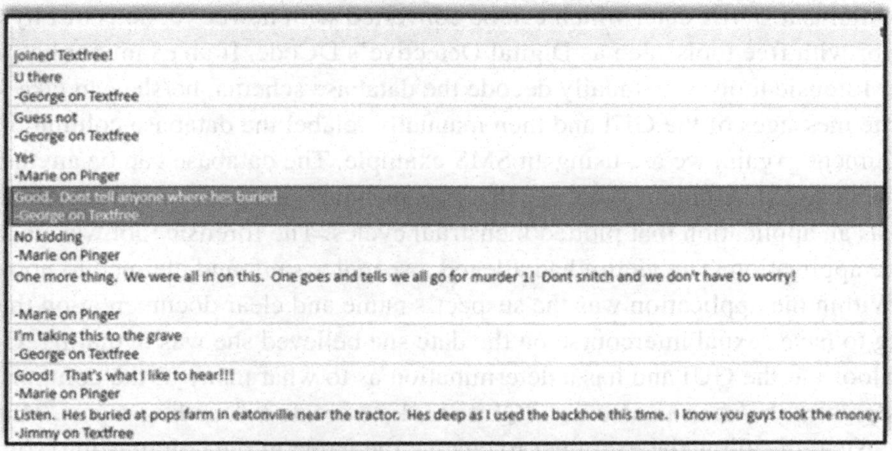

```
joined Textfree!
U there
-George on Textfree
Guess not
-George on Textfree
Yes
-Marie on Pinger
Good. Dont tell anyone where hes buried
-George on Textfree
No kidding
-Marie on Pinger
One more thing. We were all in on this. One goes and tells we all go for murder 1! Dont snitch and we don't have to worry!

-Marie on Pinger
I'm taking this to the grave
-George on Textfree
Good! That's what I like to hear!!!
-Marie on Pinger
Listen. Hes buried at pops farm in eatonville near the tractor. Hes deep as I used the backhoe this time. I know you guys took the money.
-Jimmy on Textfree
```

sender_id	recipient_id	recipient_name	tf_type	status	state	timestamp
+13603426077		rubinskeeper	1	2	0	1397059653297
12533430855	George Rubin	13603426077	1	2	0	1397059664000
12533430855	George Rubin	13603426077	1	2	0	1397060002000
13603426077	Marie Titus	12533430855	1	2	0	1397060026000
12533430855	George Rubin	13603426077	1	2	0	1397060084000
13603426077	Marie Titus	12533430855	1	2	0	1397060118000
13603426077	Marie Titus	12533430855	1	2	0	1397082301000
12533430855	George Rubin	13603426077	1	2	0	1397082352000
13603426077	Marie Titus	12533430855	1	2	0	1397082397000
19152350805	Jimmy John	12533430855	1	2	0	1397084888000

Figure 17.5
Example of columns within the database schema containing fields related to the SMS message.

If we look at the application through the phone GUI, or a test phone GUI with known data, we can visually pair up these columns with what they represent. Using Fig. 17.5, the "*sender_id*" for the top entry shows the "*recipient_name*" as "*rubinskeeper*." We can also see there are additional columns in this schema shown as, *recipient_id*, *tf_type*, *status*, *state*, and *timestamp*. These are found to represent "Inbox/Outbox," the target phone number for the contact, if the message was MMS or SMS, and if it was read. The timestamp column is a UNIX date, which can be converted with newer versions of Physical Analyzer or with free tools such as Digital Detective's DCode. If an examiner has no additional forensic tools to manually decode the database schema, he/she can take screenshots of the messages of the GUI and then manually relabel the database column titles in a Word document. Again, we are using an SMS example. The database can be anything that needs to be decoded. A unique database that was manually decoded at the time of this writing was an application that plotted menstrual cycles. The forensic tool was unable to decode the application. The victim had alleged a sexual assault and claimed to not know the suspect. Within the application was the suspect's name and clear documentation that she was trying to have sexual intercourse on the date she believed she was ovulating. Once an examiner looks at the GUI and has a determination as to what many of the columns in the schema represent, he/she can also use SQLite tools to create a decoding report. Many of these forensic tools allow the examiner to change the name of the columns into something he/she can understand, and more importantly, something a target audience (such as a jury) can visually digest.

Sanderson Forensics SQLite Forensic Browser

One of the more robust and popular SQLite forensic decoding tools is the Sanderson Forensics SQLite Forensic Browser. In this chapter, we will cover just a small aspect of the capabilities of this product. Readers can easily locate YouTube videos, as well as various articles on the Sanderson Forensic website that can provide additional clarification. We show an example that uses the TextNow application database. For purposes of briefly explaining how Sanderson Forensics SQLite Forensic Browser functions, it really does not matter if this application is now supported for decoding. What matters is that examiners understand how to conduct the fundamental steps with this popular forensic tool.

Once we have identified the database that needs to be decoded, it can be saved outside of the forensic tool. Many examiners use Physical Analyzer to view the databases in their investigations. Rather than providing advice that might miss potential target evidence, it is suggested that the entire root of the desired application be saved. This will ensure that all the subsequent directories can be accessed if needed. Simply right click on the root folder for the database in question and save as a zipped folder. In the example provided, we use only one of the databases for the SMS that needs to be decoded.

Our first step involves opening the SQLite Forensic Browser. In the upper left cover, click *File—Create case file*. A window will present to the user titled "*Create new existing Case DB*." This is where the user can select the name and location of where to save the file. In our example, we name the file Test 1. Step 2 involves locating the database from your case that you wish to decode. In the example provided, **textnow_data** (database) is loaded. A secondary window will present, which has various settings to enable. The additional settings are the following: *Make a working copy of the DB, Process associated journal/WAL, Recover Records,* and *Attempt to carve partial records*. We will briefly address the WAL file later in this chapter. The remaining settings are somewhat self-explanatory, and in our example, we have enabled all these settings. Fig. 17.6 shows these first two steps.

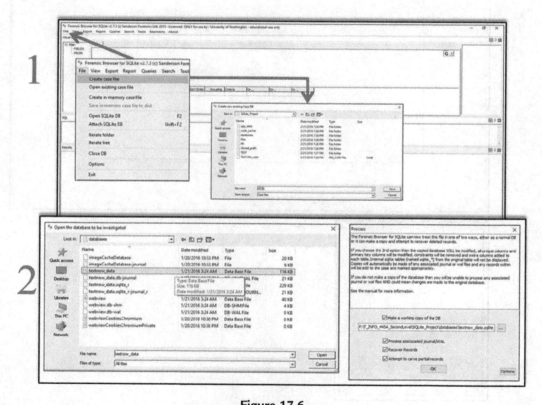

Figure 17.6

Steps 1 and 2 on using Sanderson Forensics SQLite Forensic Browser (decoding SMS application).

Once the database in question is opened, step 3 involves dragging the data you want from the database into the middle of the screen on the program. In our example, we use the column in the schema titled "messages." When this is dragged to the middle, it will show the available choices for that selection (**MESSAGE_ID, CONTACT_VALUE, CONTACT_TYPE, CONTACT_NAME, MESSAGE_DIRECTION**, etc.). Step 4 involves selecting the column names that you want to include in your final report. Fig. 17.7 shows an example of the TextNow being used to complete steps 3 and 4. Be aware that the choices shown in step 4 are based on what the application provides for the subcolumns.

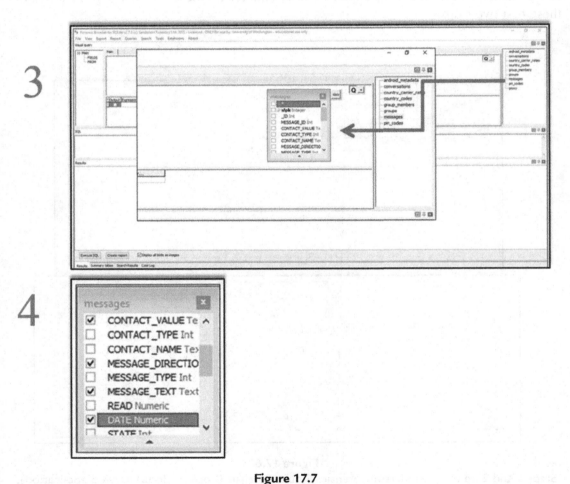

Figure 17.7
Steps 3 and 4 regarding the use of Sanderson Forensics SQLite Forensic Browser when decoding an SMS database.

The next step, step 5, involves changing the names at the top of the columns you have selected to a name that you and your audience will understand. This is called the Alias field. Once the user has created all the aliases that they want to change, the bottom left corner of the program must be selected to apply the changes. This is step 6, and the selection button is titled "*Execute SQL.*" Fig. 17.8 depicts examples of steps 5 and 6.

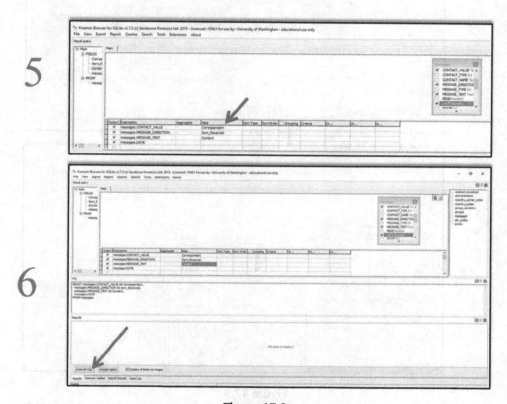

Figure 17.8

Examples of steps 5 and 6 with regard to the use of Sanderson Forensics SQLite Forensic Browser when decoding an SMS database.

The next step (7) involves changing the format of the date and time. Users can right click on the date in the database column and select "View Column as…," which pops up as the top choice in the right click window. This will present the *Select data conversion* window. The user can select the appropriate date from the *Dates* selection: *Date display* format and *Date/Time format*. Users can then select the time zone from the *Set Time Zone* choices and enable *Adjust for DST* if desired. Step 8 involves creating Alias values for Sent or Received SMS entries. Users must make certain to validate what type of Alias will represent the direction of the SMS. In our example, we apply the value of 2 as *Sent* and the value of 1 as *Received*. Once these selections are made, click the "OK" button on the *Select Data Conversion* window. Fig. 17.9 shows steps 7 and 8.

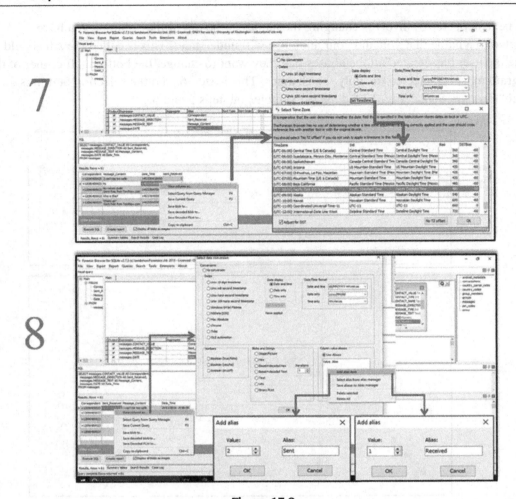

Figure 17.9
Examples of steps 7 and 8 with regard to the use of Sanderson Forensics SQLite Forensic Browser
when decoding an SMS database.

Step 9 involves creating a report. In the left bottom corner, to the right of the Execute SQL button, is the "Create Report" button. Once this is selected, the user will be presented with a pop-up window allowing them to create a file name and select a location to save the file to. It is important at step 9 to also view the report and make any correction as needed. One of the more common problems with the final report is the date and time conversions. Step 10 involves using the GUI of the phone (or test phone), to compare the line items in the report users made with the forensic tool. This validates the report. Fig. 17.10 depicts how the GUI was used to compare against the report.

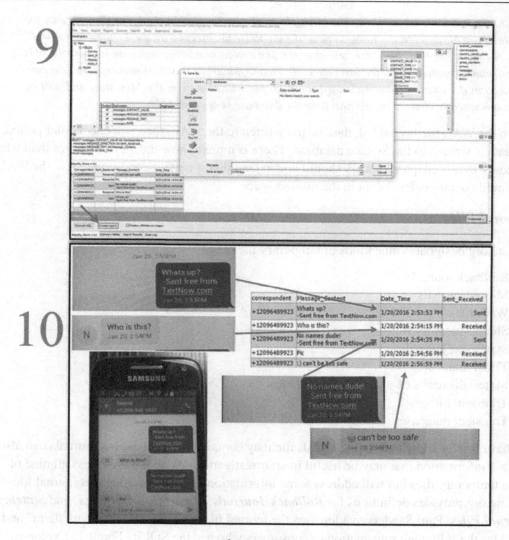

Figure 17.10
Examples of step 9 and 10 with regard to the use of Sanderson Forensics SQLite Forensic Browser when decoding an SMS database.

Write-Ahead Log Files

In this chapter, we will briefly explain the definition of the WAL file and possible evidence value. Additional information on how to process the WAL file can be contained in Paul Sanderson's website:

> A write-ahead log or WAL file is used in place of a rollback journal when SQLite is operating in WAL mode. As with the rollback journal, the purpose of the WAL file is to implement

atomic commit and rollback. The WAL file is always located in the same directory as the database file and has the same name as the database file except with the 4 characters "-wal" appended. The WAL file is created when the first connection to the database is opened and is normally removed when the last connection to the database closes. However, if the last connection does not shutdown cleanly, the WAL file will remain in the filesystem and will be automatically cleaned up the next time the database is opened. [4]

When the WAL file is enabled, data is first written to the WAL, then at a checkpoint period, the data is written to the SQLite database. There is more to how the WAL operates than what we cover in this chapter; readers should understand that if certain conditions exist, the WAL file could contain deleted data in the unused space.

Journal Files

SQLite.org designates nine kinds of temporary files [5]:

1. Rollback journals
2. Master journals
3. WAL files
4. Shared-memory files
5. Statement journals
6. TEMP databases
7. Materializations of views and subqueries
8. Transient indices
9. Transient databases used by VACUUM

We have briefly addressed that the WAL file may contain deleted data, but journals can also contain information that may be useful in an investigation. We will not address all nine of these temporary files but will address some information related to the various journal files. SQLite.org provides definitions for **Rollback Journals**, **Master Journal Files**, and **Statement Journal Files**. Paul Sanderson addresses the journal files and "how to deal with them" and provides the following information to consumers who use the SQLite Forensic Explorer:

Journal files have a simple structure. The file starts with a Journal header section which is specified as the size of a sector on the device on which the master database exists, so this would typically be 512 bytes. This is followed by:

- *A 4 byte page number.*
- *A complete page of data (the page size is stored in the header)*
- *Then a 4 byte checksum.*

The pattern then repeats. How do Journal's work and how do we deal with them:

Journal files are the opposite of WAL files in that they contain a copy of pages of a database before a write occurs. i.e. when a page needs to be updated, the existing page is appended to a journal and the database is then updated. A journal file has the same name as the parent database but with journal appended, i.e. if the parent database is main.db the journal will be main.db-journal in the same manner as a WAL file, journals can contain multiple copies of a page.

Journal files employ a cumulative checksum on each page, the checksum is seeded from a salt value (known by SQLite as a nonce) which is stored in the header. After a set of write operations is committed, SQLite also overwrites the journal from the first page with new pages and uses a new nonce value to ensure any old pages do not have a valid checksum. So to follow that through if you calculate the checksum from the start any page with a valid checksum is a copy of the page from the main database prior to the most recent transaction. Any page after the last valid page should by definition have an invalid checksum and these pages will be from a previous transaction (note a previous transaction, not the previous transaction). As always there is a complication. When a new transaction is committed, the journal can be deleted, truncated or the header can be overwritten with zeros (hence clearing the nonce). In practice the latter of these events seems to be the most common. If, however we have the parent database to go with the journal file we can still make sense of it by a) using 512 bytes as a header size (most disks are 512 bytes) and b) taking the page size from the parent database. Of course, we won't know what nonce to use to seed the checksum process so we won't be able to determine if any of the pages are from the last transaction or from a transaction previous to the last. But we will be able to correctly decode the records and we can say that at some time in the past the pages in the journal were part of the parent database. SQLite Forensic Explorer will prompt the user if a database with a matching name is found so that it can use the schema from this database. If the journal header is present SQLite Forensic Explorer will use the values from the header, but if the header is blank it will "guess" the values from the settings in the parent database. [6]

What is important regarding these files (WAL and Journal) is that they may contain additional information related to the investigation. Also, and more importantly, there can be a wrong way in which to investigate the WAL files. Again, we do not expand on the "do's" and "don'ts" of what goes into properly reading the WAL files, and the reader should visit Paul Sanderson's forensic site to read more on this topic.

Blobs and Attachments

Another point related to databases that is not addressed are the various instructions on how to link and include the blobs or attachments during the decoding of a target database. This information is also found online and will require more advanced steps than what is outlined within this chapter. On Android Operating Systems, if the attachment is media related, it will generally be linked to a location within the microSD card (if present). The user, however, may choose to install applications on the actual device, not the microSD. The point of addressing this is to first understand where the specific blob or attachment is located. A column within the actual schema of the application will provide the path, and advanced steps (online) will show investigators how to link the targeted artifact (blob or attachment) during the manual decoding of the specific application.

Chapter Summary Key Points

The number of mobile applications has grown into the thousands and continues to grow. This creates a unique journey for specific forensic vendors who are at the "never ending finish line" when it comes to decoding them. Popular vendors such as Cellebrite do support decoding several applications for Android, iOS, Windows, and BlackBerry. With each update released to their paid consumers, comes additional decoding support for more popular applications. The support list is small in comparison to what is available to the consumer. It would be impossible for the forensic vendor to ever decode every application on the market. What seems to be taking place is that there are additional tools and features that make it easier for the examiner to decode a target application that might be missed by automated decoding.

Examiners must first recognize if UIAs were used in the incident in their investigation and if missed by commercial forensic tools, they may need to be decoded by hand. If so, one of the first steps is to determine the naming structure of how it will appear in the file system. They must not assume the name used in the download store is the same name given to the application as it appears in the file system. This will allow them to locate the database and, in turn, begin the process of either manually decoding it or using a stand-alone decoding tool.

There are specific steps involved in decoding the database. In this chapter, we have provided 10 basic steps when decoding a simple, unsupported, SMS database using a product developed by Paul Sanderson Forensics. The WAL and journals located in some databases may, at times, assist the forensic investigator in locating additional information.

This chapter only lightly touches on application decoding. It utilizes a popular decoding tool, and focuses on the fundamental concepts of application database naming, file system locating, renaming columns, creating aliases, converting timestamps, creating a report, and validating the report with the GUI of the target device. In turn, the reader should have a basic understanding of what is required to begin to manually decode a database or utilize a forensic tool such as SQLite Forensic Browser.

References

[1] The Statistics Portal, Statista.com, Mobile App Usage, 2016. https://www.statista.com/topics/1002/mobile-app-usage/.
[2] The Statistics Portal, Statista.com, Our Sources Database, 2016. https://www.statista.com/sources/1/.
[3] The Statistics Portal, Statista.com, Forecast of Mobile App Downloads, 2016. https://www.statista.com/statistics/266488/forecast-of-mobile-app-downloads/.
[4] SQLite.org, Temporary Files – Write Ahead Log Files, 2017. https://sqlite.org/tempfiles. html#write_ahead_log_wal_files.
[5] SQLite.org, Nine Kinds of Temporary Files, 2017. https://sqlite.org/tempfiles. html#nine_kinds_of_temporary_files.
[6] SQLite Forensic Explorer, Sanderson Forensics, SQLite Forensic Explorer Manual, Version 1.0.0, 2014, pp. 23–24.

CHAPTER 18

Advanced Validation

Information in This Chapter

- USB Monitoring
- UltraCompare Professional
- Binary comparing (physical)
- Folder comparing (file system)

Introduction

It was in the late 2008 when the author took the stand to testify on a criminal case involving the very popular Motorola V3 (Razr). The defendant's attorney had represented clients in the past where computer evidence had been introduced. He began his questions with regards to training. His questions were formatted around the differences between computer and mobile forensics. He asked about "imaging" a hard disk, and why the same type of imaging could not be performed on his client's phone. (The phone had yielded deleted text messages with regard to a shooting investigation.) He then asked the million dollar question: *"Did the forensic tool that you use make any changes to the phone?"*

At that time, his question was answered *"no."* Many of you reading this know this answer is incorrect. He followed up this question with, *"If no changes were made, did you performed steps to confirm or validate this?"* The answer back was, *"Yes, two different forensic tools cross validated the findings."*

The defense attorney argued that the forensic tools could have made changes to the file system during their communications with the device, and that steps were not taken to confirm what changes were made. He argued that because the data recovered was deleted, there was no way of knowing if the first tool made changes. During the judicial proceedings we used the findings from the second tool, and his argument was that we were merely validating the changes the first tool made. The prosecutor objected, and arguing continued back and forth. Finally the judge asked, *"Did you at any point confirm what changes your forensic tool(s) did to this model phone?"* The author's answer was *"no."* This answer was given at the time, because the author did not know exactly how to validate the changes that do take place at the binary level. Training vendors had mentioned these changes but would simply show that no changes took place in the containers that housed our evidence, such as calls, SMS, and images. They would show how to use visual validation before and after the examination to confirm their tool did not make any changes.

This may sound a bit ludicrous. In court, questions may be asked that deal with how some of these forensic tools work. In this chapter we will address two validation tools that can help provide answers to these questions and will help illustrate what some of this may look like. In our earlier chapters, we have addressed protocols that need to take place between the forensic program and the target mobile device. Most agencies or companies that are tasked with performing mobile forensics will not have the ability to pull off the chip in the examination. This technique is very invasive, not to mention unnecessary in most investigations. Write blocking is not an option, unless we were trying to image the media storage area. As such, the tool must communicate with the mobile evidence. Because of this, there can be changes that take place on the target evidence. Do most investigators who understand advanced validation techniques conduct the examples explained in this chapter on every case? The answer is of course not. They generally do not have the time to undergo such techniques. They should, however, understand how to articulate changes that may take place. This may be where the laboratory validates a new tool, or at the very least, they replicate some of these steps on a "test" phone.

USB Monitoring—Can You Hear Me Now?

In our scenario introduction, defense council questioned what changes took place when we used our forensic tool(s). The truth was lots of things. Ultimately, however, the first tool made very minimal changes to the phone at the binary level. As explained, this may have been understood but was not actually ever validated on any phone in the laboratory prior to that testimony. It certainly was after that case!

Within Chapter 9, readers may recall the use of "Port Monitoring" software (AKA: USB Monitoring). This chapter will use the same example, and expand on explaining this program in more detail. USB Monitoring allow the examiner to "see" or "listen" to the lines of information going to and from the forensic tool to the phone? This can also be referred to as *Serial Sniffing* and *USB Sniffing*. HHD company is located in London, United Kingdom. On their website, they refer to their USB Monitor software with the following explanation:

> *"USB Monitor is a basic tool for monitoring and analyzing USB devices and any kind of application working with them on Windows platform.*
>
> *Universal Serial Bus Monitor allows you to intercept, display, record and analyze USB protocol and all the data transferred between any USB device connected to your PC and applications. It can be successfully used in application development, USB device driver or hardware development and offers the powerful platform for effective coding, testing and optimization.*

USB analyzer can be successfully used for:

- capturing data transfers between any Windows application and USB host controller
- capturing and analyzing USB data exchanged by any device and Windows application
- capturing data flow from USB communications in binary, ASCII, and HEX format
- Universal Serial Bus hardware development
- USB device driver development
- debugging any Universal Serial Bus related software and hardware
- research the functionality of any third-party software and hardware
- implementing, debugging and testing protocol between device and device driver
- USB protocol analyzing and reverse-engineering protocols
- recording and replaying logs while debugging the implemented protocol
- USB analyzing, spying and logging USB communications
- capturing USB data transfer in log file. USB data logger

USB analyzer can be successfully used by:

- software developers
- hardware engineers
- IT support specialists
- programmers
- beta-testers
- industrial control personnel
- SCADA software engineers
- science technicians
- systems integrators, consultants
- lab experts
- University students

USB protocol analyzer usage areas:

- Cameras
- Card readers
- KVM switches
- USB Keyboards
- MP3 players
- Mass Storage devices
- USB Adapters
- Printers
- Scanners
- Universal Serial Bus Ethernet adapters
- USB Hubs
- TV Tuners
- Modems
- Joysticks and Steering Wheels

- *Universal Serial Bus Audio*
- *Universal Serial Bus Midi*
- *USB Serial ports*
- *Human Interface Devices*
- *Pocket PCs*
- *Mobile phones*
- *Ipods*
- *Smartphones*
- *Bar-code readers*
- *Universal Serial Bus Zipdrives*
- *Universal Serial Bus floppy" [1]*

At the basic functional level, if we execute the "Device Monitoring Studio" icon after the USB Monitor is installed (author is using the paid, Ultimate Edition), users can see all the devices that are plugged into the host machine via USB connection. As addressed in Chapter 9, we will be using HyperTerminal to communicate to a Motorola V3 cellular phone that has been set up as a modem.

If we double-click on the device we want to monitor, another window presents to the user. This window is titled **Session Configuration**. The user can select the **Visualizers** they desire. In our example, we use the Raw Data View. This will allow us to see the Read and Write locations in the phone based on a hex view format. The images that pertain to all the steps on using the USB Monitor are contained on the companion site. Fig. 18.1 depicts these first three steps: (1) select device to monitor, (2) select Visualization type, and (3) begin viewing Read/Write to the device.

Our next example utilizes the same Motorola V3. Using HyperTerminal, AT commands are sent to the phone. To start with, we send the command of **at+gmm**, which requests the Make and Model of the connected device. The reply back from the phone is **+GMM: Motorola V3m-Sprint Phone**.

The next command sent is **at+cpbr=?**, which requests to display the starting and ending range of the phone book contacts stored on this device. The reply back is **ERROR** as the phone needs to be in **Mode=2** for this command to work. Mode=2 is then sent to the device, and the phone replies back, "OK." The command **+cpbr=?** is re-sent, with a reply of +CPBR: (1–1430),48,30. The command of **at+cpbr=1,1430** is sent to the phone. The response back provides any stored entry found within the range of 1–1430. To the left side of Fig. 18.2 (in the companion site) the referenced commands are there that were sent to the phone using HyperTerminal. The right side of Fig. 18.2 displays each of these commands as how they appear in the **Raw Data View** of **the Device Monitor Studio** tool. The "**Read**" area displays what the phone has replied back with, and the "**Write**" area displays the AT commands sent to the phone. Fig. 18.2 (companion site) shows the start of these commands and Fig. 18.3 (companion site) displays the remaining entries from the stored phone book entries. This example uses very deliberate and small commands that show how the USB Monitor can provide insight as to what is being sent *to* and *from* the phone. If an examination involved a more complex commercial forensic tool, this could be used to see what information was sent to the phone during the entire acquisition. Once the "Write" area is finished, the entire area that was copied can be selected and then saved (right click). It can be saved as a simple text file. Specific values within the text can be used to reference the examiner to a specific area in the logical, file system, or physical binary pull using a forensic tool such as Physical Analyzer or WinHex. Generally with tools that are used to locate and report data from mobile devices, the top "Read" area is the result of "Write" commands from the tool to a specific location within the file system. For example, if we used a simple CDMA LG flip phone that is supported by BitPim, and selected the SMS to acquire, and then execute the tool with the USB Monitor tracking the activity, the bottom area with "Write" may show the overall *.dat* area where the SMS entry is being read from, while the top "Read" area would show the content of the .dat, such as the timestamp bytes, to/from numbers, and content.

The use of a USB monitoring tool can certainly help the examiner see what information is being transferred to and from the evidence. Now that we can "listen" to what is taking place, let us discuss how we can show if any changes are taking place.

UltraCompare Professional

In the previous chapters, validation was discussed and even included as a keyword in defining cell phone forensics. Forms of validations included the Call Detail Records, visual, manual hand carving, and cross tool. As this chapter has suggested, examiners may find the need to understand additional concepts with regard to how a tool or utility may make changes within a file system or at the binary level.

Addressed several times throughout this book, is the understanding that mobile forensics is not like computer forensics. Examiners typically do not have an exact bit-by-bit copy of the evidence. Instead, they must connect to a device by various means and in turn elicit a response back. Some vendors within the commercial mobile forensics market even go so far as to say that their "tool" does not make any change to the target phone. They may have advertising claims such as "*Read only*" or we can create a "*Forensic copy without making changes to the original data.*"

It is important for experienced examiners to understand that the simple act of connecting a cable to a mobile device will generally always make changes to the file system. How would an examiner go about explaining this process to a jury or possibly supervisors within the private sector? Let us attempt to address and answer the following questions:

Q. What happens to a mobile file system when a "forensic" tool, utility, or process pulls data via logical, file system, or physical means?
Q. Cross-tool acquisitions—do changes take place on the target device?
Q. What changes take place at the binary level?
Q. What changes take place at the file system folder level?
Q. Does our evidence used in court change, and how should we explain all this?

To assist with answering these questions, we can utilize commercially available programs to aid in understanding where changes take place. In our upcoming examples, we will use *UltraCompare Professional*. The program can handle larger files and allows the user to compare two binary files side by side or up to three folders side by side. It can indicate a byte for byte comparison, as well as folder line entry comparison. The differences show as a default color of red (which can be changed). It is distributed by IDM Computer Solutions who also make **Ultra Edit, UEStudio, UltraFinder, UltraSentry,** and **the Mobile Solution**.

We will discuss just a few of the settings and features that are available within the UltraCompare software. The example used a supported phone that can be acquired at all levels (logical, file system, and physical) and forensic tools that can be used to pull data, thus showing changes. We will use Samsung SCH-U365 Gusto II (flip phone).

UltraCompare's Interface

Fig. 18.1 depicts UC's main screen that will appear after the program is launched. In this chapter, we will not go over all the features and settings within UltraCompare. Instead, users will be shown how to bring binary and folder files into the interface and compare the changes.

Binary Example

To start, click on the upper left folder icon—*New Session* (Fig. 18.1). For *Binary* compare we will be using the **Binary (fast)** setting. When we select this, a tab will populate within the program interface (Fig. 18.1). The first file (binary) will need to be entered. This can be accomplished by clicking on *File—Open First* or the folder icon next to the first file window (Fig. 18.1 shows screenshots of each of these settings within the figure).

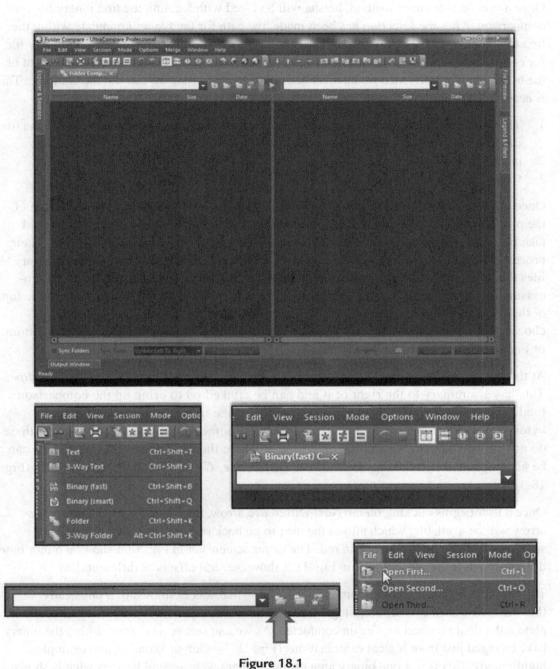

Figure 18.1
UltraCompare's main screen, New Session, Binary (fast), Open folder, and Open First settings.

Once a user selects either method, he/she will be faced with locating the first binary file for comparison. After the selection has been made, the path for the file will populate within the first file window and show in the tab. Users will repeat this process for the second binary file for comparison. They will have the choice of "Open Second" or the file folder to the right of the blank file window. Once we have loaded the two binary files we can run the compare. This is accomplished in three ways:

1. Through the "Go" icon, which is a green sideways triangle—it is located between the two file fields *or*
2. under **View—Go**, or
3. **Ctrl+F5**

Once users click on the "Go" icon, they will see the files being processed at the bottom of the program window. The size of the files will determine how long the processing would take place. In the examples used for this manual, the two binary files are of 135 MB. Their processing time is relatively fast. If, however, users were to take larger smartphone binary files that are in the gigabyte ranges, the processing can take a few minutes. After the processing is completed, users may change the way in which they view the two files. At the top of the program near the center are the Vertical and Horizontal Layout icons. Users can choose accordingly. Fig. 18.2 contains screenshots to each of these steps, and at the bottom of Fig. 18.2, the layout options are shown.

At the bottom of the screen is a tab that is enabled by default and titled *Output Window*. This has a summary to the right of it and can be clicked on to bring up the comparison total. The example in Fig. 18.3 begins at the top of the figure; it indicates how many bytes are different, how many match, and the total number. We can already see that these do not entirely match. We can begin to look at where the differences are noted. This can be accomplished by clicking, *Edit—Next Difference, Go to Next Difference*, or *F3* (Fig. 18.3).

Once a user begins clicking on the Next Difference arrow, the Go to Previous Difference arrow will be available, which allows the user to go back one area at a time. The default settings will show the difference in red. The larger screenshot in Fig. 18.3 shows a minor byte difference while the one below it in Fig. 18.3 shows several offsets of different data.

The example in this chapter is from the same phone that was examined first physically (baseline), and then two different logical tools were used to parse data. Once it was completed, the final physical was again conducted. As we can see, several areas within the binary have changed just from logical examinations (Fig. 18.3—Output Window, and examples highlighted). This is just one binary area example; there were several besides what is shown in Fig. 18.3.

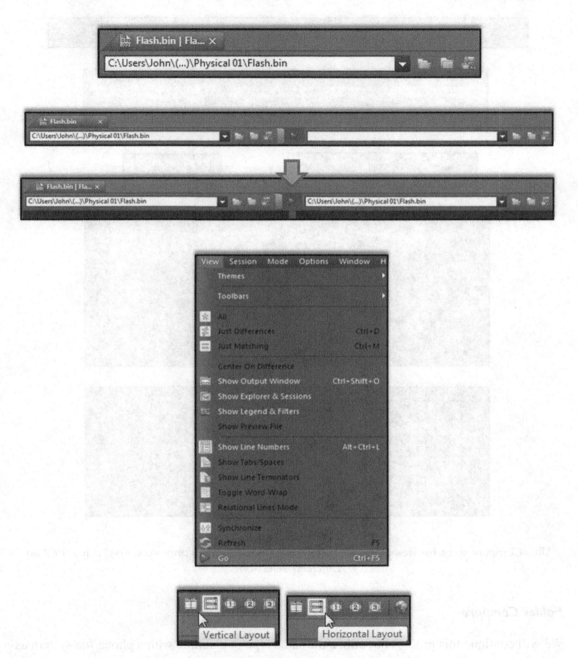

Figure 18.2
UltraCompare's binary compare entry fields, *"Go"* button, *View* settings, and *Vertical* and *Horizontal* settings.

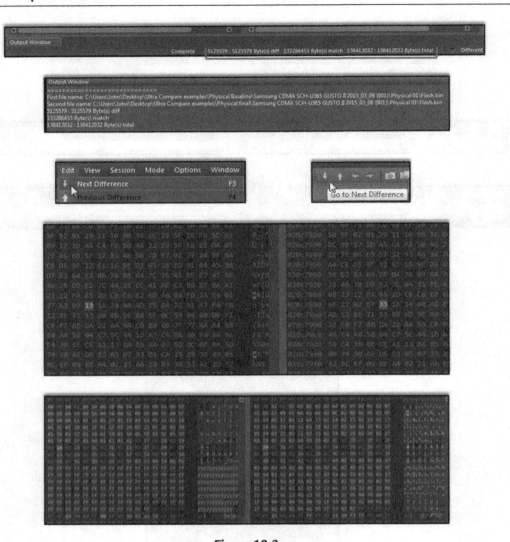

Figure 18.3
UltraCompare steps for viewing binary differences (in red (gray in print versions)) using the *Next Difference* selection.

Folder Compare

We will continue this process but utilize the same type of example with a phone file system as the comparison. This will be easier for the user to see exactly where the changes took place. The file compare option will be selected. Unlike the binary, which only allows two files, up to three folders can be compared at once. We will only be comparing two folders in the example.

The two file systems are titled baseline and a final file system. Users can title them whatever they desire. The *final file system* was acquired after two different logical tools acquired data from the phone. The same steps of importing them into UC and selecting "Go" applies when using the *Folder* compare. Once the processing is complete, the *Output Window* tab can be used to show the summary differences. It is important to understand that even though two logical tools were used between the baseline and final, it really did not matter that how many were used to illustrate the changes that take place. Fig. 18.4 depicts the Folder selection; the Output Window show the differences between the two file systems and the side-by-side comparison view. Notice the ***sysinfo.j*** area indicating a red star.

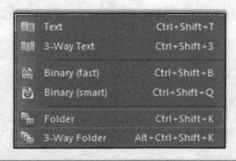

Figure 18.4

UltraCompare folder compare steps—select Folder, view Output Window for changes, and view the side-by-side for areas of change.

Users can look at the file systems side by side. Any area that has a change will have a red star in the root of the folder and then a corresponding red star in the actual folder that contains the change. Users can double-click on the actual folder and bring up the contents of the folder in a side-by-side comparison. Fig. 18.5 depicts the *sysinfo.j* folder in hex view. As indicated in Fig. 18.5, there are 36 bytes with differences between these two file systems.

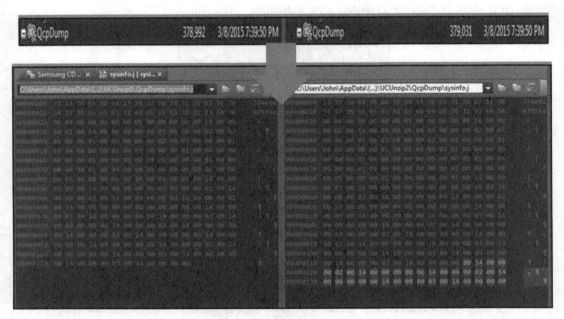

Figure 18.5
Comparing the byte differences with the side-by-side view in hex.

Replicate This Test

The following steps may be used to replicate this binary and file system comparison. Also, if desired, users can connect the HHD USB Monitor tool to see the activity on the baseline binary as well as the baseline file system. First, here is a list of forensic tools and the phone to conduct specific examinations.

- **UFED 4PC**—Used to obtain a baseline and final physical acquisition, and baseline and final file system. This program was also used to conduct a logical examination between these two primary examinations.
- **Secure View For Forensics 4**—Used to obtain a logical examination between the two baseline physical and file system examinations.
- **Device used**—Samsung SCH-U365 Gusto II with user SMS and call history.

Create four separate folders titled "***Base Line Physical Exam***, ***Final Physical Exam***, ***Base line File System Exam***, and ***Final File System Exam***." Using UFED Touch or UFED 4PC, conduct a Physical Exam–target the examination to extract to the ***Base Line Physical Exam*** folder.

Next, use UFED Touch or UFED 4PC to conduct a File System examination. Target the examination to extract into the ***Base Line File System Exam*** folder. Now conduct a logical examination using Susteen. (Pull all supported data.) When this is finished conduct another logical examination using UFED Touch or UFED 4PC. It is not necessary to keep track of the output folders for the two logical exams—all that is important is that examiners perform at least one logical examination. Next, conduct another physical examination using UFED Touch or UFED 4PC. Target this examination to extract into the ***Final Physical Exam*** folder.

Lastly, conduct another UFED Touch or UFED 4PC file system extraction. Target this examination to extract into the ***Final File System Exam*** folder. Go into the two File System examination folders—Base Line File System Exam and Final File System Exam—unzip each to the same folder location. Although UC supports zipped containers, it will become important that examiners see the unzipped folder structure when comparing the differences. Bring in either the Folder examinations (file systems) or the binary examinations and compare the results. Note: Use UltraCompare Binary (Fast) settings to compare the baseline binary against the final binary.

In this example, we could explain that both the binary and the folder comparisons changed between examinations. Although the binary showed a number of bytes that changed, the folders showed that our target containers (SMS, Calls, etc.) that we typically use in judicial proceedings as exhibits went unchanged. In some cases, it may be more difficult to show changes depending on what type of examination some are limited to. The USB Monitor can help show where the tool is reading to, if the examiner can plug the phone into the forensic machine running Windows. The "writing" aspect of the USB Monitor does not necessarily mean that it is making changes. The tool interface is using that type of GUI to show the activity, and as a command is sent to the phone, it can show in the bottom of the interface as a *Write* entry, when in fact, a binary compare may show that no actual "writing" was in that area. Another way to use the USB Monitor is to connect it between each tool that is being used to conduct the examination, even a logical pull. Both the Read and Write views can be saved as logs when the examination has completed. Then connect another logical tool and repeat the same steps. Compare the logs and note the differences between the tools.

Chapter Summary Key Points

The use of the HHD USB Monitor tool can assist investigators with documenting the activity between a forensic tool and a target mobile device that is being acquired in real time. This program can show what is being sent *to* and *from* the device. The program works by allowing the examiner to select a device through Device Manager, which is plugged into an available USB port. Once the device is selected, the user can use the *Raw Data View* in the *Visualizer* to see the activity. The interface allows the **Read** and **Write** activity to be saved as logs. These logs may be used as a reference point to "look" into the file system or binary image with other viewers.

To show changes to a file system or a binary, examiners can utilize the UltraCompare Professional program. This allows two different binary files, or up to three different folders to be compared at one time. Examiners who have specific devices that either support binary or file system acquisitions can use this tool to compare a before and after examination, or examinations between different tools. The interface of this tool allows the user to see the changes in the default red color. Users can also use the Output Window to see the number of bytes that represent changes between the binary or folders being compared.

When performing extractions, examiners should have an understanding as to what changes may take place at both the logical and physical level. Performing validation testing with the commercial forensic tools used in your laboratory can help address potential issues that may arise during the judicial process. Forensic utilities based on their design will make changes. This does not equate to changes to the direct folder or database that stores the incriminating evidence. Hopefully you now understand how to validate a tool and articulate what exactly it has changed on the phone during its extraction.

Reference

[1] USB Monitor, HHD Software, 2017. http://www.hhdsoftware.com/usb-monitor.

PART 3

Advanced Concepts

CHAPTER 19

Android User Enabled Security: Passwords and Gesture

Information in This Chapter

- Security on Androids
- Simple security values
- The password lock
- Hashcat
- The pattern lock (gesture)
- Using a rainbow table
- SHA-1 exercise

Introduction—Security on Androids

Since their inception, Android devices (the first being the HTC G1) have provided the user the ability to employ simple security measures. As the operating system versions changed, different types of security also evolved. Today, the consumer can rely on embedded security features from a specific OS or exclusive settings based on the make and model. There is also an ability to download and install specific applications for the same purpose. Some of the more popular and embedded by OS and/or make and model, include but are not limited to:

- PIN
- Password
- Pattern (gesture)
- Fingerprint
- Facial recognition
- Knock lock

It would be unnecessary to dedicate an entire chapter showing each of these security types. Instead, this chapter will primarily address the password and gesture lock. This is continuing to be one of the more popular user enabled security measures employed on Androids. Some of you may be reading this and saying, "*My _____ (fill in the blank) unit/machine/utility can get past that security. What do I need to know more about this process?*"

Yes, in the forensic utility market, many makes and models *are* supported for bypassing the gesture lock. There are some examiners, however, who may find the need to testify on the process or, in some cases, manually obtain the lock value(s) to enter the phone for visual validation, manual documentation, or to enable/disable a setting to perform an additional examination. The content in this chapter will allow the examiner to have more insight into at least one of the more popular security measures that is stored on an Android.

Simple Security Values

Before the advent of smartphones, the operating system on some phones would simply store the actual user value within the operating system. This means that if the user placed a handset lock code of 1325 on a simple bar or flip phone, that value would be stored in the basic encoding for the phone, usually in ASCII or Unicode. It could easily be located by employing encoding search techniques using popular tools such as Cellebrite's Physical Analyzer. Also, many of the devices will contain the user PIN and user security code just a few offsets from one another within the file system. On some phones, the security code is used to bypass the PIN if it is unknown. In a past criminal investigation several years ago, a homicide victim decided to change his 4-digit PIN and 6-digit (default) security codes. The phone was a Motorola iDEN. At the time of this incident, automatic tools were limited, and large vendors such as Cellebrite did support the phone for physical extraction, but the parsing on SMS and other user areas was limited. Logical settings, however, would parse the required fields for the case. A test phone of the same model was used to place a different (known) value for the PIN and 6-digit security code. Using the ***Find—Code*** tab in Physical Analyzer, the values on the test phone were easily located. They were an offset apart and had unique characters before and after these security codes. A RegEX expression was then used to locate the values on the victim's phone, unlock the GUI, and allow a logical parsing of several SMS messages related to his death. The point of explaining this case is to convey that these values were on the phone, in their original state. This was typically how phones stored the security imposed by the user. There are many phones still sold today that work this way. These generally fall into the pay-as-you-go, simple "burner-phone" categories. They lack sophisticated operating systems and have limited features. Many are supported by several commercial forensic tools, while others may lock down their USB data port.

Fig. 19.1 is a file system from an LG VX8100 that was acquired from Bitpim. Within the ***nvm_security*** folder we can see the default 6-digit security value of ***000000***. The user enabled security PIN is below this, toward the end of offset 90 as ***1397*** (bottom image in Fig. 19.1).

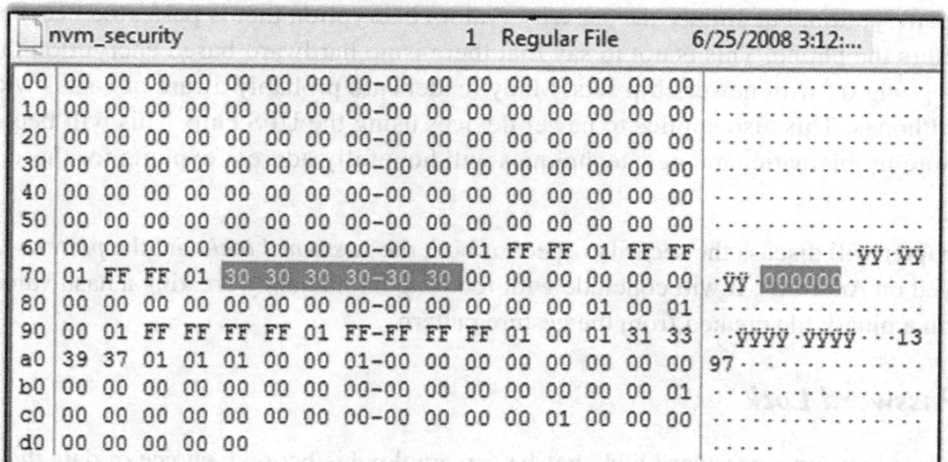

```
 nvm_security                          1   Regular File      6/25/2008 3:12:...

00  00 00 00 00 00 00 00 00-00 00 00 00 00 00 00 00   ................
10  00 00 00 00 00 00 00 00-00 00 00 00 00 00 00 00   ................
20  00 00 00 00 00 00 00 00-00 00 00 00 00 00 00 00   ................
30  00 00 00 00 00 00 00 00-00 00 00 00 00 00 00 00   ................
40  00 00 00 00 00 00 00 00-00 00 00 00 00 00 00 00   ................
50  00 00 00 00 00 00 00 00-00 00 00 00 00 00 00 00   ................
60  00 00 00 00 00 00 00 00-00 00 01 FF FF 01 FF FF   ..........ÿÿ.ÿÿ
70  01 FF FF 01 30 30 30 30-30 30 00 00 00 00 00 00   .ÿÿ.000000......
80  00 00 00 00 00 00 00 00-00 00 00 00 00 01 00 01   ................
90  00 01 FF FF FF FF 01 FF-FF FF FF 01 00 01 31 33   .ÿÿÿÿ.ÿÿÿÿ...13
a0  39 37 01 01 01 00 00 01-00 00 00 00 00 00 00 00   97..............
b0  00 00 00 00 00 00 00 00-00 00 00 00 00 00 00 01   ................
c0  00 00 00 00 00 00 00 00-00 00 00 00 01 00 00 00   ................
d0  00 00 00 00 00                                    .....
```

Six-digit security (Non-smart phone OS)

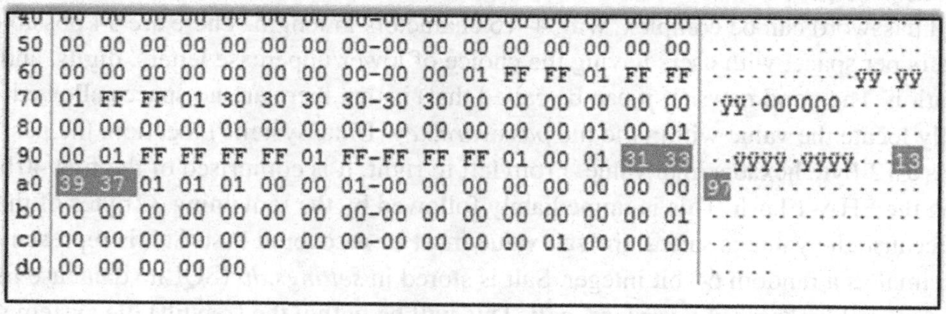

```
40  00 00 00 00 00 00 00 00-00 00 00 00 00 00 00 00   ................
50  00 00 00 00 00 00 00 00-00 00 00 00 00 00 00 00   ................
60  00 00 00 00 00 00 00 00-00 00 01 FF FF 01 FF FF   ..........ÿÿ.ÿÿ
70  01 FF FF 01 30 30 30 30-30 30 00 00 00 00 00 00   .ÿÿ.000000......
80  00 00 00 00 00 00 00 00-00 00 00 00 00 01 00 01   ................
90  00 01 FF FF FF FF 01 FF-FF FF FF 01 00 01 31 33   .ÿÿÿÿ.ÿÿÿÿ...13
a0  39 37 01 01 01 00 00 01-00 00 00 00 00 00 00 00   97..............
b0  00 00 00 00 00 00 00 00-00 00 00 00 00 00 00 01   ................
c0  00 00 00 00 00 00 00 00-00 00 00 00 01 00 00 00   ................
d0  00 00 00 00 00                                    .....
```

Four-digit user enabled security (Non-smart phone OS)

Figure 19.1

Example of default security and user set PIN values of an LG VX8100 mobile phone.

Smartphones

In most cases when the user employs a specific type of security on a smartphone, the actual value is converted out of this simple format shown in Fig. 19.1. Depending on which type of security the user chooses, it runs a check against a specific hash value of that security when the user wants to enter the GUI. It is important that examiners understand that when it comes to the gesture and password locks, we are not addressing the entire file system encryption, but simply the security (value) encryption that is performed each time a user enters the phone. This is not to say that there is no hardware-based encryption that may be going on with newer chip sets. Many readers are probably aware of issues with newer iPhones. This also applies to newer devices using the UFS chip. This will become even more problematic, and new techniques will hopefully address exploits for these issues.

This chapter will discuss the security aspect of both the *password lock* and the *pattern lock* employed on Androids. It will conclude with focusing on manually creating a hash value based on a binary file created from the gesture pattern.

The Password Lock

When a user sets up a password lock, he/she can employ his/her own choice of data that contain special characters, numbers, letters, or any combination of the same. If the user sets up a password lock, it is given a hash that uses a combination of SHA-1 and MD5. The value is also salted. Salt or salting is the process of adding additional security, as it randomizes the hash. This can prevent dictionaries and rainbow tables from breaking the hash values that are always the same, such as what readers will see when we discuss the gesture value. The Android password can be complex, with 4–16 characters in length. There are 94 possible characters per space, with users having the choice of lower/uppercase letters, digits, and punctuation. The good news (if it can be called that) is that there are no spaces allowed. If we manually locate the value within the file *password.key* (Data/System/) location, the password hash has a 72-byte hexadecimal value. From left to right, it is comprised of the first 40 bytes showing the SHA-1 hash. This is immediately followed by the remaining 32 bytes of the MD5 hash. Because the value is salted, the salt value must be recovered first. Salt is represented in hexadecimal as a random 64-bit integer. Salt is stored in *settings.db* (SQLite database file), which is named *lockscreen.password_salt*. This will be within the (rebuilt) file system shown here:

data/data/com.android.providers.settings/databases/settings.db

If examiners have pulled a binary that has not been rebuilt and decoded with tools such as Physical Analyzer, it is a little bit more time-consuming to locate the password.key and the salt value. If examiners conduct an ASCII search for "lockscreen.password_salt," they will obtain at least one hit that places them in general the area they need to look for the entire salt value. The salt is a string of the hexadecimal representation of a random 64-bit integer. The value along with the MD5 or SHA-1 from the password key location can then be used to brute force attack the values with Hashcat. Here are some steps to help examiners locate the salt when they have a physical file from a JTAG, ISP, or chip-off examination.

Hashcat

Hashcat is a free, open-source tool, which supports several different algorithms, and can be installed in multiple operating systems [1]. Using their latest list from the version available at the time this was written (3.30), the following algorithms can be attacked:

- MD4, MD5, Half MD5 (left, mid, right), SHA1, SHA-224, SHA-256, SHA-384, SHA-512, SHA-3 (Keccak), SipHash, RipeMD160, Whirlpool, DES (PT=$salt, key=$pass), 3DES (PT=$salt, key=$pass), GOST R 34.11-9, GOST R 34.11-2012 (Streebog) 256-bit, GOST R 34.11-2012 (Streebog) 512-bit, Double MD5, Double SHA1, md5($pass.$salt), md5($salt.$pass), md5(unicode($pass).$salt), md5($salt.unicode($pass)), md5(sha1($pass)), md5($salt.md5($pass)), md5($salt.$pass.$salt), md5(strtoupper(md5($pass))), sha1($pass.$salt), sha1($salt.$pass), sha1(unicode($pass).$salt), sha1($salt.unicode($pass)), sha1(md5($pass)), sha1($salt.$pass.$salt), sha1(CX), sha256($pass.$salt), sha256($salt.$pass), sha256(unicode($pass).$salt), sha256($salt.unicode($pass)), sha512($pass.$salt), sha512($salt.$pass), sha512(unicode($pass).$salt), sha512($salt.unicode($pass)), HMAC-MD5 (key=$pass), HMAC-MD5 (key=$salt), HMAC-SHA1 (key=$pass), HMAC-SHA1 (key=$salt), HMAC-SHA256 (key=$pass), HMAC-SHA256 (key=$salt), HMAC-SHA512 (key=$pass), HMAC-SHA512 (key=$salt), PBKDF2-HMAC-MD5, PBKDF2-HMAC-SHA1, PBKDF2-HMAC-SHA256, PBKDF2-HMAC-SHA512, MyBB, phpBB3, SMF, vBulletin, IPB, Woltlab Burning Board, osCommerce, xt:Commerce, PrestaShop, Mediawiki B type, Wordpress, Drupal, Joomla, PHPS, Django (SHA-1), Django (PBKDF2-SHA256), EPiServer, ColdFusion 10+, Apache MD5-APR, MySQL, PostgreSQL, MSSQL, Oracle H: Type (Oracle 7+), Oracle S: Type (Oracle 11+), Oracle T: Type (Oracle 12+), Sybase, hMailServer, DNSSEC (NSEC3), IKE-PSK, IPMI2 RAKP, iSCSI CHAP, Cram MD5, MySQL Challenge-Response Authentication (SHA1), PostgreSQL Challenge-Response Authentication (MD5), SIP Digest Authentication (MD5), WPA, WPA2, NetNTLMv1, NetNTLMv1+ESS, NetNTLMv2, Kerberos 5 AS-REQ Pre-Auth etype 23Kerberos 5 TGS-REP etype 23, Netscape LDAP SHA/SSHA, LM, NTLM, Domain Cached Credentials (DCC), MS Cache, Domain Cached Credentials 2 (DCC2), MS Cache 2, MS-AzureSync PBKDF2-HMAC-SHA256, descrypt, bsdicrypt, md5crypt, sha256crypt, sha512crypt, bcrypt, scrypt, OSX v10.4, OSX v10.5, OSX v10.6, OSX v10.7, OSX v10.8, OSX v10.9, OSX v10.10, AIX {smd5}, AIX {ssha1}, AIX {ssha256}, AIX {ssha512}, Cisco-ASA, Cisco-PIX, Cisco-IOS, Cisco 8, Cisco 9, Juniper IVE, Juniper Netscreen/SSG (ScreenOS), Android PIN, Windows 8+phone PIN/Password, GRUB 2, CRC32, RACF, Radmin2, Redmine, OpenCart, Citrix Netscaler, SAP CODVN B (BCODE), SAP CODVN F/G (PASSCODE), SAP CODVN H (PWDSALTEDHASH) iSSHA-1, PeopleSoft, PeopleSoft PS_TOKEN, Skype, WinZip, 7-Zip, RAR3-hp, RAR5, AxCrypt, AxCrypt in memory SHA1, PDF 1.1–1.3 (Acrobat 2–4), PDF 1.4–1.6 (Acrobat 5–8), PDF 1.7 Level 3 (Acrobat 9), PDF 1.7 Level 8 (Acrobat 10–11), MS Office <= 2003 MD5, MS Office <= 2003 SHA1, MS Office 2007, MS Office 2010, MS Office 2013, Lotus Notes/Domino 5, Lotus Notes/Domino 6, Lotus Notes/Domino 8, Bitcoin/Litecoin wallet.dat, Blockchain, My Wallet, 1Password, agilekeychain, 1Password, cloudkeychain, Lastpass, Password Safe v2, Password Safe v3, Keepass 1 (AES/Twofish) and Keepass 2 (AES), Plaintext, eCryptfs, Android FDE <= 4.3, Android FDE (Samsung DEK), TrueCrypt, VeraCrypt [1].

The use of Hashcat could easily take up a couple of different chapters. We will not spend too much time covering the exact steps of this program. In previous versions, the user needed to specify if they needed oclHashcat, for AMD graphic cards, or CudaHashcat, if they used Nvidia. They have combined the use into one program, and some of the examples used in this chapter used version 3.30.

When we attempt to break the password on an Android, Hashcat has the ability to break the entire string of 72 bytes, along with the salt, but the time evolved tremendously increases. If we focus on separating these hashes, and then locating the salt, it makes the attack much easier to manage. Of course, the longer the password, the more time needed. Most individuals do not use all 16 characters and generally keep their password relatively short. The food for thought here is if you have a robust forensic machine, why not try it? Hashcat usually runs an estimated time on how long the process will take. From there you can decide if you want to continue or keep it running and hand it over to your replacement after you retire with 30 years of service.

If we are dealing with a raw physical pull that has not been decoded, we can use the search technique previously described (*lockscreen.password_salt*) to locate the general area to find the salt. As we look at the search results, we need to examine the byte value directly in front of this search hit. It will be in a range between 0×0F and 0×35. That byte provides the examiner the length of the salt. Directly in front of these series of bytes, there will be a byte displaying the value of 0×3D. This byte represents a string length of 24, which is the length of our value we are looking for. Fig. 19.2 depicts an actual salt value that represents these values we just explained and the ASCII search hit that was used. For readers who are viewing this book electronically, they are color coded and labeled to illustrate this further. Once we locate the salt integer, it needs to be converted to hexadecimal. In older versions of Hashcat, the uppercase letters in the converted value must be converted to lowercase to conduct brute force attempts. The newer version of Hashcat (3.30) no longer requires this step. Fig. 19.3 depicts the salt value from the *settings.db* area, which is much easier to locate. Again, depending on which type of extraction examiners have performed, the method needed for locating the salt will be determined. Obviously, the database is much easier and preferred, if this is possible in your casework.

00 = Constraint value that will be in front of length, **3D** = Length, **35** = Salt length

ASCII search: "**lockscreen.password_salt**"

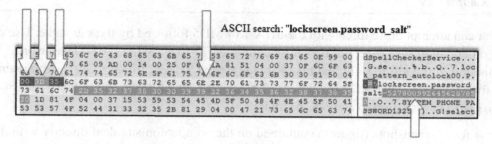

Salt value (integer) must be converted to a hexadecimal value. The upper letters are
lower cased for *HashCat* to brute force (**b6c0bdef9c965d96**)

Figure 19.2

Breakdown of locating the salt value in Hex View and converting the integer value to hexadecimal.

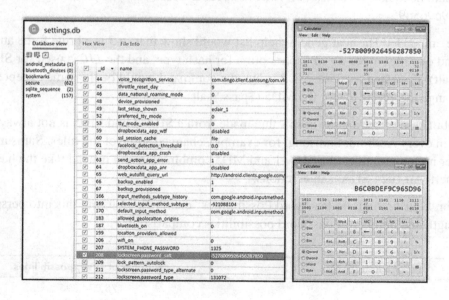

Using the *settings.db* to obtain the salt value. Use the same conversation of the integer to hexadecimal.
Use lower case letters for HashCat brute force (**b6c0bdef9c965d96**)

Figure 19.3

Breakdown of locating the salt value from the com.android.providers.settings/databases/settings.
db location and converting the integer value.

Hashcat can attempt brute force with the SHA-1 or MD5 followed by the salt value. Use one or the other, but to save time, not the entire combined 72-byte (SHA-1/MD5) password combination. From left to right, the first 40 bytes are the SHA-1, followed by the remaining bytes for MD5. Since the MD5 is shorter (32 bytes), it is much easier to use that value from the *password.key* location to attempt the attack.

The first four screenshots (figures) contained on the companion site deal directly with the help list from Hashcat. The first figure, Fig. 19.1 (companion site), is obtained from Hashcat 3.30. This is directly from the help command (C:\>hashcat64.exe -h), which displays the various options and commands that can be used. This first screenshot is just some of the choices, there are more. Fig. 19.1 (companion site) shows the first choice, which is the "Options." Fig. 19.2 (companion site) is a few of the "Hash modes." Again, not the entire list of all the choices. Fig. 19.3 (companion site) depicts the "Attack Modes." The last figure from Hashcat 3.30 (companion site, Fig. 19.4) shows some "Basic Examples" and links to where people can locate additional help.

Obviously, the tool runs in the command line (*Run As Administrator*) and, depending on the video card used, will represent which additional line codes a user would use. If we install Hashcat in the root of C: drive in Windows, we could use a command line on a 64-bit Windows machine that is running a supported GPU as the following:

C:\.Hashcat64.exe-a3-m110 AE36A990BF8300123E43EBF01E39EE41335F1406: b6c0bdef9c965d96

Using the embedded Hashcat general help list would show that *-a 3* is a brute force attack option, and qualifier noted as *-m* is our option for hash type, and the *110* is used for SHA-1 ($pass.$salt). If we had used the MD5 value, the command would be the same except we would change the *110* to *10* for the MD5 ($pass.$salt).

This combination of salting the hash value made from a SHA-1 and MD5 is not always followed in every Android. Samsung, for example, changed some of the rules. Samsung III and higher no longer utilize the SHA-1 and MD5 combination and instead take the hash and salt and perform 1024 SHA-1 interactions.

Using John Lehr's "Android Password Possibilities" chart [2], let us put this into perspective with a length and number of password possibilities comparison:

Length (PW)	Number of (PW) possibilities
4	78,074,896
5	3,339,040,224
6	689,869,781,056
7	64,847,759,419,264
8	6,095,689,385,410,816

Length (PW)	Number of (PW) possibilities
9	572,994,802,228,616,704
10	53,861,511,409,489,970,176
11	5,062,982,072,492,057,196,544
12	475,920,314,814,253,376,475,136
13	44,736,509,592,539,817,388,662,784
14	4,205,231,901,698,742,834,534,301,696
15	395,291,798,759,681,826,446,224,359,424
16	37,157,429,083,410,091,685,945,089,785,856

As we can see, tools such as Hashcat are needed to speed up the process of brute force cracking passwords. Readers can locate additional information regarding Hashcat through Internet searches. Another interesting way some examiners are tackling the problem, is by daisy chaining several high-end graphic cards and create a machine dedicated to cracking passwords.

Q. Why decode the password lock?

In most forensic scenarios, the examiner has performed a physical pull, and for various case-related reasons, decoding of the password lock is needed. It may be a case where a file system or logical pull is necessary, and the examiner must get into the GUI of the device to enable the USB debugging. There may also be cases where the examiner needs to view application data under an exigent situation or validate data. Whatever the reason, there may be times when the physical examination is not enough for the case requirements.

The actual pull itself when there is a password lock enabled can be accomplished with rooted Androids, debugging being enabled already, or in some cases using JTAG or ISP pulls. There are some newer Androids that will not support rooting and/or JTAP/ISP. Because of the complexity of some passwords, python scripts could take in some cases, over 8500 millennia to complete. However, forensic machines that employ higher-end graphic card or multiple cards could crack the same password in hours. There are specific limitations and there may be situations where the passcode cannot be brute forced in the examiner's lifetime or at least without more hardware costs being employed on the host machine.

The Pattern Lock (Gesture)

The GUI of the Android shows the pattern lock as a series of round dots as shown in the simple illustration in Fig. 19.4. There are totally nine—three in three rows. If we number each of these and begin counting from left to right and continue counting left to right, each will have its own number. Like the password lock, the security does not store the values of each of these as a number, but SHA-1 hashes the value, and stores the SHA-1. Users who create a pattern are not allowed to move over one point several times, and there are only 895,924 variants to the pattern on an Android. The hashed SHA-1 value given to the bytes is placed in the file system in the **gesture.key** file, again with the same path as before: /data/system. Computers begin counting at value 0. The first gesture is not a value of 1 converted to bytes then SHA-1, but rather a value of 0. This means that the values start at zero and end with eight, not nine. The hexadecimal equivalent of each single point is 0×00, through 0×08.

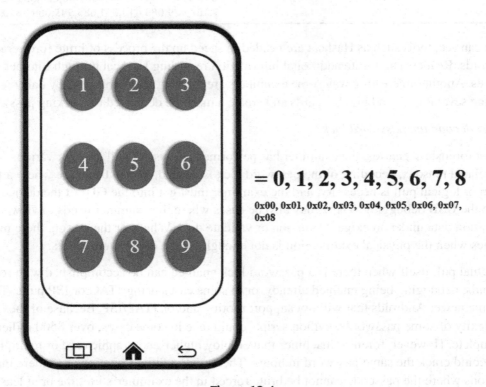

= 0, 1, 2, 3, 4, 5, 6, 7, 8

0x00, 0x01, 0x02, 0x03, 0x04, 0x05, 0x06, 0x07, 0x08

Figure 19.4

Illustration to show the numbering of the 9 pattern (*dots*) on the screen of an Android and how they are counted in hexadecimal.

If we created the minimum length of a gesture pattern of four areas and begin with the numbered values used 1,2,3,4 (left side image in Fig. 19.5), this would utilize corresponding bytes 00 01 02 03, which would in turn perform a SHA-1 hash. The resulting hash algorithm would be stored on the Android in the *gesture.key* location as:

A02A05B025B928C039CF1AE7E8EE04E7C190C0DB

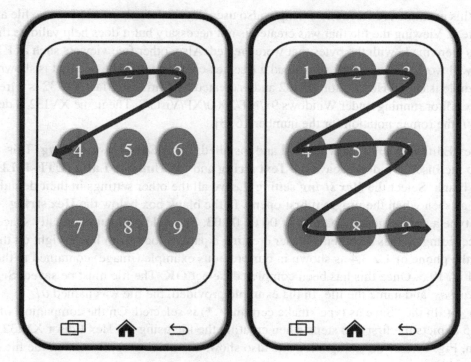

Figure 19.5
Two different examples of gesture security patterns (1,2,3,4 and 1,2,3,4,5,6,7,8,9).

If we create the gesture combination of 9,8,7,6,5,4,3,2,1, it would show as what is depicted in the right side image in Fig. 19.5, and convert the bytes to the SHA-1 value, which is also stored in the *gesture.key* location as:

853822DCEE4C6B59D4A9F0C4CDAF97989E29C83A

Extraction Summary

There are commercially available forensic programs that can decode the gesture pattern and display it in the summary of the report. For example, if we decode the gesture pattern on an LG LS-670, it may display within the summary as unlock pattern
1->2->3->6->9->8->5->4->7.

SHA-1 Exercise

To help better understand the values that are stored in the gesture.key location, there is a simple exercise that replicates the stored gesture that is hash as a SHA-1. Several of the tools used in this example are free. The example also uses Physical Analyzer to view the file after we create it. Viewing the file that was created is not necessary but it does help validate that no mistakes were made with the bytes that were created. Also, other free viewers such as FTK Imager will work. To start with, download a free hex creation tool. The one that is shown in this example is called Hex Editor XVI32 and is created by Christian Mas. XVI32 is a freeware hex editor running under Windows 9x/NT/2000/XP/Vista/7. The name XVI32 is derived from *XVI*, the roman notation for the number 16 [3].

Once Hex Editor XVI32 is downloaded and installed, go to ***Edit—Insert String***. This will bring up the Insert window. Leave the **Text string** and "**as Unicode Latin (UTF-16LE)**" settings blank. Select the ***Hex string*** setting. Leave all the other settings in their default settings as seen when the program first opens. In the blank box below the **Hex string** setting, type a simple gesture pattern of 00 01 02 03. The field will automatically space the bytes accordingly. This represents a user creating a pattern lock from left to right on the GUI of the phone of 1,2,3,4 as shown in our previous example (image) contained in the left side of Fig. 19.5. Once this has been completed, select **OK**. The file must be saved. Select *File—Save as*, and name the file. In the example provided, the file was named *01_ through_04*. In the "Save as type" make certain (****.****) is selected. On the companion site, Fig. 19.5 depicts the first two steps when creating the file using the Hex Editor XVI32 program. Fig. 19.6 of the companion site also shows the naming configuration the file needs to be saved in.

This file can be opened with a hex viewer or FTK Imager. The next step is to create a SHA-1 hash value. Again, there are several free programs available, and FTK Imager can create both an MD5 and SHA-1, exporting the values to a .csv file. In our example, we use DigitalVolcano Hash Tool 1.1. "*A freeware utility to calculate the hash of multiple files. This is a 128-bit number usually expressed as a 32-character hexadecimal number. It can be said to be the 'signature' of a file or string and is used in many applications, including checking the integrity of downloaded files. This compact application helps you quickly and easily list the hashes of your files*" [4]. This free utility allows the user to hash desired files using MD5, SHA-1, SHA-256, SHA-384, SHA-512, and CRC-32 algorithms.

Once the program is downloaded and installed, we select SHA-1, and then select our saved **. ** file, and in our example of 1,2,3,4 (bytes 00 01 02 03), the SHA-1 value created is:

a02a05b025b928c039cf1ae7e8ee04e7c190c0db

If we take a dictionary of possible SHA-1 patterns (Rainbow Table) that use all the variants possible, we will see that this SHA-1 matches our pattern of 1,2,3,4 (or 0,1,2,3). The companion site (Chapter 19), contains text file titled "*Gesture Dictionary_Rainbow table—Notepad.*" This was used to compare the SHA-1 value we created from our bytes of 00 01 02 03. Fig. 19.6 shows the SHA-1 value created using DigitalVolcano Hash Tool 1.1 followed by pasting the value using Ctrl+F keys into the dictionary. The matching values are highlighted in the bottom image of Figure 19.6.

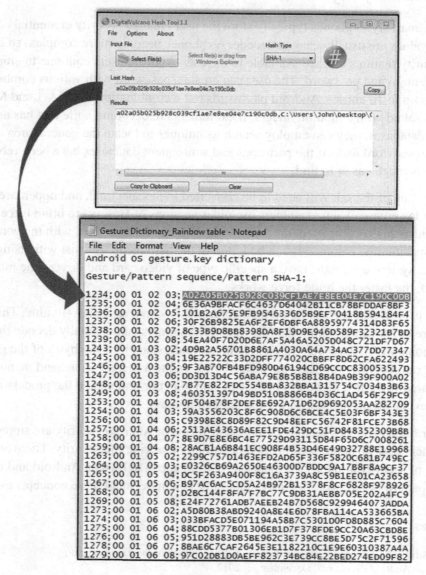

Figure 19.6

DigitalVolcano Hash Tool and comparison with an Android Gesture dictionary (Rainbow Table).

This rainbow table can be utilized to decode any SHA-1 value that is in the gesture.key location. This is also how Physical Analyzer decodes the same entry. By understanding how the pattern is stored, as well as how to replicate and decode the same SHA-1 byte values, examiners should now have a better understanding of this security feature on Androids.

Chapter Summary Key Points

Simple (nonsmart style) phones typically store the user enabled security credentials on the phone. The values are usually easy to decode. As phones become more complex, so do the types of security features that are available to the user. Android users continue to employ both the gesture pattern and password. The user can create a password with various combinations of characters up to 16 entries. Android passwords use a combination of SHA-1 and MD5. The value is also salted with a random integer. If examiners are decoding a file that has not been rebuilt with databases, they can employ search techniques to locate the general area of the salt value for the password lock. If the partitions and subsequent databases have been rebuilt, the salt location is much easier to find.

The integer value of the salt will need to be converted to hexadecimal, and uppercase letters converted to lowercase, when examiners use older versions of Hashcat to brute force the password. Once this is completed, the SHA-1 or MD5 can be combined with the converted salt value. Specific line commands can be found in the help menu to assist with using Hashcat. The system used must have a specific type of video card and driver. The more cards that are used, the faster the brute force works.

The gesture pattern that users store on their Androids is stored as a SHA-1 value. This will be in the gesture.key location within the file system. Examiners can manually decode this value using a dictionary (Rainbow Table). To help better understand how the bytes of the gesture are stored, examiners can replicate the actual bytes, create a SHA-1 value, and manually locate the same value in a dictionary. This can help to better understand the process and assist during any explanations needed during the judicial process.

This chapter briefly touches on how two popular forms of Android security are stored, and how examiners may go about locating and potentially cracking the security. There are many more forms of security at the user's disposal. If you happen to own an Android and use either the gesture pattern or password security, hopefully you understand these concepts even more.

References

[1] Hashcat, Advanced Password Recovery, January 6, 2017. https://hashcat.net/hashcat/.
[2] What's in an Android Password?, December 31, 2012.
     http://linuxsleuthing.blogspot.com/2012/10/android-pinpassword-cracking-halloween.html.
[3] Freeware Hex Editor XVI32, June 26, 2012. http://www.chmaas.handshake.de/delphi/freeware/xvi32/xvi32.htm.
[4] Digital Volcano Software. https://www.digitalvolcano.co.uk/hash.html.

CHAPTER 20

Nondestructive Hardware and Software Solutions

Information in This Chapter

- MFC Dongle
- IP Box
- UFED User Lock Code Recovery Tool
- BST
- MTP and PTP
- XPIN Clip
- Other techniques
- Flasher boxes
- Bootloaders

Introduction

If you are a mobile forensics practitioner, you have probably been approached by friends and family and asked questions about phones. If you are like the author, you try to be as brief as possible when describing your field of work.

The reasons for this is that most people believe what they hear in the news, which is not entirely accurate. This is usually the result of a government case that has made national headlines. It could involve terrorism and the need to get into a phone. People rightfully want to protect their rights and employ any choice of security method that will protect their electronic property. Often, they want to hear what you have to say about these topics and can, at times, view *you* as the entity that is imposing on their rights.

As you get closer to the end of this book, you may find additional techniques that can help you with your own investigation(s). As you read, remember what the title of this book is. The tools discussed in this chapter are used just for that purpose. What is found here is not an exclusive, list by any means. To close this introduction, consider the subject of firearms. This topic has gained national attention. School, church, and workplace shootings have become far too commonplace. Yet, we as a society realize that we need to protect ourselves and others. Our military and law enforcement cannot function without them. Now think of a camera. A camera documents wonderful moments as well as tragic moments in time. It may also be used by people to help create immoral images of children, animals, or other engaged in deviate acts.

It will always be the end user of the weapon, camera, or, in the case of the topic of this chapter—the nondestructive exploit. Many of these tools discussed come from other countries that may have had questionable national views or beliefs. There are utilities that are made in a country that at the time of this writing, may have influenced the outcome of a presidential election.

So we will now discuss some of the tools that can help examiners into many devices. Most of these are commercially available to the public. Next time someone asks you how you get past cell phone security, just tell them *"with tools purchased from Russia and China."*

MFC Dongle

MFC Dongle is a hardware and proprietary software-based tool that allows access into specific phone models that have user enabled security. The tool targets iOS, Samsung, and HTC devices and utilizes a sensor that is affixed to the screen of the target phone. It attempts to gain access through a "brute force" attack, which tries all combinations until it gains access to the device. It has many limitations and supports certain products based on which version of the operating system (OS) is running.

Here is a list of some key features for the supported devices. This comes directly from their user manual [1]:

- General iOS iDevice (iPhone & iPod and MacBook):
  Support all iOS iDevice read general information, support super restore & update & custom flash ISPW, automatic iOS version detecting, even in disabled or untrust mode, support multi iDevice operating in the same time, history recording by real-time logs, support all iDevice debug mode do button testing, support all iOS iDevice activate/deactivate by USB cable, support all iOS apps from IPA package, support management user's/system and archives apps, support update, install, uninstall, backup apps by one button, support all iOS iDevice mode change by USB cable, support all iOS iDevice iCloud status check (black/white list), support one button bypass iPhone 4 iCloud account, support all iOS iDevice recovery iCloud data (IPR), support all iOS recovery email access (IPR), support all iOS iDevice read the restrictions access (IPR), support all iOS iDevice diagnostics check by USB cable (beta), support all iOS 7.x iDevice screen passcode unlock (4 digits), support all iOS 7.x iDevice permanently disabled remove, support all iOS 8.0–8.1 iDevice screen passcode unlock (4 digits), support all

iOS 8.0–8.1 iDevice temporarily disable remove, support all Apple MacBook model unlock 4 digits by EFI boot mode, support all apple MacBook model unlock 4 digit iCloud PIN.

- iOS Jailbreak iDevice (OpenSSH required—iOS 6.0–8.4):
  Support read 4-digit passcode, support jailbreak statue check, support using cable detect data via SSH, support fast brute force SSH passcode, support one button open SSH tunnel, support one button read iCloud account, support one button deleted iCloud account, support change phone general/about info (model & color, etc.), support hide/show application icon, support all iOS super backup.
- Samsung & HTC Android Mobile Models V4.3+—4 PIN Lock Unlock:
  All Samsung & HTC Android based mobile phones.
  The MFC Dongle–Full Set includes the hardware and iPower adaptor, and the 3-in-1 OTG charging USB cable. Fig. 20.1 depicts the full set currently sold at the time of this writing.

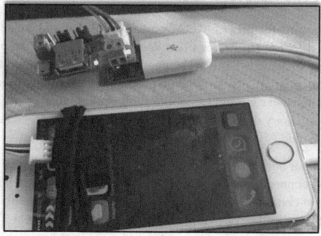

Figure 20.1
MFC Dongle Full Set.

IP Box

Another vendor who utilizes a screen sensor "brute-force" approach is IP Box. The device is limited and only supports the iPhone and iPad up to iOS version 8.1.0. The hardware interfaces with its own proprietary software and displays the brute force attempts on its own screen. Fig. 20.2 depicts the IP Box connected to an iPhone 4. They also sell an adaptor for iOS 8.

Figure 20.2
IP Box connected to an iPhone 4.

UFED User Lock Code Recovery Tool

Cellebrite has taken the same features of MFC Dongle and IP Box and created their own recovery software called *UFED User Lock Code Recovery Tool.* Unlike the previous stand-alone tools, the interface prevents wiping of the phone from occurring when this setting has been enabled on the target phone. The installation process and overall interface is also much easier to use. Clients who have a current Cellebrite subscription (yearly renewal) can download the software and necessary drivers from the Cellebrite Portal and then launch the program, which runs in a Windows command prompt.

There are special cables for both Android and Apple devices. The prompts in the command line will advise users to connect a specific cable. Just like the MFC Dongle and IP Box, this method will only support certain model Apple devices that are installed with specific iOS versions. The supported Android devices must also support USB OTG (On-The-Go). Some Android devices that are supported may not be accessed if the user has enabled two forms of security such as a user PIN and biometrics (finger print security).

Best Smart Tool

Another nondestructive tool we discuss is a product made by GsmBest Technology called *Best Smart Tool*, or BST. BST is not commercial law enforcement targeted forensic tool. It utilizes some of the same features of a flasher box but is a dongle-based utility.

BST is primarily made for mobile device servicing. Examples of a few of the features built into BST are full flash, network unlock, repair IMEI, NVM and EFS, root devices, and remove the screen lock. The tool supports many different model cell phones from makers of HTC, Samsung, Xiaomi, and MTK Android devices.

What makes BST unique is that on certain model devices, it does not require the target phone to have the ADB enabled (USB Debugging). USB Debugging, by default, is not enabled on Android devices. Because of this, most forensic tools will not acquire data from the evidential phone. Obviously, when users have enabled security (gestures, passwords, etc.) on their devices, the USB Debugging setting cannot be accessed. BST would be an option when previous tools mentioned (Cellebrite, MFC Dongle, IP Box, etc.) cannot defeat the security. On the companion site, Fig. 20.1 depicts the splash screen from BST.

When an Android phone does not have the USB debugging enabled, it can at times be seen by a host machine through the Media Transfer Protocol (MTP). MTP has limitations but does allow access to certain folders on the phone, generally multimedia based such as photos, videos, and music. BST uses this limited access to exploit the user PIN or gesture SHA value, which it completely removes. If the phone is supported and the user has installed the proper drivers, the user enabled PIN, password, or pattern lock may be removed. On some models, the phone does not need to have USB debugging enabled and the unlock can work through the MTP mode. On the companion site under Chapter 20 is a PDF titled, "BST use.pdf". This document shows how a Samsung (Android) device was enabled with a gesture pattern, and the pattern was removed using BST. The UltraCompare Professional (addressed in Chapter 18—Advanced Validation) was used to show the changes to the file system that occurred when the pattern was removed. The steps in this document can be followed to replicate your own removal of the security using BST. This can be very useful in court if you need to testify as to what this tool actually did to the file system.

It is important to note that if the user/owner of the Android device has enabled the *Picture Transfer Protocol* (PTP) mode, removing these types of security using BST will not work. PTP mode is not enabled by default. On the companion site a screenshot under Fig. 20.2 shows the MTP and PTP connection area within the settings of an Android.

Once the software, drivers, and firmware are brought up to date on BST, users can select the supported model device from the drop-down. Once selected, use the *Unlock* tab to determine if the device can be unlocked without ADB being enabled. Fig. 20.3 contains the overall BST interface, followed by a Samsung being selected, then the drop-down arrow displaying the available choices.

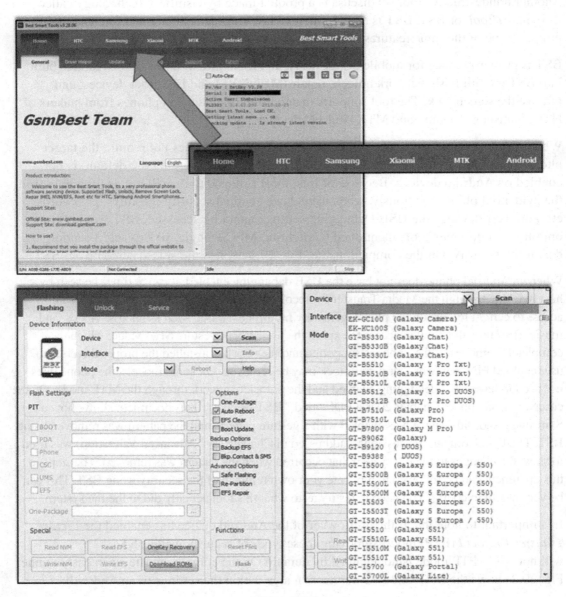

Figure 20.3
BST interface with choices in the model drop-down (Samsung shown).

FuriousGold

The following definition of FuriousGold was obtained from their website:

> *FuriousGold is the world most advanced mobile phone unlocking platform for mobile store owners and service center. Unlock, repair, change language, reset security code, read unlock codes or even generate unlock codes without having the phone in hands this is only few features supported on FuriousGold. With over 6000+ Supported phones for unlocking including exclusive software and services, 60000 worldwide users and over 10 million mobile phone unlocked since the last 8 years. FuriousGold is a must have tool if you are working in the mobile phone unlocking industry [2].*

At the time of this writing, FuriousGold supported several phone models by various manufacturers. Like many of these flasher boxes, not all the units they support will enable bypassing the user enabled security. Here is a list of models (as on February 2017):

Acer, AEG, Arness, Airtel, Alcatel, Allview, Amgoo, Amoi, Apple, Arima, Azuma, Be-Mobile, Be, Bea-fon, Beeline, BenQ/Siemens, BlackBerry, Bleu, Blu, Bouygues Telecom, Cat, Coby, Coolpad, Coral, Cosmote, DBTel, Dell, Digicel, Discovery, Disney, Doro, Dragon, Emblaze, Emporia, eStar, FNB, Foma, G-Tide, Gionee, Go, Gradiente, Haier, Hisense, HP, HTC, Huawei, Hyundai, i-Mate, idroid, Infiny, INQ, IPLUS, Irbis, iTel, Konka, Kyocera, Lanix, Lenovo, LG, M4TEL, Maxon, Megafon, MEO, Metfone, Micromax, Microsoft, MobiT, Mobiwire, Modelabs, momodesign, Motorola, MOVITEL, MTN, MTS, NATCOM, Nec, NEO, Newgen, Nokia, NYX, O2, odyssee, Onda, Option, Orange, OYSTERS, Palm, Panasonic, Pantech, PCD, Philips, Phone House, PIXO, Plum, PLUS, POLAROID, QMOBILE, Sagem, Samsung, Sanyo, SendTel, SFR, Sharp, Siemens, Sonim, Sony, Sony Ericsson, Spice, STARMOBILE, TCL, TECMOBILE, TECNO, Tele2fon, Telenor, TELMA, Telstra, Thomson, TMN, Toshiba, True, UMI, Verykool, Viettel, Virgin Mobile, Vitel, VK Mobile, Vodafone, WIKO, Windows Mobile, XOX, Yezz, ZTC, ZTE.

There may be specific steps that need to be performed to obtain the user enabled PIN. For instance, on specific model Alcatel (Android's) that is locked with a PIN, the examiner must first obtain a physical acquisition of the entire range using FuriousGold. This creates a proprietary file with an extension showing as ".*osp.*" The file needs to be renamed with a .bin extension. Attempts to open the file as .bin file will result in a needed passcode. If the examiner looks at the manifest from FuriousGold, he/she will see a value called *Rid*. This is an MD5 hash value, which is the passcode to unlock the .bin. There will be chunks of files, around 700 MB. These will need to be combined into one file using command prompt or a hex editor tool. Pay attention to the sequential offset order when combining the files. Using the same hex editor, remove the bootloader information that is embedded from FuriousGold. Once this is completed, the edited .bin file can be saved and decoded using a PIN carver in Physical Analyzer. Fig. 20.4 shows an extraction manifest from an Alcatel. Notice the Rid value.

```
Using library Brom_DLL_v7.1413.5
Searching phone in normal mode;
[connect the phone powered off to the usb cable]
Phone detected (MTK USB Port (COM27))
Preparing to start flash mode;
Preparing to open COM27
Requesting authorization;
Connecting;
Downloading DA;
Initializing;
Rid: eb5ea3ddb558b4eb7da6fe25e42a45f9
Requesting baudrate change;
Done;
USB SPEED: USB_FULL_SPEED
Switching to DA_HIGHSPEED_VCOM;

Drivers location \usb_driver\Driver_Auto_Installer\SmartPhoneDriver\x86;
If the detection fails, install manually the port from the device manager using usbvcom.inf;
```

Figure 20.4
Example of an MD5 Rid value, which is the passcode to open the .bin file.

XPIN Clip

XPIN is stand-alone device used to read a screen lock code using brute force method. XPIN clip can read Passcode (in iOS devices) as well as PIN/PIN Backup and character code (PatternLock) Android phones that support OTG functions [3]. The features of XPIN Clip are listed as the following:

- *XPIN Clip allows you to get user passcode from iPhone, iPad 7.x.x, iPhone 8.0–8.1 and PIN, Backup PIN, PatternLock from Android phones/tablets that supports USB OTG.*
- *XPIN Clip does not require resetting your device, which entails deleting data and reverts the device to factory settings.*
- *XPIN Clip work without: USB debugging, root, custom recovery, lost data, lost warranty—KNOX flag or unlocking bootloader in some devices.*
- *XPIN Clip is also helpful for forensic investigation where in some cases you cannot undermine the integrity of the data (like: root, custom recovery, etc.) [4].*

The utility has several recovery methods:

- *RANGE: range of 4-digit PIN (increase and decrease)*
- *MASK: 4-digit mask that allows to speed up recovery PIN code if we know at least 1 digit and its position*
- *DATE: this method check all PIN combination that could be a day-month or month-day configuration*
- *POPULAR: this method checks all most popular 4-digit PIN*
- *ADVANCED: this method allows you to check PIN that is longer than 4 digits (maximum 8 digits); also with mask, you can set increase or decrease direction*
- *PATH (Only for PATTERN): length of PatternLock—four or five dots*
- *PATH SD (Only for PATTERN)*: length of PatternLock—from four to nine dots reading from SD card [4]*

As of February 18, 2017, here is a list of current supported models:

Acer: Liquid Gallant E350, Liquid X1, Iconia Tab A200/A500/A700, ICONIA A1-810

Archos: G9, Notion Ink Adam

Apple: iPhone 4/4S, iPhone 5/5C/5S, iPhone 6/6S, iPad 2/3/4, iPad Mini, iPod

ASUS: Zenfone Max ZC550KL, Zenfone Max 2016, Zenfone Selfie, Zenfone 2 Laser ZE550KL, Zenfone 2 ZE551ML, Zenfone 2 Deluxe, Zenfone Zoom ZX550, Padfone II, New Padfone Infinity, Padfone mini A11, Padfone E A68M, Padfone S PE500KL, Zenfone 4/5/6, Google Nexus 7 (I/II ver.), Memo Pad 7 ME172

Coolpad: Note 3 Lite, Note 3, Note 3 Plus, Dazen X7

Gionee: M5 Lite, Elife S7, Marathon M3, Elife S Plus, Marathon M4, Elife E8, M2 4 GB, Elife S5.5, M5 Lite CDMA, Elife E7, M2 8GB

HTC: Desire 828, Desire 620G, Desire 826, One A9, M9 Plus, One M8, One, One (M8) Dual Sim, One X, One X+, One Mini, One Mini 2, One Max, One (M8) CDMA, Desire 500, Desire 601, Desire 600, Desire 700, Desire 700 Dual Sim, Desire 816, Desire 820, One M8 Prima, Desire X, Desire U, J, Butterfly, Butterfly S, Desire EYE (M910X), EVO 4G LTE

Huawei: Ascend P7 Sapphire Edition, Ascend P7, Ascend P7 mini, Ascend P6, Ascend P6 S, Ascend P1, Ascend Mate7, Ascend Mate2, Ascend Mate2 4G, Ascend G7, Ascend G700, Ascend Honor 3, Ascend D, Ascend D1, Ascend D1 XL U9500E, Ascend D quad, media-Pad 7 Lite, MediaPad, Mediapad S7-301w

Honor: Holly 2 Plus, Honor 4C, Honor 7

iBall: Andi 5.9 Cobalt Plate, Andi 5K Panther, Andi 5F Infinito, Andi 4.5 Enigma, Andi 4.7G Cobalt

Lenovo: Zuk Z1, K4 Note, Vibe K5 Plus, Vibe K5, K3, K3 Note, Vibe P1, Vibe P1m, Vibe P1 Turbo, A7000, Vibe Shot, P70, Phab Plus, K3 Note Music, CG Slate, P700, P770, P780, A859, K900, Vibe X S960

Lava: Pixel V1, Iris X10, Iris X8, Iris X1, Iris Fuel F1, Iris X1 Selfie

LG: G5, G4, Nexus 5, G Flex, G Pro 2, G2, G3, G3 (CDMA), G3 LTE-A, Vu 3 F300L, Optimus G Pro, Optimus G Pro lite, Optimus G2, G Flex, GPad 7.0, G Pad 10.1

MicroMax: Canvas 6 Pro, Canvas Juice 2, Canvas Spark, Canvas Juice 3 A392, Canvas Xperss 2 E313, Canvas Knight 2, Canvas Doodle 4 Q391, Unite 2, Canvas Doodle 3, Unite 3 Q372, A110Q Canvas 2 Plus, A116 Canvas HD, A110 Canvas 2, Canvas HD Plus A190, Canvas Hue, Canvas Magnus, Unite 2

Motorola: Moto X Play, Moto G (3rd Gen), Moto G (2nd Gen), Moto Turbo, Droid RAZR MAXX, Razr HD, Moto G, XT910, XT912, Droid 4/4G, MB865 Atrix 2, Xoom

OnePlus: OnePlus X, OnePlus 2, OnePlus One

OPPO: F1, F1 Plus, R5, N3, Neo 5, Neo 3, N1 mini, N1, Find7, Find7a

Samsung: J7, J7 (2016), J3 (2016), On7, S7, S7 Edge, J5, J2 (2015), J5 (2016), A5 (2016), A8, On5, A7, Core Prime, Core Prime VE, Grand Max, S6, S6 Edge Plus, S6 Edge, Note 5, Note Edge, Note 4, S5 Plus, S5 Sport, S5 LTE-A G901F/G906S, S5, K/S5 Zoom, S5 Octa-Core, S5 G9009FD, S5 CDMA, S5 Active, S5 Duos, S4 I9500, S4 I9505, S4 zoom, S4 Active I9295, S4 I9506, S4 Active LTE-A, S4 I9502, S4 CDMA, S III I9300, S III I9305, S

III I747, S III T999, S III CDMA, S II I9100G, S II HD LTE, S II Duos I929, S II T989, S II I9100, S II I777, S II LTE I9210, S II Epic 4G Touch, S II 4G I9100M, S II X T989D, Note N9000, Note N7100, Note N7000, Note I717, Note T879, Ace3 S7270, Ace S5830i, Nexus I9250, Mega 6.3 I9200, J, F, N810, Note 8.0 N5100, Note 10.1 2014, Tab 2.7.0 i705
Sony: Xperia Z3+, Xperia C4 Dual, Xperia Z3, Xperia Z3 Compact, Xperia Z2A, Xperia Z2, Xperia Z1, Xperia Z1 Compact, Xperia Z1S, Xperia Z, Xperia Z Ultra, Xperia ZL, Xperia ZR, Xperia M, Xperia M2, Xperia M2 Aqua, Xperia E3, Xperia E3 Dua, Xperia M2 Dual, Xperia U, Xperia S, Xperia P, Xperia Miro, Xperia Go, Xperia T, Xperia SL, Xperia ion LTE, Xperia LT29i Hayabusa, Xperia Acro S, Ericson Xperia Arc S, Xperia Neo V, Xperia J, Xperia Sola, Xperia SP, Xperia TX, Xperia V
Xiaomi: Redmi Note 3, MI-5, Redmi 2 Prime, Redmi2, MI4i, MI-4, MI-3, MI-2, MI-2S, MI-2A, Redmi Note, Redmi Note 4G, Hongmi 1S, Hongmi, Mi Pad 7.9
XOLO: Era 4G, Era 4K, Black 3 GB, Black X1, Black, Q1010i, Play 8X-1100, Q600S, A500S Lite, Q1200, Play 8X-1020, Q1011, Q900T [4]

XPIN Clip can be sold with accessories. These include the ReSTART Adaptor, Pattern Adaptor, OS800 Adaptor, TRS Light Sensor Cable, Charging Cable for Android, 4-in-1 Cable, and USB A-A Cable. Fig. 20.5 depicts the XPIN Clip and all its available accessories, minus the Charging Cable for Android, which is just a standard microUSB cable.

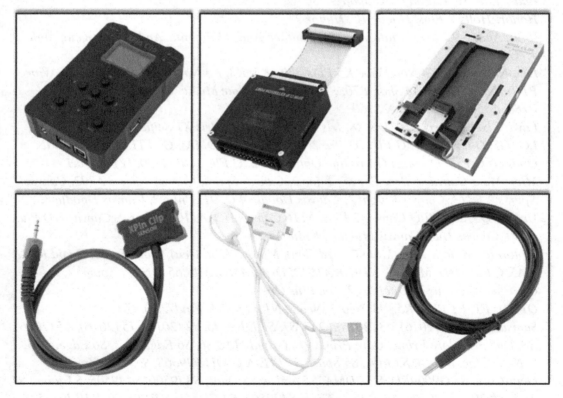

Figure 20.5
XPIN clip with accessories.

Other Methods

In-System Programming

Another method is reverse engineering by mapping the flash memory. In the later chapters of this book, we will focus on two main techniques, one being nondestructive (JTAG) and the other destructive, chip removal. Mapping the processor is a technique that is destructive on a test phone. It uses concepts from both JTAG and chip removal. This is also referred to as *In-System Programming (ISP)*. ISP examinations are explained in the last chapter of this book. They are by far, one of the most time consuming advanced techniques. To start, if the examiner is unable to locate the correct mapping configuration on the evidence phone from other investigators, he/she obtains an exact replica of the evidence. The specific flash memory on the test phone is removed. Using a data sheet from the memory manufacturer, the specific required contacts are mapped in connection with where they sit on the main board in line with the BGAs (Ball Grid Arrays). These are located by using continuity testing, and the necessary contacts are mapped to parts on the main board such as resistors. Once all the required locations are mapped per the supported flasher box, the examiner takes the evidential phone and, using fine gauged wire, solders to each of these points. The other ends of the wires are connected to a specific model flasher box. Just like JTAG, a binary pull is conducted. This technique can require a test phone, a specific model supported flasher box, and a very precise solder unit. Did we mention lots of *time*? Once a specific model phone has been mapped, the same technique can be utilized again if the phone is used in a new case. The only time new mapping occurs is when a phone has not yet been mapped.

One product also allows the examiner to pull the data through the board locations without the use of soldering. **CODED** is a hardware based-product that is made by Forensic Navigation. CODED has a series of arms that can be moved and locked into position anywhere on the main board. The tips are spring loaded. The examiner maps out the TAPs on a test phone. Once this is completed, the (evidence) main board is held in the center of the arms. The tips are positioned where they are needed and wires are plugged into each one then back to specific model flasher boxes for the binary pull. Fig. 20.3 on the companion site depicts the CODED unit. A less-expensive alternative to the CODED product is a tool created by Multi-Com, called the VR-Table. This product is currently used in the author's lab. It does not have all the accessories that are included with the CODED product, and buyers can also choose how many arms they wish to purchase. Both of these products can also be used for JTAG examinations.

Flasher Boxes

We previously discussed one popular device that is considered a "flasher box" and that was FuriousGold. There will be many other boxes that support additional phones. As mentioned before, these devices are mainly used to repair phones but, in some cases, can be used to pull the binary off a locked device. The ways in which they communicate with the target phone are usually through a specialized cable. Because the flasher box may utilize other ways to process commands to the device, it makes little difference that the user has enabled security. Some vendors support different types of *Bus* communications within their flasher boxes or can autoswitch. Fig. 20.4 of the companion site shows two different flasher boxes, which allow the user to manually change between the FBUS and MBUS.

The input to the flasher box will generally be through an RJ45 port or a standard USB. Within Fig. 20.4 (companion site) is an older UFS-3 box. This shows support for both types of input.

Diagnostic Connections

Specific vendors who sell flasher boxes may also provide the option or include the proprietary cables. Some will also have connection areas that are under the battery or sometimes beneath a special rubber or plastic plug on the back of the phone. When these are removed, specialized cables may be utilized, which clip to the area and generally do not require the user to disassemble the phone.

On our companion site, Fig. 20.5 depicts a specialized cable that is used with a Samsung model phone. This cable uses pins that would connect under the battery, and this would be used with a Z3X (Samsung) box. Fig. 20.5 (companion site) also shows the pins used for communication with the target handset.

Nokia was at one time one of the most supported devices for flasher boxes. The reason behind this was that Nokia had proprietary connections under their batteries on most of the early model phones, which allowed "flashing" and other diagnostic work. Nokia was also at one point the world's largest seller of mobile phones, and therefore most vendors wanted to support repairing them.

Bootloaders

Examiners can also utilize bootloaders to access a device partition to unlock or bypass user enabled locks. Some HTC devices, for instance, can be accessed through Fastboot—Fig. 20.6 on the companion site. A token key can be obtained from the phone, which is submitted to the HTC site. The site will in turn provide another key to unlock the phone, depicted on the bottom image of Fig. 20.6 on the companion site. Another way bootloaders can be used is using ClockworkMod. Some devices such as Nexus utilize a custom recovery through TeamWin Recovery Project. These features may be built into tools such as Cellebrite, and with Cellebrite the examiner does not need to know how to manually use a bootloader to access the memory.

Chapter Summary Key Points

When encountering devices that have user enabled security, the examiner should try and determine if the evidence is supported by a nondestructive technique. Generally, this would take place after commercially available tools indicate that they have no support for bypassing or exploiting the security. The choices will depend on the model and OS version running on the mobile evidence. Choices can include MFC Dongle, IP Box, UFED User Lock Code Recovery Tool, BST, FuriousGold, XPIN Clip, ISP, various flasher boxes, and custom boot-loaders. This chapter only touches on a few of the choices available for nondestructive examinations. It will be up to the examiner to frequently check online, with training vendors, online groups, and others performing mobile extractions to determine what "new" product is out there that can help them without the risk that comes with destructive techniques.

References

[1] MFCBOX, Manual – Features. https://www.mfcbox.com/manual/#features/3.
[2] FuriousGold, What Is FuriousGold. http://www.furiousgold.com/en/homepage.
[3] XPIN Clip, Instructions. http://www.support.multi-com.pl/XPIN/Instruction_EN%20.pdf.
[4] XPIN Clip, Features, May 20, 2016. http://xpinclip.com/features.php.

CHAPTER 21

Phone Disassembly and Water-Damaged Phones

Information in This Chapter
•   Fastening methods
•   Common screws used
•   Common tools used
•   Drying water-exposed devices
•   Use of ultrasonic cleaner
•   Commercial rework ovens
•   Suggestions—Saltwater exposure

Introduction—Holding It All Together

The remaining chapters will require the examiner, in most cases, to tear down a phone. If this is something you have never done, it is not a difficult task. With the invention of YouTube, it is fairly easy to locate videos on how to take apart just about everything. There are also a number of commercial vendors who focus on repairing mobile equipment and also sell tools for this purpose. The author has attended an actual repair school for mobile phones, which also addressed how to repair damaged USB connections and techniques that dealt with water-damaged devices.

The course has come in handy, as there have been several different "types" of moisture-damaged phones related to felony assaults and homicides over the past few years.

When the time comes to disassemble a device, you will need to understand what exactly holds the various pieces in place. At first, every effort online was used to determine exactly which parts needed to be removed, and in what order. Now, when phones need to be torn down, the author relies on the type of fundamental fasteners used to guide him. It's these basic elements, that hold everything together.

Seeking the Truth from Mobile Evidence. http://dx.doi.org/10.1016/B978-0-12-811056-0.00021-2

Fastening Methods

Manufacturers of mobile equipment will use three methods to affix their components together. This is important to understand when trying to dissemble a device. Breakage may occur if care is not taken to determine what is "holding" a particular piece together. Here are the three common types along with image examples:

1. **Screws** (Fig. 21.1). These can vary in size and type. Some will also come with specialized heads that require a specific driver. Apple, for instance, likes to use what is called a *Pentalobe*. It is not uncommon for mobile devices to utilize many different types of screws to assemble just one phone. This can include *Flat Head*, *Cross-tip* (aka: Phillips), *Torx*, and *Triwing*. Fig. 21.1 depicts some of the common types.

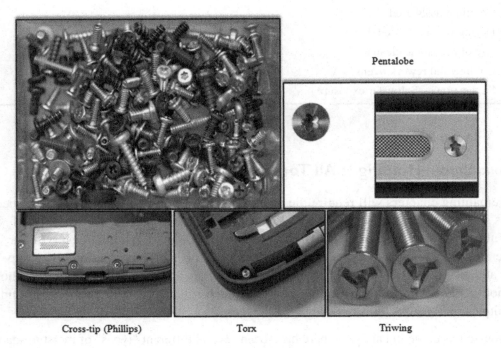

Pentalobe

Cross-tip (Phillips)   Torx   Triwing

Figure 21.1
Example of the common types of screw fasteners located on mobile equipment.

Manufacturers will also cover the head of the screws with a small sticker. These can be used to indicate that the phone has been tampered with, thus voiding the warranty in some cases. ***During the disassemble process, it is important to recognize that not all screw heads will be visible.*** Look for areas that may contain round stickers. They can vary in color—Fig. 21.2 shows a Blackberry with a white tamper sticker over a Torx screw. These stickers may also have the word "Void" printed over them. Fig. 21.2 (right image) also depicts the same tamper sticker of the Blackberry being pushed through with a proper Torx driver for removal.

Examples of a tamper sticker from a BlackBerry phone. These can be removed, or simply penetrated with the appropriate driver.

Figure 21.2
Example of tamper stickers and one being penetrated with a Torx driver.

2. **Clips**. Parts will also be fastened together through the use of clips. Clips will be found in various makes and models of phones and can be used in conjunction with other forms of fasteners. Fig. 21.3 shows a common style that is utilized on the popular Samsung Galaxy phones. The bottom cover of this phone uses several clips around the molding. The cross-tip screws are removed first, and then each clip is carefully pried around the entire case until it is freed from the main housing. Also contained in Fig. 21.3 are clips from a BlackBerry. The removal of this piece reveals hidden Torx screws that would need to be removed for further disassembly.

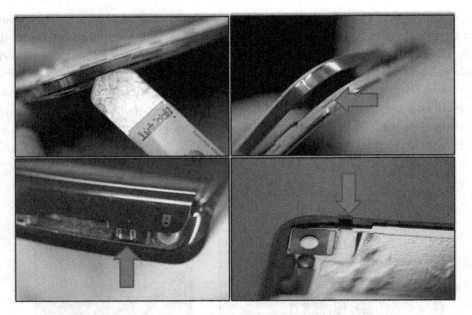

Figure 21.3
Examples of clips being located on Samsung and BlackBerry.

3. **Adhesive**. The use of glue or adhesive will also be encountered when disassembling mobile devices. Here is the area where glue or adhesive would commonly be encountered:
    a. Screens. Most vendors will use a specific type of glue to adhere the protective (outside) glass to the touch style LCD/digitizer. For the purpose of repairing a phone for forensic examination, it is much easier to replace the entire assembly. This process requires the examiner to ensure that bubbles are removed between the new glass and the LCD.
    b. Battery. If the target phone does not have a removable battery, the internal battery will usually be stuck to the case using glue or adhesive strips. It is also not uncommon for the battery to have screws in conjunction with the adhesive or glue.
    c. Internal parts (varies). Glue and adhesive can be applied to a number of internal parts on mobile devices. An example on the iPhone would be the home button. This has a small round rubber piece of material that adheres to the surrounding area. Parts such as speakers (mics) for both the ear and mouth piece will commonly either have glue or adhesive strips. Fig. 21.4 depicts the upper cover of the Blackberry cover that was shown in Fig. 21.4, as well as the back cover to a Samsung S7.

Figure 21.4
Examples of adhesive of BlackBerry and Samsung phones.

Tools Used

Individuals who repair mobile devices will generally take care not to cause damage to the parts during disassembly and repair. During disassembly for mobile forensic purposes, focus is generally given to ensure that the device can still function. Marks caused by pry tools on parts such as the housing are usually less concerning. The tools used in this course may not necessarily be the same tools that would be used for commercial mobile repair services. Here is a common list of tools used for disassembly:

1. Headset magnifier. These can include built-in lights and or secondary sets of lenses that apply different levels of magnification.
2. Drivers. These will include various (small) sizes of Torx, Flat and Cross-tip (Phillips), Triwing, and Apple-based Pentalobe.
3. Spudger. Plastic and metal spudgers of various sizes and shapes. Guitar picks can also be used as a spudger.
4. Magnetizer/demagnetizer tool. This is very helpful in magnetizing your drivers it helps with screws falling off the tip during disassembly and reassembly.
5. Tweezers. Tweezers assist with a number of various tasks, and their applications are endless.
6. SIM Card Tray ejection tool. This can also be a small paper clip, bent for the same purpose.
7. Hair dryer or rework hot air. This is helpful when removing damaged screens.

Removing Moisture (Water Damage)

Often, phones will need to be disassembled when they have been exposed to or submerged in water or other fluids. At present, the author has examined devices that been exposed to toilets, snow, saltwater, and freshwater. Recently, however, the author experienced a phone exposed to bodily fluids of a decomposing body. The body was dismembered, and stuffed into a duffle bag and buried. The human fluids, over several months, had seeped into the main board of this phone. As grotesque as this may sound, this should serve as a reminder that phones may be exposed to nearly any type of moisture. It will be the forensic examiner's responsibility to try and clean and dry the device to acquire user data.

Hold the Rice

For years, people have believed that placing a phone in a bag of rice would dry out the phone and make it operational again. This technique may have worked, but it was only because the moisture exposure was not severe or the phone did not succumb to internal damage. It does not mean that the rice removed moisture from deep inside the phone. Moisture may also have some degree of bacteria. Some moisture will have more bacteria than another, such as water from a pond that is stagnant. This will lead to mold which typically comes in three different colors based on how long the bacteria were growing: white, green, and black. The presence of black generally means the most damage has occurred and in some cases, it is irreversible. There is also general oxidation (rust) that can occur. Most phones have specialized circuitry inside their batteries that will detect excess charging or shorts. This prevents the battery from damaging the phone. Most water-exposed devices will need a new battery, which is the least of the overall problem that the examiner will need to deal with.

Examiners must ensure that they completely disassemble the phone, clean, and inspect all parts. The parts must be dried and, in some cases, heat dried with specialty ovens used for electronic parts. Compressed air is not usually recommended as it can "push" residual moisture into small component parts including chips located on the main board. This can lead to additional problems. Often, the bacteria damage will be near the Molex connections. If the device was partially exposed to moisture, or a screen was cracked and not repaired, an inspection can reveal where the moisture entered the phone.

Ultrasonic Cleaning

The use of an ultrasonic cleaner may greatly increase the likelihood of salvaging a water-exposed device. This is especially true when there is a great degree of fungus present or other types of foreign items are adhered to the board. These cleaners have multiple "frequencies," which vibrate at a specific rate. They also have features that heat the source material (fluids) used for cleaning. It is not uncommon to see these small items vibrate off the main board while the sonic cleaner is in use.

The cleaning may have to be administered more than one time, using different frequencies until the desired results have been achieved. The author has several ultrasonic cleaners, but the one used often is an inexpensive Baku BK-3550. This model works at 35 and 50W. It can hold more than one board at a time. Since most tablets use a similar size board to what is found on their mobile phone cousins, this size cleaner works with 99% of all encountered mobile devices. If you plan to clean a main board of a laptop or computer, you will need to purchase a much larger ultrasonic cleaner. There are ultrasonic cleaners that have trays that sit inside the bowl of the cleaner. This is a small metal screen with a handle, similar to how fries are cooked at a fast-food restaurant. This can come in handy and can help the examiner in reaching dirty water to retrieve the board. If you ever need to clean a board that was in a toilet with a person's "#2" waste, this will more than pay for itself on the first use.

Steps for Cleaning

As previously mentioned, in nearly all cases of a water-exposed device, the item will need to be disassembled. The main board and associated parts should then be inspected. Here are the general steps for cleaning and repairing devices that are exposed to moisture. Steps 3 and 4 will vary based on visual inspection once the phone is apart.

1. Disassemble the phone and inspect the degree of moisture exposure. This will usually include removing the screen. If the phone was fully submerged in a water source, it is recommended to tear down the phone completely. Often the moisture will reside under parts that may not be visible or discovered simply by removing the main screen.
2. Inspect all parts under magnification. If fungus is severe, consider cleaning with an ultrasonic cleaner. If parts have mild fungus or oxidation is present, cleaning by hand with a nylon brush can be accomplished. The use of alcohol, denatured alcohol, or bacteria removal solutions may be used. Be aware that after using some solutions, the parts should be rinsed with distilled water. Distilled water can also be used to clean parts, especially phones that show no signs of fungus. Do not scrub parts too hard, as damage may occur.
3. Is fungus severe? Consider disregarding the nonessential parts with parts from a replacement phone or new parts. This would be the screen, case, cables, etc. Examiners should always **focus on repairing the main board when the water damage is severe**. There is no need to clean severely damaged parts that do not contain user data and can simply be replaced.
    a. Soak the main board in a bacteria solution for ~10min. Scrubbing Bubbles (yes, the bathroom cleaner) is highly recommended for this.
    b. Place in ultrasonic cleaner that has distilled (clean) water. Clean at two different frequencies for 5min each (total time 10min). Heat can be adjusted to high.
    c. Allow the board to dry enough to inspect for fungus under magnification. If fungus is present but is minimally present, consider *lightly* scrubbing these areas with a bacteria solution dipped onto a nylon brush. Extreme care should be given not to damage the specific area that is being scrubbed. Make certain the area that is scrubbed is also rinsed with distilled water. If the fungus is still severe, repeat the steps used for ultrasonic cleaning. Increase the ultrasonic time to 20min (10min intervals). Dry, and inspect. It is not uncommon for examiners to have to repeat this process multiple times. Make certain the distilled water is replaced from the ultrasonic cleaner after each use.

4. If fungus is light or there is none present, clean parts by hand. It is recommended to rinse the main board in distilled water. Distilled water is also cheaper than alcohol. This will remove any potential bacteria. If the water source that the device was exposed to was rich in bacteria to begin with, i.e., toilet, pond, etc., consider scrubbing the parts lightly with alcohol. This would be a scenario where the phone was submerged in that type of water but was removed before fungus began to show.

5. Dry parts. <u>This step is often the most rushed in the process</u>. Failure to allow enough time to dry out the components can cause other problems. The main board should be the part that is allowed enough time to thoroughly dry. If the plan is to attempt to salvage the phone, and not perform a chip off extraction, the use of compressed air is not recommended to assist in drying. Compressed air does contain moisture, which generally is not the real issue. On the main board are additional chips that provide various functions for the mobile device. Many of these do not have adhesive around them and, unlike the processor, coprocessor, RAM, and NAND memory, are unprotected from moisture. What this means is that if compressed air is used, it can "push" moisture and other foreign items into these unprotected areas. To help illustrate this, the companion site contains Fig. 21.1 that is from a Blackberry main board. The top of the image shows the package on package (RAM/Processor) that was removed and separated. Below this is the NAND memory, which would contain all the evidential data. Each of these chips has a high level of black adhesive around them, shown with arrows. This along with solder protects the chip and can aid in preventing moisture from entering. Manufacturers place this adhesive around such components to protect them and aid in their longevity. These components are also the most expensive items on the main board and are tasked with complex functions that may be difficult to repair or diagnose.

Fig. 21.2 on the companion site shows chips on the main board of a Motorola that do not have adhesive around them (redacted chip names). These areas would be susceptible to moisture or other minuscule items being forced under them when compressed air is used for drying.

Drying Boards

If your intent is to dry a water-exposed device, ***or to remove a chip through a thermal process***, the target board should be dried in a rework oven or preheater. Even if the phone was never submerged in water, moisture can still be present. The temperatures do not need to be high enough to melt solder, but should be warm enough to allow any moisture that may have penetrated the board, and chip, to dry out. What typically happens when there is moisture between the chip and the board is that the chip will swell during the removal, as high temperatures are being applied to the top. Any residual moisture begins to boil, and the chip will rise and usually crack. The time applied to the drying should be at a minimum of 30 min but can be quite longer depending on other circumstances. Drying times should be increased if your evidence has any of these issues:

- Cracked screen or case.
- White, green, or black fungus anywhere on the board.
- Signs of rust on the board.
- Device was recovered in water, blood, or other liquids. In those cases, the board may need to be cleaned first. Even if your plan is to remove the chip, cleaning blood or saltwater off the chip is much easier while the item is still attached. Not to mention the smell you will create if you do not clean contaminate(s) such as blood first.

There are a several commercially available units that can be used for drying. Most are designed for rework or preheating. Here are two examples used by the author. One costs around $100, and the other around $400:

- Preheater. BAKU 853. This is primarily designed for heating the bottom of a board. This unit has an exposed heating element affixed to the top of the box. It is also sold with the aluminum, adjustable board holder. This can be used to preheat under the chip to help aid in removal, or it can be used to dry the chip/board. Since this holder is open, the author has used an aluminum cooking pan to help enclose the heat. Fig. 21.5 is an image of this modification. Due to the exposed design on this product, the temperatures will not reach what is set on the front of the unit. The use of an infrared thermometer will indicate this. See an example on the companion site, Fig. 21.3.

Figure 21.5
Using a cooking pan to help hold in the heat on a preheater.

- Infrared IC Heater T-962. This unit is designed for rework and can handle larger components, to include computer main boards. One of the things to consider is the amperage this unit draws. It will average 21–27 amps, which means a traditional 20-amp breaker will throw when this is connected to a standard 110-V outlet. When this was installed, the main wire feeding to the wall also had to be increased by a gauge. This should be secured with a lockable outlet and male connector, called *"Locking Plug, 20 Amps, 125VACm NEMA Configuration: L5-20P, Number of Poles: 2."* The unit purchased by the author came from China, and there were bare wires to connect to, not a wall plug present. The wires also used International Electrotechnical Commission standards for their colors.

Suggestions—Saltwater Exposure

If any of you have recovered firearms from saltwater, you may be familiar with the basic premise behind this technique. If a phone has been submerged in saltwater, and it will be some time before an examiner can work with it, it is suggested to collect it with the source water. This can easily be accomplished using a clean (new) paint can with a lid. If it is a larger device such as a tablet, plastic, square, Tupperware-style containers can be used. The reason for this is that the device will deteriorate much quicker once it is removed from the water and exposed to air. Although saltwater is very corrosive, there can be instances where it is actually better to leave it in the water than to take it out. There are of course conditions to this. The author is not suggesting that you leave the device in saltwater for months at a time. This would be a situation where the examiner may not be able to examine the mobile device for a few days, and the device has been in the saltwater for a few weeks or months already. This would not apply if the item was recently dropped in the saltwater, and you were able to retrieve it in a timely manner. If you can also remove the battery, this can also help. Removing the battery can be applied to both situations—short-term exposure and collection with the source water.

Chapter Summary Key Points

The three main types of fasteners that hold mobile components together are screws, clips, and adhesive. It is very common to encounter more than one type of fastener on a target device. The screws used can vary. Manufacturers may develop their own proprietary screw that is only used on their particular models.

Standard tools that are used to disassemble phones will include magnifiers, various drivers, spundgers, magnetizer/demagnetizer, tweezers, SIM card ejector, and a hair dryer or rework hot air unit.

Water-damaged devices will generally always require disassembly. Units should be inspected for fungus and oxidation. Parts that are severely damaged and expendable such as screens, batteries, and housing units should be replaced. Examiners should focus on repairing and cleaning the main board, to include the use of an ultrasonic cleaner if necessary.

When using the ultrasonic cleaner, the use of distilled water is recommended. Small areas on the main board that show signs of fungus can be cleaned by hand using a nylon brush, denatured alcohol, and light scrubbing. The use of compressed air is not recommended. Ovens and preheaters can aid in drying the main board.

CHAPTER 22

JTAG (Joint Test Action Group)

Information in This Chapter

- JTAG
- IEEE
- 1149.1
- How JTAG works
- Test Access Port (TAP)
- Test Mode Select (TMS)
- Test Clock Input (TCK)
- Test Data Input (TDI)
- Test Data Output (TDO)
- Test Reset (TRST/NTRST/NRST)
- Return Clock (RTCK)
- Ground (GRD/GND)
- Test data resistors
- Boundary scan register
- Molex connections
- JTAG issues

Introduction

"You need to open a window—you're stinking up the house!" That comment was often yelled to the author by his mother while he was growing up. No, it had nothing to do with the bathroom or smelly socks left on the floor. Soldering, welding, brazing, and cutting metal were introduced to the author during his childhood years, growing up on a farm. His late father spent 44 years working for the telephone company, spicing and repairing landlines. He spent his spare time on 320 acres of land, raising cattle, and drilling water wells. It was in this setting, the author's love for electronics germinated. It started with vacuum tubes, then 555 timer kits found their way into the house, which followed with solder smoke filling the air.

You may be reading this and asking yourself, how these are all relevant to the work of Joint Test Action Group (JTAG)?

There will be some of you who may never need to perform a JTAG extraction. As case "luck" would have it, you could go through your career and have every target phone be supported with tools that never require the phone to be disassembled. Then there will be some of you who will need to locate specified Test Access Ports (TAPs) and make connections with tiny wires to tiny contact points. The point here is that for some of you, this may be very easy, and like the author, you have experienced soldering and working with electronics. If so, the remaining chapters may be easy to understand and follow. The remaining chapters will also contain the most images. Most will be contained on the companion site. This will help others who may have little to no experience with these techniques, and hopefully, they can gain enough knowledge to work their way through a JTAG examination.

It still amazes the author that most of the IT students who decide to attend the digital mobile courses at the university have never soldered and have never had to conduct a simple continuity test. They may even be living at home while attending college, and when their parent yells, *"Open a window—you're stinking up the house!"* It has nothing to do with the smoke from melting solder.

Joint Test Action Group

As circuit boards developed over time they were found to be more difficult to program, test, and debug. Multilayer boards and extremely close pin spacing were contributing factors. There were many designs requiring a vast number of test programs to perform this function.

JTAG developed test architecture for printed circuit boards, integrated circuits (ICs), and system level testing to help address these issues. This was recognized and accepted by the Institute of Electronical and Electronic Engineers (IEEE). IEEE is a not-for-profit organization that promotes the advancement of technology. IEEE Standard Test Access Port and Boundary-Scan Architecture is officially labeled the *IEEE Standard 1149.1*. This is also called JTAG or Boundary Scan. Most mobile forensic examiners who utilize this technique will always refer to it as "JTAG." The *History of JTAG* is outlined by Corelis, a company that specializes in JTAG/Boundary Scan software and hardware:

> In the 1980s, the Joint Test Action Group (JTAG) set out to develop a specification for boundary-scan testing that was standardized in 1990 as the IEEE Std. 1149.1-1990. A few years later in 1993, a new revision to the standard—1149.1a—was introduced to clarify, correct, and enhance the original specification. An additional supplement, 1149.1b, was published in 1994 to add Boundary-Scan Description Language (BSDL) to the standard, paving the way for fast, automated test development and spurring continuous adoption by major electronics producers all over the world. The lessons that were learned became formalized in an update to the core standard in 2001 and IEEE-1149.1-2001 was published.

As new applications of JTAG were discovered, new standards were developed to extend the capabilities of JTAG. Standards such as the IEEE-1149.5 module test and maintenance bus standard in 1995 and the IEEE-1149.4 standard for mixed-signal testing in 1999 were met with low adoption rates and are not widely used at present. The IEEE-1149.6 standard introduced in 2003, on the other hand, began with slow adoption but has since become standard in many ICs as the technology it addressed—high-speed, AC-coupled signals—became a common feature of electronic systems. IEEE-1149.7, published in 2009 to address the need for JTAG in low-pin-count systems, is now standard on many popular microcontrollers [1]. Since the inception of JTAG in 1990, there have been over 12 JTAG-related standards through 2014.

How Joint Test Action Group Works

Corelis also provides an explanation on how JTAG works:

The JTAG/boundary-scan test architecture was originally developed as a method to test interconnects between ICs mounted on a PCB without using physical test probes. Boundary-scan cells created using multiplexer and latch circuits are attached to each pin on the device. These cells, embedded in the device, can capture data from pin or core logic signals as well as force data onto pins. Captured data is serially shifted out through the JTAG Test Access Port (TAP) and can be compared to expected values to determine a pass or fail result. Forced test data is serially shifted into the boundary-scan cells. All of this is controlled from a serial data path called the scan path or scan chain.

Because each pin can be individually controlled, boundary-scan eliminates a large number of test vectors that would normally needed to properly initialize sequential logic. Using JTAG, tens or hundreds of test vectors may do the job that had previously required thousands. Boundary-scan enables shorter test times, higher test coverage, increased diagnostic capability, and lower capital equipment cost [2].

Test Access Port

JTAG, in simple terms for mobile forensics, refers to a way in which we can communicate and pull stored data off the target device. Specific pin points were designed that, along with specific performing resistors, allowed programming, testing, and debugging to take place. These points are called *TAPs*. Many phones will have TAPs that can be mapped directly to the processor or embedded memory. JTAG is performed through specific TAPs and requires a minimum of four. There are five pins that are associated with the TAP and they are referred to as Ports. These are Test Mode Select (TMS), Test Clock Input (TCK), Test Data Input (TDI), Test Data Output (TDO), and an optional TAP of Test Reset (TRST). There will be times when additional TAP locations are used for acquiring data from mobile devices. We will address the main four and include additional common access ports used:

- **TMS**
  The TMS refers to a serial input that will test the logic control. Using an internal resistor, bits of data are grabbed as they rise on the edge of the test logical clock.
- **TCK**
  The TCK is a logic test clock that is used to apply changes to the specific commands as needed, specific test data and input controls that take place on the rising edge of the clock. It can shift the output data serially on the falling edge of the clock. There will be a maximum frequency for the clock. We will discuss this frequency in a later chapter.
- **TDI**
  TDI is a serial input that takes specific commands. The data are retained on the rising edge of the test logic clock and will have an internal resistor.
- **TDO**
  TDO refers to the output serial data. This would be the data that are the result of the specific commands after they have executed the test through the other TAPs. These four pin locations can also be referred to as "TAP" signals. During mobile forensics, examiners may find other TAP locations that are necessary for a specific flasher box to communicate with the target phone. The following are some that will be commonly needed with most flasher boxes.
  - **TRST**
    The TRST can also be referred to as **NTRST** and **NRST**. This is typically an optional setting and is used to reset the signal and will have an internal resistor.
  - *Return Clock (**RTCK**)*
    The target device being JTAG analyzed can have an RTCK feed. This will generally have a resistor that is attached in series with this input.
  - *Ground (**GRD** or **GND**)*
    Within the IEEE Standard 1149.1, the Ground is generally not addressed. For mobile forensic examiners, it will be a common TAP that must be used. In a later chapter, we will discuss the flasher boxes that work directly with JTAG. The boxes often will show, within their own software, the exact location for the required TAP connections to connect with their tool.

Fig. 22.1 shows a diagram of the JTAG communications protocol that uses the four main TAP pins. The optional TRST is also shown along with a Ground. Resistors are also displayed as previously referenced.

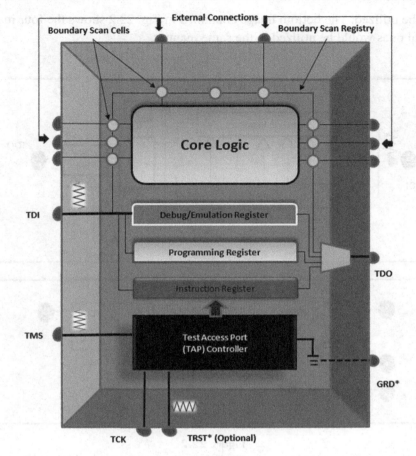

Figure 22.1

Diagram showing the Joint Test Action Group communication protocol that uses the four main Test Access Port (TAP) pins. *GRD*, Ground; *TCI*, Test Clock Input; *TDI*, Test Data Input; *TDO*, Test Data Output; *TMS*, Test Mode Select; *TRST*, Test Reset.

The scan will work on supported devices by allowing the "in data" operator clock into two shift registers: (1) the actual instruction the examiner has chosen and (2) the data register of the TAP controller. Based on the instructions, the data can be executed to read or set by the values of the boundary scan register. Each bit within the boundary scan register is linked to the external pins of that circuit. This allows the user to set or read the values to and from the system bus. Fig. 22.1 illustrates this and is a simpler version of what is depicted in the top of Fig. 22.2. The top image in Fig. 22.2 also shows where the addition TAPs are located within the scan. Within the main board of the target mobile device, this layout can be designed for using the JTAG standard. These can apply to each IC and can be designed as test points that may access each pin for that specific target circuit. The design may be interconnected, allowing the same commands to take place, but only those requiring the need for one set of

TAPs are to be utilized. The bottom image contained in Fig. 22.2 shows the four main TAPs, but additional ones would be utilized in the same manner.

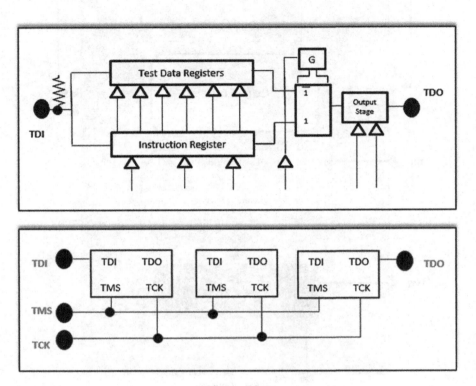

Figure 22.2
(Top image) Diagram of the test data registers, instruction register, and additional Test Access Port locations. (Bottom image) Interconnected example, using one Test Data Input/Test Data Output/ Test Mode Select/Test Clock Input (TDI/TDO/TMS/TCK) to communicate to all circuits.

Using more recent memory configurations, specifically the Ball Grid Array (BGA) technology, we can obtain the data sheet from the manufacturer and get a clearer understanding of how the TAPs may be mapped back to their source. Fig. 22.3 are screenshots from an example of this type of packaging directly from a data sheet (note these are two different configurations shown). The data sheet can show the examiner the exact Ball of the processor or eMMC that uses the instruction for that TAP.

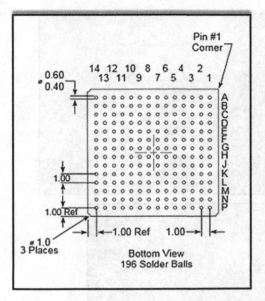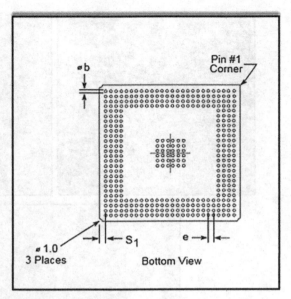

Figure 22.3
Ball Grid Array data sheet example.

The data sheet, for example, will advise the location of the TDI by using the horizontal and vertical positioning that is depicted in Fig. 22.3. For instance, TDI may be located at the 6-C BGA position.

In-System Programming (ISP) was previously addressed. JTAG is very similar to ISP, but ISP communicates directly with the memory and does not involve the processor.

The following figure will help illustrate the BGA locations in correlation with the TAPs. In most cases, the TAP locations will be very close to the processor or eMMC memory (if supported for JTAG). At the top of Fig. 22.4 a Qualcomm processor that has been removed from a Samsung Android device is shown. The TAPs are on the opposite side of this same board positioned directly under the processor. In this example, the TAPs are under the label that is affixed where the battery sits. The label indicates the model, MEID/IMEI, FCC, and other typical values. On this model, this is simply peeled off. The TAPs in this example are covered with board materials and must be cleaned for the scan to take place. The middle image on Fig. 22.4 depicts the TAPs before cleaning. The bottom image contained on Fig. 22.4 shows them ready for the JTAG process. It is important to understand that not all TAP locations will be laid out the same.

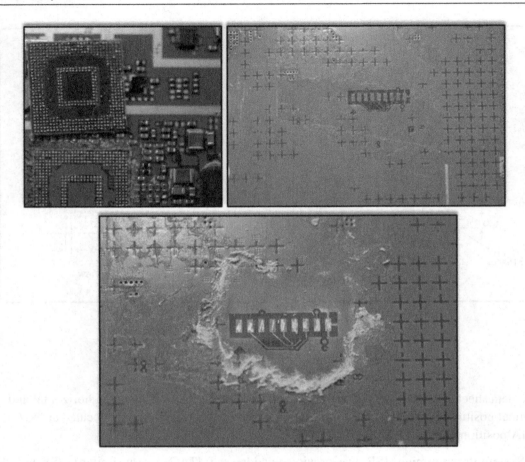

Figure 22.4
Processor and opposite side main board Test Access Port correlation.

Here is another example of the TAP locations being located under the product label. This is a Casio C771, and the TAPs do not require further processing for them to be used. The top, left image in Fig. 22.5 shows the phone with the label in place, then peeled back, shown in right, top image in Fig. 22.5. The bottom image in Fig. 22.5 depicts the eight TAPs that would be used for the JTAG acquisition. The location was revealed through the GUI of the flasher box used for the pull. This is outlined in additional detail in the next chapter.

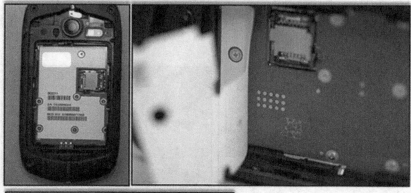

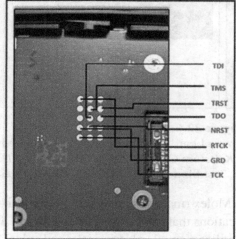

This board uses 8 of the 15 exposed TAPs. As previously mentioned, the requirement will vary based on the target device examiners are attempting to scan. In almost all cases, the four main TAPs (TDI, TDO, TCK and TMS) will be required for JTAG.

Figure 22.5

Example of Test Access Ports (TAPs) located under the label of a phone along with the correlation of the necessary TAPs needed for the Joint Test Action Group (JTAG) extraction. *GRD*, Ground; *RTCK*, Return Clock; *TCK*, Test Clock Input; *TDI*, Test Data Input; *TDO*, Test Data Output; *TMS*, Test Mode Select; *TRST or NRST*, Test Reset.

Molex (Connections)

Another method in which TAP locations can be identified (and accessed for JTAG) is through Molex connections. Many of these are premade by the manufacturer on the main board of the phone. The top, left image in Fig. 22.6 is from Samsung SCH-i535. The right image contained in Fig. 22.6 depicts the associated TAP locations in relationship to the Molex connection for this i535 model. The bottom, left image would be the required female connector and associated cable. These specialized parts will be discussed in an upcoming chapter.

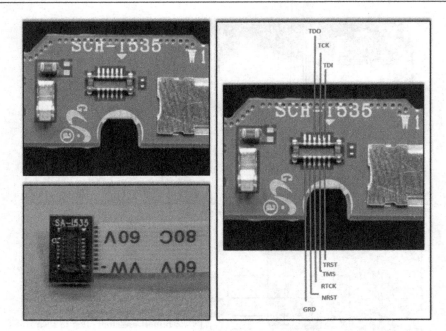

Figure 22.6

Example of a Molex connector built into the main board of a phone and the associated Test Access Ports with required cable. *GRD*, Ground; *RTCK*, Return Clock; *TCK*, Test Clock Input; *TDI*, Test Data Input; *TDO*, Test Data Output; *TMS*, Test Mode Select; *TRST or NRST*, Test Reset.

Some main boards will not have the actual Molex (male or female) connector affixed to the board. Instead, they will have the solder locations that can be used for the Molex. In this case, the examiner would have two choices: (1) utilize a small soldering iron and solder the necessary wires to the TAPs, or (2) purchase the necessary Molex and solder it to the main board. This type of soldering can be extremely difficult because of the connections being so close to one another. In most cases, it is easier to utilize solder paste, set the male (or female) Molex adaptor on the board joint, and use hot air rework to make the necessary connections. On the companion site, Fig. 22.1 depicts an LG D500 main board that has a supported location where a 14-pin male Molex would be soldered.

Fig. 22.2 on the companion site indicates the TAP locations for this LG D500 along with an aftermarket 14-pin male Molex adaptors that can be soldered to this location. The examiner would in turn use a 14-pin female Molex to quick connect to this area. The female connector would look more like the one depicted in Fig. 22.6 for Samsung SCH-i535.

Joint Test Action Group Issues

The use of this nondestructive mobile forensic examination technique can come with various issues. For example, although Boundary Scan is a recognized standard, it does not mean that all manufacturers are required to equip their main boards with a circuit that supports this testing. Also, there will be times when the board is capable of JTAG access, but the actual TAP locations are not documented, or the documentation is difficult to locate.

The next chapter addresses equipment involved in Boundary Scan reading; examiners will soon realize they will need several flasher boxes or specialized equipment to conduct these (JTAG) types of exams. Like most of the forensic equipment used for mobile acquisitions, there is no such thing as one tool doing it all. The JTAG process is no different and will require several different hardware tools (generally, flasher boxes) to pull the target memory.

Examiners will also find that these tools will require specific voltages and clock speeds and other proprietary settings that must be used for the process to work correctly. This may or may not be sufficiently documented by the vendor who sells the equipment because of the vast number of processors and memory configurations that are available. Vendors' target audience for their equipment is the mobile repair industry, not law enforcement. As such, they may not address issues in an easy "cop-friendly" format. Three common JTAG problems are the following:

1. *Device does not support JTAG (no TAP locations present on main board).*
2. *TAPs are present but not properly mapped or documented (this does not include ISP).*
3. *Device fully supports JTAG, however, inadequate documentation of proper settings for the hardware that will be used to conduct the pull. This is usually regarding suggested voltages and clock speeds.*

Chapter Summary Key Points

JTAG is part of an IEEE standard. Examiners can use JTAG to communicate with the processor and flash memory on a mobile device. This allows them to bypass user security and, in some cases, a damaged phone that previously would not be acquired through commercial forensic tools. Communications take place through specific designated TAPs. TAP locations vary and may be covered by board finish or, in some cases, communicate through a Molex connection. Common TAP signals communicate with the following input or output standards:

TMS, TCK, TDI, TDO, TRST (also referred as NTRST and NRST), RTCK, and GRD or GND.

It will be up to the examiner to determine if their target device is supported for JTAG. JTAG is considered a nondestructive physical examination.

References

[1] Corelis, What is JTAG? http://www.corelis.com/education/What-Is-JTAG.htm.
[2] Corelis, How JTAG works. http://www.corelis.com/education/What-Is-JTAG.htm.

CHAPTER 23

JTAG Specialized Equipment

Information in This Chapter

- Pogo pins
- Jigs
- Premade boards
- JTAG clip
- Dolphin clip
- Molex flex cable kit (MOORC)
- Assorted wires and RJ45 style cable blanks
- 20-pin ribbon cable
- Jumper wires (copper)
- JTAG Finders
- BSDL file library for JTAG
- Precise soldering units
- Hot glue, rubber bands, and cardboard

Introduction—Slow and Deliberant

A few years back, a neighboring police department needed assistance with a homicide case. The phone required a Joint Test Action Group (JTAG) extraction and had a place on the main board where a 14-pin male Molex could be soldered. This was one of the smallest connections (at that time) that the author had encountered (prior to In-System Programming (ISP)). The solder tip was too big, and the solder was the incorrect gauge. Molex male parts were on back order, which meant the actual contacts needed direct soldering.

The situation required practicing on the same model test phone, obtaining a precise solder station and using hot glue. The use of hot glue from that point forward became a standard practice that continues today. There will be times when the use of commercially available products will be needed. Manufacturers have more and more items that are being developed and sold for JTAG purposes. There will be many adaptors, jigs, holders, premade connection boards, pogo pins, and other items available for purchase. Remember, success will come from the ingenuity of the examiner. When training and experienced examiners encounter a specific problem, they modify simple, everyday products to make the JTAG extraction work.

Examiners who have conducted several JTAG exams will understand this. Cardboard will now come to your rescue. Rubber bands and plastic clamps will save gray hairs from growing out of your head. Most importantly, JTAG requires patience. It is certainly not something to rush.

Your boss wants answers, the case detective is waiting in your lab, the suspect is unknown, and the pressure to hurry is very real. To slow down and do precise work can be difficult, but it is necessary. Remember, modify anything to make the JTAG extraction work, and slow down. Remember the old search term: *SLOW AND DELIBERANT*, it more than applies with this type of extraction.

Pogo Pins and Jigs

In our last chapter, we showed a couple of examples of Test Access Port (TAP) locations on main boards of phones. For understanding TAPs, the images supplied indicated the proper address associated.

Vendors who support various tools for JTAG extraction will often sell jigs. The adaptor's purpose is for continued use. They make contact with the TAPs on a phone without the need of soldering to the actual device. There are many of these jigs available to the examiner. Most work through a pin that is spring-loaded, which helps make a better connection with the TAPs on the main board. These pins come in different gauges, as well as tips. They are named *pogo pins*.

Vendors will use the pogo pins in connection with a specific board that allows the examiner to choose the spacing needed for the target TAPs. Examiners can choose the pins that will fit their phone and solder to the board. The (blank) boards are specifically designed to allow wires to be soldered as needed to the printed circuit that corresponds with the pogo pin. The board is designed by the manufacturer to fit into a premade clamp. The clamp sits over the phone and makes contact with the TAPs in question. There are some vendors who make the jigs to fit specific phones. Their jigs have slotted contact boards that allow the connection to take place without the need of soldering. One such brand is called Dolphin. The Dolphin Clip is specifically designed to work with Nokia FBus speeds, which are generally in older model Nokia phones. One side of the clip allows the examiner to set various voltages and clock speeds.

The other side of the Dolphin Clip houses the main connector for the TAPs to communicate through (RJ45 style). Users can elect to feed additional 5 V through a Nano USB port. The remaining Mini USB is used to supply power to the target phone. Fig. 23.1 depicts images of various pogo pins, premade pin boards, JTAG clip, Dolphin Clip, and assorted premade jigs for the Nokia phones.

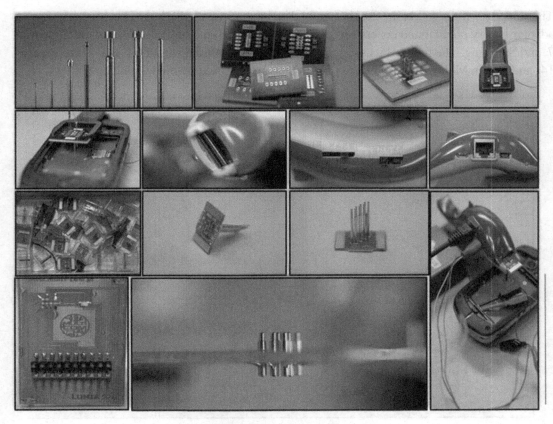

Figure 23.1
Examples of pogo pins, premade pin boards, JTAG Clip, Dolphin Clip, and premade jigs for Nokia phones.

Molex Parts

In the previous chapter, we showed an example of a cellular phone that had Molex adaptors soldered onto the board. Many vendors sell kits, cables, and various adaptors that allow the connection to take place between the (target) board Molex and the flasher box that is performing the extraction. These will generally have a list of supported make and models that can be referenced back to the Molex adaptor number. Contained within the images in Fig. 23.2 (upper left) depicts the chart for the MOORC JPIN JTAG Molex Flex cable 33-in-1 kit. These are categorized by "Z" number. These can be broken off the strip that they are affixed to and used accordingly. The Molex data cable will need to interface with an adaptor that is suited for the box that is being utilized to conduct the JTAG. Fig. 23.2 also shows examples of a few different adaptors that would connect the Molex cable for the communications to take place. Contained within Fig. 23.2 is also the adaptor board that comes with the 33-in-1 (MOORC) kit. The board offers optional soldering to the TAPs for phones that may not be Molex supported (dual purpose).

This adaptor will fit within the 20-pin (male) data input for the RIFF box. This particular Molex adaptor is very popular and covers several model phones from Asus, LG, Nokia, Google Nexus 7, and Samsung. The focus of its support, however, is for Samsung and LGs. It also has generic 14- and 30-pin Molex support for LG phones that are not listed by model number.

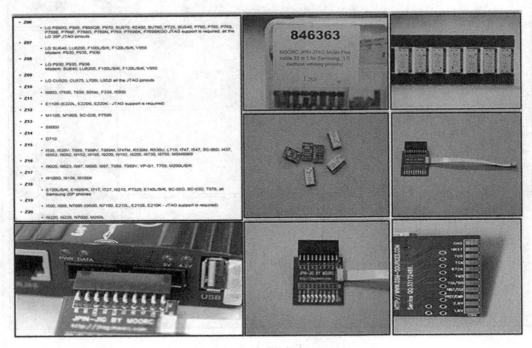

Figure 23.2

Example of the MOORC chart used to determine the "Z" number adaptor, the 33-in-1 MOORC Kit with adaptor board, and 20-pin connector for common flasher boxes.

Wires and Wire Harnesses

Examiners will primarily use wire connections during most JTAG extractions to connect between the TAPs and the flasher box that is being utilized. This would be used when jigs are not applicable, or the device does not support Molex connection.

Many vendors will sell cables that can be modified to fit the phone directly or soldered to an adaptor board similar to the ones previously shown by MOORC. The cables will vary, but the most common will be a 20-pin female or an RJ45 style. Both types will already have the cable affixed to the data head, and it will be up to the examiner to "map" these back to the appropriate TAP locations—either on the actual main board of the phone or to the adaptor board. The vendor of these cables will show a color coding (if applicable) schematic for the RJ45 cable male end. When conducting continuity testing, an examiner can ensure that the opposite end correctly corresponds to the TAP in question. Fig. 23.3 shows the "blank" RJ45 cables sold with various flasher boxes. The box being this is used which supplies a "pin-out" location used for this type of connection. The examiner can in turn correspond the opposite ends with the TAP needed for the phone or specific adaptor board (if used). The upper right image in Fig. 23.3 shows the female end of a common 20-pin. The bottom, right image contained in Fig. 23.3, is a common "jumper" board sold with the RIFF box. This allows the examiner to solder one time to either the 20-pin style ribbon cable, RJ45 style, or any other type. The smaller areas on the board (numbered) can also be soldered to one time using small wires. The board and subsequent cables/wires can be reused on different phones.

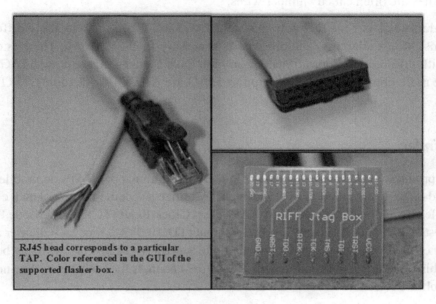

RJ45 head corresponds to a particular TAP. Color referenced in the GUI of the supported flasher box.

RIFF Jtag Box

Figure 23.3
Examples of RJ4 (style) and 20-pin cables, along with a standard "jumper" style board (RIFF Jtag Box shown).

Very often, bare copper wires are used to connect to the TAPs on the main board and back to an adaptor board, or wire harness going to the flasher box. This type of wire may or may not be sold with a fine covering of insulation (enameled). In some cases, the examiner may need to prepare the wire first before soldering it. This would involve burning of the insulation with a solder tip to ensure proper continuity. The insulation may be very difficult to see based on the gauge of wire being used. There are two suggested ways to do this:

1. Use a ball of solder on the tip of a hot solder iron, and feed the wire through the hot solder ball several times. You will only need a small portion of the wire end to be removed of its enamel. Perform this step on both ends. Check for continuity.
2. Use a spaded (hot) solder tip, and carefully scrape the ends of the wire against a solder board (wood). It is very easy to cut the wire when doing this, so scrape lightly. The wire should be rotated while you scrape it. Perform this step on both ends. Check for continuity.

There can be many problems caused by improper wire connections. If you plan on using enameled wire, make sure you use one of the two steps, and you check the wire to ensure current will flow through it. Unfortunately, this will need to be accomplished with each wire needed for each TAP, as well as the ground. The "pros" of using enameled wires is that generally you do not need to worry about the wires shorting out if they touch one another. Fig. 23.1 on the companion site is an image of small gauged copper wire. From left to right in the image are gauges 38, 28, 26, and 24. There are many vendors that sell wires for this purpose. They are often called "jumper wires."

Also, vendors such as Teel Technologies sell JTAG kits. These include many different jigs, boards, Molex adaptors, and other parts necessary for JTAG work. The kits can also be sold with different configurations of common flasher boxes that support JTAG extractions. The more common boxes that support JTAG are ATF, GPG, Octoplus, ORT, RIFF, and Z3X.

JTAG Finder

There are products available that can assist in identifying unmapped TAPs on mobile phone main boards. These are called JTAG Finders. They utilize a specific routine, which checks all the possible pins to locate the necessary TAPs (Test Clock Input (TCK), Test Mode Select (TMS), Test Data Input (TDI), and Test Data Output (TDO)). JTAG Finders will offer a specific number of channels that they can scan at one time. Since JTAG can work with any board that supports this standard, some vendors will offer more channels than what would be necessary just for mobile devices.

One vendor sells the JTAGulator. It offers the ability to scan 24 channels. This board is one of the more feature rich finders that are available. JTAG Finders will use some form of USB interface that is generally handled on the chip through a USB-to-serial universal asynchronous receiver/transmitter. Also, most of the finders will have an adjustable target voltage that provides increments of power up to 3.3 V. Nearly all the board designs of JTAG Finder will have a Parallax Propeller microcontroller. JTAGulator can be controlled through Open OCD (Open on-Chip Debugger) or UrJTAG (Universal JTAG library). UrJTAG runs in a command shell and is open source [1]. Fig. 23.2 on the companion site depicts the JTAGulator board, and Fig. 23.3 depicts the JTAG Shell in the Command Prompt.

Another commercially available product is called "JTAG Finder." This board can scan up to 30 I/O pins at one time and has its own software [2]. The software allows the examiner to look for the SRST (step 1), then the TCK/TMS/TDO (step 2), followed by TDI (step 3). Step 4 is the RTCK, and last, step 5 is TRST.

The last example is the JTAG finding solution used by the author. This board is made by 100RandomTasks [3]. The board is very simple and offers 12 channels. Also, the software that interfaces with this board is a (free) simple-to-use Parallax Serial Terminal. This allows the user to scan the registry with or without instruction. If the scan is completed using the instruction, the user must enter the instruction register width in bits, the ID command in hex, and tell the program how many channels to scan (supply a value between 4 and 12). These values for the register width and ID command can be in the Boundary Scan Description Language File (BSDL). The BSDL will also have another value that can help with the confirmation—this is the ID code value.

Examiners can look up their target processor online, locate the BSDL file, and in turn find the values needed. Once they have these, they can connect to the available TAPs that are on the target board and connect to the JTAG board. The board is then connected via USB to the Parallax Terminal, and because the processor on the JTAG Finder is flashed for this terminal, it will see the device if the COM port is set correctly. Supplying the registry values of the BSDL can help narrow down the scan possibilities greatly, thus reducing the number of TAP duplicates that need to be manually eliminated. The examiner can look up some of the values for the ID command. On the companion site, Fig. 23.4 is a screenshot from the *BSDL Files Library for JTAG* website. At the bottom of the screenshot, it indicates the "Vendors" to choose from.

Another way to look up this BSDL value is through the UP 828 and 828P Programmer software. The software can be downloaded for free, and the actual programmer does not need to be connected to see the values. Once installed, launch the program, and simply look up the chip part number and typically it will be displayed in the left pane of the utility. (The use of the UP 828/828P Programmers is covered in an upcoming chapter).

Once the scan is conducted, the user would focus on the combinations that repeat on the same ID—for instance, if TDO shows on channel 1, and repeats itself on every ID combination that was entered as TDO for channel one, then it is most likely the proper TAP location for TDO. There will, however, be times when IDs provide the same TAP, but in different pin locations. These would have to be reduced further. The options may result in manual testing, but the TAP positions can be reduced from thousands of possibilities down to just a few.

Fig. 23.4 shows the board made by 100RandomTasks, the Serial Parallax Terminal connected to the JTAG Finder, and some of the selections the user must choose from. Random Tasks calls their finder *JTAG Pin Detector*. Fig. 23.5 is an image of the "homemade" box created (crudely) by the author. Inside this container houses the board from 100RandomTasks. Connectors were mounted to the top to allow wires to be quick connected. This is just one example on how examiners could create their own box for JTAG finding, using any of these referenced boards, when the TAP addresses are unknown. At the time of this writing, the author was working with the owner of 100RandomTasks. He has developed JTAG Pin Finder 2.0, which features the ability to accommodate various voltages.

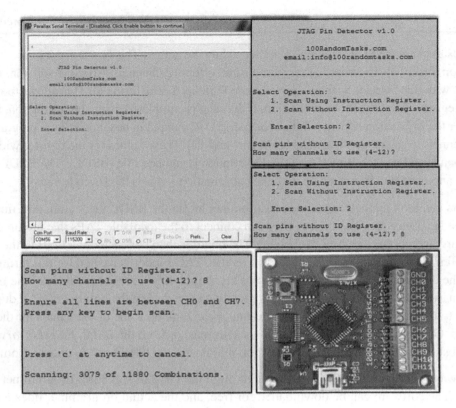

Figure 23.4
GUI of the parallax serial terminal connected to the 100RandomTasks JTAG Pin Detector.

Figure 23.5
Example of a "homemade" box that contains the JTAG Pin Detector inside.

Precise Soldering Units

In the introduction of this chapter, the author spoke briefly about the need to utilize a precise soldering unit to perform a necessary JTAG extraction. When first acquiring equipment necessary for JTAG work, many examiners find themselves cutting corners on equipment and various parts. This was true for the author as well, and the driving force behind the decision was cost. After experiencing several cheaper alternatives when it comes to the soldering iron/station, it is recommended to invest in better (precise) solder-ing unit. This not only helps the examiner, but it also cuts down on time and damaging parts, and in some cases, the target evidence. These units can help you become better at soldering in a very short amount of time. This was at least the case for the author, who never had "formal" training on soldering. If soldering electronic components is new to you, there are several free videos on YouTube that can assist with fundamental principles involved.

There are several vendors that sell these types of solder stations. Weller is a a well-established company that offers a number of products that can be used for precise soldering. Also, if you plan to conduct chip removal, you may want to consider a precise soldering unit. These units work extremely well when cleaning the excess solder and adhesive on the chip. For the author, the unit purchased was made by JBC Tools. The company is based in Spain and started making soldering equipment in 1929. Their units have a 2-year warranty [4].

Another reason this brand was selected was the size of the actual handle that holds the cartridge. This needed to fit under a microscope, and other vendors had a much larger handle length that interfered with the optics. There may be times when soldering work will be required through a microscope, such as JTAG, ISP, or chip-off. Even specific models created by JBC have handles that are too large for microscope work. There are ways around this issue. One remedy is to solder with an angled cartridge. This puts the handle off to the side, away from the optical main area. Another way around this issue is to purchase a digital microscope unit. One popular vendor is Tagarno. This allows the examiner additional room to conduct soldering, as the camera is mounted several inches from the target. Contained on the companion site is the Tagarno Magnus FHD Zip Brochure (PDF).

JBC sells single units as well as dual work. The single units are called "Precision Soldering," while the dual units are called "Nano Soldering" or "Nano Rework." The Nano units can hold two handles. These can be changed out to accommodate the Micro Tweezers or in the author's case, two different cartridge configurations. On the companion site, Fig. 23.6 depicts a JBC Nano Soldering unit. The images to the right are the two different microtips that have been configured. The upper right image is the spaded tip (used for cleaning), and the bottom right image is the tip used for JTAG and ISP soldering.

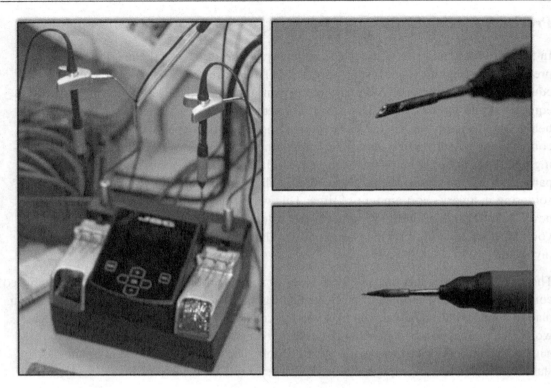

Figure 23.6
JBC Nano Soldering unit and two different microtip examples.

Hot Glue, Rubber Bands, and Cardboard

Online searches for JTAG connectors will yield several vendors that sell various specialized cables, boxes, and other tools. This chapter is not designed as an attempt to discuss every available option when it comes to JTAG tools. It is mainly to focus on items that are commonly used for assisting with JTAG extraction. Examiners who perform several JTAG extractions will realize that no one set of pogo pins, cables, or adaptors will work with every situation. In bringing this chapter to an end, a couple of examples will be provided where hot glue (glue stick), pieces of wood, and some creativity helped with this type of acquisition.

Fig. 23.5 on the companion site depicts a Casio C811 being JTAG. The jumper board was held down with two small pieces of glue from a glue stick. Small slivers are cut from the glue stick with a razor, and an old soldering iron tip is used to melt them where desired. Also on the companion site is a close-up image of hot glue being used to hold down the copper wires after they have been soldered. Fig. 23.6 (companion site) depicts the 38-gauge wires that were soldered to the TAPs on an LG phone. The hot glue protects the wires from inadvertently being pulled off.

It is also very common to use pieces of cardboard to glue wires, jumper boards, or other parts necessary for the extraction. Cardboard, along with rubber bands, can help hold required things in place. Some phones feed the current from and to the battery contacts through a secondary connector. This connector may need to be removed if the battery needs to be supplied to the device. In most JTAG extractions, a constant supply of power to the phone is usually required. Fig. 23.7 shows two images. The top picture depicts the various areas where hot glue was applied during a JTAG on an LG phone. This image also shows how rubber bands can be used to hold the battery against the terminals. The bottom left image in Fig. 23.7 displays how hot glue was used to hold the proprietary connector for the battery on a Samsung phone.

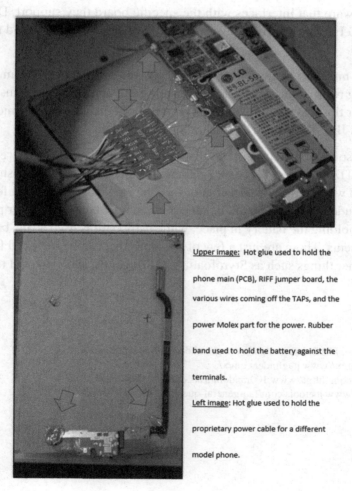

Upper image: Hot glue used to hold the phone main (PCB), RIFF jumper board, the various wires coming off the TAPs, and the power Molex part for the power. Rubber band used to hold the battery against the terminals.

Left image: Hot glue used to hold the proprietary power cable for a different model phone.

Figure 23.7
Example of hot glue and rubber band used during JTAG extraction.

Chapter Summary Key Points

JTAG extractions will require a variety of parts. These include jigs, clips, adaptors, Molex accessories , and wires. Jigs utilize pogo pins and can come prefixed to specific boards made for certain make and model phones. Other boards allow the examiner to solder the pogo pins to the board in the location needed. Some of the boards that are designed to hold the jigs can also come with a JTAG clip. The clip allows the specified jig to slide into it, and this allows the user to "clip" the pogo pins to the target device. The main reason jigs are used is they allow the JTAG extraction to take place without the need of soldering.

JTAG Finders allow users to properly locate undocumented TAPs. The finders typically use open-source software that interfaces with the specific board they support. Depending on the vendor, JTAG Finders can have several channels that can be connected to the main board.

Precise soldering units can be used for JTAG specific soldering tasks. The units can also be used for soldering related functions when performing ISP and chip-off exams. Some of these units have smaller tips and shorter handles and can work efficiently under microscopes. A popular vendor is JBC Tools, which offers both single and dual work units.

Examiners can also use a variety of items that may assist in the process as well as help reduce problems during JTAG exams. These include hot glue sticks, which can be shaved into small pieces and heated with an older solder iron or tip. The glue can be used in a few different situations, to include holding the main board, wires, jumper boards, or other parts. Rubber bands help with holding the battery in place, while cardboard is used as the base for most of the main components. These are just a few of the items that can be modified for conducting JTAG exams. Other things such as Styrofoam, plastic clamps, and electrical tape can also be useful.

References

[1] Grand Idea Studio, JTAGulator. http://www.grandideastudio.com/jtagulator/.
[2] Jtagfinder.com. http://www.jtagfinder.com/x/.
[3] 100randomtasks.com. http://www.100randomtasks.com/jtag-pin-finder.
[4] JBCTools. http://www.jbctools.com/faq-general-questions-menu-15.html.

CHAPTER 24

RIFF Box Overview

Information in This Chapter

- RIFF Box components (Original RIFF)
- RIFF Box Pinout
- Exercise (setting up a 20-pin cable)
- JTAG Manager Software
- Box Service/Get Box Info
- Show S/N
- Check for Updates/Firmware Updates
- RIFF Updates Manager
- RIFFBOX Registration
- Resurrector Settings
- Interface Pinout
- Using Ctrl + F for Fast Search
- Search for DLL for this Model Name
- JTAG Read/Write
- Connect & Get ID
- Connect to the dead body
- "The RTCK Signal Does Not Respond"
- Analyze JTAG Chain
- DCC Read/Write
- Image File is Used (Main + Spare combined into single file)
- Auto FullFlash Size
- Access MCU Address Space
- Use End Address, not length/ECC Module Enabled
- JTAG TCK Speed
- Using Resurrector Settings (Predefined)
- Custom Target Settings
- Useful Plugins
- Saving the binary scan

- Previous Read Was Interrupted!
- RIFF Plain Shrinked Files/RIFF Secured Shrinked Files
- Manual Probing TAPs
- RIFF 2 overview

Introduction

The next few chapters will deal with specific flasher boxes that can be used for JTAG extractions. The ones featured will be the boxes that are commonly used to support the most phones. Each box will have its own software interface. The warning here is that nearly all of them are not "cop" friendly. What this means to the author is that unlike many of the commercially available forensic tools, they will not provide the user with "dummy-proof" steps on how to use them. If you are new to using these types of devices, you may get frustrated during the initial install, as well as the actual use. The biggest problem when using them is that *they can easily alter the evidence*. If that were not enough, the software can be complex, and many allow advanced user access to additional features and functionality.

If possible, attend JTAG training or work directly with someone who has attended training. It is also recommended to try soldering techniques on test phones first. Examiners can use the interface of the box they are using, and determine (before their examination begins) which phones are supported. If you need to purchase test phones, this is an easy way to locate older, supported phones for that purpose. The extraction time on JTAG pulls can also be quite time-consuming, especially with newer, larger capacity phones.

In each of the chapters that deal with a specific flasher box that support JTAG, the basic steps will be shown. What is not covered are the decoding steps. In most cases, Physical Analyzer Open Advanced will be used with the specific JTAG profile. For other phones, the physical (default) profile will work.

This chapter begins by addresses the RIFF (1) box, which at the time of this writing, was hard to locate online, as the RIFF 2 box has replaced it. The features of the RIFF 2 box are also covered. The software for both RIFF and RIFF 2 works in a similar format. There is also a small exercise (lab) that provides suggestions on setting up the RIFF jumper board to the 20-pin ribbon cable. Again, the author suggests working as slow as necessary and to try and have as much patience as possible.

RIFF Box Components

RIFF (1) box is typically sold with two 20-pin cables and a jumper adaptor board. Included with the packaging, is the "RIFF BOX PINOUT" card. This is a colored reference guide, which shows the pin locations for both the RJ45 and 20-pin, male connections on the end of the RIFF box. Fig. 24.1 contains pictures of the RIFF packaging, the box, the included cables, and the jumper board.

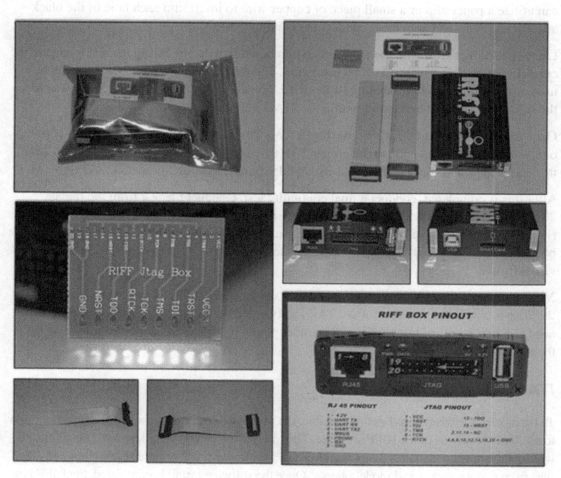

Figure 24.1
Images of the RIFF box and associated parts included.

One of the first things that can assist the examiner who plans to use the RIFF box is to prepare the 20-pin cable and solder the necessary contacts to the RIFF jumper board. This will cut down on time when an actual case presents itself and the RIFF box needs to be used for the JTAG pull.

Exercise

Identify the appropriate cables from the 20-pin cable that corresponds with the "RIFF BOX PINOUT" card. Ensure that they line up the notch on the cable with the box to properly locate each corresponding wire. The ends of the 20-pin cable would then be stripped as needed. Once the appropriate wires have been identified from the 20-pin cable and stripped, conduct a continuity test between the stripped end and the female (black) end of the cable. Examiners can utilize a paper clip or a small piece of copper wire to insert into each hole of the black adaptor end. This can help them conduct the continuity test.

Locate the proper wire with the appropriate numbered female pin during the test to ensure the correct wire has been stripped off its insulation. The **RIFF BOX PINOUT** card should be used as a reference and for labeling. If the RIFF box did not come with this PINOUT card, the same interface can be viewed within the JTAG Software.

Once each wire for the corresponding Test Access Port (TAP) has been tested as the correct one, solder the stripped ends to the proper TAP names of the adaptor jumper board. Follow the safety steps and cautions that deal with solder fumes, lead, and potential risks of burns.

After this is completed, conduct a final continuity test. Conduct the test from the female 20-pin position (again with a paper clip or wire inserted) to the opposite side of the adaptor (jumper) board you have soldered to. Use the smaller TAP solder points of the jumper adaptor board to conduct the test. On the companion site, Figs. 24.1–24.4 depict the various steps in a visual format.

Note: Once examiners have ensured that they have properly soldered the appropriate wires of the 20-pin ribbon cable to the correct TAP locations on the jumper adaptor board, they will need to apply a coat of hot glue over the solder points to protect the wires from coming off the solder joints.

JTAG Manager Software

To try to keep this chapter as brief as possible, the reader will be provided specific steps about how to use basic functions of the RIFF software. The install itself can be quite lengthy. The .dll install will be shown when the RIFF 2 box is addressed. The program will require several hundred .dll files from various makes and model phones. Once the software install is completed, the RIFF box must be connected to the PC. Users may see drivers installing during the first-time the box is connected.

An icon that can be used to launch the RIFF Box JTAG Manager program should be on the desktop. Once the program opens, users will be shown a series of tabs that allow access to different features. There will be five main tabs across the top from left to right. Depending on the tab selected, the associated tabs (that correspond) at the bottom will change. On the far right, from top to bottom will be the **JTAG TCK Speed, *Resurrector Settings, DCC Loader USB Interface, Target (Core), Reset Method, JTAG I/O Voltage**, and **TAP#** settings. ("Resurrector" is spelled in this fashion by RIFF).

Some of the settings on the far right are not accessible when a user has selected a specific Make and Model under the Resurrector Settings. The user must switch to *Custom Target Settings* to enable the features below that setting to work. During the initial install, a user name and password will need to be created to allow access to the server that supports the upgrades for the box. The serial number is in turn checked and verified that it is an authorized device that can receive additional upgrades and can be continued to use.

To create a mechanism to check for fraud, vendors will embed products with a serial number that is checked against their database for service and support. Fig. 24.2 shows the various selections available that display when the *Box Service* tab has been selected. When the *Get Box Info* button is selected, it will prompt users with a warning about the theft of your serial number as shown in Fig. 24.2. Selecting *Show S/N* will get the main (black) screen to display the serial number if the RIFF box has been properly installed (Fig. 24.2).

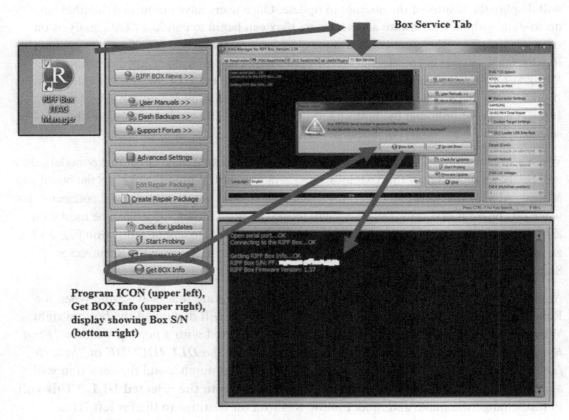

Figure 24.2
Images of the JTAG Manager Software ICON, the Box Service tab, Get Box Info button, and Show S/N—with results example.

Within this same "Box Service" tab, we will also utilize the ***Check for Updates***, and ***Firmware Update*** buttons. The image to the right of the JTAG Manager Software ICON in Fig. 24.2 displays these selections. If updates are available, they will display in another screen and allow the user to select and download each one. This will take place through the RIFF Updates Manager window. When the ***Firmware Update*** button is selected, the user will be prompted to enter his/her ***User name*** and ***Password*** to proceed. On the companion site, Figs. 24.5 and 24.6 display the Check for Updates, Firmware Update, and RIFFBOX Registration window that display the user name and password. The first time this is launched, the user will need to create his/her user name and password. Make certain this is documented and stored, as it will be needed to obtain updates in the future.

During the firmware update, the RIFF box lights will flash and the black interface (GUI) will display the results of the attempt to update. Once users have confirmed that they are up-to-date with their firmware and software, they can begin to conduct JTAG analysis on supported phones. There are two ways to select your target device. The first is to ensure the Resurrection tab has been selected on the upper left. Then go to the right and within the *Resurrector Settings* use the drop-down blue arrows to select your make and model device. If your target make and model is supported within the drop-down, you can select the ***Interface Pinout*** button at the bottom left (remember, the Resurrection tab must be selected).

When users click on the Interface Pinout button (after selecting their target make/model), they will be shown an image of the TAP locations on their board. Within Fig. 24.3 is the board and Molex TAPs for the Samsung (SPH) i535. This image does not show the actual connector, but when this board is disassembled, users will locate the male Molex, which can be used with a Z Molex female end in the MOORC 33-in-1 kit or similar. Also, contained within Fig. 24.3 is an example of TAPs from a Samsung (SGH) T589 that was selected in the Resurrector Settings drop-down.

Another option is to use the ***Ctrl+F for Fast Search*** feature that is available when the Resurrection tab has been selected at the top left. This will display at the bottom right. When these hot keys are selected, the user will be greeted with a pop-up window "***Find Required Resurrector***." This allows the user to type in the ***DLL IDCODE*** or "***Search for this Model Name***." They can simply type the model number and the selection will appear to the left. Once this is displayed select "**Switch to the selected DLL**." This will in turn change the make and model in the Resurrector Settings to the far left. This eliminates the need to have to use the drop-down arrows previously explained in the Resurrector Settings pane. On the companion site, Fig. 24.7 shows the example of the

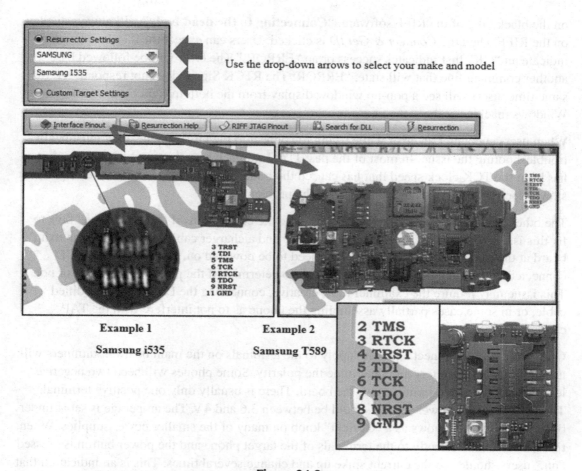

Figure 24.3
Using the Resurrector Settings to select the make and model, and the Interface Pinout that displays the settings for the Test Access Ports.

Ctrl+F for Fast Search feature using the word "*sam*" (for Samsung) to display the possible choices.

To the right of the Resurrection tab is the *JTAG Read/Write* tab. This should be used to initially check to see if the RIFF box is properly communicating with the target phone. When this tab is selected, users will have some additional choices that populate in the center, toward the bottom of the GUI. The *Connect & Get ID* can be used to determine if everything is properly connected and the phone has proper power and clock speeds, users will get a reply on the black GUI of the RIFF software. "**Connecting to the dead body**" will always display on the RIFF when the *Connect & Get ID* is clicked. Users can expect the interface to either indicate an "OK" that indicates success or an "ERROR." The error will be followed by another comment line that will state, "ERROR: The RTCK Signal does not respond." At the same time, users will see a pop-up window display from the bottom right corner of the Windows machine at the same time.

When users encounter an error while trying to connect to the target phone, they must begin troubleshooting the issue. In most of the past JTAG exams where this error has occurred, it has been the TCK clock speed that has caused the issue. This clock speed can be changed to a slower speed, which in many cases will fix the problem.

The other issue can be bad connections. Examine the connections if the clock speed fails to fix this issue. Also, devices may need the battery and a charger cable connected to the main board at the same time. Some phones will need to be powered on, and without the LCD connected to the main board it can be difficult to determine if the phone is turned on or not. This issue may require the examiner to be creative, connecting the LCD with a modified cable, or in some cases partially assembling the phone as to not interfere with the TAP connections.

One solution is to connect a power supply to the terminals on the main board. Examiners will need to look at the battery and determine the polarity. Some phones will need two negative leads connected to the terminals off the board. There is usually only one positive terminal. The voltage on the power supply should be between 3.6 and 4 V. The amperage is set at under 0.04, which usually shows as a "Current" knob on many of the smaller power supplies. When this is connected correctly to the terminals of the target phone and the power button is pressed "on," users should see the current spike up and change several times. This is an indication that the phone is receiving power. Likewise, the opposite will take place when the phone powers off or the RIFF box TAP resets the phone. The current setting will go to zero. When the RIFF has reset the phone, users may need to turn off the power supply to reset the phone (power cycle).

Troubleshooting this issue may take some time, but eventually the RIFF box should be able to connect and get the ID. Directly above the "Connect & Get ID" is the *Analyze JTAG Chain* button. This should also be used to allow the examiner to see what can be located in the scan. Typically, this will indicate the default voltage, the TCK frequency that was used, the TAP number (shown as a # sign), the ID in hex, and the IR length in hex bits. Fig. 24.4 shows an example of a phone where these buttons were selected, along with the error pop-up window when communication does not take place.

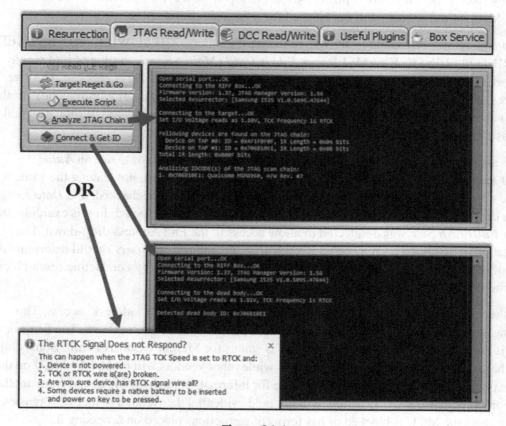

Figure 24.4

Example of the JTAG Read/Write tab, with Analyze JTAG Chain, Connect & Get ID, and the "The RTCK Signal Does not Respond?" pop-up.

In most cases this feature will also show the IDCODE(s) of the devices it locates from the JTAG scan chain. It is usually displayed with the manufacturer name and the chipset number and can include the revision or build number. Once the examiner gets a positive reading that the JTAG Chain has been read, attempts to obtain JTAG extractions should be tried.

This will be accomplished through the ***DCC Read/Write tab***, which is to the right of the JTAG Read/Write tab we just covered. Just like the previous tabs, users will have access to specific features that present when the DCC Read/Write is selected. DCC stands for ***Debug Communication Channel.*** DCC is basically a channel that JTAG uses to communicate with the host. Since the RIFF box is primarily used to repair phones, it can write to the device as well. Many of the settings will not be used for a forensic examination.

Main and *Spare* correspond to *Writing* to the flash memory. THESE WILL NOT BE USED DURING FORENSIC EXAMS! *Image File is Used (Main + Spare combined into single file)* will pull the spare and user area into one binary image when this is checked. The *Use Address as Offset for Flash Files* will use the *Address* value that is set within its box (to the right) above the *Data Length* field. The other feature that will not be used during an actual forensic examination will be the *Erase Flash* button.

RIFF also allows the user the ability to manually set the flash size or to use an *Auto FullFlash Size* setting. This setting will detect the size of the flash, not leaving the value up to the user. If the user desired to set the size, this setting will go unchecked, and *Data Length* has a drop-down allowing a file size from 1 MB to 16 GB to be selected. In this example, the *Auto FullFlash Size* was deselected to allow access to the End Address drop-down. The limitation of 16 gigabytes may be an issue with some phones, and users should determine the size of the memory by using the *Analyze JTAG Chain* feature or by conducting research on the chip(s) off the target board.

Another setting a user must select is where the JTAG scan needs to "address" access. This setting also has a drop-down that allows the scan to start at different locations. The first selection is the *Access MCU Address Space*. MCU stands for **Memory Control Unit**. Some chips will have a separate chip with just the MCU while other vendors will embed the MCU on the same profile (chip). The MCU is responsible for information (data) going to and from another portion of memory. MCU generally will not hold evidential data related to mobile forensics. In many cases the MCU is blocked or has forms of restrictions placed on accessing it.

Beneath the Access MCU Address Space will be Access ROM1 through ROM8 Address Space. This will be the most common setting that will be used to acquire the flash memory. ROM1 is used in most cases but is dependent on what the *Analyze JTAG Chain* has previously displayed (discussed previously). There may be times when more than one address (besides the spare area) will show up during the Analyze JTAG Chain. In that case, the examiner may need to acquire each one.

Directly below this setting are three additional selections: *Auto FullFlash Size*, *Use End Address*, *not Length*, and *ECC Module Enabled*. The Auto FullFlash Size setting's purpose was previously explained. The "Use End Address, not Length" setting will allow ignore the actual Data Length (size) of the target and uses the end of address. The ECC (Error Correction Code) will be used only on NAND chips. The DCC comes into play to generate the NAND spare area. Fig. 24.5 displays the DCC Read/Write tab, the Address/End Address choices, the Access ROM1 Address Space with "Use End Address, not Length" and ECC Module Enabled.

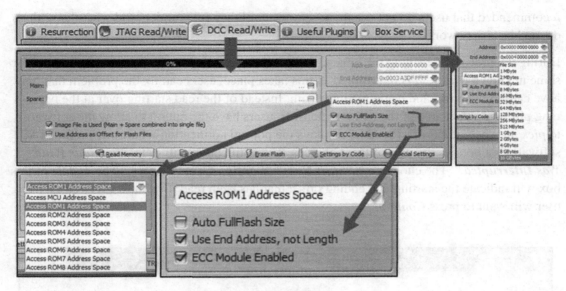

Figure 24.5

An example of the DCC Read/Write settings that includes Address/End Address, Access ROM1 Address Space, "Use End Address, not length," and ECC Module Enabled.

The *JTAG TCK Speed* setting is located to the right when the DCC Read/Write tab has been enabled. Within this setting it has a built-in drop-down that allows the user to change the RTCK speed to stay at a fixed rate of 5 kHz to specified intervals up to 18 MHz. It also allows the user to define the sample rate from "Sample at Max" to specified intervals between 20 kHz and 9 MHz. If the user changes the RTCK to a fix rate clock speed, the sample rate setting is disabled. Many mobile devices will error because the TCK speed is too fast. One disadvantage of setting the TCK speed to a slow is the acquisition time can greatly increase from hours to days.

Below the JTAG TCK Speed setting is the *Resurrector Settings*, again, these settings correspond to when users have selected the DCC Read/Write tab. This allows the user to specify the make and model of the (supported) device. The phone makes and models that are supported by RIFF are listed alphabetically. The DCC Read/Write tab would need to be enabled, and CTRL+F would allow access to search for the same profiles (DLL). Fig. 24.8 on the companion site displays the choices the user can select with the clock speeds, along with the drop-down selections available for the make and model phone (alphabetically).

The Resurrector Settings contain a setting labeled *Custom Target Settings*. When this button is selected, *Target (Core)*, *Reset Method*, *JTAG I/O Voltage*, and *TAP#* areas can be accessed. The Target (Core) allows specific processors that RIFF supports to be selected. It is recommended that users do not use these settings until they fully understand what the settings do, and how they work.

During the process of reading the binary, there may be times when the process begins, and for some unknown reason, it is interrupted. If this takes place, users can fix the problem that may have caused the error, and begin reading again. Instead of the read starting over at the beginning physical offset area of the memory address, users have the option to allow the software to *pick up* where it left off. Fig. 24.6 displays the pop-up notification window from the JTAG software that notifies the user of these choices. The notification will state, "*Previous Read Was Interrupted!*" The choices are "*Start New*," "*Continue*," or "*Cancel*." The middle of this box will indicate the starting and ending offset that has been read. In almost every case, the user will want to press *Continue*.

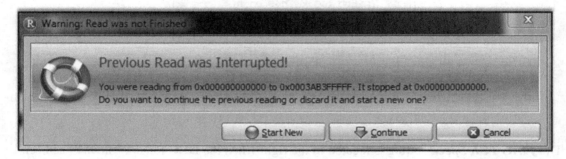

Figure 24.6
Example of the "Previous Read Was Interrupted!" window.

The last tab we will discuss is the ***Useful Plugins*** tab. RIFF offers users the ability to activate specific plugin features. At the time of this writing, these were listed in five categories. Each of these plugin options will interface with the RIFF JTAG Manager Software GUI in different ways, some launching a specific tool or manager. A couple examples of these are shown as screenshots only, showing the pops up when the Activate Plugin button is selected. Fig. 24.9 on the companion site displays the various settings in the Custom Target Settings, which includes the Target, Reset Method, JTAG I/O Voltage, and TAP #. Fig. 24.10, on the companion site, depicts the Useful Plugins tab, and one example (Global RIFF Link & Data Exchange Manager).

Saving the Binary Scan

Once the "Read" has taken place, users must press the "Save" button. Fig. 24.7 shows the process where a Samsung SPH-i535 was acquired using a Molex TAP cable. The entire 14.6 GB memory took over 40 hours to complete using the max JTAG TCK clock speed! This is normal. In this example after the examination was completed, the file was saved. Clicking the save button will present the user with another window that allows the file to be saved as a binary by default. The other choices in the "Save as" type drop-down window will be ***RIFF Plain Shrinked Files*** or ***RIFF Secured Shrinked Files.*** When saving the binary, it is a good habit to use the model name derivative. This helps with overall file management and can help examiners remember which profile to use when decoding. It is also recommended that the file be hashed before and after decoding.

Fig. 24.7 depicts an example of what the RIFF JTAG Manager software will display when saving a binary after the target memory has finished reading. Also, Fig. 24.7 shows the area near the bottom of the GUI, which will display the offset addresses being saved, the Estimated Time Left and the overall kilobyte size as it is saved, and the overall saving progress bar.

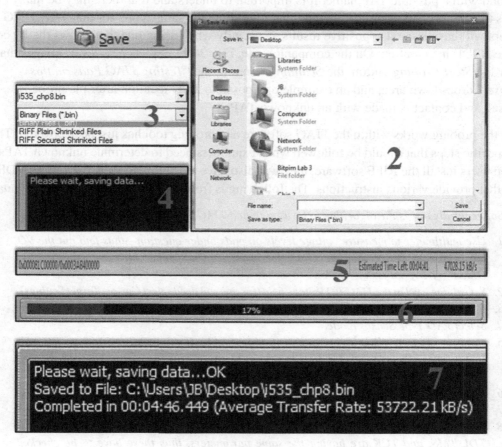

Figure 24.7
Example of saving a binary file, naming it, and the typical status bars that indicate progress.

Manual Probing Test Access Ports

Under the Box Service tab, users can use the **Start Probing** button to manually probe TAPs for possible identification. This will require a special probing adaptor, which is sold separately from the parts included with the RIFF box. The probe adaptor has a pogo pin that is attached to a push button (opened) switch. The pogo pin is spring-loaded and can be pressed against the target TAP. The user would press the switch to close the circuit and register a possible reply from the GUI of the RIFF software.

When the users have pressed the "Start Probing" button, the **Scanning** pop-up window will display. This has various settings that can be changed to include the target voltage and the type of **PAD Mode.**

As users touch and press the probe switch for possible TAP locations, the interface will respond with a possible TAP name. It is important to understand that there may be many TAPs that get probed using this method that may show the same name for that TAP. JTAG finders will have less false-positive results, especially when using one that allows the ID code of the BSDL information. On the companion site, Fig. 24.11 depicts a series of images that show the *Start Probing* button, the *Scanning* window, the *"Testing JTAG Pads on this Chipset"* drop-down area, and an example of a possible TDO location after the probe is pressed and contact is made with an unknown TAP.

How the probing works within the JTAG software and probing tool has just been covered. There are specific steps that should be followed when examiners need to determine unknown TAPs. When users install the RIFF software, they will also have the ability to view the various PDF files that provide various instructions. The following is from the "RIFFJTAG Probing Manual."

> *So, generally this is the algorithm to be used to find JTAG Pinout:*
>
> 1. *Use multimeter to measure voltage levels on pads under question—thus find out the I/O levels current device uses for JTAG (for example, Qualcomm chips are usually 2.6V, OMAP—1.8V, S5PCxxx—2.8V).*
> 2. *Set voltage level in the JTAG I/O Voltage field (for this you need select Custom Target Settings).*
> 3. *Click Star Probing.*
> 4. *Select PAD Type Sensor mode.*
> 5. *Connect separate GND signal to board, for example, if you connect device to PC with USB, do not rely on common GND. To get more accurate measurements solder dedicated GND from RJ-45 to the Device.*
> 6. *Touch with the Probe Needle the pads on device's board.*
> 7. *Use your logic to interpret readings correctly.*
> 8. *For example, you found TRST, RTCK, and TDO with big probability of truth. Usually, TDI, TMS, and TCK are having the same parameters, thus these have to be checked manually. For this:*
>   > 8.1. *Solder TRST, GND, RTCK, and TDO to the JTAG connector and connect it to RIFF BOX.*

8.2. *Out of three pins (since it is yet unknown which one is TDI, which one is TCK, and which one is TMS), pick any and connect it to TCK on RIFF BOX.*

8.3. *Click Analyze JTAG chain: in the case TCK is found ok it will report None Found error, otherwise there will be RTCK does not respond error.*

8.4. *Proceeding in such a way in three attempts, TCK will be found.*

8.5. *Now only two attempts remain to find which pinout of the remaining two is TDI and which is TMS [1].*

RIFF 2 Overview

Note: The image examples used to explain the overview of the RIFF 2 interface are all contained on the companion site. Also, in various areas within this chapter, the author will describe the second edition of the RIFF box as RIFF box 2, RIFF 2, or RIFFBOX 2. Lastly, throughout the software interface, it is simply referred as RIFFBOX.

Contents and Install

Just like the original RIFF box, RIFF 2 comes with a set of cables and the jumper board. The package configuration is similar to what came with RIFF (original). The box depicted in this chapter is white and came with one gray female 20-pin ribbon cable with a blank end, a gray 20-pin female to 20-pin female ribbon cable, a multicolored female 30-pin ribbon cable with a blank end, and a multicolored 20-pin female to 20-pin female ribbon cable. Also included in the packaging is the same jumper board. Be aware that when you purchase the RIFF 2 box, it may differ to what is depicted in this book, and the included accessories may also be different.

If we examine the RIFF 2 box, one end will have the USB (out) connection next to the eMMC/SD & GPIO male connections. On the opposite end of the RIFF 2 box is the input area for RJ45, 20-pin JTAG, and USB. (We will address some of these connections later in this chapter.) On one side of the box will be the serial number. This will be a sticker with a bar code and the actual number displayed under it. Fig. 24.12 on the companion site depicts the packaged contents of the RIFF 2 box, along with overall photos of the device.

Software and Driver Install

There are some general system requirements needed for the RIFFBOX 2 to properly function. This list covers both software and hardware and assumes the user has the actual physical RIFFBOX 2:

- OS: Windows XP, Vista, 7, 8, and 10.
- Display: 1280×1024 or more.
- 4 GB or free space for the software install. 32 GB or greater is needed for flash backups.
- USB port. USB hubs are not recommended.

The last chapter explained the JTAG software associated with the RIFF box. It skipped the steps involved with the install, to include addressing any driver issue(s). Since RIFF 2 will be the most probable version of the two RIFF boxes available, the install will be addressed in more detail. The ability to locate documentation regarding problems with the install was, years ago, somewhat problematic. Now, users can join the forum and locate additional help off the RIFF website located at www.riffbox.org. Also, after the install is completed, various user guides in PDF format will pop up. These are in the root of the program file or can be saved to a different location. The software and driver install instructions in this chapter may also be applied to the previous chapter if users are using the original RIFF box.

On this main website, users will see several choices. One will contain a download to the latest version of the *"RIFF Box JTAG Manager software setup."* This will link the user to a "RIFFSetup.exe" download file. There is nothing noteworthy regarding the initial install; users simply need to follow the prompts and standard install locations. This chapter depicts the install on a Windows 7 machine. The RIFF website indicates the following regarding Windows 10:

> *New hardware and software is fully compatible with Windows 10, which provides effortless installation. Just connect RIFF Box to Windows 10-based PC and everything will be installed automatically. For older Windows versions, there are custom drivers provided with RIFF JTAG Manager installer [2].*

If you are using an OS that is not Windows 10, you will typically have a driver-related issue after the initial install. Their driver is within the driver folder, but users must manually point to this location through Device Manager. Plug the RIFF 2 box into the machine you have installed the JTAG Manager software on. At this point, there may be a pop-up window that indicates the driver was not installed properly. In other cases, users may not see any activity related to the driver through the Home screen. Regardless of which Window's OS you are using (to include W10), users must check their Device Manager for any driver-related problems while the RIFF 2 box is plugged in. Locate the yellow exclamation mark under *Other devices—RIFF BOX2 by Rocker Team (c), 2010*.

Users must double-click on this entry. This will show three tabs—*General/Driver/Details*. Under the *Driver* tab, select *Update Driver*. The next window will be *"How do you want to search for driver software?"* Select *"Browse my computer for driver software."* The next window allows the user to locate the driver by browsing to the location. This will be called, *"Browse for driver software on your computer."* Select "Include subfolders." Then use the "Browse" button and navigate to the correct folder. This is in: *Program Files (x86)\Rocker Team\RIFF JTAG Manager\Drivers\64 Bit*.

When this folder is selected, users will see the Windows Security pop-up window. Select *"Install this driver software anyway."* If the install is a success, the final window will be, *"Windows has successfully updated your driver software."* Recheck the Device Manager.

There should be no further problems. The example used in this chapter already had the RIFF (original) software and drivers installed. If you are installing this software for the first time, there may be other areas within Device Manager that indicate a problem. These too can be remedied in the same manner. On the companion site, Figs. 24.13–24.15 provide a step-by-step (numbered) process for the initial install.

DLLs and Account Manage

Once the software is installed and any driver issues are resolved, the machine must be connected to the Internet for the remaining updates and required .dll files. Users will see a window that displays, "*Hashing for Updates Tracking*." Click "Continue" and the next window will allow you to establish connection with the RIFF server. Click "Connect Server." The top image of Fig. 24.16 on the companion site depicts the first hashing update after the software and drivers are installed properly.

At this point, a window will ask for a "User name" and "Your e-mail Address." The black GUI area may indicate that the *RIFFBOX* license shows an *ERROR*. This is normal and will eventually show with the correct values once the account is established and all the necessary updates are downloaded.

On the companion site, the upper image of Fig. 24.17 depicts the registration information window, and the lower image shows the RIFFBOX ERROR.

Next, select "*Check for Updates*." The next window users will see will be the RIFF Updates Manager. There will be several files that need to be downloaded and installed. They must be highlighted first, then select "Download." Users can also select one, then right click and select "Select All to Download" and then select "Download Selected" near the right, bottom area. This process will take several minutes to hours, depending on your connection. Also, if examiners have a specific phone that they need to immediately JTAG, that model phone can be selected first. Most of the files are .dll and .riffpkg files. Fig. 24.18 (companion site) displays the "Check for Updates" button and the "RIFF Updates Manager" window. Fig. 24.19 (companion site) depicts the right click selection (Select All to Download), the Download Selected button, and the window showing the files being downloaded.

Once all the files have been downloaded, RIFF will begin hashing the updates. Users will see a series of pop-up screens related to the install. These are usually titled, "INFORMATION DOWNLOADED!!" and contain specific information regarding various aspects of the software and RIFF features. It is common to see several of these screens after the first install.

On the companion site, Fig. 24.20 provides two images (screenshots) that depict summaries of various information that is related to the install. These are from a new install, and users may from time to time, encounter these summaries when updating the RIFFBOX.

After completion, a final window should indicate, "*License Installation is Complete! You can continue using RIFFBOX!*" Click "OK." At this point it is a good idea to check once more for updates (Check for Updates button) to ensure that no files were missed. If so, simply repeat this process. Fig. 24.21 on the companion site shows an example of the RIFF Updates Manager depicting "All files are up-to-date." Users will also want to check that their firmware is up-to-date by selecting the "*Firmware Update*" button.

Account Manage

Under the Box Service tab, one of the first selections (near the top) is the *Account Manage* button. This allows the user access to the following subchoices: *Sign In, Edit Account Details, Extend Account, Transfer Credits, Packages Global License*, and *Sign Out*. The Sign In setting will be grayed out if users have previously signed in. These settings are basically self-explanatory. Fig. 24.22 on the companion site displays images of the Account Manage button and a screenshot example of what will appear in the black GUI of the RIFFBOX. The bottom right corner shows the various subchoices previously addressed.

Connector Pinout Locations

Just like the original RIFF box, the software for RIFFBOX 2 includes a "RIFF BOX JTAG Connector Pinout." On one end are the RJ-45 port, the 20-pin (male) JTAG connection, and the USB male connection. The RJ-45 port is used for SD/MMC interface. If we look directly at the port, from left to right the small pins inside are numbered for reference. Number 1 starts from the left and ends to the right with pin 8. These correspond to the following settings:

(1) 4.2V, (2) SDMMC_CLK, (3) SDMMC_DAT0, (4) SDMMC_CMD, (5) GPIO1, (6) GPIO2, (7) (Not used), (8) SDMMC_GND

On the main board of the RIFFBOX, there are two additional contacts that can be utilized for SDMMC voltage. These are A and B. A represents SDMMC_VCC and B represents SDMMC_VCCIO.

The 20-pin JTAG Pinout is represented as the following:

(1) VCC, (3) TRST, (5) TDI, (7) TMS, (9) TCK, (11) RTCK, (13) TDO, (15) NRST. Pins 4, 6, 8, 10, 12, 14, 16, and 18 are grounds. Pins 2, 17, and 19 are not connected.

On the opposite end of the box is the USB output, which connects to the machine with the software installed. To the right of this is the eMMC/SD & GPIO, 30-pin (male) connection. If you look carefully, there are only 28 pins used. Pins 21 and 22 are missing, which is normal. The upper far right pin is pin #1. Directly below it is pin 2. All the upper pins are numbered odd and the bottom corresponds as even. The following is the representation of each of these pins, reading from right to left, top row first, then bottom (left to right also):

(1) VCC_REF, (3) GPIO_PIN01, (5) GPIO_PIN02, (7) GPIO_PIN03/SD_DAT2, (9) GPIO_PIN04/SD_DAT3, (11) GPIO_PIN05, (13) GPIO_PIN06/SD_DAT1, (15) GPIO_PIN07, (17) 3.3V, (19) GPIO_PIN08, (21) Blank, (23) GPIO_PIN10, (25) GPIO_PIN11, (27) GPIO_PIN12, (29) GPIO_PIN13.

(2) Ground, (4) SD_CLK, (6) SD_RST, (8) GPIO_PIN24/SD_CMD, (10) GPIO_PIN23, (12) GPIO_PIN22/SD_DAT0, (14) GPIO_PIN21, (16) GPIO_PIN20, (18) Ground, (20) GPIO_PIN19, (22) Blank, (24) GPIO_PIN17, (26) GPIO_PIN16, (28) GPIO_PIN15, (30) GPIO_PIN14.

The top image contained in Fig. 24.23 on the companion site shows the RIFF BOX JTAG Connector Pinout as it displays within the software interface. Below this image is a picture of the eMMC/SD & GPIO male, 30-pin area on the box. Below the image is the schematic screenshot showing the corresponding pin representation. The number 2 pin is marked with an arrow.

General Purpose Input/Output

Throughout this chapter there have been references to GPIO. This stands for *General Purpose Input/Output*. A definition of GPIO is on the Android developer site.

> *(GPIO) pins provide a programmable interface to read the state of a binary input device (such as a pushbutton switch) or control the on/off state of a binary output device (such as an LED).*

> *You can configure GPIO pins as an input or output with either a high or low state. As an input, an external source determines the state, and your app can read the current value or react to changes in state. As an output, your app configures the state of the pin* [3].

The RIFFBOX takes advantage of these inputs/outputs and allows communications to take place with a specific supported device. GPIO pins are not just confined to mobile circuits; they are generally a generic pin on an integrated circuit or other boards that usually have no predefined purpose, and go unused by default [3].

eMMC/SD Access Tab

The interface on the original RIFF box did not have the eMMC/SD access tab. Users can, however, elect to purchase this feature, which after updating the firmware on the original RIFF box allows access to some of the features. The original box itself does not have the 30-pin connector and, as such, there will be limitations on some of the features unless users upgrade to the new RIFFBOX 2.

When this tab is selected, there are several settings to choose. From left to right, these are displayed in upper and lower selections. ***Partition/Bus Width, Address/Data Length, Auto***

FullFlash Size/Use End Address, not Length/Use Address as Offset in the Source File, and *Source File* (input area for selection). At the bottom of this screen are the following buttons: *Read eMMC/SD, Save to File, Erase eMMC/SD, Check eMMC/SD Card, eMMC/SD Advanced, SD/MMC Clock Speed, SD/MMC Bus Width,* and *SD/MMC VCCIO Voltage.* The same conditions on forensic examinations apply here as they did in the previous chapter. Erasing options will never be used on actual evidence. Fig. 24.24 on the companion site shows the overall choices under the eMMC/SD access tab. These areas are described as the following:

Partition (drop-down access to the following):

- User Area Partition
- Boot Area Partition
- Boot Area Partition 2
- RPMB Area Partition
- General Purpose Partition 1
- General Purpose Partition 2
- General Purpose Partition 3
- General Purpose Partition 4
- eMMC Core Address Space

Address (not manually adjustable):

Data Length (drop-down access to the following sizes, actually written as shown):

1 MByte, 2 MByte, 2 MByte, 8 MByte, 16 MByte, 32 MByte, 64 MByte, 128 MByte, 256 MByte, 512 MByte, 1 GByte, 2 GByte, 4 GByte, 8 GByte, 16 GByte.

As the user selects each of these values, the Data Length will change to accommodate the byte number for the length.

Auto FullFlash Size/Use End Address, not Length/Use Address as Offset in the Source File:

Each of these settings will influence the previous settings (Address/Data Length). Selecting (checking) *Auto FullFlash Size* disables the user's ability to change Address/Data Length. Selecting *Use End Address, not Length,* or *Use Address as Offset in the Source File* allows the user to use any of the sizes mentioned in the End Address drop-down. Fig. 24.25 contained on the companion site depicts the *Partition* drop-down area, the *Address/Data Length* drop-down, and examples of the check marks enabled in *Auto FullFlash Size/Use End Address, not length* settings.

Read eMMC/SD & Check eMMC/SD card:

These two buttons would be selected after connecting to a target device. *Read eMMC/SD* would be used to read all of the area selected. *Check eMMC/SD* would be used to verify that the connections are valid and reading could take place. On an actual examination, users would select the Check button first, then after confirming a good connection, utilize the Read button.

Save to File:

After the entire binary address has completed the reading phase, users would select the *Save to File* button. The choices are the same as in the previous chapter that covered the original RIFF box. For forensic examinations, choose binary.

Erase eMMC/SD:

This setting will not be used during an actual forensic examination.

eMMC/SD Advanced:

When users select this button, another window titled *eMMC Advanced Actions* will appear (Fig. 24.26 on the companion site). In the upper right corner of this window is a drop-down, directly under *Select eMMC for Info & Read*. These selections are the various chip part numbers the user can select. Any entry that contains a small blue symbol to the left of the part number will have an image to reference for additional information. This will provide the *Testpoint Wire* locations for the specified chip, along with instructions. Fig. 24.27 on the companion site displays an example of this area with a selection chosen that displays the blue symbol. The figure also shows the area on the chip with the tap located for the Testpoint Wire and additional instructions. The following buttons within the *eMMC Advanced Actions* window can be used for forensic examinations:

Select eMMC for Info & Read, *Show eMMC Testpoint*, *Read eMMC Firmware*, *Display Short Help*, *Save eMMC Info File*, and *Read Info From eMMC*. The following buttons will not be used during forensic exams:

Update eMMC Firmware, *User Area Forced Erase*, *Samsung Factory Format*, *Write CID Register*, *Write CSD Register*, *Write EXTCSD Register*, *Write Selected EXTCSD Field*, *Resize BOOT and RPMB*, *Lock/Unlock User Area*, *Remove Write Protection*, and *Set Boot Operation Mode*. Fig. 24.28 on the companion site has an image that displays each of these areas with either a green arrow (OK to use), or a red "X" (do not use).

Display Short Help (within eMMC Advanced Actions):

Selecting this button will bring up a window titled "*Short Manual & Instructions*." Contained within this window are specific instructions on operation commands. Many of the commands pertain only to Samsung MMC chips. At the bottom of this document is the meaning to common error codes. Fig. 24.29 on the companion site is an example of some of the documentation located in the "Short Manual & Instructions." Exiting out of the eMMC Advanced Actions, we go back to the eMMC/SD Access tab.

SD/MMC Clock Speed/SD/MMC Bus Width/SD/MMC VCCIO Voltage:

This area allows the user choices with the drop-down of each of these fields. *SD/MMC Clock Speed* provides the user with the following choices:

KHz ranges: 400, 408, 425, 500, 510, 531.25, 600, 637.5, 680, 750, 816, and 850.

MHz ranges: 1, 1.02, 1.0625, 1.2, 1.275, 1.36, 1.5, 1.59375, 1.7, 2, 2.04, 2.125, 2.55, 3, 3.1875, 3.4, 4.08, 4.25, 5.1, 6, 6.375, 6.8, 8.5, 10.2, 12.75, 17, 20.4, 25.5, 34, and 51.

The *SD/MMC Bus Width* drop-down has two choices: 1 Bit Bus Width (DAT0) or 4 Bit Bus Width (DAT0–DAT3).

The SD/MMC VCCIO Voltage drop-down has the following voltages to choose from:

3.20, 3.25, 3.20, 3.15, 3.10, 3.05, 3.0, 2.95, 2.90, 2.85, 2.80, 2.75, 2.70, 2.65, 2.60, 2.55, 2.50.2.45, 2.40, 2.35, 2.30, 2.25, 2.20, 2.15.2.10, 2.05, 2.00, 1.95, 1.90, 1.85, 1.80, 1.75, 1.70, 1.65, and 1.60. Fig. 24.30 on the companion site provides several screenshots of the *SD/MMC Clock Speed/SD/MMC Bus Width/SD/MMC VCCIO Voltage* area and associated drop-downs described.

Most of the remaining tabs have the same settings that were encountered in our previous chapter with the original RIFF box. The steps to perform a standard supported JTAG extraction will be the same when using the RIFF 2 box. The obvious change is to the box with the 30-pin SD/eMMC & GPIO area and eMMC/SD Access tab within the software.

The next example begins by using the *eMMC Advanced Actions* button. This example also assumes that you know how to remove the chip in question and properly prepare the BGA area for reading. Removal and prepping techniques are covered in our final chapters. For now, it will be assumed that readers understand those steps and are trying to read an eMMC chip using RIFFBOX 2. This is basically an ISP technique. ISP is outlined in Chapter 30 in more detail.

First, navigate to: *Select eMMC for Info & Read* and use the drop-down to locate chip part number KLMAG2GEAC-B001. Using Google, the data sheet for this chip part number is researched. The data sheet will contain the necessary information needed to connect to the chip, as well as configure settings within the RIFF 2 box to read the memory. This chip uses an FBGA Pin Configuration. The data sheet will contain a schematic that labels the various balls. Also documented will be the voltage and speeds for data transfers. The VCC may be referenced as VDDF, and the VCCQ may be referenced as VDD. Using the *Show eMMC Testpoint* will provide the area for the *Testpoint Wire Pin* and other information regarding the required connections. The example provided that uses the data sheet for KLMAG2GEAC-B001 indicates the connections for CLK, CMD, DAT0, VCC (VDDF), and VCCQ (VDD). The data sheet also reveals that the VDD voltage has a range of 1.70–1.95 V or 2.7–3.5 V, and the VDDF (VCC) has a range of 2.7–3.6 V. Other pertinent information from the data sheet is the bus width of 1 bit default, as well as 4 and 8 bit. The speed is noted as MMC I/F Clock frequency 0–200 MHz, and MMC Boot Frequency 0–52 MHz. All these values (from the data sheet for the target chip) can be used to adjust the appropriate settings in the various areas within the eMMC/SD tab that was previously addressed. Fig. 24.31 on the companion site depicts the ball information for the KLMAG2GEAC-B001 eMMC chip. Below the main image are some notes related to some of the pins. Fig. 24.32 on the companion site shows the information related to power, bus bit width rates, and frequency speeds.

Useful Plugins Tab

Just like the original JTAG Manager software used with RIFF (1), the same plugins tab will apply to the RIFFBOX 2. In this book, we do not cover the use of these plugins. At the time of this writing there were four listed, noted as: ***Direct JTAG Access to Flash Memory, eMMC Based FullFlash Image File Processing Plugin, Qualcomm FullFlash Image Files Processing Tool, Samsung i9000-like FullFlash Image Files Processing Tool.***

Fig. 24.33 on the companion site shows a screenshot of the *Useful Plugins* tab and the four available plugins at the time of this writing.

Advanced Settings

Under the *Box Service* tab, users can access the *Advanced Settings*. Many of the settings within these two available windows (Advanced Settings/Setup Default Actions) will require the user to understand exactly what he/she is applying. This knowledge may be gained through additional research and/or conducting several examinations using RIFF and RIFF 2. Fig. 24.34 on the companion site displays images of the two windows that users will have access to under the *Advanced Settings* button.

Chapter Summary Key Points

The original RIFF box is usually sold with one or two 20-pin ribbon cables and a jumper board. Examiners should prepare the 20-pin cable by mapping the appropriate connections to the jumper board using the schematic. After they finish soldering each connection, the wires should be checked for open circuits (bad connections), using a continuity check. The solder connections that attach from the 20-pin cable to the jumper board can then be covered with hot glue to protect the wires from accidently being detached.

The RIFF box also has software that will need to be installed. Through the software interface, the user can update the firmware and download the necessary .dll files. Once this is finished, the user can manually look for the desired model in the Resurrector drop-down (from the Resurrector tab), or use the Ctrl + F keys to bring up the quick search box. While in the

Resurrector tab, the user can utilize the *Interface Pinout* button to display the TAPs of the target board that need to be connected to the RIFF box. Once this has been accomplished, the user will select the *JTAG Read/Write* tab, and *Analyze JTAG Chain,* and then *Connect & Get ID*. If these commands fail to work properly, begin troubleshooting. This can include changing the clock speeds and checking solder connections, power, and battery.

Once the JTAG Chain and Connect & Get ID are successful, the user will need to select the *DCC Read/Write* tab. From here, users will need to determine if they want to combine the entire area into one binary read, and use auto settings or manual. It is suggested that users try the following settings first, and only change if they encounter errors:

- Check "Image File is Used" (Main + Spare combined into single file)
- Drop-down—Access ROM1 Address Space
- Check "Use End Address, not Length"
- Check "ECC Module Enabled"

Again, these DCC reading settings can be changed if the user has problems reading the binary. Once a read begins, the user may encounter an error. If so, rectify the problem and begin the read again. Use the "Continue" button rather than starting the read over from the start. Once the entire process is through reading, the file must be saved as a binary in the selections. The saving process will take a few minutes. Once the file has been saved, it can be decoded using tools such as Physical Analyzer. It is recommended that the binary file be saved with the model of phone that it came from. It should also be hashed before and after the decoding process.

The RIFF box also has the ability to probe unknown TAPs. Probes are sold separately and the examiner should consult with the steps previously mentioned in this chapter, as well as the RIFF manual that addresses probing. It is important that the examiner be aware of the proper voltage of their target processor before beginning the probing process.

Here is a quick summary of how to use the RIFF Box for JTAG extractions:

1. Install software, register, update firmware, and download all .dll's.
2. Select *Resurrector* tab. Locate target phone (Ctrl + F or drop-down) and the *Interface Pinout.*
3. Connect necessary TAPs to RIFF box and phone—test for continuity.
4. Select JTAG Read/Write tab. Supply battery and power supply to phone. Turn on phone. Check connections using the Analyze JTAG Chain and Connect & Get ID. Fix problems if any arise. If the read is positive, continue to step 5.
5. Select DCC Read/Write tab. Change the settings as previously suggested. Select *Read Memory.* Fix problems if the read fails or change settings in this area (DCC Read/Write tab). Use the *Continue* button if read was interrupted. If the read is positive read, continue to step 6. Remember, the read can take hours to days, depending on the size.
6. Save to binary; rename according to model phone. Hash before and after decoding.

The RIFF 2 box allows examiners all the features that were found in the original RIFF box. RIFF 2 is also designed to allow connections through 30-pin male connectors on the end of the box, which supports SD/eMMC & GPIO. GPIO stands for General Purpose Input/Output. RIFF 2 takes advantage of GPIO contacts on various devices to allow for specific supported extractions to occur.

The software includes a tab for eMMC/SD support. This is considered an ISP examination technique. (Refer to Chapter 30 for additional help.) There are several supported chips that can be accessed within the *Select eMMC for Info & Read* drop-down. RIFF 2 can in some cases display the *Testpoint* pad. Using the data sheet for the targeted chip, users can navigate to the locations of the required (RIFF 2 box) connections; determine bit width rates, frequency speeds, and voltages; and apply those settings to the RIFF 2 box as needed.

The ability to read chips using the eMMC feature does require the user to understand how to remove and prepare the memory. If JTAG extractions are all that you plan to use RIFF 2 for, just like the original RIFF box, it certainly is equipped to fulfill that requirement on supported devices.

The use of the RIFF and RIFF 2 boxes for JTAG extractions is one of the more popular and robust tools currently on the market. This chapter has only covered some of the small steps involved with using this flasher box. This should provide the examiner some basic overview and understanding on how to use the RIFF/RIFF 2 boxes and the associated JTAG software.

References

[1] RIFF Box JTAG, RIFFJTAG_ProbingManual.PDF, Rocker Team, 2010.
[2] RIFF 2, RIFF Box v2 Software, Version-2, August 09, 2016.
     http://www.riffbox.org/category/riff-box-version-2.
[3] GPIO. https://developer.android.com/things/sdk/pio/gpio.html.

CHAPTER 25

Z3X Box (Easy JTAG) Overview

Information in This Chapter

- Easy-JTAG w/cables and ISP adaptor
- Software and driver install
- Additional activations
- Easy JTAG tool (Z3X EasyJtag Box JTAG Classic Suite)
- Reading Target Flash
- JTAG finder

Introduction

At the end of the third class in the mobile forensic course series at the University of Washington, and directly after the final exam, the author usually has a couple of tips for the students. In the last school year, they have completed over 90 labs, carved numerous deleted artifacts, manually decoded SQLite databases, had two different student presentations, assembled custom chains and plug-ins, repaired water damaged phones, and performed JTAG and chip-off extractions. They are finally advised a (joking) nugget of wisdom, *"If you can't get a job repairing phones, or any job for that matter, you may decide to turn to a life of crime. Don't—but if you do, don't take a cell phone with you."*

This chapter introduces the reader to another repair tool called *Z3X Easy-JTAG*. This is a very popular box that is also used in mobile forensic examinations. The Z3X boxes can be sold with activations that are specific to certain makes of phones.

As explained in various locations throughout this book, some of the programs, utilities, and hardware were not designed for forensic exams. Most of the advanced products are designed for repairing, and the Z3X box is no different.

You may also be thinking about retirement someday and have spent years performing mobile digital forensic examinations. Next time you are at your local mall, and you see the guy in the kiosk fixing cracked screens on mobile devices, tell your significant other who may be with you, *"I could do that—and even more."*

Easy-JTAG W/Cables and ISP Adaptor

If you perform a search for "Z3X Team," you will be directed to the main site for their product. From the home page, there are several choices that include locating a dealer. This chapter covers the Easy-JTAG box designed by Z3X. When purchasing the actual box, the buyer will have a choice of which activation comes installed on the box. There are several, and at the time of this writing included LG, Samsung, Benq-Siemens, and China Editor. What this means at the time of the purchase is that the box may only have one of these activations, various selections, or all. The box being used for this chapter was purchased by GSM Server and only had the Easy-JTAG activation. Two additional activations were added, and the steps for the purchase and activation will be addressed in this chapter.

The box came inside a plastic bag. It contained one Easy-JTAG box, one USB data cable, one 20-pin female to 20-pin female ribbon cable, one 20-pin female to blank end ribbon cable, one JTAG-ISP Adapter from Moorc.com, one RJ45 (male) to RJ45 (male) connector, and one 20-pin adaptor to read BGA162-186, BGA153-169, BGA221, and BGA529 chips. Fig. 25.1 depicts images of these items.

On one end of the box is the JTAG 20-pin (male) input area. To the right of this is the RJ45 port. On the opposite end is the input for the USB cable to connect the box to the PC. Somewhere on the box will be a sticker with the serial number. In Fig. 25.1 the serial number has been redacted.

In this chapter, we only cover the JTAG features. The components shown in Fig. 25.1 are sold when the buyer purchases, "Z3X Easy-JTAG with Cables and JTAG ISP Adaptor 5-in-1." This box is also capable of eMMC/ISP reading. Those features are not covered in this chapter. Our last chapter, however, will cover the ISP examination.

Software and Driver Install

There are two different (related) sites the user can visit to obtain details on the install process. The two sites are *Z3X-Team.com* and *Easy-JTAG.com*. In both cases, the instructions are the

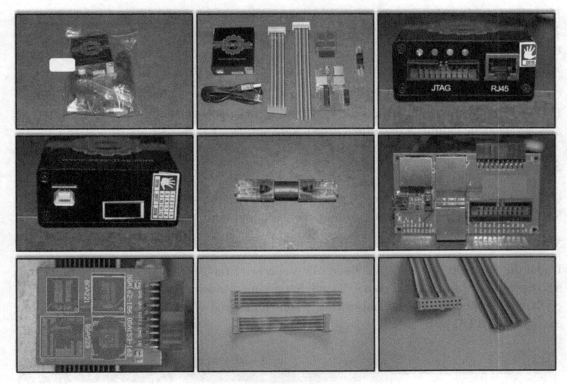

Figure 25.1
Images of the Z3X Easy-JTAG box, including cables and adaptor.

same. The install begins with downloading and installing the *Shell* software. Once this is installed, follow their steps, which the author has added to step 1:

1. *Connect Z3X-Box to PC. Open Device Manager. There should be various areas that show with yellow exclamation marks. These drivers can be in the below-listed folder paths. It is ok to try each of them if you have no idea which one applies to each of the missing drivers.*
2. *Install Z3X-Box Drivers from folder x:\Program Files\z3x\Box drivers*
3. *Install Z3X-Card Drivers from folder x:\Program Files\z3x\Card drivers*
4. *Install Easy-Jtag Drivers from folder x:\Program Files\z3x\Jtag drivers*
5. *Install additional drivers (if necessary) from folder x:\Program Files\z3x\Reader drivers*
Activation and registration:
4. *Run Shell*
5. *Click "Settings and Card tools"*
6. *Click "Run Hardware Wizard." Wizard will start*
7. *Make all necessary steps from wizard*

Download main software:

7. *Click "Support files" from Shell and browse/search software*
8. *Run downloaded exe*
9. *Choose phone model from list and click "Run"* [1]

On the companion site, Figs. 25.1–25.5 show the various steps involved in the Shell install. Fig. 25.5 (companion site) depicts the Windows Security pop-up window that commonly appears when installing an unverified driver software.

Shell Tab

Once the driver issues are corrected, and there are no issues in Device Manager, launch the Shell software. At the time of this writing, there are four main tabs within the Shell interface:

Shell, Support files, Station, and *Settings* and *Hardware tools*

Under the Shell tab, users will see three subcategories: Brand/Series/Model. To the far right is a section titled "Mini F.A.Q." When Brand, Series, and Model are selected, double-clicking on the highlighted Model will automatically launch the Easy-JTAG tool. Fig. 25.2 depicts an example on an LG LS670.

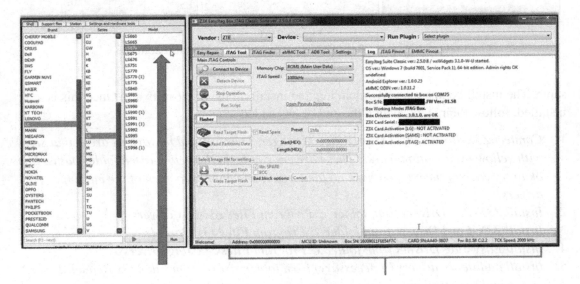

Double clicking on the Model in the Shell, will bring up the *EasyJtag Box Classic Suite*

Figure 25.2
Example of selecting a Brand/Series/Model and double-clicking brings up the EasyJtag Box JTAG Classic Suite.

The Mini F.A.Q. area allows access to additional questions related to the two main issues—"*I don't have Z3X Card/Box/JTAG*" or "*I have Z3X Card/Box/JTAG*." Users who have issues with their drivers can use the "*I have Z3X Card/Box/JTAG*" selection, and then select "*I just buy Z3X Box/JTAG—How to start using software?*" Under these selections, there are links to the exact location of the drivers that may be needed. On the companion site, Fig. 25.6 shows an example of the Mini F.A.Q. area being expanded to locate the answers. There are additional questions listed. (The actual spelling contained in this area has been used) Directly under "*I just buy Z3X Box/JTAG*" the following choices that contain answers are there:

- *I can't update card firmware!*
- *Which software can I use?*
- *Software shows "Product not activated" message*
- *Which additional activations exist for my Z3C Card/Box/JTAG?*
- *Where can I buy additional activations(s) for my Z3X Card/Box/JTAG?*
- *When I'm trying to download file—I see message…*
- *How many files can I download per day?*
- *Can I use download accelerators?*
- *Can I increase download limit?*

Under the "*I bought Z3X Box/JTAG some time ago*" the following answers are found:

- *Shell and other software can't find Z3X card*
- *When I try to download file I see message…*
- *I want to buy additional activation*
- *I bought additional activations. How to activate and use it?*
- *I can't find required model in software*

At the left bottom of the Shell, there is a section titled "*Installed modules (double click to run without model selection).*" Double-clicking does exactly as it describes: it launches the specific module selected. This may be blank until additional software is downloaded and installed. What users should be aware of is that viewing or downloading some of the files within these tabs will count against the daily downloads allowed. This is usually 20 per day.

Support Files Tab

To the right of the Shell tab is the Support files tab. In this location, users can select main categories of Software, Samsung files, LG files, China Editor files, Benq files, Nec files, and Easy JTAG files. Within each of these folders, there are additional folders with the following categories:

1. Software = China Editor/Drivers, Shell/Easy JTAG/LG Box/Samsung Box
2. Samsung files = Firmware/Recovery/SVC Manual

3. LG files = Boot/Firmware/NVM/QCN/SVC Manual/Video Manual
4. China Editor files = Add on/Firmware
5. Benq files = Firmware/NVM
6. Nec files = Firmware/IPLT Firmware
9. Easy JTAG files (numbers 7 and 8 are missing) = Over 50 models are listed in alphabetical order.

Fig. 25.3 is a screenshot showing each of these areas from the *Support files* tab. The bottom of the figure contains only a few of the 50+ models from the "*9. Easy Jtag files*" area.

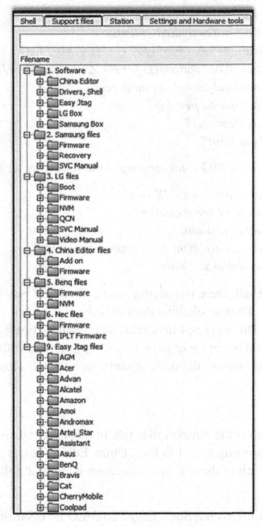

Figure 25.3
Easy JTAG Support files tab within the software interface.

Station Tab

Within the Station tab, there are three categories labeled Pinouts, Solutions, and Testpoints. If a user clicks on any one of these three categories, the drop-down of choices are the same. Once a selection has been made, any referenced image file will show. The Pinout locations are generally referencing specific cables, adaptors, or unique devices. They may or may not have any reference to your target phone. They usually have nothing to do with the actual JTAG tap locations. Fig. 25.7 on the companion site shows an example from an LG KG800 USB Cable to UFS.

Settings and Hardware Tools Tab

The last tab in the Z3X Shell is the Settings and Hardware tools. This is where users would initially set up the card for the first time. Selecting the *Run Hardware Wizard* will bring up the "Card and account wizard" window. There will be six choices, but only the ones that apply to your card will be available. The first time the wizard is run, the "Register card" should be selected. The next series of windows will populate based on what is needed on your card. The example shown indicates that the card needed the firmware updated. Next to the *Run Hardware Wizard* button is the *Show card info* button. When this is selected the card serial number, card type, card version, reseller, and card activation date are displayed. Fig. 25.4 contains several images from the *Run Hardware Wizard* and an example of the *Show card info* results.

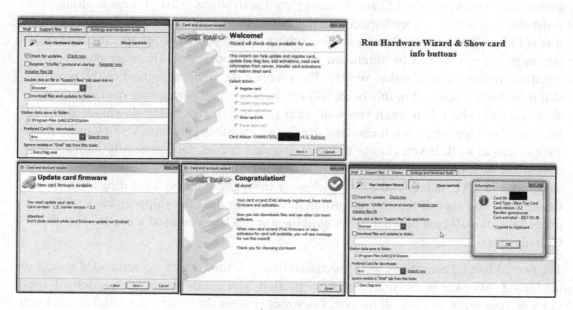

Figure 25.4
Examples of an activation of a new card using the *Run Hardware Wizard* and a *Show card* info result.

Directly below these two buttons, the following selections are found:

- Check for updates/Check now
- Register "z3xfile" protocol at startup/Register now
- Initialize files DB
- Double-click at file in "Support files" tab open link in: Shell/Browser/Torrent/Torrent via Browser
- Download files and updates to folder (allows user to select location in a dialog box)
- Station data save to folder (default C:\Program Files (x86)\Z3X\Station, or user can change the address in a dialog box)
- Preferred Card for downloads (allows user to specify a connected card—next to the drop-down is another button labeled, Search now)
- Ignore models in "Shell" tab from this tool (various secondary activations such as LG/Samsung tools will show in this area. Users can select each entry by checking the dialog box to the left of each one)

Fig. 25.8 on the companion site depicts the various settings within the *Settings and Hardware tools* tab.

Additional Activations

The Z3X box used in this book was purchased with only the Easy-JTAG activation. The author later purchased the LG and Samsung card activations. This process is straightforward and will require an authorized reseller to handle the sale. The Z3X Easy-JTAG box was sold by GSM Server. There are a few others, and if you work for specific agencies, they may require the box be purchased within the United States. There are positives and negatives to buying with either vendor. The first is cost. Generally, most of the boxes that have been discussed in this book will be cheaper when purchasing overseas. The shipping varies based on when you want your package to arrive. The downside with inexpensive shipping is that it can take over a two months. There are VAT (Value Added Taxes) fees as well. If you choose to use state-side vendors, they generally increase the cost of the box, but they handle any warranty issue. In many cases, even with 3- to 5-day shipping and VAT included, the box is cheaper from going through the direct vendors. Remember, however, if there is any problem with your box, the shipping back will exceed the overall cost of what you would have saved had you used a vendor in the United States.

The two additional activations were purchased from a United States recommended vendor off the Easy-JTAG website. No matter which activations you decide to add, the vendor will need to know your serial number off the box. Once they process the order, your serial number will be allowed access to the activations you paid for. The possible activations will present the next time you select "*Run Hardware Wizard*" within the Settings and Hardware tools tab within the Shell.

Fig. 25.9 off the companion site displays the Z3X box before and after purchasing the LG and Samsung activations. In each case, the "*Run Hardware Wizard*" was used to show which activations were available. The upper right screenshot shows the user choosing which one to activate once they are available. When they are purchased and the box is given the ability to use the specific activations, it is up to the user when they want to activate them.

Easy JTAG Tool (Z3X EasyJtag Box JTAG Classic Suite)

The Easy JTAG tool, which when launched, displays the name as "*Z3X EasyJtag Box JTAG Classic Suite.*" This software allows the Z3X box to perform additional tasks besides JTAG. It also allows the user to connect directly with eMMC Pinout locations. This functionality is discussed in the last chapter of the book (eMMC/ISP). For now, this chapter will address the JTAG steps.

At the top of the suite, from left to right, the following areas that have additional subcategories within their own drop-down arrow are found: **Vendor/Device/Run Plugin**. Under the *Vendor* selection, there are 57 choices (at the time of this writing). When a user selects a specific vendor, the devices that are available will be based on what is supported for that vendor. For instance, if Acer was selected for the *Vendor* the devices that would be available under the *Device* tab would allow access to seven models. The *Run Plugin* has two drop-downs (again, at the time of this writing); these are: *SD Card Imaging Tool (USB SD/E-Mate Tool)* and *GPT Partitioning Manager (eMMC)*. The SD Card Imaging Tool will be discussed in the final chapter.

Directly under Vendor/Device/Run Plugin are the following tabs (from left to right):

Easy Repair/JTAG Tool/JTAG Finder/eMMC Tool/ADB Tool/Settings/Log/JTAG Pinout/ EMMC Pinout. Fig. 25.5 depicts an example of the Z3X GUI showing the JTAG Pinout locations for a supported phone.

Easy Repair

This tab should not be used during mobile forensics. This can write to the phone and is used to repair damaged devices. This allows the user to rewrite specific areas within the file system of the phone, such as the ROM, BOOT, and EFS. There may, however, be areas within this tab that users may find useful for their examinations, such as a download of the JTAG Pinout

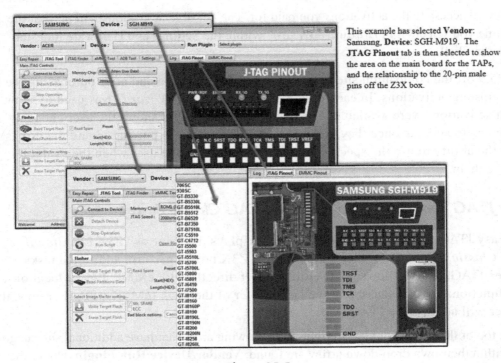

This example has selected **Vendor**: Samsung, **Device**: SGH-M919. The **JTAG Pinout** tab is then selected to show the area on the main board for the TAPs, and the relationship to the 20-pin male pins off the Z3X box.

Figure 25.5
Example of a supported JTAG Pinout location located in the GUI of the Z3X box (Samsung SGH-M919).

(image). Users would select the green sideways triangle button that states, *"Download Files From Support;-)"* There will be a brief moment where the software connects to the server, and another window will appear, *"EasySupporter [IDLE]."*

At the top of this window is displayed, *"Type part of filename here >."* To the right of this, a box to type in the phone model number can be found. In the example on the companion site, Fig. 25.10 depicts the Easy Repair tab, the *Download Files From Support* button, the EasySupporter [IDLE] window, and an example of model M919 typed into the search box, and the results from that inquiry. Examiners could at this point download the .jpg image of the JTAG Pinout. JTAG Pinout images can be located additional ways besides under the Easy Repair tab. This will be explained in upcoming pages.

JTAG Tool

The tab to the right of the Easy Repair is the JTAG tool. Users will have access to several selections in this area. To the far right is a tab titled *JTAG Pinout*. Users will need to select the

Vendor/Device, then select the *JTAG Pinout* tab. Images of the target board will show in the area below the Log/JTAG Pinout/EMMC Pinout. In some cases, there will be no images. This does not necessarily mean the target is not supported: it means the TAPs have not been documented by Z3X.

The other method is to locate the JTAG Pinout images manually. This can be accomplished by using the "Open Pinouts Directory" link that is directly below the JTAG Speed dialog box. When users click this link, they will be moved to a folder location that contains all the images the Z3X has available for the JTAG connections. Simply use the Windows search box in the upper right corner and enter a derivative of your target model number. Fig. 25.11 on the companion site reflects the use of the Open Pinouts Directory link, and a search for M919 (Samsung). Two images result in the search.

Directly below the JTAG Tool tab are the Main JTAG Controls. The user has access to the following buttons:

- *Connect to Device*: Used after establishing required connections, power, etc.
- *Memory Chip*: Drop-down access to ROM1 (Main User Data) and ROM2 (Boot Partition).
- *Detach Device*: Used to disconnect Z3X from the target device.
- *JTAG Speed*: Drop-down selections of 100, 200, 500, 1000, 2000, 4000, 6000, 8000, 12,000 kHz.
- *Stop Operation*: Stops the current job sent to the device.
- *Run Script*: Allows user access to run scripts.

The next section is the *Flasher* area. These buttons will change from gray to color, once users select the *Connect to Device*, and an error-free communication occurs.

- *Read Target Flash*: Reads only the flash portion of the memory. Generally, does not contain evidential data.
- *Preset*: Allows users access to a drop-down of size choices. Selections are 1, 2, 4, 8, 16, 32, 64, 128, 256, 512 Mb increments, and 1, 2, 4, 8, 16, and 32 Gb.
- *Read Partitions Data*: This will read the available partitions on the target device.
- *Start (HEX)*: Users can select the starting hexadecimal address (size) where the box will begin reading.
- *Length (HEX)*: The ending hexadecimal address (size) can be entered by the user to choose where the reading ends.
- *Select Image file for writing…*: This is used to write specific images to the phone. This will not be used for forensic examinations.
- *Write Target Flash*: This is used after an image has been selected for writing. This will not be used for forensic examinations.
- *Wr. SPARE*: Used to write to the spare area. This will not be used for forensic examinations.

- *ECC*: (Error Correction Code). This is used to include ECC on specific chips. This will not be used for forensic examinations.
- *Erase Target Flash*: This is used to erase the flash area of the memory. This will not be used for forensic examinations.
- *Bad block options*: This allows the user specific commands when encountering areas of the flash memory that contains bad blocks. Users may need to change this setting when reading partitions if they encounter problems at certain stages of the read. The choices available to the user in the drop-down are *Cancel*, *Ignore*, and *Skip*.

Additional fields are at the bottom of the software. From left to right these are noted as, *Welcome!/Address* (hexadecimal represented)/*MCU ID*: Unknown (if not connected)/Box SN: (your connected box serial number)/*CARD SN*: (your connected box's card serial number)/*Fw*: (your box's firmware version)/*TCK Speed*: Connected JTAG clock speed that was selected in the JTAG Speed drop-down.

Reading Target Flash

The steps involved in reading the flash memory of a supported phone will involve selecting buttons within the *JTAG Tool* tab. First, users will need to determine if their target make and model device is supported. As previously mentioned, the Z3X box can also support eMMC reading, and the JTAG Pinout may not be documented. In the next example provided, a Samsung SCH-I535 (Galaxy III—Verizon) phone was used. This device has a Molex connector already mounted on the PCB of the phone. The phone also does not need complete disassembly to access the Molex. A fully charged battery and a USB charger were used. A Moorc Molex 33-in-1 kit was used, making the connection very easy, and of course does not require any soldering. Not all the supported JTAG phones will have Molex connectors, and most will require connecting to the board, through soldering, using a jig, or a specialized tool such as the CODED kit.

This phone required several attempts to determine the maximum JTAG speed it would tolerate before producing errors. The following were the steps followed using an additional 33-in-1 Moorc Molex kit and the settings with the JTAG Tool:

1. Use one of the small ribbon cables from the Moorc kit, and locate the Z-15 head for this model phone. The Z head numbers for specific phones can be located in the vendor's website that sells the 33-in-1 Molex kits. In a previous chapter that addressed JTAG tools, a screenshot of some of the Z numbers and the corresponding phones they work with was provided. Break off the Z-15 from the strip of other heads. Connect one end to one of the loose ribbons in the kit. Be careful not to bend the ribbon when inserting it into the Z-15 head. Insert the remaining end into the

female connector of the Moorc adaptor board. Connect the Molex connector to the PCB, and to the Moorc 20-pin adaptor board, and plug in to the Z3X 20-pin JTAG area. The adaptor board faces up (should be able to see the adaptor board components). Make certain the battery is inserted into the phone and the charging cable is attached. Power on the phone and wait for it to boot completely. The Molex connector can go on in either direction on the PCB, and for this phone, the white Moorc ribbon should cross over the battery area, not away from the phone.

2. In the *Memory Chip* drop-down area, make certain the ROM1 (Main User Data) is selected, and the JTAG Speed is selected at 4000 kHz for this phone.

3. Make certain the *Log* tab is selected within the Z3X EasyJtag Box JTAG Classic Suite. Select the *Connect to Device* button within the JTAG Tool tab. If the connection is a success, the Log area will show several fields to include the *EMMC IDs* and the size of each. If there are any problems, users will see references to the issue(s) in red.

4. Under the *Flasher* area, select *Read Spare*, then select the Preset size for the size memory. In this example, the EMMC #0 is 14.7 G, and a selection of 16 Gb would be used from the drop-down in the Preset area. This will automatically place the Start (HEX) and Length (HEX) values based on the size.

5. *Select Read Target Flash.* Users will see a pop-up window, with a prefilled name of the file and default location for the .bin file. The file is named after the make and model, and starting and ending hexadecimal length. In this example, the default .bin file is named *SAMSUNG_SCH-I535_0x000000000000_0x000400000000*.

6. Wait for the process to complete. This can take more than 1 day, and if reading errors take place, pull the battery on the phone, replace it, turn the phone back on and wait for it to reboot, close Easy-JTAG, then reopen it, and repeat the steps previously addressed. The utility will allow the user to write over the existing file and pick up the read where it left off. Users will encounter a window that advises, *"Easy-JTAG has detected that a previous operation with selected file has been interrupted. If you want to continue last operation press YES if you want to discard saved state and start new operation press NO."*

7. Hash the saved .bin file. Decode as necessary. Hash after decoding. Ensure hash results match. If your results do not match, repeat the process and make a copy of the original .bin file. Use one of the copies for decoding. Compare the decoded .bin file against the copy you made using Ultra-Compare, binary compare. Note the areas of change and determine the cause and if it effects the containers with evidence.

Fig. 25.6 depicts the JTAG Tool tab and numbered steps on how to read the .bin file during a JTAG extraction. Not included in these numbers would be the *Vendor* and *Device* selection.

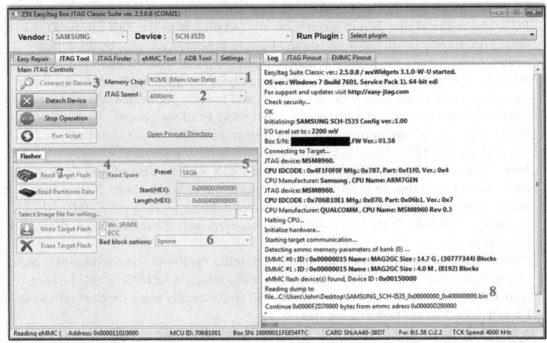

Step 8 is saving the .bin file after *Read Target Flash* has been selected. Users will encounter a pop-up default window location which can be changed.

Figure 25.6

Example of JTAG (Molex) connection steps within the JTAG Tool tab for a Samsung SCH-I535 device.

The companion site provides the following additional images (Figs. 25.12–25.15) related to this example. Fig. 25.12 shows the various *Preset* sizes the user can select for the memory. Fig. 25.13 is an example of the *"Save memory dump to:"* window that will show after users select the *Read Target Flash* button. Notice the default naming configuration for the make, model, and size of flash memory selected. Fig. 25.14 is a screenshot from the bottom area of the JTAG Tool (Suite) indicating the Reading eMMC address, MCU ID, Box SN (redacted), Card SN (redacted), Fw (firmware), and TCK Speed. Fig. 25.15 is the *"Continue interrupted operation?"* window that will populate when the user begin reading a previous (interrupted) operation.

JTAG Finder

The *JTAG Finder* Tab is located within the Z3X EasyJtag box JTAG Classic Suite software. This tab allows the user to locate unmapped TAP locations on a target board. It supports 20 channels. This chapter does not explain the use of the JTAG Finder feature. The Easy-JTAG website, however, provides additional help under the *Product—Knowledge Base (Manuals)* section. There is an example of a JTAG Finder guide that includes pictures [2].

Chapter Summary Key Points

When purchasing the Z3X Easy-JTAG box, users will have a few choices on the configurations. One of the choices is to buy the box with cables and the ISP Adaptor. Other selections include specific manufacturers for support. In any configuration, the buyer can also choose to purchase additional activations after the sale from approved vendors. The card and box serial numbers will be required for the vendor to properly activate the box.

When first installing the Z3X box, the Shell must be installed first, followed by the Easy-JTAG software. The box is then plugged in, and drivers must be manually located with the Program Files\Z3X folder. Device Manager must be free of any driver issues before proceeding.

Once the software and drivers have been installed, the Shell can be used to register and activate any of the paid activations. The Shell is also used to locate various drivers, additional software, and other information.

The Easy JTAG Tool (Z3X EasyJtag Box JTAG Classic Suite) is used to perform the actual JTAG acquisition. Within this interface, the user can locate the JTAG Pinout for their target phone many ways. This includes using the *Easy Repair tab*, the *Open Pinouts Directory* link (under JTAG Tool tab), and the *JTAG Pinout* tab after selecting the *Vendor* and *Device*.

After users have selected their *Vendor, Device, Memory Chip ROM1*, and *JTAG Speed*, they will ensure the device is powered on with a charged battery, charging cable attached, and select *Connect to Device*. If no errors are noted in the *Log* tab, ensure to select the *Read Spare* box, select the *Preset* memory size in the drop-down, select *Ignore Bad block options*, and select *Read Target Flash*. Users can use the default naming configuration, or change the name to suit their needs. Once the file has been saved, the reading will begin. The bottom of the interface will show information as the read takes place. Once the process is complete, hash the results, decode, and hash afterward. The results should match. If hash results differ, repeat the process and make a copy of the first examination to compare with the .bin file after the decoding. Use Ultra-Compare, Binary Compare feature to locate the changes. Examiners who need to utilize the JTAG Finder features can locate additional help on the Easy-JTAG website. Help on this subject is in the Knowledge Base (Manual) section.

The Z3X Easy JTAG is a popular repair tool that is commonly used for law enforcement forensics. This chapter has provided a basic overview on the steps and features of Z3X Easy JTAG.

References

[1] Easy-JTAG Installation and Registration Procedure, Jaipur Telecom, December 6, 2013. http://forum.gsmhosting.com/vbb/f672/read-1st-tutorial-easy-jtag-installation-registration-procedure-1671862/.
[2] Easy-JTAG.com, Knowledge Base (Manuals). http://easy-jtag.com/?page_id=1461.

CHAPTER 26

Thermal Chip Removal

> **Information in This Chapter**
> - Steps involved in chip-off
> - Research the phone—and chip
> - Is the chip encrypted?
> - Prepping the board
> - Removing moisture
> - Thermal removal process
> - Basic steps

Introduction—Chain of Command Knowledge Phenomenon

If you work for a law enforcement or federal agency, you may encounter the *"chain of command knowledge phenomenon"* (*COCKP*). This is the process by which specific people above your pay scale, and who manage you, want you to perform digital forensics, but do not necessarily want to understand what is needed logistically for you to succeed. This can be equated to running a marathon without shoes, or in some cases if you are lucky, one shoe. Here are some more precise examples of *COCKP*:

- *"We just bought you a $10,000 extraction tool for phones. Why doesn't that get what we need off this (bad guy's) phone?"*
- *"Can't you see if another agency has that _____ (insert the tool) for us to borrow?"*
- *"You just went through digital training 5 years ago, why do you need to go again?"*
- *"How come the last chip reader we bought you doesn't work on this other phone?"*
- *"What's that smell coming from the lab? Why are you using a soldering iron? Don't catch anything on fire!"*
- *"After all those certifications, tools, programs, and hundreds of cases, you're telling me you still can't get into the phone?"*

- *"Why is your lab always a mess? This needs to be cleaned up before you do anymore work."* (2 days later after the lab was initially cleaned, new cases come in, this question repeats itself, and the cycle never ends.)
- *"You need a test phone to validate what?"* Which is usually followed up with you getting cut off midsentence, *"Never mind, don't answer, how much will it cost?!"*

If any of these examples apply to you, you have suffered from *COCKP*. The cause of this phenomenon is unknown. It seems to exist around the country and in various facilities big or small. There is no known cure for *COCKP*. As we start another chapter, it will become very important that your relationship with your supervisors is one where they have a working knowledge of digital forensics. Chip-off extractions are not cheap. Some of the tools needed are consumable, and others will become obsolete in a few years. There are also hot and cold ways of removing memory. Each have positives and negatives, not to mention costs. If you work in law enforcement, and if you can perform chip-off examinations, it is also important to network with surrounding agencies. They may not be able to conduct advanced, destructive techniques and will eventually "need" your abilities to assist with their own case(s). This may seem to your agency to tax its own resources, and in some cases affect internal casework. There was even one administrator who said, *"why should we be the agency who has the expert in this field, and has to assist others with their work?"* The answer is quite simple: that's what we are paid to do. We assist the public, and when another agency needs assistance and we have the capabilities to help, we should give them what they need. Of course, this will always be within reason, and in many cases, they would need to provide compensation for the examiner's time, parts, or other logistics involved. In many of the cases, laboratories shared specialized flasher boxes, readers, and even precise solder stations for services that were needed by smaller agencies. Like many other tasks, more can be accomplished if resources are shared among a group. The most important thing that should be shared is not tools or unique tactics, it is, and will always be, knowledge.

The author has also had many situations where *COCKP* lasted for hours, days, and even months. He began to seek help from his local (Tech) university, and after a few years, instances of *COCKP* grew fewer and fewer, but it has never been eradicated. For the author, the exposure to new cases of *COCKP* is usually just a promotion, or career rotation away.

Steps Involved in Chip-off

When it has been decided that a chip-off extraction is the only option left for the examiner, there are a series of steps that need to be conducted before tearing into the phone. Just like Joint Test Action Group (JTAG) and In-System Programming, some research needs to be conducted first. This can help prevent problems and, in some cases, prevent the examiner from realizing, after the fact that the target chip was encrypted or unsupported with the tools in your laboratory. There are also special unlocking services that some commercial forensic vendors can employ on specific phones that have specific chips installed. If your agency or business can afford these specialized unlocking services, they should be exhausted first. There may be times your agency will not pay for the unlock and may feel that they have invested money into chip-off tools and training and want to proceed even if it can be unlocked through nondestructive (paid) methods. If that is the case, or it is an older phone that is not supported with a paid unlock, the following steps can be used to assist. The first four of these sections will be expanded on within this chapter. Again, this is only a suggestion, and your actual mileage may vary:

- Research the phone and chip.
- Is the chip encrypted?
- (Prepping) Drying the board.
- Techniques to remove the chip.

Research the Phone and Chip

Prior to disassembly, the first step is to research the target board. This can help establish if your device is supported by the readers you have in your laboratory. Some of you may have purchased a chip-off kit, which would come with a set of common chip readers. This can be proprietary to a flash programmer or be a simple SD style reader. The actual reading process is covered in the next chapter. Before removing the actual memory that contains the user data, examiners will need to know which chip contains the evidential data and which does not.

Many of the chips will be covered with heat shields. Some of these can be pried off with little effort, while others will require heat, or other techniques to remove them. There are some online sites that may assist in identifying the chips on your target board. There are also chips that are package-on-package (POP). Many of the POP configurations pertain to the processor and RAM. However, the older BlackBerry 9700 and the newer Samsung Galaxy S6 use this method. Obviously, you are less likely to examine a 9700, and at the time of this writing, more likely to encounter the S6. Even though the S6 is POP, most current phones are not, and as such, you will need to understand some basic identification techniques.

Phonescoop.com—FCC IDs

Using Phonescoop.com, users may be able to locate internal photographs of their target phone. Using the standard search bar in the left corner of the main site, the model is searched. Once the results show, scroll to the bottom of the page, directly under the features. In most cases, there will be an FCC ID link in blue that has the complete model number. In the example provided a Galaxy Stratosphere II (SCHI415) was used. The initial search in the upper left search bar (Phonescoop.com home page) was for an I415. Notice Phonescoop.com shows the FCC IDs as A3LSCHI415 in a blue hyperlink. Clicking on this will launch the user to the FCC site for that product code (SCHI415). At the top of the page is usually the most recent entry. Click on *Detail* under the *Display Exhibits* area. The next window will be a warning about the exhibits being viewed with virus protection software. Click *OK* to continue. The next window will display all the possible exhibits that the FCC has for the device. Look for a link for *Internal Photos*. Clicking the link will bring up the internal images. Typically, there will be images of the heat shields in place, as well as an image of the shields removed. On the companion site, Figs. 26.1 and 26.2 depict the steps starting with the FCC link in Phonescoop.com.

In the example provided in the companion site, users may or may not be able to see the chip part number. This is common. The actual part numbers on your evidence may differ, and this is not necessarily the reason for researching the board. The goal is to see how the board is laid out, and which heat shields cover specific chips. In the example provided, there are two main (larger) chips that should be examined closer. If this model was your actual target, you would now have an idea of the heat shield location, as well as which side of the board contains your possible evidence.

Confidentiality Request Letter

Using the FCC link of Phonescoop.com does not always allow the user access to the internal photographs of the board. There may be times when the manufacturer has requested that this information remains confidential. In those cases, they will submit a letter as an exhibit, and there will not be a link to internal photographs. This will apply to related models using different carriers. Our next example uses the Samsung Galaxy 4 (SCH-L720). In the search bar from Phonescoop.com the entry of L720 was submitted, and the results show the Samsung Galaxy 4. At the bottom of the page there are three different FCC IDs related to this phone: A3LSCHI545, A3LSPHL720, and A3LSPHL720T. Each of these models represents different carriers. It is common for the internal boards and case to be laid out slightly different between carriers. In fact, if you are ever replacing screens with the LCD all in one piece, make certain you get the actual carrier correct, as many are not interchangeable. The main hardware is usually the same, however. This means that the processor, RAM, video, NAND memory, etc., will most likely be the same.

If the same steps are followed, we eventually end up at the exhibits page. Notice a link to the *Confidentiality Request Letter*. This allows the manufacturer to keep from the public specific exhibits. In this case, there are no images of the internal components. These letters have been a common occurrence with newer phones. Fig. 26.3 on the companion site shows the example using the SPHL720 phone.

If you encounter this situation in the FCC site, continue to research the device for board images. If the phone is an older device, it is very common to locate images of the main board in sites such as Ebay.com. There are technical sites that can provide the types of processor(s), memory, RAM, and other components. This typically does not include images of the board. Google Images is another source, which can also reveal positive results.

Further Research the Location

The examiner will need to determine the exact location the memory is located. Remember, in almost every case, we are not removing the processor. As mentioned, there will be some BGA packages that are POP, and the actual evidential information would need to be acquired from the top portion of the configuration. These will require a special adaptor which is covered in an upcoming chapter. This chapter focuses on the most common forms of memory. These will be UFS, eMMC, eMCP, NAND, and iNAND configurations. These configurations will be a chip that is affixed in a separate location from the processor or coprocessor on the main board. Many times, the FCC site will show us the board without the heat shields (called "cans") in place. If examiners were to disassemble most phones without researching the chip locations, they would still run into the issue of the heat shields and end up removing unnecessary shields to locate the target memory. There may be times when FCC research does not show the internal image of the target phone. This is common with many pay-as-you-go devices or some HTC devices. Examiners would need to conduct Google searches or visit sites such as gsmarena.com. There will be instances where no matter how much you search, you still are unable to locate information related to the layout of the board. In those cases, you will have no recourse but to dissemble the device, and try and determine what layout you have. Here are additional steps that can assist:

1. Remove each can (heat shield) as needed. Some of the cans can easily be pried off the board without the use of heat. Always attempt to remove them manually first. There are other methods, such as the use of Dremel style cutting tools. If you do decide to use heat from a rework station, apply liquid solder flux around the seam of the heat shield first. The flux will aid in removal when the heat is applied. If you need to use heat REMOVE THE ON-BOARD (AFFIXED) BATTERY IF EQUIPPED.

2. Do you see a chip with the name Qualcomm? This is a processor and is *NOT* your target. Keep looking.

3. Do you see two chips with the same make name such as Samsung? Look at them carefully, aiming your attention to the side of the chip. Can you make out a clear line around the side of one of the chips? Is that chip thicker? The thicker chip is POP (RAM/processor or RAM/coprocessor) and is usually *NOT* your target. Keep looking, or look up the part number and make certain it is not a newer UFS style chip.

4. Do you see a separate chip with the name SanDisk, Toshiba, SK Hynix, or Micron? This is *usually* your target and will be an eMMC, eMCP, iNAND, or NAND and, in some cases, the older NOR memory with evidential data. NOR will be found on some flip phones and cheaper older phones. NOR memory will be smaller in size and usually rectangle in shape.

5. Last resort: look up the chip number using the UP 828 or UP 828P software, which is discussed in the next chapter. You can also look up the number using Google. The use of magnification will assist, as some numbers may appear to be a letter when they are numbers, and vice versa.

6. Is the chip a Micron? Micron chip numbers will need to be looked up in the Micron website to determine the chip configuration. This is called the Fine Pitch Ball Grid Array (FBGA) and Component Marker Decoder. Examiners will need to enter the FBGA Code in the actual chip affixed to the main board. This will provide the complete part number that is used by chip programmers such as the UP 828 and 828P. Micron uses an abbreviated number to save on space. The website to search for the complete part number can be found here: https://www.micron.com/support/tools-and-utilities/fbga. This site contains instructions and an example of a chip with the FBGA Code to look for. By looking up the complete part number, examiners can determine if they have the proper adaptor to read the chip before they decide to remove it.

Of all these steps, locating the processor will help in elimination of which chip is _**NOT**_ your target. When examiners are new at chip removal all these components will look the same. After a few removals, the identification process will become easier. It will be removing the exact "_can_" that covers the memory in question that can become difficult. This is especially true on newer phones that have little or no online documentation. Older BlackBerry phones have very difficult heat shields to remove.

Just remember that Qualcomm will generally be the most common processor on newer smart phones, followed by Samsung, and then Texas Instruments (TI). Most new phones will have a POP configuration and the chip is clearly thicker than the target memory that needs removal. Also, the TI processor is usually under a Samsung RAM in a POP configuration. On the companion site under, Fig. 26.4 depicts a BlackBerry main board with the cans being pried off. The seam around this had liquid solder flux brushed on it prior to applying heat. Fig. 26.5 (companion site) shows a Motorola XT912 board with numerous cans in place on the left image. The image on the right shows only the can that was removed, along with the actual eMMC chip (also removed). This is an example of how (only) the actual can that covers the evidential memory was removed. Maybe you simply you do not know which _can_ will reveal your target memory. Simply remove all of them and inspect and research what is underneath. This may be your only option, and it may not be the best option as heat needs to be applied. If you must apply heat, make certain you use solder flux around the seams of the cans to help aid in the removal.

Is the Chip Encrypted?

One of the more problematic issues that examiners will be facing with chip-off exams are situations where the chip is encrypted. This can take place at the software or hardware level. In the past, it was entirely software related. BlackBerry and iOS devices were the most common. Pulling off the chip on an encrypted device is of little use to an examiner unless they have the means to decrypt the data. Within the past couple of years, the UFS chip became more popular and is common in Samsung S6, S7, and S8 devices. UFS stands for Universal Flash Storage, which is basically a faster chip that allows both reading and writing functions to take place at the same time. These chips can employ hardware-based encryption. This means that by default, they may not be able to be decoded if they are removed and read. At the time of this writing, the S6 chip did not have the encryption turned on by default, but the S7 did. There are other phones that may also employ encryption at the user partition level. If you are facing a newer style phone, it is imperative you conduct research into what type of chip the phone is using. This is especially true with Samsung devices. The UFS chip is not only in the S6, but other models as well.

Prepping the Board

Before applying heat to any board, it needs to be inspected for a battery, plastic, wires, and other items that can melt or catch fire. Since the technique is destructive, many of these items can be removed for safety. If you are lucky enough to have equipment in your laboratory that can be used to rework the board and put the chip back on, then these steps may not apply to you. The other option is to cover these areas with Kapton tape, which is heat resistive. Fig. 26.1 shows an example of a phone equipped with a battery. This battery can be broken off or pulled off with pliers. Fig. 26.1 also shows plastic from the battery terminal area that can also be removed. This would typically melt and create an awful odor, which in turn may elicit a *COCKP* solicitation.

Remove battery (if equipped) or break off board where battery resides. Remove plastic areas if needed.

Figure 26.1
Example of a printed circuit board equipped with an onboard battery and plastic areas that can be removed.

Removing Moisture

Chapter 21 addressed phone disassembly and water damaged phones. As a reminder, if you intend to remove a chip using a thermal process, it is highly recommended to dry the board—even if the device was not suspected of being exposed or submerged in water. Moisture over time can still find its way into the components. The little time it takes to dry a board will help ensure that there is no problem during the thermal removal. Think of it as buying insurance, you may need it, but if you never buy it and get into an accident, you have even more problems.

Board Holder

Once the determination has been made that you will begin removing the chip, it will need to be secured in a board holder that allows access to the memory and stands up to the heat. The common holders sold should be affixed to a piece of scrap wood. This will allow the high temperatures of the heating unit area to disperse the heat without damaging the bench, table, or work area. This same piece of wood will also be used when examiners need to conduct JTAG or other soldering.

The next chapter addresses cleaning, re-tinning, and reballing of the memory. Again, the wooden board can be used for those functions as well. Fig. 26.6 on the companion site is an image of a main board holder. This particular holder has been involved in several hundred JTAG and chip-off examinations and shows wear. On one end of the holder is a spring loaded retention clip. An old heat shield (can) was used to take up some of the slack of the spring. The set screw that comes with the unit eventually wears out during repeated use (or is misplaced), and the use of an old heat shield can fix the problem. This allows a firmer hold on the board you may be working on. On the other end are two small hooks that are used to grab the edge of the board. These can be moved apart to accommodate different configurations. Fig. 26.2 depicts the board holder with a phone main board being held in place. The extra space at the end of the spring has an old heat shield taking up the slack and applying additional tension on the board.

Figure 26.2
Example of the board hold with old heat shields being used for tension.

Using Heat for Memory Removal

There are two general techniques used for removing the evidence memory off a mobile device. One is using heat and the other is a cold process. In most investigations, the author's preference is the cold process—which should also be the first choice for others (in most cases). The cold methodology may not be a choice for you, as it can cost more to perform the technique. Most companies or law enforcement agencies that began preforming chip-off examinations in the last few years were more than likely using heat to get the chip off the main board. This is still common, but it is being replaced by the much safer cold technique. There are split opinions over the time involved to complete a cold versus heat removal technique. For the author, the cold technique has generally always taken additional time.

High-End Tools

Many smaller law enforcement agencies will utilize equipment that is relatively inexpensive at removing the target memory from the main board of the phone. This does not always mean this is the best way in which to conduct the removal. The tool(s) selected will always have to do with the resources the agency or private business can invest into this work. Before addressing some actual (cheaper) hardware components that are used during the heat technique, a couple examples of more expensive units are provided that can be used to remove the memory using heat.

ZEVAC and Weller

The author has had the opportunity to consult and instruct with two different federal laboratories within the United States. A highly regarded training vendor that is used to instruct on the chip-off process is the Netherlands Forensics Institute (NFI). The NFI provides training to law enforcement personnel only. Their laboratory uses a high-end rework station manufactured by a company called Zevac. Zevac is headquartered in Switzerland. The company produces several of these rework machines, each varying in features. At the time of this writing, the NFI was using the Zevac Onyx 24 to perform chip removal from mobile evidence. As of April 2017, Zevac offers the top of the line Onyx 29. Their lower-end unit is called the Onyx 21. The companion site contains a .PDF file from the Zevac website, titled "ONYX 24 E.pdf." This is the product download for the Zevac Onyx 24. Additional downloads are available directly from their site: http://www.Zevac.ch/en/downloads/brochures.php?navid=21.

One of the outstanding features of the Onyx 24 is the *Site Cleaning Option. "By means of the contactless site cleaning option the residue solder after removal of a component is removed without touching or damaging the surface of the printed circuit board. The site is cleaned and ready for a new component to be soldered in after applying flux and paste if necessary"* [1].

When Zevac sells any of their high-end machines, they offer on-site, customized training and setup. They fly a representative from their company to the customer site. They in turn spend several days with the actual hardware target that is expected to be worked on. There are a number of other high-end rework stations. One that is around half the price of the Zevac (at $33K) is the Weller WQB4000SOPS. On the companion site there is a PDF titled "WQB4000-Brochure," which provides the technical data for this model.

The financial impact of purchasing these high-end machines will keep these out of the reach of smaller municipal agencies. Instead, most nonfederal laboratories will utilize a more cost-effective means at removing the memory. Because of this, the acquisition is called a destructive process, as they only allow the chip to be removed from the board and not reapplied to an operational status. The units are not usually precise and will usually combine a solder gun element in many of the configurations. Some offer a preheater, allowing the bottom of the board to be exposed to a desired temperature. The top work area that would contain the chip, however, would still use a manual nozzle. There are substantial risks to the evidence when using these lower-end rework stations.

- Manual use only. The users will "hand-hold" the hot air nozzle. This can in some cases cause problems with applying too much or too little heat to the target. Because the user has the nozzle in one hand, this may also tie up a hand that is needed to work on getting the memory removed from the main board.
- No precise controls. Unlike the other high-end models, the user must set up the board in a separate holder and introduce the hot air to the memory location. Again, the distance between the hot air nozzle and the chip does not stay the same and temperatures may fluctuate. This may expose the chip to longer periods of high temperatures.
- Chip is manually lifted off the board. Some of the higher-end units allow the chip to be lifted through an aligned suction, which keeps the BGA area from smudging solder across the ball area. Examiners are using tweezers or other tools to get the chip (which is hot) off the board. Smudging the BGA points will increase the time it takes to clean and retin the memory.
- Simply damaging the chip. This can take place at any of the previous addressed stages or at the corner of the chip if the examiner is prying on it too hard, or too soon, before the solder on the BGA area has enough time to heat up. In the upcoming pages examples of damaged chips due to incorrect prying will be shown.

These are just a few examples of some of the issues. They all have a common theme, and that is heat. Obviously, heat can cause damage to almost every type of electronic component over time. The good thing is that many of these chips are very durable and can be exposed to temperatures they were not necessarily designed to withstand. This by no means should be interpreted that an examiner should disregard how long they apply hot air to the memory or disregard how they use preheater or other hardware tool.

Less Expensive Rework Station Examples

One of the first hardware tool examples is the T-862 IRDA. This unit has a hot plate, infrared (pulse) heat, and a terminal that allows a soldering iron to be plugged in. It also has a work clamp to hold the main board. The clamp does not have the ability to hold the board tight, which renders it useless during the chip removal. This is mainly due to the need of the examiner to scrape around the edges to remove adhesive. The temperature adjustment is in Celsius. On the companion site, Fig. 26.7 shows the rework station without the soldering unit present. These examples display a main board that is being held down with Kapton tape, as well as the included clamp. During the infrared pulse, users would place the protective screen down to avoid exposure to the harsh IR light. The unit allows independent controls of heat to each of the components. The user can control power to each of these, as well as electing to keep them on or off. Examiners should also be aware that the temperature being displayed in Celsius is generally hotter than what it should actually be. In this example, the Fahrenheit temperature should be 219°F, or close to that range, as laser thermometers can be off (Fig. 26.8 on the companion site). In most cases, it is around 20–25° hotter than what is displayed. It is better to start out with a lower range and gradually increase the temperature.

The next example is the YIHUA 862BD+ SMD Rework Station with soldering iron. This rework station combines the use of SMD (hot air) and a soldering station (iron). It allows the user to select power as needed to each. It also features a switch that can be toggled to *auto* or *manual*. This allows the hot air nozzle to detect that it has been set down in the cradle, which, when placed there, will gradually turn off the air flow. The air flow rate is adjustable through a knob in the center of the unit. Although the specs on this unit indicate the temperatures are in Celsius, testing has confirmed the unit heat output (displayed) is in Fahrenheit.

The last rework example is the Best 902D. This has been rebranded a number of times. The author has this same model as the Wild PCS 559. Other than the name, the unit functions exactly the same. At the time of this writing, the unit was being sold under the Best 902D make and model name. Originally, this was also sold as a YIHUA. These units function very similar to the 862BD+. An exception being that the SMD hot air does not have the option to turn on auto; however, the nozzle does automatically stop after a few seconds once it is placed back into its respective cradle. Another useful feature is that the soldering unit knob on some models will display both Fahrenheit and Celsius settings. The air flow has a 1 through 8 setting. The SMD Rework knob has a *DOWN–UP*, which is used to adjust the temperature of the hot air. Like the 862BD+, the specifications indicate the temperature displayed is Celsius, but it has been confirmed as Fahrenheit.

These three examples are considered less expensive options. The major complaints are generally related to the soldering iron. If examiners can afford spending more money for their hot air unit, they may want to consider Hakko FR-801/802/803 models. The models in the 800 series are also sold with letter identifiers within the model, such as the FR-803B-11. These are configured just for the hot air and are not designed with a soldering iron on the opposite side. Hakko offers a number of unique nozzles for these rework stations, which can be configured for specific applications. Hakko also has a dual solder unit, the FM-203. This can be configured with several different attachments, such as the thermal tweezers, or micro solder handles.

Basic Removal Steps When Using Heat

At the point where examiners are ready to remove the chip using heat, as a reminder, they should have already addressed these points we previously covered:

- Researched which chip is the correct one to remove.
- Removed or protect any item on the board that may melt or explode (battery).
- Removed any "can" necessary to allow full access to the memory. You need access to all four sides of the chip.
- Dry the board (chip) prior to removal, even if the device was never submerged in water.

Examiners should be aware of the safety issues associated with whichever rework station that they choose. Also their work area should be free of any unnecessary items that could melt. At a minimum, eye protection should be worn during chip removal and proper ventilation or fume extractor should be used.

Temperature on the 559 or 862BD+ should be set to the number on the display of 450. If using the T-862, this will be the IR Heat Lamp setting and needs to be set to 232°C. The IR preheater plate can be set at 150°C. These are recommended settings, and in the case of the rework being set at 450°C, this does not mean the chip should reach this temperature. There will be some heat loss taking place between the end of the nozzle and the target memory. If there is concern about overheating, examiners can also use a thermal (wired) temperature probe to monitor the chip. This is especially useful on the first few chip-off pulls, as most individuals tend to leave the heat on the chip too long. Most people have the nozzle too far away from the memory; they work too slowly, and as such, they slowly overheat the target. The thermal probe can be taped to the board/chip area using Kapton tape. An inexpensive unit that is recommended is from Extech. Their *Mini MultiMeter MN15A* sells complete with the wired thermal adaptor probe for around $29.99 on Amazon. This can help monitor the temperature until one feels comfortable with the process and has a general idea or "feel" for how long to apply the heat and the distance.

Another issue is that vendors will commonly utilize adhesive around the chip to add additional stabilization and longevity to the mobile device. This can be removed with solvents or by applying heat and scraping at the same time. Many of the solvents available are extremely toxic and will require scraping and cleaning—and in some cases, heating the solvent after it has been applied.

There are specific phones that use adhesive that can be carefully scraped away from the memory without the need to apply solvents or heat. This will not be the case with most BlackBerry devices. Using a thin bladed tool, begin scrapping the edges of the target memory to remove the adhesive. The tool pictured in the upcoming examples is from a square blade of an "Exacto" style knife set. This was a generic set, which came with a number of other blades. It was less than $5.00 for the entire set. On some phones there may be no adhesive showing and on others, there can be a large amount of it. It is very important that examiners do not pry up on the memory during this process. Damage to the chip can occur if prying is used. Remember, you will need to clean and retin the memory. In some cases, you may also have to reball the chip. If you pry off the chip from the board, it can pull off actual BGA (round) points from the memory, rendering that specific contact useless for data transfer. If this takes place, there may be times when the damage is not catastrophic and did not actually affect the circuity of the memory. The damage is completely avoidable if you take your time and do not rush trying to "force" the component off the main board. Fig. 26.3 contains images of the square spade tool being used on both a Motorola and BlackBerry main board. The three images at the bottom of Fig. 26.3 show the damage that can occur to the chip if users pry too hard on the edges while trying to remove it. The edges of the chip are one area where damage typically takes place if you are new to chip removal using heat.

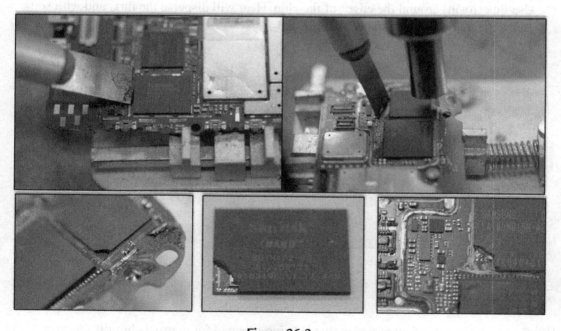

Figure 26.3
Example of square spaded tool/heat nozzle distance and damaged edges of chips from prying too hard.

The suggestion here (if you have never performed a chip-off using heat) is to practice removing as many chips as you can before an actual case. This includes the processor, coprocessor, video memory, and POP configurations. Here are some additional suggestions when using heat:

- Bring the nozzle close to the target, and do not use an oversized or undersized nozzle. Remember you are trying to heat the BGA area. A small nozzle will isolate heat to one area, and even if you heated one corner and moved to another, that corner you came from may begin to cool down if the nozzle is too small.
- Preheat from underneath the chip you want to remove. This can significantly help, and generally the heating time needed through the top of the chip is much less.
- Wave the nozzle around the entire chip, but do not stay in one spot. Try to evenly distribute your heat. Work fast, but do not rush the removal by prying. Make sure the adhesive in the sides is removed first. This is where it is acceptable to use a smaller nozzle if you did not use solvents to remove the adhesive. It is also acceptable to use your spade to see if the chip is loose, but only on a middle area, away from the corners. These areas are stronger than the fragile corners. You are using your tool to determine if the chip is loose, not to pry it off. If you pry too soon on the chip, even though you did not damage the corner, you may inadvertently pry off the necessary solder from the BGA. The chip will need some solder to remain on the BGA contacts for the reader to function properly.
- Use flux (rosin) around the edges of the chip. Heat will disperse the flux, and with some chips, the flux will travel under the chip and assist with removal.

Figure 26.4
Example of scraping around the chip and excess glue that may be located on the chip (thermal process).

Fig. 26.4 is a close-up view of a chip that is being prepped for thermal chip-off removal. Directly on each side of the chip the excess glue is being scrapped off. The right-hand side image in Fig. 26.4 shows the excess glue that these types of phones could have (BlackBerry).

Chapter Summary Key Points

- Research the phone and chip
- Is the chip encrypted?
- Prepare the board
- Remove moisture
- Remove adhesive (if necessary)
- Don't pry on corners

When a decision has been reached that the chip will be removed, examiners must perform some standard steps if they are unfamiliar with the phone. The first is to begin researching the phone and the chip. Do not remove the chip if it is encrypted. The FCC website of Phonescoop.com can be of assistance with this task. There will be some phones that have confidentiality letters, and the interior photos are not disclosed. Internet searching may help, but in many cases, the phone will need to be disassembled to determine the chip number. Most chips will be covered with heat shields (cans). Only the can covering the target memory will need to be removed, but typically all of them may need to be removed if you have no idea where the chip is located. In cases where a Micron chip is located, the FBGA Code will need to be researched to determine the entire (complete) part number. Micron abbreviates their numbers. The full number will be used by programmer boxes such as the UP 828 and 828P.

When using heat to remove the chip, the board will need to be thoroughly dried. In cases of water-exposed (submerged) devices, the examiner will need to clean the board. After the board has been dried, there are basic steps for removing the memory using heat. These involve the examiner prepping the board and removing the battery and/or any plastic that may melt. Another option is to cover any area that you want to protect with Kapton tape.

There are several rework stations to choose from. Do not use a nozzle that is too small or too large. Use a square style "Exacto" blade to help remove the chip. Make certain the adhesive around the chip is removed first. This can be removed using solvents or heat. Do not pry on the corners of the chip, and move the heat around the entire area of the chip, being careful not to stay in one spot too long.

If you are new to chip removal, practice many times before working on an actual case.

Reference

[1] Zevac Onyx 24. http://www.Zevac.ch/en/rework_products/smt_systems/onyx_24.php.

CHAPTER 27

Nonthermal Chip Removal

Information in This Chapter

- Removal through a cold process
- Cut out the chip
- Dremel style tools
- Band saw
- Milling
- Lab and polishing
- Ultra Tec products

Introduction—"Step Away From the Heat"

For those of us familiar with chip-off extractions, there are different ways to remove the chip other than through a thermal process. Within the corporate world, the tools, training, and availability of skilled personnel are generally not an issue. Businesses will pay whatever is necessary to properly process devices through advanced techniques. Some of these same logistical requirements may not be an issue for federal law enforcement agencies. For state and local municipalities, this will generally be a different story. Most small agencies who are able to perform advanced chip-off techniques may be utilizing less than idea tools to do so.

More vendors are coming on board with nonthermal solutions. Two types are discussed very briefly in this chapter. The trend seems to be to get away from thermal chip-off exams all together, thus increasing the likelihood of a successful read. Since most of us were street officers first, the nonthermal method needs to be "cop-proof," just like the popular forensic tools that tell law enforcement what to do on the screen. *"Plug cables X into your phone, and insert a thumb drive into port A of the machine. Press Continue for the exam to begin."* Yep, that is pretty "cop-proof" indeed. Nonthermal solutions are, at the present moment, in their "infant" stages. The other issue is encryption. All the methods for removing the chip are meaningless when our high-end phones have encrypted chips. This is a hot topic in the forensic field. For the most part, really "bad-dudes" do not go out and buy smartphones when they are planning to commit a crime or on the run from law enforcement. We still have the need to process low-end phones, which for years have not had a reason (or cost benefit) to be encrypted. So, put down the rework station nozzle, and "*Step away from the heat.*"

Removal Through a Cold Process

Why, you may ask, do we have nonthermal chip removal methods? The easy answer is that it significantly reduces the risk of damaging the chip, and increases the likelihood of reading the contents. There are two basic techniques discussed in this chapter: milling, and the lap and polish method. Both require an investment into specialized tools, which we will address. Before beginning the extraction, many factors or steps from our previous chapter will apply: research the chip to determine if it is encrypted or not; and prep the board or chip. Since we are not applying heat to the chip, it is not necessary to dry it in an oven. If the device was exposed to water, or was not operational at the time of seizure, drying would be recommended. Remember, dry the board at a constant low temp so as not to melt solder or damage components. In most cases, however, if the phone is operational, drying will not be necessary for a nonthermal removal. The tools we used in our last chapter may also be useful for this purpose as well, minus the rework station. Both techniques require the examiner to work through the materials that are affixed to the target chip. These materials consist of board layers, other chips, and various materials including tin. The number of materials can vary. For instance, a chip cut from a newer Motorola has nothing other than the board on the other side, whereas an older Samsung Galaxy does. Figs. 27.1–27.3 help illustrate this.

Target chip in question (Samsung)   Materials on the opposite side (waste)

Figure 27.1
Chip cut from a Samsung Galaxy phone.

Target chip (Motorola)   Materials on the opposite side (waste)

Figure 27.2
Chip cut from a newer Motorola.

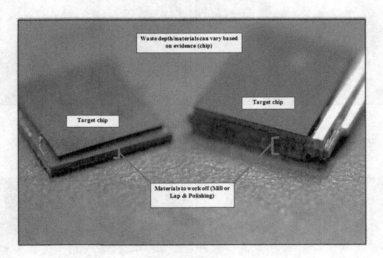

Figure 27.3
Side-by-side comparisons on how board materials (waste) will vary from one phone to another.

Removing the Chip From the Board

Milling is a process that can be used to cut the chip from the board. It is a relatively easy concept: drill small holes around the chip and the chip can be pushed off the board. This chapter will also detail some other alternatives. These techniques can be used prior to milling or lap, and polishing.

Dremel Style Tools

The "Dremel" style cutting wheel can take several minutes to cut out the chip and may also produce lots of dust. A dust mask should be worn during its use. There is a degree of vibration, which according to some experts may cause damage to the Ball Grid Array (BGA) areas. The author has never experienced damage from the vibration, and if there is a vibration damage risk, it is far less than what thermal removal poses. Fig. 27.4 depicts a chip being cut from a main board using a very inexpensive cutting tool and wheel. This tool costs significantly less than the entry level "Dremel" brand. It works, but takes time to get through the materials. There is little to no torque on this inexpensive ($10—Harbor Freight) tool, and as such, the user must take more time, applying light pressure with the cutting wheel. The heat shields can also be removed using the same tool. Fig. 27.5 displays the "can" being removed from a BlackBerry.

Figure 27.4
Example of a Dremel style cutting wheel being used to remove chip.

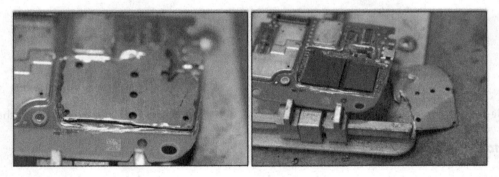

Figure 27.5
Heat shield (can) removed with a cutting wheel.

Band Saw

Another method that can be used to cut out the chip is to use a small band saw equipped with a metal blade. The band saw takes a few minutes compared to the Dremel style tool. There is more noise, but less dust. Fig. 27.6 shows an inexpensive Craftsman 9-inch Band Saw ($129) with 18-TPI (teeth per inch) metal blade ($10.99). The heat produced on the actual chip as the band saw cuts is minimal, and the chip is warm to the touch but not hot. There is also less vibration. Be aware, there may be occasional small sparks, depending on what is being cut around the chip. There may even be small embers when a component is cut through burns for a brief second. We are not talking about the 4th of July in Washington D.C., just a few glows reminding you that you are alive.

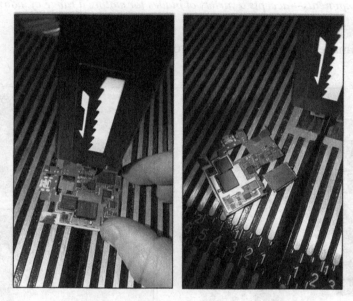

Figure 27.6
Images of a band saw being used to cut out the memory from a main board.

An alternative to the cheap band saw is a product that is currently being offered by Ultra Tec Manufacturing Incorporated, called the Ultraslice Macrotome. This cutting device feeds cooling liquid to the cutting wheel and ensures a heat-free method for removing the chip off the main board of mobile evidence. (No more sparks) Specifications from Ultra Tec provide the following information on the Ultraslice Macrotome:

> ***ULTRASLICE*** *macrotome precision diamond saw, is a quiet, direct drive design for smooth, chatter free slicing system for important and fragile industrial, hard tissue, biological and certain industrial specimens. The system suits Fish & Game applications, such as Otolith and Statolith samples. Specimens can be oriented to ensure a flat surface is parallel to the desired section plane such as sagittal, frontal or transverse. Macrotome can also be used in many other industrial applications where the best price/performance ratio is required. The wheel (spindle) rotation is variable speed, to allow for optimized cut quality. An easy access coolant reservoir, allows for quick efficient coolant changes.*

PRODUCT HIGHLIGHTS:

*   ***Suits Low Budgets***—*The system is price "to sell" for all lab sizes and budgets*
*   ***Z-Spindle Option***—*Make Cutting height changes quickly—even during cutting operations*
*   ***Manual Crank Motorized-Feed Option***—*all feed are possible for achieving optimum cutting results*
*   ***Otolith, Statolith, undecalcified Bones & Teeth***—*the system cuts most hard tissue*
*   ***Industrial Components***—*accepts a variety of blades for cutting a range of industrial materials [1].*

Fig. 27.7 depicts images of the Ultraslice Macrotome unit.

Figure 27.7
Picture of the Ultraslice Macrotome unit made by Ultra Tec.

Milling

Another technique that may be available to examiners is called milling. Milling does not involve the introduction of heat to remove the chip, and it is considered a cold, nonthermal technique. It involves going through the layers of the board on the BGA side of the chip. There are several different milling machines that are commercially available that can be used for this purpose.

Milling can have a catastrophic risk to the chip if the user was to proceed too far into the material. There are also experts who believe milling poses risks to the chip based on friction and vibration caused during the process. This type of error for the author is no different than running a Dremel cutting wheel, or band saw blade into a chip. Yes, there is the possibility of error, but the milling depths could be predetermined on test boards or gradual to allow inspection. There are other experts who have not experienced any issues or damage caused by the friction or the vibration. One would also assume that if examiners are using the milling process, they are fully aware of how to use the machine and have taken measures to minimize damage to the chip.

One of the more popular models being sold for chip milling is the *Othermill Milling Station*. These milling machines are designed for creating parts and single or double-sided PCB boards, and utilize a Computer Numerical Control router. Ultra Tec Manufacturing, Inc. sells a machine called *Blue Mill* [2], which is also designed for cold chip-off forensics.

At the 10th annual International Conference on Systematic Approaches to Digital Forensic Engineering, David Billard and Paul Vidonne produced a six page, unpublished document titled, "*Chip-Off By Matter Subtraction: Frigida Via.*" The document can be located using Internet searches and is also included on the companion site, titled "*Chip-off-by-Matter-Subtraction-Frigida-Via.pdf.*" David and Paul document the milling process, which they refer to as micromilling, and outline some of the pros and cons of using this type of technique. The document compares the hot and cold processes of removing the chip in a side-by-side comparison. Fig. 27.8 is an image of the Blue Mill unit sold by Ultra Tec. This unit offers a digital camera that allows the examiner to easily view the process of an attached monitor.

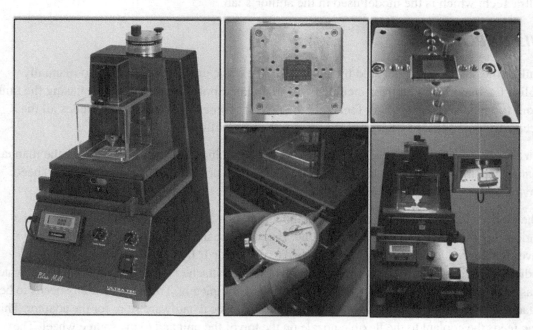

Figure 27.8
Image of the Blue Mill (Milling) unit sold by Ultra Tec.

Lap and Polishing

The last cold technique addressed is called "lap and polishing." This is a machine that pumps water to the polishing wheel, and the chip materials are sanded or "polished" off from the bottom to the BGA area. An examiner would cut the chip out using one of the previous described techniques. The chip is then attached to a specialized holder and placed onto the wheel. The wheel can be affixed with silicon carbide (SiC) abrasive paper (sandpaper) that is available in different abrasion levels (grits). Some vendors also refer to the paper as carborundum. Most people will call this "sandpaper" or "wet-dry sandpaper." Because water is being used to cool the material during the sanding/polishing, there is no heat introduced to the chip.

The Scientific Working Group of Digital Evidence (SWGDE) created a document titled *"SWGDE Tech Notes regarding Chip-off via Material Removal Using a Lab and Polish Process."* Again, the article can be located using Internet searches but is included on the companion site (Chapter 27), under a PDF originally titled, *"SWGE_Tech_Notes_regarding_Chip-off_via_Material_Removal_Using_a_Lap_and_Polish_Process.pdf."*

The referenced article from SWGDE describes the lap and polish process. Within their article, they use and refer to features of an Ultra Tech, ULTRAPOL Advanced lapping and polishing tool. The next section describes additional use of the ULTRAPOL Basic model also made by Ultra Tech, which is the model used in the author's lab.

ULTRAPOL Basic

Unlike the advanced model sold by Ultra Tech, the basic unit allows the user to manually polish the materials with their included "manual planar polishing tool." If purchasing the unit from forensic vendors such as TeelTech, the product comes with a kit that includes all the necessary parts, except what is necessary for the hose fitting.

On the companion site, Fig. 27.1 depicts everything included in the kit, except for the manual planar polishing tool. There are 25, 8″ (three different abrasions) discs included. The sheets have adhesive backings that affix to the wheel.

The kit does include a printed manual, but it does not provide any details on how to set up the various hoses, and submergible water pump. Based on the included hose adaptors, the setup gives the impression that it would be attached to the larger 1″ hose, as there are no adaptors indicating it goes to the other 3/8″ sized line. The author attached it this way and found that water was being pumped into the basin drain area, filling it completely. The pump actually needs to be attached to the 3/8″ line, which will require a trip to the local hardware store for the adaptor. This line feeds the coolant to the flexible nozzle on the top of the unit and to the source wheel. The two plastic fittings included in the kit will not fit this line. Users will need a 1″ NPT Male x 3/8″

Straight Hose Barb Fitting as pictured in Fig. 27.2 on the companion site. Fig. 27.3 on the companion site is a labeled overview of the back of the unit. This image provides the user with a description of the input power areas and the two different hose lines.

The kit comes with a small bucket, which has little use for either coolant or drain, as it fills (or empties) rather quickly. The author uses two 5-gallon buckets. This allows for approximately 10 chip-off polish jobs. The most practical connection to this unit would be to have a constant water source line installed as well as a permanent drain line.

The manual planar polishing tool comes with four small aluminum pieces called *Parallel polish sample mounts* that are approximately 3/4″ long. These are inserted between the blocks and held in place with spring tension. Only one of these is used at a time and the remainders are spares. The opposite end has two *Teflon wear feet* that are used as guides from preventing the metal block from being damaged. The kit is sold with a small stick of wax and can be used to affix the chip to the parallel polishing mount. The wax softens at 160°F and melts at 250°F. Wax is not the only way to affix the chip to the mount, and thanks to Bob Elder from Teel Technologies Canada, for determining another method that does not require heat. Bob utilized double-sided carpet tape. The examiner traces the chip onto the tape and cuts the required piece with scissors. When the polishing is finished, the tape is very easy to remove compared to the wax. Fig. 27.4 on the companion site shows an example of the double-sided carpet tape and an inexpensive level used by the author.

The polishing process begins by using the coarsest abrasive sheet from the kit. Approximately 2–3 chips can be polished with one 8″ sheet. After affixing the chip, it is checked for level. As mentioned earlier, and depicted in various chip examples, mobile devices will vary as to how much material is affixed to the opposite side of the chip. As the high points are removed, the surface will eventually become even. Examiners need to be aware that the *manual planar polishing tool* needs to be held in place with your hand against the wheel. Even though you may have leveled it, it still may polish one area more than another. Rotate the chip by releasing the spring tension and removing the entire *Parallel polish sample mount* to a different angle, this helps to keep the polish consistent if high spots developed. Since the chip is adhered to the *Parallel polish sample mount* with wax or tape, it only takes a second to remove and rotate it back into the *manual planar polishing tool*. Do not push the block into the spinning wheel. The only weight applied should be the weight of the actual tool, and you are merely holding its level as it polishes. The author also found that the wheel RPM (rotation per minute) worked best at the highest setting during the initial stage (removing large items). Once paper is switched to the finer grit, examiners may want to also decrease the RPM, to allow more control over precise polishing.

Fig. 27.5 on the companion site contains a few images of the author performing the lap and polishing process. Included are images of the chip in the early stages of the polishing process. As he polishes through the layers and begins to see the BGA area, the coarse paper is swapped for a fine grade, and he reduces the RPM to nearly half the maximum speed. This will prevent polishing too deep into the BGA area. A recommendation is to purchase additional 8″ lap plates for each grade of adhesive material. Using one disc requires removing a used, viable paper, reinstalling the back of the paper for future use, drying the plate for the next grade paper, and eventually removing the finer grade to replace back the coarser grade for a new chip. Using a minimum of two discs keeps two grades of paper attached until they are worn out.

Lap and polishing things to consider:

- It is time consuming, and involves constant monitoring of the work area. Whereas, with the thermal process, the cleaning always took much longer than the removal.
- Leveling is mainly a "visual" process. Even though the initial setup involves leveling the "manual planar polishing tool," the majority of the removal will depend on holding the tool in a "level" position. As the polishing takes place, the examiner will be able to see if they are holding the tool correctly and can easily adjust as needed before any over polishing occurs.
- The Teflon feet on the manual planar polishing tool can wear out quickly. This is caused by the heavier abrasive paper. A way to prevent this is to hold the tool in the middle, adjust the chip down further, and prevent the feet from touching the surface of the paper. These should not be thought of as resting points as the polishing takes place, but as a guide to prevent the block from becoming scratched.
- As suggested, purchase another 8-inch lap plate for the other grades of paper. This will save time and paper. Taking off these sheets then reapplying them for the next job can be time consuming, and the adhesive does not adhere as well the second (or third) time around. Not to mention you must remove and dry any water that is on the disc before replacing the paper. Storing a used disc is also an issue, as the original cover needs to be reapplied exactly as it came off. Reapplied discs as they spin can also "throw" more excess water (coolant) during the process. This is usually because the adhesive was previously used, and the paper does not lay entirely flat against the plate.
- If you are accustomed to scraping off the excessive solder and glue from the surface of the chip (BGA) area (thermal), it is not necessary to clean all the way down to the chip board. Polish until the BGA area is nice and even, each of the balls can be seen, and all the copper is gone. If you view the chip under a microscope, it may surprise you to see a thin layer of clear glue (or black glue) still sitting around the BGAs. Try to read the chip. In nearly all of the lap and polishing exams the author has completed, the chip is hardly ever polished all the way down to the chip board, because it is not necessary to go that far.
- Do not be afraid of using tweezers and gently pulling off the layers of copper. As you get closer to the BGA surface, you can actually see the pattern. Make sure you change to the lighter (grit) paper. The copper materials are usually held in place with glue at this point, and can be peeled off. Prior to the release of this book, Ultra Tec contacted the author

regarding a video they created to assist with the lap and polishing process. The video includes how to use their included wax to mount the target chip. It also depicts how to level the polishing jig, and the use of their Long Arm. The Long Arm holds the jig, keeping the item at a consent pressure. The link to the video can be found here: https://www.youtube.com/watch?v=hntMNV-FdUQ&t=13s.

Chapter Summary Key Points

Before examiners utilize a nonthermal method of removing a chip, they must conduct research into the phone (and chip) to determine if it is supported and not encrypted. The actual removal process will depend largely on which type of tools the examiner is using—milling, or lap and polishing.

There are two inexpensive ways to remove a chip: one is with the use of a cutting wheel affixed to a Dremel style device. The second method is to use a band saw with a metal cutting blade. Both methods expose the chip to little to no heat.

Milling involves removing the waste material by using a cutting bit and shaving through it, moving around the (waste) area until the BGA surface has been reached on the chip. Lap and polishing involves mounting the chip to a block and sanding off the materials using water cooling. Lap and polishing requires different grades of paper and is less prone to catastrophic operator error compared to milling. The process does require additional time to complete, and the chip does not need to be polished all the way down to the chip's board. Once the BGAs are evenly polished, attempts to read the contents can be tried. Examiners can also pull small pieces of copper off the BGA area once they get closer to the contacts.

Just like anything else that has been discussed in various chapters of this book, it will be necessary to try this nonthermal method out on some test chips. Determine which removal process works best in your lab. Hopefully your lab can afford some of the tools offered by such vendors as Ultra Tec, which can aid in chip removal, milling, or lap and polishing. On the companion site are some additional PDFs that provide an overview of the milling unit, and Ultraslice equipment offered by Ultra Tec. These are titled *Blue Mill Brochure 2014 (2)*, *ULTRASLICE 2015*, and *Cold Chip-off for Digital Forensics(1)*. Also included on the companion site is the SWGDE Best Practices for Chip-Off PDF. This is titled *SWGDE_Best_Practices_for_Chip-Off*.

References

[1] Ultra Tec, ULTRASLICE 2015.pdf, p. 5.
[2] Ultra Tec Manufacturing, Introduction to Cold Chip-Off Equipment for Digital Forensics, January 20, 2017. https://vimeo.com/200313794.

BGA Cleaning

Introduction—Your First Car

The year was 1983. A 1967 Mercedes Benz 200D just had the 4-cylinder motor rebuilt by the author's father. The car was to be a high school graduation present, but the arrangement made between the author and his father involved hours helping with the motor rebuild. The four-door sedan had over 300,000 miles. The floorboard in the left rear passenger area was rusted out, and you could see the ground while sitting in the back. At that time, this was easily remedied with a rubber floor mat. The speedometer was a vertical bar, which changed colors as you increased speed. The windshield wipers also had a foot petal on the floor, which could be depressed to activate the wipers when there was a mist and you did not need them on full time.

The driver and passenger side windows had the small vent window, which had a black knob that when turned, opened or closed the vent. At that time, this car was the coolest thing the author owned. It was an oxidized brown color. The body was straight and, other than the rust, had no issues. Being a diesel, it averaged around 40 miles to the gallon. It was no "get-away" car, but there was no hurry when you drove it. At the time, the author had no idea it was a classic, it was simply his first car.

When you work hard at getting something, it seems to take on a new flavor, feel, and even a smell. During these teen years, there was a sense of pride that permeated the author's heart when he would sit, stare, or talk about it with his high school friends. It was washed and vacuumed every weekend, and usually waxed too. The unnecessary cleaning seemed to be endless and included the engine and undercarriage. Thinking back on his first car always involves images of scrubbing some part of it.

Fast forward over 30 years later. Now the excitement has manifested itself in another way. It is contained in the prospect of pulling a small memory chip, and getting it to "read." This time, the cleaning is completed in a macro area. It takes time and patience. Instead of finding the freedom that comes from your first ride, you may experience how satisfying it is to work on something which eventually leads to some answers in your case, or someone else. Or maybe someone lied to the case agent or other investigator. You scrub, clean, inspect, and repeat. Your car "wax" may now be compared to re-tinning or reballing. Your final reward is answers to this very small and delicate component. Maybe it is not your first exam, but you will more than likely be proud if you can get the chip to be recognized. Your first chip might even be "pretty ugly" and surprise you that it does read.

Do you remember your first car? It may have always got you where you needed to go, and you may have been quite proud to own it because of the work that was involved for you to get it to run. Cleaning was not necessary to make the car work, but you will soon realize how important it is to retrieve your answers from the memory.

Examples From Thermal Use

Once examiners remove the target chip from the board, they must begin the process of preparing the memory to be read. This will usually require cleaning the surface area. Just like the removal process, heat is again applied to the area for this cleaning purpose. In the last chapter, there were examples of adhesive on the sides of the memory during its removal. There can also be adhesive on the bottom, which can be around the Ball Grid Array (BGA) area or all over the bottom surface. This may be mixed in with the BGA solder. This is very common with Blackberry. In fact, Blackberry will coat this area under the chip quite heavily with their signature black glue.

There is no way of predetermining how much glue or excessive solder will need to be cleaned until the chip is lifted off the board. Some manufacturers will use adhesive on some models and not others. For instance, the Motorola XT912, which is shown in the previous chapter, uses little to no adhesive around the edges of the eMMC or on the bottom, near the BGA area. Fig. 28.1 shows a few different chips which have been removed using heat. The upper chip shows two different solder balls that are missing and remained on the main board (circled). The bottom image shows a chip that has solder smudging. This will cause shorts if not corrected, or damage the reader.

Figure 28.1
Examples of various chips removed using heat. Missing solder balls and solder smudging.

Equipment Used in Cleaning (Thermal)

There are different methods in which this BGA area can be cleaned. This chapter addresses the use of a spade soldering tip, liquid solder flux, cleaning brush, and denatured alcohol. Isopropyl alcohol of 90% and higher can also be used, but it will generally cost more than denatured.

- **Liquid solder flux.** Purpose: This keeps the solder from adhering to itself. When this is applied to the surface, the BGA solder points begin to get "re-tinned." Downside: The rosin is left behind and will need to be removed. This creates more work, but it is necessary for cleaning of the BGA area.
- **Spaded solder iron tip.** Purpose: The angle of this tip is ideal for cleaning the BGA area and re-tinning. The flat area allows more surface cleaning than a standard straight tip. Downside: It may at times be too big for the surface of the chip when trying to clean a specific area. Microsoldering units will also have angled tips available.
- **Cleaning brush (antistatic).** Purpose: The brush will be used in conjunction with the denatured alcohol. This will get heavy use as it is also needed to clean any solder flux that is left behind during the retinning process.
- **Denatured alcohol.** Purpose: A more cost-effective alternative to isopropyl alcohol. This is used to remove flux, glue, and other materials while scrubbing. It is applied to the cleaning brush and then to the surface area of the target chip.

When cleaning the BGA area, examiners should utilize a work board to keep their bench or counter top clean. The author uses the wooden board that is attached to the main board holder for this purpose. Fig. 28.2 is an image of the described items. The solder flux pictured is very sticky, and an alternative is the flux that is sold in a large syringe. It is more of a gel and does not have the stickiness of the flux shown. It will generally cost more.

Common items needed for cleaning the BGA area. (When heat is used for removal)

- Solder Flux (gel type also used)
- Spaded solder tip
- Cleaning brush (anti-static)
- Denatured Alcohol (or Isopropyl of 90% or higher)

Figure 28.2
Examples of the supplies recommended for cleaning the Ball Grid Array (BGA) area when the chip is removed using thermal.

Steps Involved in Cleaning (Thermal Removed)

- **Step 1—Use solder flux.** The first step in cleaning the chip is to apply a drop (small) of liquid solder flux to the BGA/adhesive area that needs to be cleaned. Make certain all the BGA solder balls have flux on them. This will prevent them from sticking to one another.
- **Step 2—Use the spaded solder tip.** Examiners will need to use a dental pick tool to hold the memory—**do not hold the chip with fingers, burns will occur.** Try initially to set the rework station soldering tip to 350°F. This temperature may need to be adjusted depending on how accurate your rework station is as well as how it performs at this temperature. If your chip has excess glue or raised BGA solder, the tip will be placed over the area of the memory to allow the entire area to make contact. Do not push too hard or scrape into the green area of the chip. The finesse involved here is hard to describe, but with repeated practice, you will understand how much pressure is correct and how much is too much. You will need to gently remove glue and raised solder off the BGA and surrounding area without damaging the circuitry underneath. You want the surface to be even, and not have some BGAs higher than others, or glue left behind. An uneven surface will affect the reader. Make certain a smoke absorber is on near the work area as the flux (rosin) will produce smoke immediately after the hot iron touches it. This vapor is harmful. With a light coat of rosin (flux) on the chip, it will be a common occurrence to

see small pieces of solder, glue, and rosin start to build up while you are scraping with the angle solder tip. Fig. 28.3 shows an example of what this may look like. This can be scrubbed away afterward. Dipping the nylon brush in the denatured alcohol (Fig. 28.2) and scrubbing vigorously (Fig. 28.3).

- **Step 3—Scrub, inspect, and repeat (if necessary).** Fig. 28.3 shows the chip after the initial scraping and scrubbing. Most of the glue is off the edges, but inspection shows that additional attention is needed to remove the remainder. Go back to the angled solder tip and hold the edge with a dental tool. Begin scraping the necessary areas. Again, do not push too hard or the important green material will come off the chip revealing and possibly damaging the circuits underneath. Fig. 28.3 shows the remaining glue being removed. During this scraping phase, it is not necessary to use the hot solder tip for the entire process. Using a plastic spudger, or even the handle end of a brush. You can work at getting off the pieces of rosin or glue. It is not uncommon for an examiner to have to scrape, inspect, and clean several times. The goal here is to try to get the entire area free of anything that would keep the chip from sitting evenly on the adaptor. The bottom right corner image within Fig. 28.3 is the finished memory before attempting re-tinning. It is not always necessary to retin every chip. The reason is that most of the adaptors have small spring loaded pogo pins that push up on the BGA area. If this area has been properly cleaned and there is enough solder to contact the pogo pins, then acquisition may take place.

✓ Apply Flux
✓ Clean with spade
✓ Scrub, inspect, repeat

Figure 28.3
Example of applying flux, using solder spade, scrubbing, inspecting, and repeating as needed (thermal removed chip).

- **Step 4—Retin if necessary.** This step is not always required. If you have cleaned your BGA area and all the areas have a good amount of solder left and it is evenly distributed on all the contacts, proceed to reading the memory. This is explained in upcoming pages. If some of the BGA areas need additional solder, then it may be necessary to retin. Most of the readers just require contact with the pinouts, and reballing is not necessary.
- **Step 5—Reball if necessary (S6/Note 5/others).** Many of the newer chips used in newer devices utilize a UFS (Universal Flash Storage) chip. The reader uses an adaptor that has conical pogo pins that will require contact with an actual ball instead of the pinout. Examiners will not be able to read these chips unless the chip is reballed.

The Re-tinning Process

There will be times when examiners will remove the chip from the main board, inspect the BGA area, and if there are no shorts (smudge) from the solder, they can try and read the memory using the supported adaptors. If the read is unsuccessful, they will begin the process of cleaning the BGA area, using the steps outlined earlier in this chapter under *"Step 3—Scrub, inspect, and repeat."*

If the binary fails to read through the supported adaptor, re-tinning may be necessary. Since most of the (non-UFS) adaptors utilized spring-loaded pogo pins, it is not necessary to reball the BGA.

The BGA area should be initially cleaned and inspected to see which BGAs under a microscope need additional work. Once it is determined that re-tinning is needed, the area must have rosin applied very sparingly to keep the solder used for re-tinning from smudging the BGAs.

Fig. 28.4 shows a small drop of liquid solder flux (rosin) being applied to the BGA area that needs to be re-tinned. The entire area may need rosin. Using a spaded tip can assist in this process. It helps move the solder evenly around the area. There are two ways to get the solder introduced to the BGA area for re-tinning:

1. Place a very small amount of solder paste onto the BGA area of the chip that contains the drop or drops of rosin as depicted in the left image within Fig. 28.4.
2. Hold the bladed tip and introduce solder to the tip until there is a small ball sticking on the blade—depicted in the right image within Fig. 28.5.

Using a solder wick alone is preferred to remove solder as shown earlier. This most likely should be applied prior to the chip, since it discolors/solidifies both metal flow's surface.

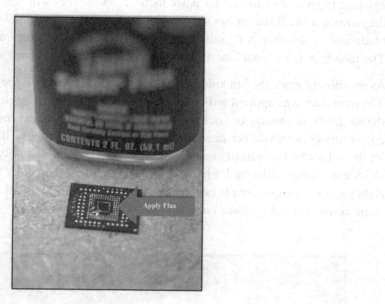

Figure 28.4
Example of how much solder flux to apply to chip.

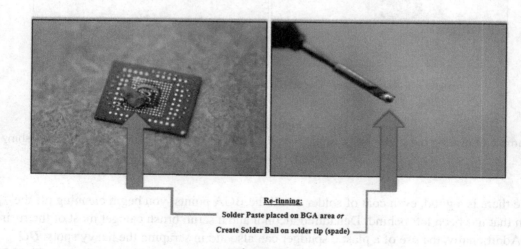

Re-tinning:
Solder Paste placed on BGA area *or*
Create Solder Ball on solder tip (spade)

Figure 28.5
Example of using solder paste or solder ball on spaded tip to retin the Ball Grid Array (BGA) area.

Using a solder iron (spade tip preferred) begin gliding the solder across the BGA area. There should be no "pushing" into the chip, simply allow the solder to ball up and flow over the existing BGAs. With the solder paste method, examiners will need to go back and forth until they create a small ball of hot solder. Eventually the ball will move to the tip of the solder blade and be the only part contacting the BGAs. The spade does need to scrape this area. The idea here is to "coat" the BGAs coming out of the chip with a fine coat of solder.

As examiners work the hot solder over the BGAs, they should see the points getting shiny. The rosin that was applied will help keep the solder from smudging or shorting the BGAs. If the solder does smudge or stick to each BGA, apply additional rosin sparingly. Note: The edge (copper) spots do not need re-tinning. During this process, do not scrape the BGA area; let the solder ball you have created "float" over this area. The only thing that should touch the BGA area is the solder ball. Fig. 28.6 is an example of the solder ball, and the image to the right shows the BGA area is becoming shiny. Roll the solder ball until all the points are the same consistent color (shiny) and are even.

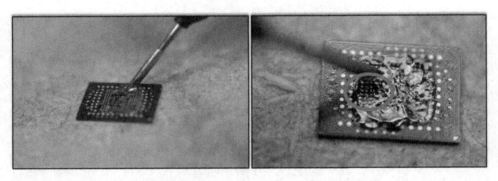

Using solder paste to create ball for tinning.

Using a solder ball on tip of solder iron to create ball for tinning. Note the shiny coating of solder now appearing on the BGA.

Figure 28.6
Example of moving the solder ball across the Ball Grid Array (BGA) area until the points are shiny and evenly coated (tinned).

Once there is a good, even coat of solder on all the BGA points, you begin cleaning off the rosin that has been left behind. Denatured alcohol and a scrub brush can get most of the rosin off. Additionally, the use of a plastic spudger can also aid in scraping the heavy spots. ***DO NOT USE ANY METAL TOOLS*** in this area to scrape off rosin—BGAs could get pulled off inadvertently, or the chip board could get scraped and damaged. The process of re-tinning may be necessary more than once. Fig. 28.7 is an image of a static-free scrub brush being used to clean off the rosin left behind from re-tinning. The brush would be dipped in alcohol or denatured alcohol prior to scrubbing.

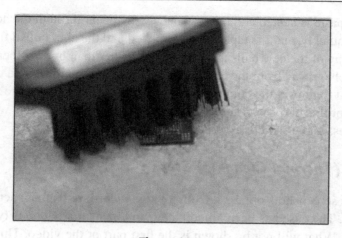

Figure 28.7
Image of an antistatic scrub brush being used to clean off the rosin left behind—dipped in alcohol or denatured alcohol first.

A typical work flow would be as follows: Using a heat process, examiners will pull the memory, and inspect the BGA area. No BGA (smudge) shorts—try to read. *No read*—clean and scrape glue, and excess solder from the BGA area as needed. Try to read again. *No read*—retin the BGA surface and clean off rosin. Try reading again. *No read*—inspect under microscope and just retin the BGAs that need it. Clean and try reading again. Repeat these steps as necessary. If re-tinning has failed after a few attempts, the chip may need to be reballed.

Reballing

There are common methods used for placing new balls onto the chip. One involves a stencil with solder paste. Another method uses premade BGA balls that are sized based on the configuration of the chip. The last would employ automated equipment that performs this function, and in some cases like the Zevac machine, can suction up the old solder prior to reballing.

Most businesses or police agencies will not invest in a high-end machine dedicated to reballing chips. Instead, examiners will utilize inexpensive stencils to reball. The most common chips encountered that will need reballing (at the time of this writing) are UFS. As previously mentioned, this is caused by the type of reader being used.

Stencils are designed to align the chip with the preconfigured holes for that model chip. The stencils are usually made from tin or aluminum and must be the same width BGA as was originally on the chip. Once the chip is properly aligned with the holes in the stencil, it is held in place with aluminum or Kapton tape on the opposite side. Low heat solder paste is gently spread through the stencil holes on the opposite (taped) side. Excess paste is wiped off. Using hot air, the solder paste is heated and the new balls will appear through the holes in the template. It cools quickly, and the tape can be removed and the chip pulled from the stencil and inspected. If any of the new balls are irregular or higher than one another, a heat gun can be used several inches away from the chip to allow the solder to reform to a consistent height. It will be important to not get the chip too hot during this process. There are several vendors who sell stencils for this purpose. There are numerous videos on YouTube, which document the reballing process using stencils.

Case Example (Thermal Cleaning) Steps

The following are screenshots obtained from a video recording from an actual case in the Puget Sound area. The case has been adjudicated, and the actual video is typically used for training purposes. What will not be shown is the first part of the video. This contains a dry erase board with the case number, date of exam, case agent, examiner name, type of crime, and make and model of phone. The dry erase board is used to take still images of the evidence as it is disassembled. Once the heat shields are removed, the process is video recorded using a microscope camera. The still images and video are then combined into one video. This was surrendered to the prosecutor and defense. In Chapter 4, we discussed the destructive court order. If you recall, it explained that the process would be recorded. So in this example, it provides some of the steps without images, and others with still images of the video. Be aware that some of the images will have blurry aspects as there is a lag. Most of the items that are blurry are the nozzle from the rework unit, the solder spade that is moving back and forth during the cleaning, and the spade. All of these images are contained on the companion site.

- Step 1—Slate image of the evidence (grease board). Contains necessary information about the case and the evidence in stages of disassembly. Use still digital photography. (No example shown.)
- Step 2—Remove any necessary heat shield (cans) and place the phone main board into a holder for thermal removal. (No example shown.)
- Step 3—Begin the process of removing any adhesive around the sides of the chip using rework heat and spade. Feather in the heat from the sides of the chip. Do not keep the heat in one place too long. See Fig. 28.1 (companion site).
- Step 4—Once the adhesive has been scrapped off, move the heat evenly over the top of the chip, covering the entire area, pry very softly to check the chip to determine if it can be lifted off. Do not pry on corners or force the chip off the board. See Fig. 28.2 (companion site).
- Step 5—Lift the chip off. In this example, Step 5 is a continuation of Step 4, and the chip is simply flipped over to be documented. See Fig. 28.3 (companion site).
- Step 6—Document the removal at this state. This may or may not apply to your lab. See Fig. 28.4 (companion site).

- Step 7—Apply flux (rosin) to the BGA area and begin cleaning using a spaded tipped soldering iron. Hold the chip with another tool. Clean, and repeat as necessary. This example does not show the scrubbing, as the video was blurry during that step. See Fig. 28.5 (companion site). In this image, the bottom right picture shows an example of scrubbing too hard during the cleaning process. Part of the copper is showing through the board. This did not affect the read, but easily could have. This is an easy mistake to make if you do not take your time.
- Step 8—Use an appropriate model chip reader, a validated write blocker, and begin imaging the chip (steps are shown in the next chapter—*Creating an image*).

Chapter Summary Key Points

When an examiner has used a thermal process to remove the memory, the BGA area will need to be inspected prior to placing it into a reader. In many cases, there will be adhesive and excess solder that will need to be addressed prior to reading. Solder flux, a solder iron spaded tip, isopropyl alcohol (or denatured alcohol), solder paste or solder, and an antistatic brush will be key components and equipment needed to clean, and retin the area for the contents to be read. Depending on your department or work policy, the process may need to be recorded.

There will also be some chips that need to be reballed in order for the reader to make contact with the required BGAs. One method used in reballing is the use of stencils that fit the target chip pattern. These can be held in place with Kapton or foil tape. Use low heat solder paste when reballing as some chips are very sensitive to heat and can be damaged.

Cleaning memory chips will require finesse and patience. Also, has there been a mention in this book of practice?

CHAPTER 29

Creating an Image

Information in This Chapter

- Examples from thermal use
- Reading the memory
- Using the UP 828 and 828P Programmers
- DediProg NuProg-E Programmer
- SD style adaptors
- Imaging with FTK
- Regular expression searching

Introduction—Fish On!

When you have been involved with local law enforcement for over 25 years, you become accustomed to working with equipment that "fits" within a specified budget and training parameters. Your duty weapon may be one choice, or you may even have to purchase it yourself. The vehicle you drive on duty may be a marked unit, or a specific fleet of unmarked vehicles, all the same make and model.

These choices may carry over to the forensic laboratory as well. The "tool box" for chip-off examinations may require proprietary readers, specific adaptors, and programming equipment that may or may not fall into the purchasing requirements that local municipalities often are subjected to.

Let us pretend that you have everything you need for your chip-off examination. The chip was removed using a nonthermal process, and the Ball Grid Array (BGA) area looks great and is ready to read. You utilize one of the adaptors discussed in this chapter and follow imaging steps also suggested. There will be a moment when you plug in the reader, and you stare at a screen, hoping to see proof of all the labor you have invested up to that point. It is the same feeling if you have ever rebuilt an engine and turn the key over for the first time. Or if you are trying to fish and your pole tip jiggles, then suddenly bends downward. It is that anticipation that you will get to see something that up until

Seeking the Truth from Mobile Evidence. http://dx.doi.org/10.1016/B978-0-12-811056-0.00029-7
Copyright © 2018 Elsevier Inc. All rights reserved.
429

that point was just visualization. It sounds funny saying it, but the author still feels a sense of satisfaction when he can look into the partitions of the chip from a homicide or other crime, and know that everything appears to be ready for one of the last steps in the destructive forensics process.

There will be times when the screen on the forensic machine will populate with a window that asks the user if he wants to format the disk. You may know already what the author is relating to, or you may be brand new to the chip-off process. Either way, your hope is that the window shows up after all the work that went into the removal, cleaning, retinning, and maybe even reballing. It is the same celebration some of us shout sitting on a boat, floating on a body of water. We get up early, drive for miles, pack all the gear in. Then we cast out and watch (just like the computer screen). After minutes or hours, then suddenly it is, *"FISH ON!"* Big smiles appear on our face, and at the same time, there is a little adrenaline release.

Reading the Memory

If the chip has been cleaned and it appears that the BGA will make contact with the adaptor pogo pins, the examiner may elect to try and read the memory. As previously mentioned, some chips will come off the phone and can be imaged with no cleaning whatsoever. If there is glue residue or large amounts of solder across the BGA (smudge), *DO NOT try and read the memory*. Again, if the surface is uneven for these reasons or the BGAs have solder shorting them, damage could occur to the adaptors.

Several examples of various readers used by the author; and many others in law enforcement, will be provided in upcoming pages and on the companion site. First, let us address a more elaborate reader used in such laboratories as the Netherlands Forensic Institute (NFI). The NFI created their own chip reader. This is called the NFI Memory Toolkit II. The NFI Memory Toolkit II combines both hardware and software into one unit. Most readers are independent of the software that is used to read the contents of the chip. NFI's GUI is written in C++ and Qt. It can be configured with the pins for the memory chip in signal layouts. XML files are used to access the memory. Such things as signal layout, memory type, power supply, and size can be edited through this XML file.

Many law enforcement agencies will utilize chip programmers. These were designed to "flash" data to blank chips. For forensic purposes, they can also be used to read the contents of a chip. They will often support many models and configurations of memory on the market. Here are just a few examples:

SU-6808 eMMC Gang 8 Programmer/Duplicator

This is a stand-alone unit that uses one master source and up to eight blank spots. The source memory/configuration can come from eMMC, SD card, or a PC.

C-Ming Technologies: IPM-1DX eMMC—eMCP Production Programmer

This unit works similar to the SU-6808; however, it also supports programming to the eMCP. This is also a 1-to-8 unit.

XELTEK Superpro 6100

This programmer supports flashing files up to 256 GB. It also supports a number of variants to the BGA configuration. Even though the unit has one adaptor, they can be configured to work simultaneously (similar to a daisy chain).

FlashPAK III

There are some law enforcement laboratories in Canada that use products from *Data IO*. One of the models used is called the FlashPAK III. This is a 1-in-4 programmer. It supports a number of different flash memory types, to include NOR, NAND, MCP, MMC, eMMC, SD, MoviNAND, OneNAND, iNAND, Serial Flash, EEPROM, EPROM, and devices with microcontrollers built in.

Data IO has a standard 5 years of support with an option to extend the support yearly. It not only can perform read and write functions, but also has advanced testing abilities. Here are a few additional links to various model adaptors that can be used to read and program flash memory:

http://www.deepspar.com/products-pc-3000-drive.html
http://www.xeltek.com/industries/digital-forensics/computer-mobile-chip-off-forensic-tools-for-data-extraction-from-mobile-device-chips/
https://www.dataman.com/
http://www.bpmmicro.com/
https://www.elnec.com/en/

Using the UP 828 and 828P Programmers

A popular model programmer being used by law enforcement agencies is the "UP" brand. These units are commonly used with various training vendors who instruct chip-off forensics. Compared with the previously described "gang" and high-capacity programmers, these are somewhat more affordable. Fig. 29.1 depicts images of the UP 828P Ultra Programmer with an adaptor inserted. The UP 828 Ultra Programmer looks identical to the 828P.

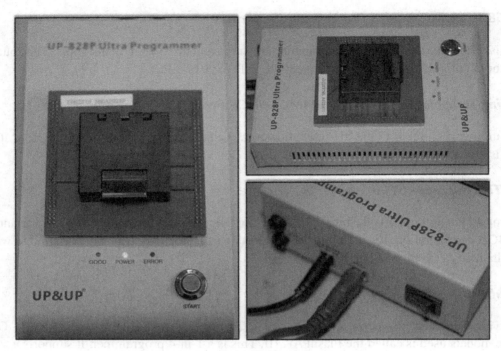

Figure 29.1
Image of the UP 828P Ultra Programmer with an adaptor inserted.

The use of the 828 and 828P UP programmers will require specialized adaptors that are designed to fit specific memory types. The GUI of the software allows the examiner to look up the supported memory by make and chip part number printed on the chip. The adaptors for the 828 and the 828P will fit into the programmer, but they are not backwards compatible with one another. The adaptors can cost anywhere from $200 to over $700 each. *These are memory programmers—settings that "write" or "erase" should never be used for forensic acquisitions*. Forensic examiners should not use the silver "START" button located on the front of the programmer. This would be used for writing data to a blank supported chip. When the software and drivers are installed, and the unit has been powered on and plugged into the PC, the interface will indicate that the programmer is "online" in the lower left corner. The software can also run in demo mode when the programmer is not attached to the PC.

Once the actual tool has been confirmed within the GUI of the 828P Programmer, click on the *Select* button. This can also be located under *Device—Select Device* or hot key *F3*. When the Select (Device) setting has been clicked, users will see another window present itself. This will contain all the supported devices the 828P Programmer supports. The manufacturers and chip part numbers are listed alphabetically or numerically, depending on which way a user is searching. Directly below the Manufacturer box will be the ***Device Info*** pane. This will populate with information as it corresponds with what has been selected in the main ***Device/Package/Adapter*** pane.

Examiners can use the keyword search box at the top of this window and begin typing the part number that is printed on the chip itself. There may be times when the use of magnification and/or cleaning the area will be necessary to view the chip part number.

As the letters and numbers of the chip part number are typed into the keyword search box, the user will see only the available choices that are supported display in the *Device/Package/Adaptor* area.

Adaptors (828/828P)

The appropriate adaptor must be inserted into the UP 828P Programmer prior to selecting the part number. Fig. 29.1 depicts the programmer with an adaptor already inserted. Fig. 29.2 shows examples of the SBGA202AP adaptor being selected and inserted into the appropriate slots of the unit. The arrow in Fig. 29.2 shows the direction of the adaptor opening in conjunction with the programmer. The opening points toward the start button on the unit. It is very important that examiners insert the required adaptor(s) for their examinations in the correct manner to avoid damage to the small pins.

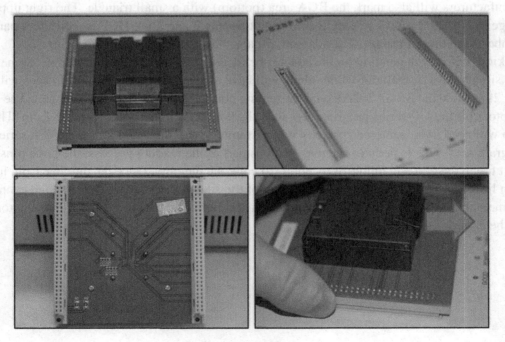

Figure 29.2
Image of the correct way to insert the adaptors into the 828/828P Programmers.

Once the adaptor has been properly inserted, users would select the appropriate selection for their target chip number. Once the device selection is made, the GUI will display that particular memory configuration within the interface of the software.

The *Device Info* pane will show at this point. The ***NAND Organization*** reveals our size. Also of importance is the ***Device ID***.

Side note: In the JTAG chapter, some of these values are discussed when explaining the JTAG Finder tool from *100RandomTasks*. The BSDL file is also addressed, which would narrow down some of the possibilities during the JTAG scan.

In this case, if we need to JTAG map this phone using our ***RandomTask*** finder, and the laboratory you worked in also had this 828P Programmer software installed, a user could locate the values needed for the JTAG scan registry fields. The software for the UP Programmers is free and, as mentioned, can operate in demo mode without a programmer attached.

Examiners must properly place the chip in the adaptor for the contents to be read properly. This must be done in a particular manner, ensuring the number 1 pin is lined up correctly within the adaptor. Fig. 29.3 shows the correct orientation using a Samsung chip (redacted). A circled location of this pin is shown in Fig. 29.3. There is usually a round circle printed on the top of the chip. It may be white or black, which can be hard to recognize. Some manufacturers will also mark the BGA area (bottom) with a small triangle. The right upper image in Fig. 29.3 shows an eMCP chip depicting this (Note: the eMCP is a different part number from our Samsung). The adaptor will also have a corresponding marking. This marking will vary depending on the adaptor being used. Some will have a triangle; some will simply have a small dot while others will have a clear arrow. The bottom images within Fig. 29.3 show the SBGA202AP adaptor seating correctly in the 828P Programmer. The adaptors for the UP-series programmers will all show this circle for the number 1 pin. The chip will need to be centered correctly when examiners use the adaptors for the 828 series programmers. This is perhaps the most tedious part of the reading process: the pogo pins must touch the corresponding BGA points to copy the memory. Once the number 1 pin has been lined up against the same number 1 pin of the adaptor, examiners must try and center the memory evenly on each side. When this has been accomplished, the lid of the adaptor can be closed.

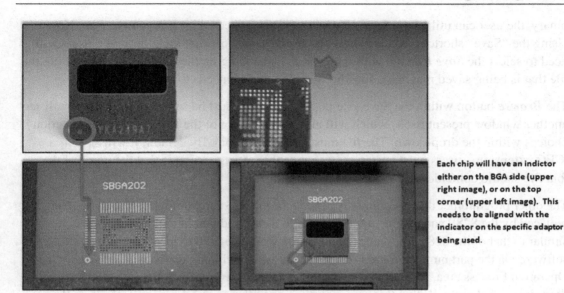

Each chip will have an indictor either on the BGA side (upper right image), or on the top corner (upper left image). This needs to be aligned with the indicator on the specific adaptor being used.

Figure 29.3
Example of the chip #1 indicator, and the #1 indicator on the programming adapter (828P depicted).

At this point, you would go back to the GUI of the 828P software and select the ***Read*** button from the interface, which can be accomplished in a couple different ways. After selecting the ***Read*** button, another pop-up window will present itself. This will be the ***ONENAND_Skip— Ready to read*** window. The next step would be to uncheck the "Check Device ID" and ensure that under the ***Read Options*** the ***Verify after Read*** and ***Read all blocks*** are checked. The remainders of the settings are left as default.

After these settings are set click on "Ok." The next pop-up window will show the users the pin configuration. The pins that display red are "Poor contact" connections and the green pins are "Good contact" connections. Examiners will need to move the chip around and/or continue to clean the BGA area until they establish a 100% green pin connection.

During this phase, examiners may need to clean, scrub, and inspect the BGA contact area several times. The use of a microscope can help troubleshoot areas that need to be focused on. There may be times when a thermal extraction results in a chip that comes off "clean", and can be read without any cleaning. After several chip-off examinations, users will become better at inspecting the BGA area to determine this. Unless there is an obvious short (BGA smudge) across two of the BGA points, reading can certainly be attempted before cleaning. Examiners should also make sure that the surface is even and there are no areas with "high spots" that may bend the pogo pins. Hold the chip sideways while inspecting, and if necessary, use magnification.

After the memory read has taken place, the checksum will follow. At this point, the memory has only been read into the program buffer. It still needs to be saved. To save the file as a binary, the user can utilize the *Save File* button. This is located in: *File—Save File*. Note: Using the "Save" shortcut icon will also access the same software area; however, users will need to select the *Save File* tab within this area. Depending on the memory configuration, the file that is being saved may have specific ways in which it needs to be saved.

The *Browse* button within the Save File pop-up window must be selected next. Users will see another window present itself, which will allow the naming of the file and two file selection choices within the drop-down. The file must be saved as .bin. By default, it will save as a .CEO extension—<u>users must ensure they change this</u>. A suggestion is that the name of the .bin file should coincide with the model of the phone.

The other programmer that is commonly used is the UP 828 Programmer. The 828 has been replaced by the 828P and may be more difficult to locate and purchase. The software is very similar to that of the 828P. The same *Select* button would be used to locate the chip within the software via the part number. *Read* is clicked next, which will pop up the window. Under the Operation Process area, there is a subarea labeled *Check Device*. Click the (+) sign to open the drop-down of choices. Within this area, users can open the *Access Area* and *Operation Process* settings. The Check Device (+) button being pressed will reveal the additional settings (*Insertion Test/Short Test/Check Device ID*). Ensure that the *Check Device* selection is unchecked and the *Insertion Test* is checked. The remaining boxes from all other fields in this "Ready" window can remain set with their default settings. The *Insertion Test* screen is like the *Insertion State* screen that displays on the 828P software. Once the BGA pins all line up correctly in the adaptor, the memory will begin reading. The file can be saved and labeled based on the model of phone it was removed from. Users will see a pop-up window that shows after the memory read has completed. This is to allow the calculation of the checksum. Once the file has been read, it needs to be saved. This can be accomplished under the *File—Save File* area, which will present a window allowing the user to save the memory. There are three different types of files within the drop-down of the Save: *Project Files, Binary files,* and *INTEL HEX files*.

Again, the model phone should be the name inputted into the *File name* area. After creating a binary file from either the 828P or 828 Programmers, the file must be hashed prior to being read. Free hashing tools such as MD5Summer can be used for this purpose.

SD Adaptors

Another popular type of flash memory reader is the *SD* style. These will be made with specific chip size configurations. Some can read more than one type of chip by changing the holder that is used to line up the BGA points to the pogo pins. Unlike the 828/828P adaptors, the user does not need to manually align the memory within the adaptor, as the chip snuggly fits into the area based on its size. The number 1 pin still needs to be properly aligned, and that is generally the only issue. A properly cleaned chip would be placed into one of the supported SD readers, connected to a validated hardware USB write blocker, and then imaged with FTK Imager or a similar imaging tool.

Sireda Adaptors

This brand of memory reader is usually built with a metal housing. They will usually cost more and can be sold in kits by such vendors as Teel Technologies. Some of the common sizes for eMCP profile are 11.5×13 and 12×16 mm. The eMMC common sizes are 14×18, 12×18, 12×16, 11.5×13, and 11×10 mm.

ANDK All-in-One SD Adaptors

There are also some cheaper alternatives available. One such brand is the ANDK all-in-one SD adaptors. These come equipped with interchangeable inserts to read six different configurations as follows: eMCP: 12×16 and 11.5×13 mm, eMMC: 9×11, 11×10, 11.5×13, 12×16, 12×18, and 14×18 mm. When using any of these SD adaptors, examiners will need to ensure the 1 pin location is correctly orientated each time the selected holder size is inserted. Two screws hold the holder in place.

These ANDK readers cost a fraction of the price of the Sireda adaptors, and there are some experts who frown on using "cheaper" equipment. The author has a set of both ANDK and Sireda. The ANDK brand has been used for a few years during lab practical assignments at the university, as well as with criminal cases. They have in many cases been able to read chips when the Sireda has failed. They are definitely not built as well as the Sireda, but they do function properly.

Fig. 29.4 provides examples of the Sireda adaptors at the top of the image and ANDK all-in-one adaptors at the bottom.

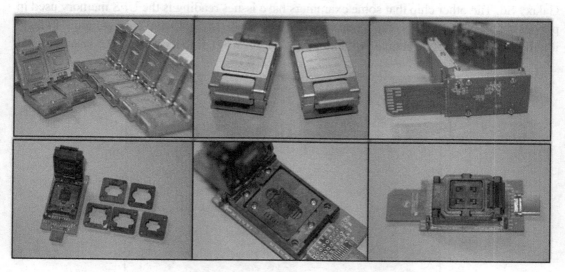

Figure 29.4
Examples of the Sireda and ANDK all-in-one SD Adaptors to read memory.

DediProg NuProg-E Programmer

Examiners may find the need to use a programmer that can obtain the data from some of the newer designed chips. This will include UFS memory and other eMMC configurations. There will be some phone models that contain UFS chips that will be encrypted. This was previously addressed, and the chip number should be researched prior to removing the memory. If, however, the chip is not encrypted, users will need a specific programmer to read the information if it is a newer chip not supported by other programmers. At the time of this writing, one common programmer is manufactured by Depiprog Technology Company, called the *NuProg-E*. This programmer works like the UP Programmer but is one-third of the size and weight. It uses interchangeable adaptors. Of significant importance is that <u>examiners must reball the chips before attempting to read them using this adaptor.</u>

One common adaptor that may be needed is the FBGA153, which fits the UFS chip used in many of the Samsung S7's and other phones. The other adaptor is the BGA095, which fits the Samsung S6 phones. This chip has BGA points on only two sides of the chip. The chip will be a package-on-package configuration. This type of chip was popular on older style BlackBerrys. The chip is very susceptible to damage through thermal removal. There are a couple recommendations. One method employs the use of a electric "hot" knife. These are designed for cutting foam core board. The author used one that is sold at a hobby store, and is made by Walnut Hollow (walnuthollow.com). It comes with two angled razor blades, (screw-in style) tips.The other method is to cut the entire package on package configuration off the main board and polish from the bottom. If the polish method is used, do not polish too far. Removing too much material is easy to do, and remember that only two sides are necessary for reading. The center does not contact any BGAs but may have adhesive present. Fig. 29.5 is a UFS chip from an Samsung Galaxy S6. The other chip that some examiners have issues reading is the UFS memory used in phones such as the S7. This chip looks very like an eMMC 11.5×13 mm configuration. In fact, it will fit into an SD style adaptor without any issue but will fail to read. Fig. 29.6 is an image of

Figure 29.5
Image of a UFS chip from a Samsung S6.

Figure 29.6
Image of a UFS chip from a Samsung S7.

this UFS chip. As mentioned at the start of this section, this chip and all chips read with the NuProg-E adaptor, will require reballing.

The NuProg-E is sold with the programmer, power supply, USB cable, and the software. The software included in the box will more than likely be an older version than what is available online. The adaptors can only go into the programmer one way. Once the installation is complete, plug the device into the computer and ensure that it is also powered on. Correct any driver issues within Device Manager before continuing. Once the software has acknowledged that it sees the programmer, unplug the device from the machine, and close the program. After the targeted chip has been reballed, place it correctly into the adaptor. With the BGA095 chip, the BGA area will have two different widths that will correspond with the adaptor. One will have two rows of pins and the other three rows. Line the chip up accordingly. The FBGA153 adaptor will have a round circle indentation on the bottom left side of the adaptor. Line this up with the one pin indicator on the chip. Once the chip has been reballed and properly inserted into the adaptor, the adaptor should be seated into the programmer (if not already). Plug the programmer into the host machine and power on the programmer. Examiners may see Windows recognizing the device with pop-up windows related to Device Manager. When users first installed the program, there are four different aspects of the program that may be confusing. If shortcut icons were created during the install, these are called ***Dediware, Dediware CLI, NuProg_UFS,*** and ***NuProg_eMMC***. **If you are attempting to read a UFS chip, you will need to launch the NuPog_UFS icon**. This is one of the most common mistakes made when using this programmer: UFS chip models will *not* be located under the NuProg_eMMC software.

The GUI of the program will have an icon near the upper left titled ***Detect.*** This will begin autodetecting the supported chip. If the chip is seen by the programmer, it will populate the information in the dialog box within the program. The next icon to select is the ***ReadIC*** button. This will bring up a window that by default shows the ***RPMB*** (Replay Protected Memory

Block) subsystem area. From this window, near the top, users can choose to move off the default RPMB selection and select other partitions. These are referred to as *LUN* (Logical Unit Number). Look for the LUN that shows a high number of megabytes of information. This can be seen by looking at the main log window screen or going down and looking at the hexadecimal address length for each LUN. It is usually LUN0, and the other LUN locations will have just a few megabytes of nonevidential data or none at all. Once the correct partition is selected, select the *Save Memory From* button (leave the settings alone—as it will default to the entire partition size). After selecting the Save Memory From button, another window will pop-up and display, "*The data of regional automatic alignment to 0x00000000 ~ 0x772bfffff*", would you still want to save?" Be aware the ending address will vary based on the size of *your* particular chip and how much data has been stored on it. Select "Yes." The next window that will show will be the "*Editor Save*" option. Choose a location to save the file. Be aware of the size you are saving and ensure there is adequate space on the target location. Again, it is recommended to create a file name that coincides with the model of the phone, and in the *FileFilter* drop-down, choose the *Binary File(*.bin)* option. These steps are fundamental steps on how to use this programmer to read a UFS chip. Most investigators will purchase this reader for that exact purpose. Be aware there are other settings within the software GUI. These settings allow the user to navigate to the chip in question, and can be used instead of the autodetection. On the companion site (Chapter 29), the author has created a PDF titled "*NuProg-E_steps*." Examiners can refer to this as a quick reference guide for reading a UFS chip. It contains images along with five simple steps. It is important to understand that DediProg Technologies is not liable for improper use or loss of data while using this product. Also, DediProg Technologies creates support for chip manufacturers who currently share their configurations. This information is subject to change, and as such, DediProg Technologies has no control over which models are contained within their software. This section of the book only covers two adaptor models. There are many other adaptors available, and if necessary, readers should contact the vendor directly for additional models that may be supported.

Imaging

One of the last steps involved with a chip-off examination is the actual reading of the contents. If your laboratory has invested in the SD style readers, many of the phones examined will have chips that fit in these styles of readers. They are easier to use and obviously do not require proprietary software to interface with the adaptor.

If the decision is to use any of the previously mentioned SD memory readers, or any other brand, the device will need to be hardware write blocked during the process. If you already performed computer forensics, you are more than familiar with write blockers. This part of the chapter will be straightforward for you: simply write block the reader and create a complete image. Hash the results. Do not fragment the image; keep the entire .bin file in one single file.

For the rest of the readers that may have never experienced creating an image file from flash memory, the following is a recommendation on the process. This will include using a cheaper hardware-based write-blocker and free software to conduct the imaging.

Hardware Write Blocker

There are many hardware solutions when it comes to write blocking. Some cost more than others. If you already have a Cellebrite kit, then you should have their memory card reader included. This is very useful for this purpose. Before using this card reader, examiners should ensure that they validate that it write blocks on a nonevidential chip. The reader can accept SD/MMC series products, which is where the SD memory adaptor you used will be inserted. The writer blocker models that were used by the author also had the ability to R/W (Read–Write) or Read Only. This will need to be set to Read Only. The card reader will illuminate an LED that signifies "Write Block" is operational. Fig. 29.7 depicts a hardware write blocker and a Sireda adaptor inserted.

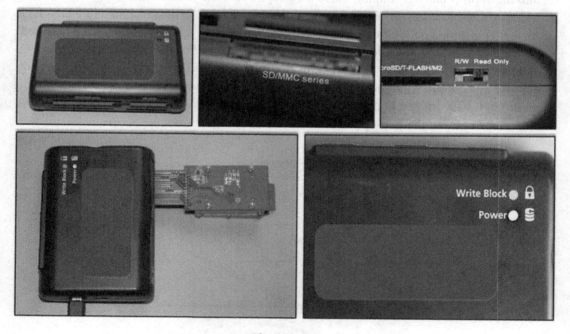

Figure 29.7
Example of the Cellebrite Forensic Memory Card Reader being used with a Sireda SD adaptor.

Using FTK Imager

AccessData's FTK (Forensic Tool Kit) Imager is a free program that can be used to create an image from the memory. There are other free utilities that can create an image, and

EnCase also has the same ability. In this chapter, we will only address the use of FTK Imager. When the card reader is inserted into a Windows machine to be read, users may see the "Microsoft Windows" pop-up window that displays, *"You need to format the disk in drive C: before you can use it. Do you want to format it?"* Because you are using a write blocker, selecting "Format disk" will not do anything to the target chip. The best practice is to select "Cancel." Here are some general steps when using FTK Imager to create an image from your target chip. These steps include a preliminary step of viewing the actual partitions of your target memory. Viewing the partitions is not actually necessary—but can save time if the examiner actually images a chip that does not show valid or incomplete partition information. It may take a few examinations for some of you to completely understand how the partitions should look. The author's preference is to view the partitions before creating an image. You can jump directly to step 6 if you prefer to not look at the partition structure first:

1. The chip should have already been removed and properly cleaned/inspected and placed into the appropriate SD adaptor. Place the adaptor into the Cellebrite USB (Forensic Memory Card Reader) write blocker. Plug the device into the host machine in which FTK Imager is installed on. Some machines will show a pop-up window as they have detected the chip as a mass storage device and will prompt users to Format disk. Select "Cancel" and proceed to step 2. Note: <u>Not all chips that are connected using the write blocker will activate this pop-up window. If examiners do not see this window present itself, they must go through FTK Imager to determine if they can see the drive letter for the chip.</u> Fig. 29.8 shows examples of the pop-up window and FTK settings.

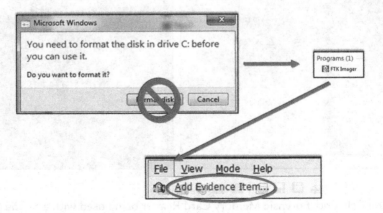

Figure 29.8

Example of the "format the disk" window that may appear after write blocker insertion, and the "Add Evidence Item" selection within FTK Imager.

2. Open FTK Imager and ensure that you can see the partitions to the chip. Select *File— Add Evidence Item.*

3. If the chip has been properly connected to the host machine, it will be "seen" as a storage drive. Examiners will select *"Physical Drive"* from the *Select Source* window. Fig. 29.9 provides an example of the "Select Source" window with "Physical Drive" selected.

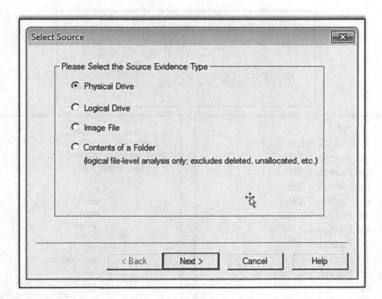

Figure 29.9
Example of the "Select Source" window in FTK with "Physical Drive" selected.

4. The actual drive letter for the chip must be located within the drop-down. If examiners do not see their drive for the chip, then they have either not cleaned it properly, inserted the number 1 pin wrong, or may have damaged the chip. To help facilitate not making a mistake, unplug any peripherals (thumb drives, phones, etc.) from the host machine.

5. Once the proper drive for the memory is selected, double-click on the physical drive that should now show in the *Evidence Tree* within FTK. Examiners should see many partitions for the memory if they selected the correct drive letter. If you are examining an Android device, look for the partition that contains all the application data. These will begin with a "com." naming configuration. This will be where most of your evidence will reside. With an Android OS, these are contained in the *userdata/root/ data* folder.

Fig. 29.10 is an example of the drive letter for a 16 GB chip that was connected through the write blocker. Like any other drive, the actual size will vary from what actually appears for the size (16 is listed in the phone specs, but 15 GB is shown).

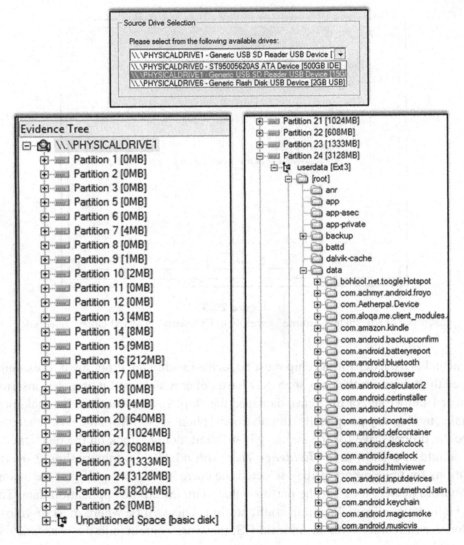

Figure 29.10

Example of selecting the appropriate drive letter for the chip, and viewing the *userdata* partition area.

6. Once examiners have verified that they have a valid memory configuration showing within FTK Imager, they must now create an image of the memory. To create an image using FTK Imager, select *File—Export Disk Image.* This will bring up the *"Create Image"* window. Select the location where they want the image file to be stored, by clicking the *"Add"* button underneath the "Image Destination(s)" area. When the "Add" button is selected, the *"Select Image Type"* will present to the user. Select *"Raw (dd),"* which is the default selection. Fig. 29.11 provides an example of these settings.

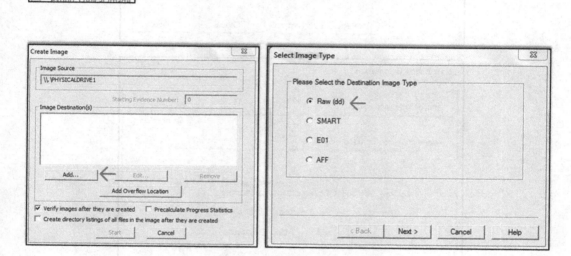

Export Disk Image > Select Add > Select Raw (dd)

Figure 29.11
Example of the *Export Disk Image* button, *CreateImage Window*, and *Select Image Type Windows*.

7. After the Raw (dd) Image Type has been selected and examiners have selected "Next," the *"Evidence Item Information"* window will present itself. This will be part of the image manifest that provides information regarding the case, most importantly the verified before and after hash results. *"Select Image Destination."* Select a location for the image to be stored by clicking on *"Browse."* Under the *"Image Filename (Excluding Extension),"* examiners must create a name for the file. Examiners must change the "Image Fragment Size (MB)" to "0". Figs. 29.12 and 29.13 show these settings. Fig. 29.13 depicts examples of the required fields entered with the model name of the phone and the Image Fragment Size (MB) set to the required "0" setting.

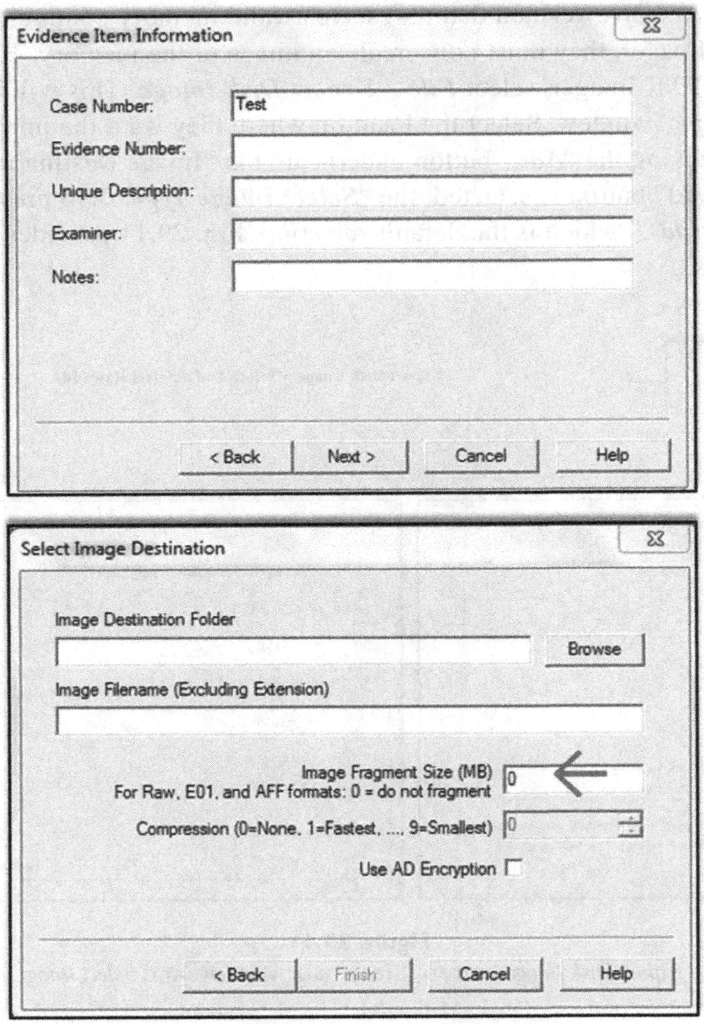

Figure 29.12
Example of the required fields showing blank.

8. When the required areas within the "***Select Image Destination***" window have been addressed, select "Finish." After "Finish" is clicked, the "***Create Image***" button will populate. The "***Verify images after they are created***" should be checked by default. Click "Start."

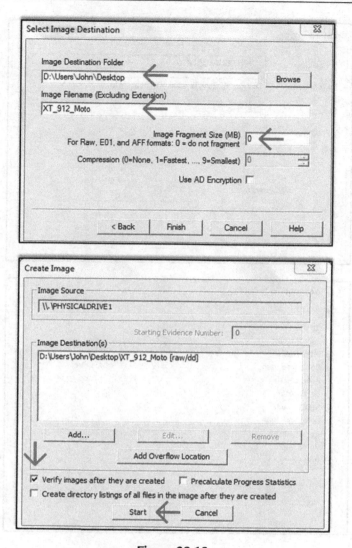

Figure 29.13

9. Examiners will see a "Creating Image…" window that displays the progress of the image they are creating. When this process finishes, the status will change to verifying. When the verifying process has finished, examiners will see a *"Drive/Image Verify Results"* window. The top image within Fig. 29.14 shows the "Creating Image…" window after the imaging was started. The bottom image shows the finished "Drive/Image Verify Results" window that will pop up after the imaging finishes.

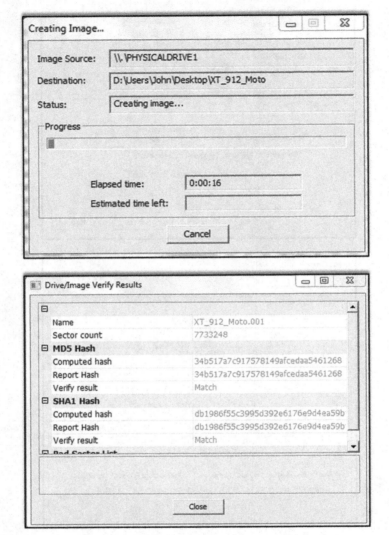

Figure 29.14
Examples of the *Creating Image and Drive/Image Verify Results* windows.

10. Examiners will navigate to the location where they created the image. Next to the actual image file will be a text file manifest. Open this file and inspect the results to ensure the image file is verified. The before and after hash results should match. Be aware, there are some flash memory configurations that have their own built-in controller. This can affect the hash result. In this case, hash the partition that contains the user data independently from the entire .bin file. This situation is not commonly encountered. Fig. 29.15 provides an example of the text manifest file with a close-up of the verified areas.

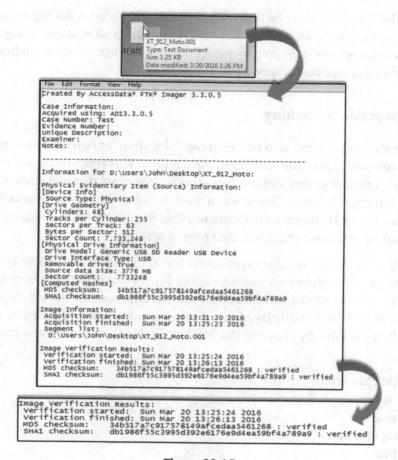

Figure 29.15
Example of the hash verification manifest from FTK Imager.

There is also another way to simply create a disk image with FTK. *Select File—Create Disc Image*. Examiners will have to follow some of the previously described steps and point to the drive letter, *Select Image Type, Evidence Item Information, Destination Folder, Image Filename,* and *Fragment size.*

Users should focus on the hash results and address any discrepancy if noted. On the companion site is a PDF document titled "*FTK_Chip_Imaging_Steps.*" This document includes these same 10 steps and is a quick reference guide that readers can print.

Once examiners have successfully created an image of their target memory chip, the file can be decoded using tools such as Physical Analyzer. Use the Open Advance feature and first attempt to select the actual model number. The selection in almost every case will be to use the physical selection. There may be times when your target phone is not supported. In these cases, another profile can be used within Physical Analyzer. As an example, many of the Android devices that are not supported by model number will use the same Android Physical chain profile from a device that is supported.

Regular Expression Searching

The term regular expression can also be called *regex* for short, or *regexp*. There are some who refer to it as a *rational expression*, but today, most refer to it as regex or regular expression. In simple terms, a regular expression involves specific characters that will allow a search of programming language. Stephen Kleene was a mathematician who lived from January 5, 1909, to January 25, 1994. Based on his work in 1956, Stephen described regular languages using mathematical notations which he called regular sets [1].

It took over 10 years before regular expressions found their use, and others began adapting the work of Stephen into various editors for several different computer languages. Here are some very basic concepts of regular expressions that are shown within Physical Analyzer. These are displayed as a pop-up window under the RegEx (GREP) tab (right of the Find tab), by pressing the ">" button. Users will see these choices displayed:

. Any single character
* Zero or more
+ One of more
^ Beginning of a line
$ End of line
\b Word boundary
\s Whitespace
| Or
\ Escape special character
( ) Group/Capture
\ Line break
[ ] Any one character in a set
[^] Any one character not in a set

Tools such as EnCase, AccessData FTK, and Physical Analyzer could be used to search the forensic image using regular expression. This chapter could easily be devoted to explaining the various aspects of the regular expression. Many investigators simply need specific expressions that have already been developed for specific purposes, which we will include in this chapter. If you want to know more about writing your own expressions, and how to work with them, additional information can be located in several sites:

https://developer.mozilla.org/en-US/docs/Web/JavaScript/Guide/
Regular_Expressions
https://regexone.com
http://regexr.com/
http://www.rexegg.com/
https://www.codecademy.com/courses/javascript-intermediate-en-NJ7Lr/0/1

GREP

The word GREP stands for *globally regular expression print*. It was originally developed for the Unix OS and debuted in Unix version 4. Grep is a powerful tool for matching a regular expression against text in a file, multiple files, or a stream of input. It searches for the *pattern* of text that you specify on the command line and outputs the results for you [2]. The grep command may encompass four different types of commands—*rgrep, fgrep, egrep*, and *grep*. A Basic Regular Expression (BRE) and Extended Regular Expression (ERE) may differ based on how specific characters and patterns function and get interpreted.

What should be important to understand is that many of the examples used in this chapter will rely on the image we are working with having the ASCII string content for the expression. With mobile devices, the encoding of the data will not always be in ASCII, and as such, the search hits being used may not have positive results. This does not necessarily mean that what you may be looking for is not there. By comparison, if we used the same expressions, say on an image from a computer hard drive, the results would, in many cases, be higher based on more ASCII source encoding. The working examples that follow in this chapter may use both formats (BRE/ERE) and, for simplicity, will be referred to as "regular expressions."

Working Examples

Within the Physical Analyzer manual, one example of a regular expression (GREP) that uses is provided: **[a-zA-Z0-9._%+-]+@[a-zA-Z0-9.-]+\.[A-Za-z]{2,4}**. This searches the Memory Images within of the rebuilt partitions for all the email addresses that match common format structure of: <string>@<string>.<2 to 4 letters> [3].

Since we do not dive into all the details regarding each of these characters, it does not take much to understand the range of what we are looking for. We see the letters represented in lowercase and uppercase of the entire alphabet, along with zero through nine.

If we continue with this search format, it allows for any beginning string from the start of an email, followed by an "@" symbol, followed by any following string, then a dot (.), followed by the ending part of the email that has two to four letters.

Common Email Regular Expressions

Email regular expression patterns can be limited down to the domain. The common ones are .com, .edu, .gov, .net, and .org; however, any one desired can be entered. The examples shown here can limit the results based on the domain near the end of the string. Used in the example is *.com*:

[0-9a-zA-Z._%+-]+@[0-9a-zA-Z._%+-]+\.com\>

Obviously, this could be replaced with any domain that is needed in your investigation simply by replacing the value with what is being requested:

[0-9a-zA-Z._%+-]+@[0-9a-zA-Z._%+-]+\.edu\>
[0-9a-zA-Z._%+-]+@[0-9a-zA-Z._%+-]+\.gov\>
[0-9a-zA-Z._%+-]+@[0-9a-zA-Z._%+-]+\.net\>
[0-9a-zA-Z._%+-]+@[0-9a-zA-Z._%+-]+\.org\>
[0-9a-zA-Z._%+-]+@[0-9a-zA-Z._%+-]+\.us\>

In the next example, we included several email domains all at once in the search. This type of expression may take several minutes to show the results, depending on the size of the Memory Image being searched:

[0-9a-zA-Z._%+-]+@[0-9a-zA-Z._%+-]+\.([a-z]{2}|biz|cat|com|coop|edu|gov|info|int|
jobs|mil|mobi|museum|name|net|org|pro|tel|travel)\>

Domain Only Expressions

If we did not want to utilize the email domain and instead were looking just for the domain hits, we would remove the @ symbol, and the second string that would follow the "@" symbol. This first example is for the .com domain:

[0-9a-zA-Z._%+-]+\.com\>

Again, the domain could be replaced with whatever is needed in the search:

[0-9a-zA-Z._%+-]+\.edu\>
[0-9a-zA-Z._%+-]+\.museum\>
[0-9a-zA-Z._%+-]+\.tv\>
[0-9a-zA-Z._%+-]+\.net\>
[0-9a-zA-Z._%+-]+\.org\>
[0-9a-zA-Z._%+-]+\.gov\>
[0-9a-zA-Z._%+-]+\.info\>

Just like our email domains, we can include several different ones (domains) at the same time in the expression search. What is listed here is just an example. These can be edited according to what is needed. This may or may not slow down the processing time, depending on the size of the source drive and how many hits are appearing in the early stages of the search. If examiners find that this method takes too long, limit the number of entries accordingly:

[0-9a-zA-Z._%+-]+\.([a-z]{2}\biz\cat\com\coop\edu\gov\info\int\jobs\mil\mobi\museum\name\net\org\pro\tel\travel)\>

Fraud-Related Regular Expressions

If the owner or user of the device has enabled specific settings on the mobile device, it is possible to locate values related to social security or credit card numbers. These are not always fraud cases and may be a situation where the specific values were not necessarily used in a criminal incident but simply needed to validate the investigation. With credit cards, some of the expressions can be used based on the type of card. The first digit, in some cases, can represent the financial institution for the card. The first example here will be an Amex card. This will begin with 3. Exclude the colon (:) sign.

Amex: \<3\d\d\d[\-\.]\d\d\d\d\d\d[\-\.]\d\d\d\d\d\>
Visa: \<4\d\d\d[\-\.](\d\d\d\d[\-\.]){2}\d\d\d\d\>
Mastercard: \<5\d\d\d[\-\.](\d\d\d\d[\-\.]){2}\d\d\d\d\>
Discover: \<6011([\-\.]\d\d\d\d){3}\>
American Express: \<3[47]\d{2}[\-\.]?\d{6}[\-\.]?\d{5}\>
Mastercard and Visa: (\<5[1-5]\d{2}[\-\.]?(\d{4}[\-\.]?){2}\d{4}\>|\<4\d{3}[\-\.]? (\d{4}[\-\.]?){2}\d(?:\d{3})?\>)

If the investigator does not necessarily know which type of card value could be stored on the file system, there are a couple of different choices with the expression. The first can be a simple standard format for most credit cards:

\<(\d\d\d\d[\-\.]){3}\d\d\d\d\>

The other method, which will generally take longer to get the results, is to combine all the different credit card regular expressions at once:

\<(?:4[0-9]{12}(?:[0-9]{3})?\5[1-5][0-9]{14}\6(?:011\5[0-9][0-9])[0-9]{12}\3[47] [0-9]{13}\3(?:0[0-5]\[68][0-9])[0-9]{11}\(?:2131\1800\35\d{3})\d{11})\>

Purchases that take place on the web that utilize a credit card may contain a value of *x* or *#* within the receipt. They will usually only show the last digits of the credit card used. The *x* or *#* is used to block the actual number for the card. The receipt may be stored in the file system in this format. The following regular expression can be used:

([#x][#x][#x][#x][\- \ ]?){3}\d\d\d\d\>

To search for a social security number, try either of the following regular expressions:

\<\d\d\d[\-]\d\d[\-]\d\d\d\d\>
\b[0-9]{3}(|-)[0-9]{2}(|-)[0-9]{4}\b

Internet and Miscellaneous Related Regular Expressions

Locating various Uniform Resource Locator (URL) addresses of *http, https, ftp,* and *ftps* can be accomplished using this regular expression:

\<(((((ht\|f)tps?)\://))?[0-9a-z._%+-]+\.(biz\|cat\|com\|coop\|edu\|gov\|info\|int\|jobs\|mil\|mobi\|
museum\|name\|net\|org\|pro\|tel\|travel\|[a-z]{2})(\.:[0-9]{1,5}){0,2}
(/($\|[a-zA-Z0-9\.\?\+*\$\~-&%/#_,;'=-]+)))+\>*

There may be instances that are specific to Hotmail, searching, IP, US dollar amounts, and orphaned files:

MSN Hotmail Beginning: *[/<]input type[/=]hidden name[/=]msgFromName value[/=]*
MSN Hotmail End: <\^-\- S\: [0-9]\-\->
HTML Search Engine Return—Google Search: *href=/advanced_search\?q=*
INDEX.dat entries and Search Engine Return—Google Search: */search\?hl=..&q=*
HTML Search Engine Return—Ebay.com, search.aol.com, mamma.com: *[/?]query[/=]*
HTML Search Engine—Ask Jeeves: *href="\?q=*
Orphaned Index.dat Files (with date): *url.{12}\x01.{7}\x01*
Orphaned Index.dat Files (without date): *url.{101}http\:\/\/*
Orphaned History Index.dat Files: *url.{101}visited\:*
Orphaned Index.dat Cookie Files: *url.{101}cookie\:*
IP Address: \< *[1-2]?[0-9]?[0-9]\. [1-2]?[0-9]?[0-9]\. [1-2]?[0-9]?[0-9]\.*
[1-2]?[0-9]?[0-9]\>
US dollar amount: \<\$ *((([1-9]\d{0,2}(\.\d{3})*)\|([1-9]\d*)\|(0))(\.\d{2})?\>*

GPS Devices

For GPS-related devices that are being examined, the following regular expressions can be utilized:

Mio MyRecent.xml: ^\x3c\x3f\x78\x6d\x6c.*\x3c\x2f\x52\x65\x63\x65\x6e\x74\x4c\x6f\
x63\x61\x74\x69\x6f\x6e\x73\x3e
Garmin GPX: *^\x3c\x3f\x78\x6d\x6c.*\x3c\x2f\x67\x70\x78\x3e*
TOMTOM cfg: *^\x04\x00\xDD\x0F.*\x1B\x1B\x1B\x1B\x04.bif=\x5B\x54\x6F\x6D*

Chapter Summary Key Points

Reading the contents of the chip can be accomplished with either a programmer and its associated adaptor for the target memory, or an SD style adaptor that is designed for the target, and imaging software. A common programmer used today is the UP series. The 828 and 828P use adaptors that are not interchangeable. Both adaptors (828 or 828P) will require the user to install the appropriate software. The software can also be used in demo mode. Besides reading supported memory, it can assist examiners who are using the JTAG Finder from 100RandomTasks; as it helps identify BSDL information.

Some newer UFS memory may need a unique programmer and adaptor. DediProg Technologies produces a programmer that can be used to read these newer style chips. The DediProg NuProg-E Programmer will require the examiner to reball the memory. The memory off certain Samsung S6 devices will be a package on package style chip. Additional care should be rendered when removing this memory. A hot (razor) knife or careful polishing are two recommended ways of removing it.

Two recommended SD style adaptors are the Sireda and the ANDK all-in-one. If the chip can be read using an SD style reader, programs such as FTK Imager can assist in creating a binary image of the contents. A hardware write blocker will need to be used to prevent changes from taking place when the chip is connected to the host machine. A recommended inexpensive write blocker for this purpose is the Cellebrite Forensic Memory Card Reader. Examiners should ensure that the entire image is created in one single binary file and not fragmented. Check to ensure that the image hash results match. In rare cases where the hashes are not valid with one another, hash just the user partition, as this type of flash memory has a controller that generally causes the overall hash to be different.

Once the image has been created and decoded, examiners can conduct additional searching using regular expressions. Tools such as EnCase, FTK, and Physical Analyzer can assist in the search.

The process you employ in preparing the memory will depend on which method of removal was used. There was an old joke that is traced back to Jack Benny: *"How do you get to Carnegie Hall? Practice, practice, practice!"* It will take several test chips before you begin to feel comfortable with cleaning, milling, or polishing. You will not end up at Carnegie Hall, but hopefully another party ends up walking down the halls of a penal institution.

References

[1] Regular Expression, 2016. https://en.wikipedia.org/wiki/Regular_expression.
[2] GREP, 2016. http://www.computerhope.com/unix/ugrep.htm.
[3] Cellebrite Physical Analyzer 5.3.5.14 User Manual 5.2, July 2016, p. 174.

eMMC Reading and In-System Programming

Information in This Chapter

- What is ISP?
- How does communication occur?
- Understand eMMC support versus ISP
- Researching ISP connections
- Probing ISP connections
- Probing example
- Undocumented phones
- Medusa Pro and Octoplus Pro JTAG

Introduction—Model Building

Wikipedia provides the following definition for model building: "*Model building as a hobby involves the creation of models either from kits or from materials and components acquired by the builder. Categories of modelling include:*

- *Scale model building*
- *Live steam models*
- *Matchstick models*
- *Military models*
- *Model aircraft*
- *Model cars*
- *Model commercial vehicles*
- *Model construction vehicles*
- *Building models*
- *Architectural models*
- *Model figures*
- *Model military vehicles*

Seeking the Truth from Mobile Evidence. http://dx.doi.org/10.1016/B978-0-12-811056-0.00030-3
Copyright © 2018 Elsevier Inc. All rights reserved.
457

- *Rail transport modelling*
- *Model rockets*
- *Model ships*
- *Freelance model*
- *Cardboard engineering*
- *Firearm models (See Airsoft guns)*
- *Gundam Models"* [1]

Another childhood hobby of the author was building model cars and airplanes. The completed cars sat on a shelf, and the airplanes were suspended from the ceiling using fishing line. They were often traded to friends for their models, or model parts. Initially, the stickers that came with the model were the only items that ended up on them. After a few years on the basics, additional details were being applied through fine paintbrushes, Q-tips, and toothpicks. Magnifying glasses were always a necessity, but most of all, a high degree of patience.

As we begin our last chapter, many of you reading may have never experienced what model building was all about. Those techniques certainly apply to our last advanced technique— *In-System Programming*. This technique can be quite time-consuming, will require magnification, steady hands, and most of all, a great degree of patience. The good and bad news is that we will not be using model glue that can get you "high" from the fumes.

What Is In-System Programming?

Examiners have another choice when it comes to advanced techniques. The last acquisition process that will be addressed is called *In-System Programming (ISP)*. This may also be referred to as *In-Circuit Serial Programming (ICSP)*. ISP was not designed exclusively for mobile forensics, and like JTAG, it allows communication to take place with a target chip without the need to remove it. Think of ISP as your own ability to communicate directly with the eMMC or eMCP chip, bypassing the CPU altogether. Just like the SD style readers and programmers that read directly off specific Ball Grid Array (BGA) points of contact, ISP works the same way. JTAG was previously explained as a way in which we could debug various boards that supported it, through Test Access Ports (TAPs). ISP is like this, but may use a serial protocol, single protocol, or a hybrid of JTAG protocols for communication to occur.

Manufacturers designed devices to support ISP based on revenue. They could program, reprogram, or test devices without buying additional chips. The changes that were needed could be applied to the current line of products.

How Does Communication Occur?

Just like JTAG, there are specific contacts that will be of interest to the examiner. But unlike JTAG, the contacts are directly off the chip BGAs and do not go through the processor. These contacts will be necessary for ISP to function properly. The following are pin descriptions from Integrated Silicon Solution, Inc. [2].

- *DAT0*

Function: Data. This is the data transfer bidirectional line. These DAT signals operate on a push–pull mode. The chip will have several DAT channels, but only DAT0 will be utilized for data transfer after a power up or reset.

- *CMD*

Function: Command/Response. This signal is a bidirectional command channel used for device initialization and transfer of commands. The CMD signal has two operation modes: open-drain for initialization mode and push–pull for fast command transfer. Commands are sent from the eMMC host controller to the eMMC device and responses are sent from the device to the host.

- *CLK*

Function: Data Input. Each cycle of this signal directs a 1 bit transfer on the command and either a 1 bit (1×) or a 2 bits transfer (2×) on all the data lines. The frequency may vary between zero and the maximum clock frequency.

- *Vcc*

Function: Vcc is the power supply for the core. This is usually 2.85 V.

- *VccQ*

Function: VccQ is the power supply for I/O. This is usually 1.8 V.

- *Vss*

Function: Ground for the core. This may also be referred to as ground or GND.

Understand eMMC Support Versus ISP

Many vendors who produce flasher boxes for ISP exams may not actually refer to the process within their software as "ISP." Instead, they will indicate "eMMC Supported" or "eMMC Device Programmer." The Easy–JTAG interface, for example, uses this type of terminology. In the previous chapter that addresses the RIFF 2 box, there was an example of an eMMC chip that supported direct download. Readers should be aware that the technique of connecting to a removed chip via the BGA is not the same as ISP. The main purpose of the ISP exam is that it does not require the chip to be removed. However, examiners may connect directly to a chip that *has* been removed using the same required points of contact that are used in an ISP pull. In most cases, when an examiner has pulled a chip, a reader is used to create an image of the contents. There may be times, however, when the reader will not read the chip. In those cases, the examiner could utilize a datasheet for their chip and solder directly to the required locations. Fig. 30.1 was obtained from a supported eMMC chip of the GUI of the RIFF 2 box. This Samsung model shows instructions on the various steps to perform the connections. Note that RIFF 2 supports this feature on repairing "dead" chips. Fig. 30.2 is from the Easy–JTAG GUI. This is within the drop-down: *Vendor—Samsung eMMC, Device—BGA 169 Type C*. Both examples are for reading memory after the chip has been removed using the same type of connections required for ISP. Just be aware that some flasher box vendors support eMMC/eMCP reading within the interface that also support pulls through ISP. If you have performed a chip-off, and the memory supports direct reading, you may try pulling directly from the chip if your adaptor or reader fails to acquire the contents. Some examiners may call this "chip-off" ISP acquisition. Be aware of the primary use of ISP for digital forensics, and how vendors may show support for both types (chip on and off the board).

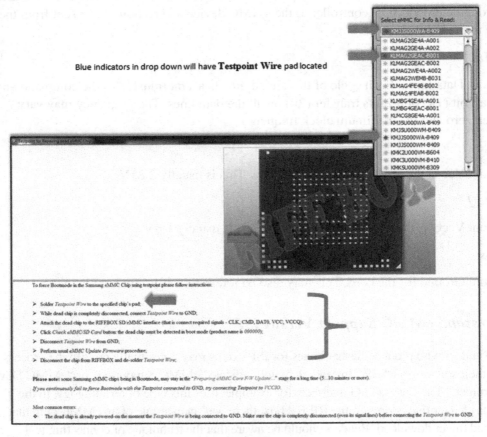

Figure 30.1
Example from RIFF 2 showing support for specific eMMC memory with pinout locations and instructions for reading/repairing.

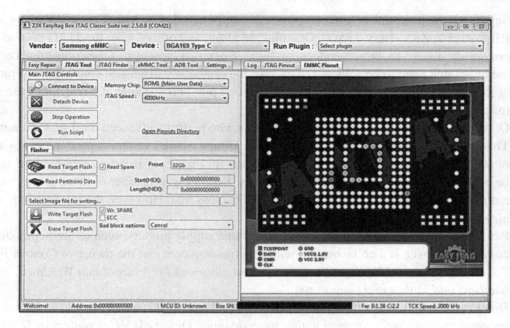

Figure 30.2
Example from Easy-JTAG showing specific support for Samsung eMMC memory and pinout
locations.

Researching ISP Connections

The process of locating these specific required contact points may require the examiner to obtain a nonevidential (exact make/model) phone and remove the target eMMC or eMCP memory. This is addressed later in this chapter. Before any manual work takes place, make certain the chip number of the evidence is researched. Some of the newer phones do not support ISP, such as phones with UFS chips. Although it is not necessary to have chip-off and JTAG experience when conducting an ISP exam, it certainly helps. Having a working knowledge and past JTAG extractions aids in understanding the ISP protocols. Experience with chip-off extractions, will assist in manually removing the chip from a test phone and conducting the continuity test. Many of the flasher boxes that were previously discussed support ISP. If readers go back to the RIFF 2 chapter, it provided some of the steps involved in reading directly off the actual eMMC memory (Fig. 30.1). The entire purpose of an ISP acquisition is that it can be applied to a chip that is still attached to the main board. There will be a few overall ways in which an examiner will locate the (pinout) connections necessary for their target memory for ISP.

1. Supported documentation (pictures) from the supported flasher box. This will include RIFF/RIFF2, Z3X (Easy-JTAG), Octoplus, Medusa, and others. Like the JTAG pinouts previously discussed, these vendors can include detailed closeups of the connections of the board that need to be soldered to each of the previously discussed connections. Many of these will require soldering (or the use of pogo pins) on one side of a resistor of the main board.

2. Obtain the connections from other investigators who perform advanced forensic techniques. This is common with law enforcement online groups where examiners pose questions and others supply assistance. It is also very common for images of ISP connection points to be posted to users to aid in their investigations. Becoming a member of these groups may require attendance to an ISP, JTAG, or Chip-Off class first. However, the information gleaned from these sites is invaluable.

3. Pay for the information through subscriptions that supply pinouts, such as emmcpinouts. com. This website is a collaboration with fonefunshop.com and the owner of Control-F, *"...is a repository of high-quality tested pinout diagrams for Android and Windows handsets and tablets and satnavs too.*

   Dumping smartphones, tablets, and satnavs via direct eMMC (also known as ISP) is becoming increasingly common within forensic units. Direct eMMC is replacing JTAG not only as a method for performing physical extractions of locked devices but also for situations where a logical extraction is incomplete and a physical extraction is not possible within commercial forensic tools. The biggest challenge with direct eMMC is finding the test points on the printed circuit board (PCB) of the device to connect to!

   Which is why we have launched emmcpinouts.com – a subscription based repository of high quality reliable documentation.

   The repository currently contains pinout diagrams for 54 devices including
   - *Sony eMMC ISP pinouts*
   - *Samsung eMMC ISP pinouts*
   - *Motorola eMMC ISP pinouts*
   - *HTC eMMC ISP pinouts*
   - *TomTom eMMC ISP pinouts*
   - *Plus and we are committed to growing that number each month.*

   All of the pinout diagrams were researched and tested by Control-F so you can rely on them. The site also includes chip-off schematics for 30 BlackBerry devices" [3].

4. Probe for the necessary connections on a test phone (not the evidence). This requires removing the target memory, locating DAT0, CLK, Vcc, VccQ, and Vss. Use a continuity tester and determine where each of these connections respond to points on the main board. These will usually be one side of a resister, or other specific areas around the chip or processor. This is discussed in more detail later in this chapter.

Note: Option 4 should be examiners last resort when they need to perform an ISP exam. This will require a test phone, continuity tester, magnification, lots of time, and patience.

Boxes that support ISP will have a diagram for the pins that represent the required connections of DAT0, CMD, CLK, Vcc, VccQ, and Vss. The examiner will need to locate a datasheet for their target eMMC or eMCP chip. This will contain locations for DAT0, CMD, CLK, Vcc, and VccQ. Vss can be connected to a heat shield (can) or the seam, where the can was soldered before it was removed. Fig. 30.3 is an image example from a datasheet from the

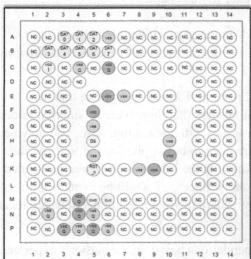

This data sheet example is from a 153FBGA Top View (Ball Down). When examiners are locating the correct connections, be aware of the orientation and the number 1 pin marking. Once this chip is lifted off the board on the **test phone**, use the datasheet and locate the required connections for the ISP exam off the mainboard. The picture to the right is from Easy-JTAG. VDD off the Easy-JTAG box equates to VccQ. It does not matter which Vcc, VccQ and Vss contact you use – as there will be more than one. You must determine the voltages of Vcc and VccQ for your target device.

Figure 30.3

Datasheet example that contains BGA areas for required In-System Programming (ISP) connections. Example of ISP supported flasher box—Easy-JTAG connections for ISP.

BGA area of a 153-FBGA chip. Next to the pinout locations is the diagram from the Easy-JTAG box. This gives the examiner a location where to begin probing for the required pinouts connections. Whichever ISP-supported box you use, each will have its own diagram for the ISP connections.

Probing In-System Programming Connections

If you have determined that your chip supports ISP and you are unable to obtain any information on the pinout locations from the box you are using online groups, or through paid services, you will need to manually locate the areas on the main board. There will be a few tools and reference items that will be required for this purpose, and others that are recommended. Recommended items will be noted with an asterisk (*) symbol.

- **Datasheet for the target chip.**
- **Flasher box that supports ISP**.
- Exact duplicate of the target phone (two may be required).
- Rework station to remove (test) memory.
- Small pry tools (spade).
- Solder flux.
- Continuity tester (Ohm meter). This will require some minor modification to hold small pins for probing. (Example images supplied later in this chapter.)
- Digital camera to document locations.
- Magnification*: Most examiners can use head-mounted magnifiers for this purpose. Recommended is a digital zoom microscope such as the previously mentioned *Tagarno Digital Microscope*.

The process of locating the connections will need to be performed on a phone that *was originally working prior to the chip removal*. This ensures that there were no internal issues with the main board to begin with that may cause issues with the testing. Also, you may need a second test model to determine what voltages are need to be supplied to the Vcc and the VccQ. Often this can be located on the chip datasheet. If the information cannot be located by any research means, there is another way test for the voltages. This will be explained after the probing instructions, as it will be required to know where the required connections are located first before determining the correct voltages.

The overall steps involved in probing are recommendations based on the author's experience. They will be expanded on in additional detail. You may have already performed ISP exams, and as such, may include additional steps, or better approaches to manually locating the connections.

1. Research the target chip. Locate the datasheet and corresponding connections required for ISP. Determine if you have a box that will work with the ISP pull.
2. Obtain a test phone that is the exact model of your target evidence. If you were unable to locate information on the proper voltage for Vcc and VccQ, consider getting two test phones, one for probing (chip removal) and one for determining the correct voltages. Remember—both test phones must be in working order.
3. Document the chip orientation as it relates to where it sits on a working phone. Remove the chip using a thermal process only. It is imperative that you take extra steps not to damage surrounding components when removing the cans, and eventually the chip. Some of these components (especially resistors) may be where the contact you need resides. There are techniques here that can be useful to prevent damage to surrounding areas.

a. Use Kapton tape around the chip components. Although this is not a 100% preventative measure on damage, it can help preserve them.

b. Protect the areas around the target chip with heat shields. The author uses old battery covers that are made from metal. Motorola is one of the vendors that produce these types of covers. They can be located in first-generation Droid phones or older flip phones. Remember, we are suggested old parts, use whatever may be at your disposal—even previously removed heat shields will work. They can be taped in place with Kapton tape.

c. Remove the adhesive around the chip using small amounts of solvents (sparingly). Be mindful not to get the solvent on other components. The other method is to carefully scrape the adhesive using a tool that has a heated tip. This may be a precise solder tip, or a dental tool that you heat up with a rework station. This again, must be completed with very careful placement, as you want to prevent contact with any other component. Some manufacturers will coat the resisters around the chip and the edge of the chip with adhesive. These parts may be hard to see under normal vision. Use magnification to check around the chip before scrapping the adhesive off. If you do see resistors that are hidden under the same adhesive that holds on your chip, work under a microscope and scrape carefully.

4. Once the chip is removed from the main board, clean the BGA area on the board. The BGAs should not have any smudging (shorts). Retinning can assist with making them more consistent for manual probing.

Practice, Practice, Practice

If you have never performed an ISP exam, it can be extremely helpful to try the technique before working on an actual case. A method that helped for the author was to utilize a supported phone that has the pinout locations already mapped out for you. Boxes such as Easy-JTAG, Medusa, and RIFF 2 would be a great choice to start your first ISP extraction on. Use a test phone that is in good working condition. The suggestion would be to have two of these working phones. The first would be used to connect to the required locations, which would be available through images of the GUI of the supported box. The second could be used as an aid to help you with manual mapping and continuity testing. It is also a good idea to practice at soldering, which can be very difficult on the small components that need connections. If your lab has a VR Table (or similar) manually probing tool, this could also be used to practice with. The example in this book will use a supported Motorola model XT912. Using Easy-JTAG, users can locate the image that corresponds to the eMMC connections. Fig. 30.4 is the interface of Easy-JTAG with the Motorola XT912 pinout locations.

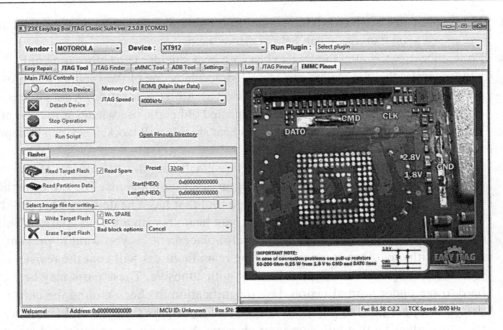

Figure 30.4
Easy-JTAG interface showing the Motorola XT912 pinout locations.

Locate the specific locations on the main board, and practice soldering to the required pinouts. There is really no way around the fact that a precise soldering unit and tip will be required. If you plan to conduct ISP extractions, and have been using a larger solder iron, it will become painfully clear that you will need better equipment.

When soldering to the required locations on the main board, it is recommended that copper, enameled wire is used. This is often referred to as "Jumper Wire." In the example provided, 38-gauge wire is used, which may also be sold in millimeter sizes. This type of wire will need to be "prepped" first. Since the wire is coated in enamel, the coating on the ends that are making connections must be removed to allow continuity to occur. Also, the length of the wires needs to be kept short. Because the wire is very thinly gauged, the signal can degrade as it increases in length. Examiners should use a solder board to connect the thin jumper wires to larger wires that go into the actual flasher box. The board can be taped or hot glued to one side of the main board. Let us review from our JTAG chapter regarding two techniques that can be used to prepare the enameled wire.

1. First, cut all your required wires and simulate where exactly you want to run them in conjunction with the main board, jumper board, and flasher box.
2. Create a medium-sized solder ball on the tip of your soldering iron. Run the ends of enameled wires through the solder ball several times. You will only need approximately 3/16th to 1/8th of an inch on each end to be pushed through the hot solder. This burns off

the enamel. When the solder begins to stick to the copper, the enamel has been burned off. Make sure you repeat this process for the opposite end. When you have finished both ends, check the wire for continuity. If you are unable to see continuity, repeat the process and continue testing until you have a closed circuit (continuity). Repeat this for all your required wires needed for the ISP exam. *Or*:

2. After cutting each of the required ISP wires, use a precise, angled solder tip and begin scrapping the enamel off each of the ends. Again, 3/16th to 1/8th of an inch should be the amount removed. It is very easy to scrape through the entire wire during this process, and apply pressure gently to the enameled wire. Also, the heat on the soldering unit should be turned down to a minimum temperature, as the higher heat can burn through this thin wire. The wire will need to be rotated as you scrape it, which due to the size, is hard to determine if you are rotating it at all. Once you feel you have scraped enough of the enamel off each end, check the wire for continuity. Continue scrapping if necessary, and retest until the circuit is closed. Repeat this scrapping process for all your required wires. Fig. 30.5 is an image of the process of burning off the enamel from the ends of the wires using a hot solder ball. Whichever method is used, make sure you check the wire for a closed circuit (continuity). The tip used in Fig. 30.5 is a small, angled tip for a JBC rework unit.

Figure 30.5
Example of using a hot solder ball to remove the enamel off wires.

Once your wires are prepped, you can begin soldering them to the specific locations on the main board. Since our first example uses the pinout locations supplied by the flasher box vendor (Easy-JTAG), it is unnecessary that we will need to pull a test chip, and map the locations. By first looking at the locations of a supported phone, it can help examiners who may be new to ISP, better understand what is required when they encounter an unsupported phone. This first technique has explained suggestions on what type of wire to utilize, how to prep enameled wires, and how to use a supported (pinout) mapped phone for your first attempt at ISP. The next example uses the same phone (Motorola XT912). This time, however, let us assume the phone does not show the pinout locations on any of the commercial flasher boxes for ISP.

Probing Example

Using the XT912 scenario (board), we assume that one is our evidence and the other is our test phone. For this example, we ignore the fact that Easy-JTAG supports the device. For learning the technique of manual probing (mapping), we will, however, refer to the pinout locations within the GUI of Easy-JTAG to check our work.

For sake of simplicity, it will be assumed that you have already researched this device and determined that it will support an ISP extraction. Your next step would be to locate a datasheet for the eMMC chip. The chip in our example is a Toshiba, part number THGBM4G7D2GBAIE. Not every XT912 will have this exact make and model chip. This model will have a 12×16 mm, eMMC model memory configuration housed in a 169 BGA package. This means that it will *not change* where the required pinout locations are on the board, even if you decide to practice using this model, and the chip manufacturer and model are different.

Using the datasheet for this Toshiba model, Fig. 30.6 contains information that would be necessary in probing. Also contained in Fig. 30.6 is the voltages for both Vcc and VccQ.

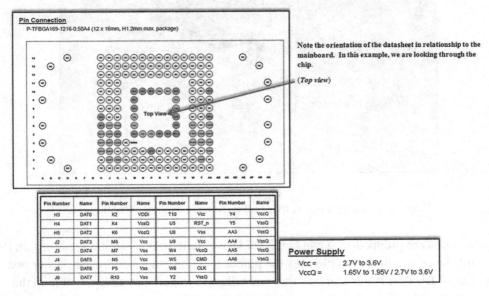

Pin Number	Name	Pin Number	Name	Pin Number	Name	Pin Number	Name
H3	DAT0	K2	VDDi	T10	Vcc	Y4	VccQ
H4	DAT1	K4	VssQ	U5	RST_n	Y5	VssQ
H5	DAT2	K6	VccQ	U8	Vss	AA3	VccQ
J2	DAT3	M6	Vcc	U9	Vcc	AA4	VssQ
J3	DAT4	M7	Vss	W4	VccQ	AA5	VccQ
J4	DAT5	N5	Vcc	W5	CMD	AA6	VssQ
J5	DAT6	P5	Vss	W6	CLK		
J6	DAT7	R10	Vss	Y2	VssQ		

Power Supply
Vcc =   2.7V to 3.6V
VccQ =   1.65V to 1.95V / 2.7V to 3.6V

Figure 30.6
Datasheet information for the Toshiba THGBM4G7D2GBAIE chip.

Our next step would be to pull the chip using a thermal process. Care should be given not to damage, or alter the surrounding components. Once the chip is removed, clean the main board BGA area to allow proper probing to take place.

After the BGA area on the main board has been cleaned, the continuity tester will need to hold small pins to conduct the testing. There are a couple ways by which this can be accomplished. Examiners can use test probes that have Alligator Clips on the test end to clap to pogo pins or even sewing pins. Another method is to temporary fasten pins to the straight probes that most multimeters already come with. This can be done using electrical tape or wire and hot glue. Fig. 30.7 displays how sewing pins were affixed to the standard test probes. First, they were wrapped with 28-gauge bare, copper wire. Then they were held in place using hot glue. A side note on cooling hot glue (for ISP, JTAG, or other applications) is to turn a can of compressed air upside down and carefully spray the cold liquid (that will flow out) onto the hot glue. This will instantly chill and solidify the glue so examiners do not have to wait for it to slowly dry. Whichever method you use, make sure you test the pins for continuity prior to probing.

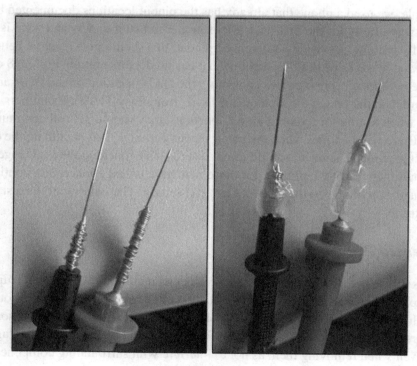

Figure 30.7
Sewing pins wrapped with copper wire and hot glued to standard multimeter probes to use for manual probing In-System Programming.

Using the Easy-JTAG eMMC pinout locations as your reference, start with the DAT0. If you reference the datasheet, DAT0 is in the H3 position. Place one of the (pin) multimeter probes on the BGA location on the board for the DAT0 (H3). Using the GUI of Easy-JTAG, locate the area where they have probed for the DAT0 of a component on the main board. Touch the other probe to this location. You should get continuity (closed) results on your meter. If you do not, you may not be making proper connection to either the BGA for DAT0 or the components of the main board. Be aware that many of the components will have a coating of glue or other board material that can interfere with continuity. This is where a secondary magnification unit can come in handy. Once you have completed this, repeat this process for the remainder of the connections. Be mindful that the power settings Vcc/VccQ can come from any of the Vcc and VccQ areas on the BGA area of the board. If you use the Easy-JTAG for the reference, and have one probe on one side of a known resister for Vcc, and you do not get continuity on the first Vcc of the datasheet location, move to another one. Eventually you will locate which Vcc/VccQ BGA Easy-JTAG used. Locating the correct Vcc and VccQ pinouts that Easy-JTAG uses on its GUI (in the example, Toshiba chip) is just for practice. In a real scenario, you would just pick one Vcc and VccQ and document the location.

In this example, we used a phone that already has the pinout locations documented by a vendor. This was strictly for the first-time ISP examiner to better understand what is entailed when manually probing. By using a referenced pinout, this should give reader a better understanding of what needs to be done on a phone that has no documentation. Fig. 30.8 contains images of the multimeter (pins) probes contacting the DAT0 location on the BGA area from the main board, and the pinout location on a resister (from Easy-JTAG). Examiners should be mindful that when testing for required pinout locations, they should get full continuity on their meter. There will be times when the meter moves partially. This should not be considered a correct location. The meter should jump to zero—like touching the leads together when testing the multimeter. Just a reminder, for those who have no experience with continuity testing, the meter should be on the highest Ohm (Ω) setting. The polarity of the test leads does not matter.

Undocumented Phones

For the cases where you are unable to locate any documentation on a supported chip, you will need to complete the same steps that we previously outline. This time, however, you will need to take a high-quality image of the test board (phone)—mainly around the processor and target chip area. The photo should be created with the heat shields removed. Care again should be given when removing them as not to interfere with surrounding components.

Motorola XT912 – DAT0 pinout
location (confirmed with Easy-
JTAG). Full continuity. Using a
known, documented pinout to
practice.

Figure 30.8
Example of using premapped pinout location (Easy-JTAG) to practice replicating manual probing.
DAT0 pinout used.

If possible, use a nonthermal method. It will be up to you to decide which pin you locate first. The author starts from left to right (on the BGA area). Test the resisters around the processor first. Make note of continuity on each side of the resister. Look at the GUI within the Easy-JTAG (eMMC tab) on different support phones. You will see that many of the required pinouts use only one side of the mapped resister for that specific pin. Fig. 30.9 is a closeup of the area around the eMMC that was removed from the XT912. If we assumed that it was not properly documented by Easy-JTAG, this figure has various color-coded references on where to probe. This is just a guide, and examiners will find several different locations for the necessary pin locations that may certainly differ from this example. Start by staying near the area between the removed memory and the processor—the closer the better. Again, you want full continuity to take place when probing.

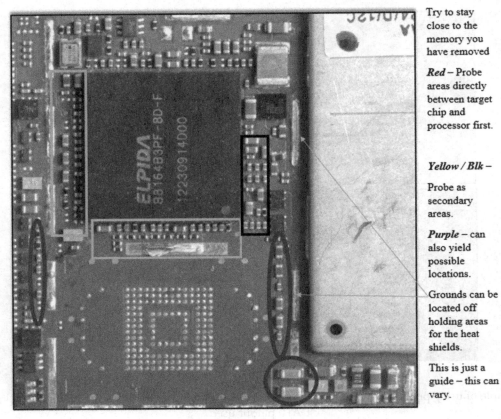

Try to stay close to the memory you have removed

Red – Probe areas directly between target chip and processor first.

Yellow / Blk –

Probe as secondary areas.

Purple – can also yield possible locations.

Grounds can be located off holding areas for the heat shields.

This is just a guide – this can vary.

Figure 30.9
Example of color-coded areas on where to manually begin probing (will vary per phone).

When you start to locate the required pinout locations, begin documenting using the high-quality digital image you have previously taken. The way in which you document is completely up to you. Some training vendors will suggest color-coding the pinout connections. Other investigators like to document the connection back to the BGA spot on the board. Whichever way you decide to document your probing, make sure it is clear to you what each contact represents. Fig. 30.10 is from our XT912. This was obviously already documented within the GUI of Easy-JTAG, but this example shows how it was created using a digital closeup and Microsoft Word. Fig. 30.11 is also from the XT912. This pinout shows the corresponding area on the BGA that resulted in continuity.

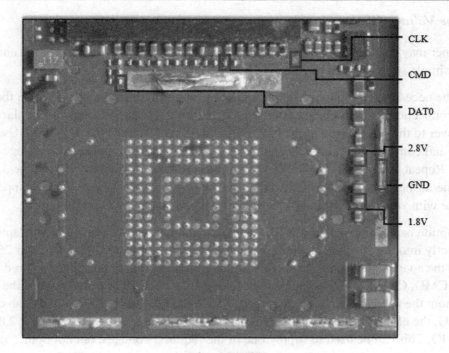

Figure 30.10

Example of manual documenting In-System Programming probing using digital photography and MS Word.

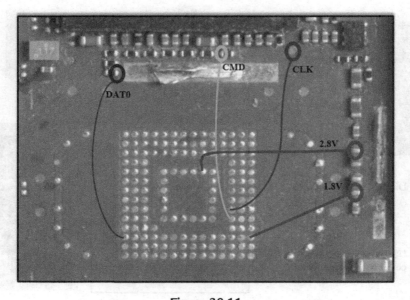

Figure 30.11

Example of manual documenting In-System Programming probing with the corresponding areas on the Ball Grid Array.

Determine Voltage (If Necessary)

An examiner may have times when they will need to determine the voltages for the chip. Here are some simple steps that can be of assistance:

Perform the necessary probing and make note of the areas on the main board where the required connections reside. Obtain your second, working test phone (chip still in place). Apply power to the board through the battery or power supply. Turn the device on. Use a voltmeter and complete a circuit between the Vcc and GND. Make note of the voltage for your Vcc. Repeat this process for VccQ. Vcc will usually be 3.3 V, and VccQ will be 3.3 or 1.8 V. Some flasher boxes for ISP may only produce one range of voltage. If this happens to be the case with your (supported) box, one solution is to utilize a DC power supply.

Another option is an adaptor. The eMMC adaptor supports a USB input, and the adaptor plugs directly into the 20-pin connector on the back of the Easy-JTAG box. Chapter 25 explained the adaptor that can be ordered with the Z3X Easy-JTAG box. The required connections (CMD, CLK, DAT0, etc.) are connected off this board. The board applies the 1.8 and 2.8 V without the need of two power supplies. Within the GUI of the eMMC Tool tab on Easy-JTAG, the eMMC voltage settings (in the drop-down) are 1.8 V IO, 1.8 V ISP, 2.8 V IO, and 3.3 V IO. This can be used to supply one of the required voltages, but not both. Fig. 30.12 is a diagram that shows how our sample XT912 board, the adaptor with USB power supplied,

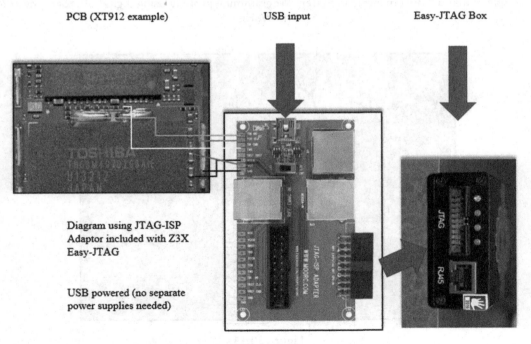

Figure 30.12
Diagram example of the Motorola XT912 board being connected to the eMMC adaptor, USB power, and the Easy-JTAG box.

PCB (XT912 example)   Easy-JTAG Box

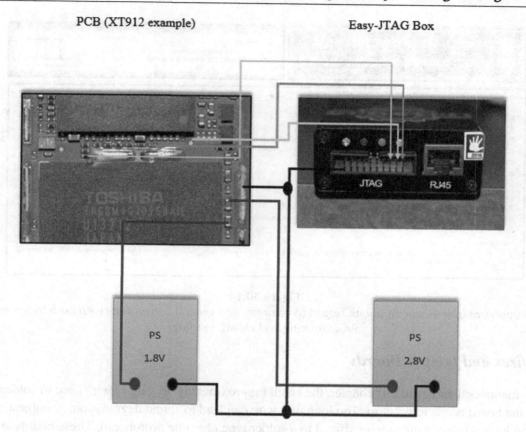

Figure 30.13
Diagram example of the Motorola XT912 board being connected to the Easy-JTAG box and two separate power supplies for Vcc and VccQ.

and the Easy-JTAG box would all be connected. Fig. 30.13 is a diagram showing the use of two DC power supplies to connect the 1.8 and 2.8 V.

Most of the commercial flasher boxes will also inform the examiner of any special requirements that are needed for voltage or other connections. These will vary. Fig. 30.14 was created from specific instructions contained in both Easy-JTAG GUI and RIFF 2 interfaces. The two top images are from Easy-JTAG, and the bottom image is from RIFF 2. Boxes such as Easy-JTAG also can perform both JTAG and eMMC/ISP exams. On the companion site, Figs. 30.1–30.3 show screenshots from the FAQ/Pinouts for both JTAG and eMMC mode, as well as the common eMMC chip pinouts. Noted in the image to the right within Fig. 30.3 is the chip configurations of 153-FBGA 11.5 × 13, 169-FBGA 12 × 16, 12 × 18, and 14 × 18, all have the same locations for the required pinouts. If you were unable to locate your specific data sheet for your exact model chip, utilize these images for common eMCP, and eMMC configurations, in various sizes.

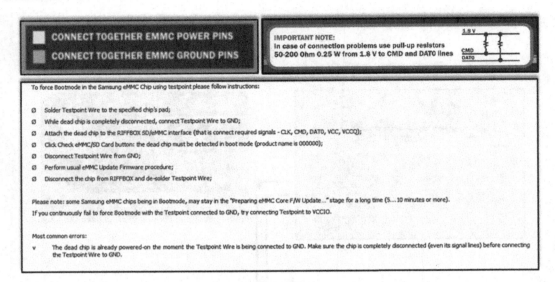

Figure 30.14
Examples of user instructions with regard to voltages, and general connectivity with both In-System Programming and eMMC reading.

Wires and Jumper Boards

As mentioned earlier in this chapter, the small (approximately 38 gauge) wire used to solder to the board needs to be short. Too long of a wire can lead to signal degradation. A suggestion is to have a larger gauged wire affixed to a solder type phenolic protoboard. These boards are inexpensive and have copper donut holes that work well with ISP and JTAG applications. The board can be a jumper to the smaller gauged wire. Fig. 30.4 of the companion site depicts the connections between the wires leading to the flasher box, and the smaller wires that are used for ISP. Another useful adaptor is the 20-pin female with exposed (10) wire in the opposite end. This allows direct connections to the desired box and adaptable ends to a protoboard. Fig. 30.5 from the companion site shows how the adaptor was connected to a piece of cardboard and protoboard. These boards should be as close to the main board of the phone as possible. They should also be taped or hot glued down to prevent solder joints from being pulled off. Since soldering to the main board is the most difficult, the better you prepare the connections, the more protection it will provide. Fig. 30.6 of the companion site is one of the author's original protoboards used for JTAG and ISP work. Notice how some of the donut holes have eventually burned out from repeated use. What is convenient about these boards is that users can jump to another (unused) set of holes. It is not pretty, but it works!

Medusa Pro and Octoplus Pro JTAG

Another popular box used for eMMC and ISP extractions is the Medusa Pro and Octoplus Pro JTAG. This last section of this chapter will briefly cover some of the features of both boxes. At the time of this writing, the Medusa Pro/Octoplus Pro JTAG supported JTAG and eMMC reading on many makes and models of mobile devices. The interface used for Medusa Pro and Octoplus Pro JTAG will have their respective names at the top, but the software is nearly identical for eMMC and ISP. One of the attractive features of both boxes is that they support both common voltage ranges (Vcc/VccQ) directly off the box. There is no need for an adaptor.

Both boxes support a few Samsung model chip numbers. This would be for direct eMMC (chip-off) reading. Users can change the setting to *Custom Settings* and manually download supported eMMC configurations for the devices that it does support. After the download is complete, users can select the "*? Pinout*" button to display a high-definition image of the ISP pinout locations. The image allows the user to zoom in and see the specific contacts without image loss. Fig. 30.7 on the companion site contains screenshots of some of the features of the Medusa Pro box. The left upper image displays the drop-downs that are available under the Model Settings—Brand. The upper right image displays the available chip numbers for direct eMMC support (chip-off), and the lower left image shows the eMMC pinout location on the back of the box. Fig. 30.8 on the companion site is the download manager, which is accessed when users select the "*Download *.srf*" button. Fig. 30.9 on the companion site shows an example of the Samsung SM-G530P model being downloaded for eMMC support. Once this is downloaded, "Samsung" will show as one of the choices under the *Model Settings—Brand*. When this is selected, the user can display the pinout for that model–as shown in the example in Fig. 30.10 on the companion site. Fig. 30.11 is a side-by-side comparison of the GUI from Octoplus Pro JTAG and Medusa Pro.

Chapter Summary Key Points

A nondestructive technique that is like JTAG extractions is the In-System-Programming (ISP) acquisition. This physical exam typically utilizes pinout contacts that consist of CMD, DAT0, CLK, Vcc, and VccQ. Vcc is usually 2.8 V while VccQ is 1.8. ISP bypasses the processor and allows the acquisition to take place by communications directly with the supported memory. Unlike chip-off forensics which is destructive, ISP allows the exam to take place without the need to remove the memory. Not all flash memory configurations support ISP. Instead of using TAP locations, the examiner solders directly to defined points on the main board that communicate with the required pinouts. There are several vendors that provide the pinout location for specific make and model phones. However, some devices that support ISP will not necessarily have documentation on the specific pinouts readily available. After exhausting the GUI of various ISP supported boxes, online (paid) ISP documentation sites, and online groups, the examiner may need to resort to manual probing.

Some key steps that can assist with ISP (and probing) are to obtain the datasheet for the specific model chip. Use a working test phone and remove the chip. Configure a multimeter (Ohm) using Alligator Clips or glue to hold pogo pins or sewing pins. Using magnification, locate the required pinouts that are needed for the acquisition of the GUI of the specific box that supports the ISP. Begin testing around the location of the removed chip. Using digital photography, map out and document the locations. Microsoft Word can be useful for this purpose. If necessary, use a working phone to determine the proper voltages of the target phone for Vcc and VccQ. If the box does not independently support both voltages, utilize an eMMC adaptor, or power supply. Examiners can also opt to use two power supplies independent of the box.

Techniques that can be useful are to properly prepare the enameled wires. The ends can either be scrapped or burned off using a hot solder ball. The small enameled wires should be kept short and soldered to a jumper board. Test wires for continuity before connecting them to the pinout locations on the board. Other adaptors such as the 20-pin female with bare wire ends are also helpful when used in conjunction with a jumper board. Just like JTAG, examiners can become creative with different materials that may be required for ISP such as hot glue, cardboard, tape, etc.

Vendors often support both eMMC and ISP. eMMC can mean direct contact to the BGA area of the chip—using the same pinouts required for ISP. eMMC can also mean that the chip is supported for ISP. eMMC is often listed (named in the GUI as eMMC) as a supported feature on some boxes when it is supported for ISP. Other vendors support both (eMMC and ISP) within the GUI of their software. Although the names at the top of Medusa Pro and Octoplus Pro JTAG software are different, they both utilize the same software for eMMC (direct) and ISP exams. One of the more useful aspects of both Medusa Pro and Octoplus Pro JTAG boxes is that they support both common voltages used for Vcc and VccQ. ISP exams are one of the more time-consuming exams that are currently available. These physical acquisitions are becoming more popular for examiners as they are nondestructive and utilize less resources than chip-off. If the phone pinouts are undocumented, it will require investing in a working test phone and like any form of hobby modeling, lots of patience.

Closing Remarks

The author has in the past 30 chapters attempted to convey techniques, processes, steps, forensic methodologies, and investigative suggestions to the reader. Hopefully you have found something that helps each and everyone of you. What you may locate could help solve a case, bring closure to a family or loved one, or exonerate a wrongfully accused person. Thank you for taking the time to read all of these suggestions. Remember: "Truth is just like a thorn—it may hurt even when it's pulled out." Best wishes to all of you—and stay safe.

References

[1] Model building, June 2010. https://en.wikipedia.org/wiki/Model_building.
[2] IS21ES04G/08G/16G/32G/64G, 4GB/8GB/16GB/32GB/64GB eMMC with eMMC 5.0 Interface Advanced Data Sheet, April 26, 2017. http://www.issi.com/WW/pdf/IS21_22ES04G_08G_16G_32G_64GB.pdf.
[3] eMMCpinouts.com 1 Year Subscription. http://www.fonefunshop.co.uk/cable_picker/100309_eMMCpinouts.com_1_Year_Subscription.html.

Index

'Note: Page numbers followed by "f" indicate figures, "t" indicate tables and "b" indicate boxes.'

+CGMR, 128
+CGSN, 128
+CIMI, 128
+CLAC, 128
+CMGF=?, 129
+CMGF=0, 129
+CNUM, 128
+CPAS, 128
+ICCID=, 128
PM. *See* Permanent Memory (PM)
PM Key 58, 195, 195f
POF. *See* Plenty of Fish (POF)
Pogo pins, 336, 337f
"Point-and-shoot" camera, 164
POP. *See* Package on package
    (POP)
Pop-up window, 148, 360, 385
    Microsoft Windows, 441–442
    Save File, 436
    Scanning, 360
    Windows Security, 362–363
Port(s), 325–326
    COM, 148
    damaged USB data, 143
    HyperTerminal commands, 136
        Data View HHD logged data,
        136, 136f
        Raw Data View HHD logged
        data, 136, 137f
    manual probing test access,
        360–361
    monitoring, 134–137
    phantom, 143
    tab, 147
    unsupported phone and locked
        USB, 156–157
Portable Operating System
    Interface time (POSIX
    time), 219–220
"Powered-on" mobile phone, 15–16
"Precision Soldering", 343
    units, 343
Preferred Roaming List (PRL), 65
Preheater. BAKU 853, 319, 319f
Premade jigs for Nokia phones,
    336, 337f
Premade pin boards, 336, 337f
Premapped pinout location, 470,
    471f
Prepping board, 395–396, 395f

board holder, 396, 396f
    removing moisture, 396
Printed circuit board (PCB), 324,
    395f, 462
PRL. *See* Preferred Roaming List
    (PRL)
Project-A-Phone, 159
    Flex, 159, 160f
    ICD-8000, 159, 160f
Property list files (Plist files), 227
Proprietary cable
    to RJ45 connection, 121
    to USB connection, 121
Proprietary files, 181
Proprietary physical file system,
    195
Proprietary readers, 180
Proprietary systems, 206
Protocol, 120
    communication, 124
    Description Unit format, 195
    logging, 152
    Protocol Log, 150
Protocol Description Unit (PDU),
    129, 195, 211, 237–238,
    238f, 242f
PST. *See* Pacific Standard Time
    (PST)
PSTN. *See* Public Switched
    Telephone Network
    (PSTN)
PTP mode. *See* Picture Transfer
    Protocol mode (PTP mode)
Public Land Mobile Network
    (PLMN), 77
Public Switched Telephone
    Network (PSTN), 66, 68
    cellular to cellular call, 69f
    cellular to landline call, 69f
PUK. *See* Person Unlocking Key
    (PUK)
"Pull behind"–type trailer, 144

Q

Quad-band, 56–57
Qualcomm, 394
Qualcomm BREW, 225
Query Modem, 127, 147, 147f
Quick Access ISP Information, 38
Quick filter, 41

R

R/W memory. *See* Read–Write
    memory (R/W memory)
Rainbow tables, 286, 294–295,
    295f
RAM. *See* Random access memory
    (RAM)
Random access memory
    (RAM), 74
RandomTask finder, 434
Rational expression, 450
Read Partitions Data, 383
Read Target Flash, 383
Read-only memory (ROM), 74
Read/reading
    area displays, 270–271
    button, 435
    eMMC/SD card, 366
    JTAG Finder, 386
    memory, 370, 437f
    target flash, 384–386
        example of JTAG, 386f
Read–Write memory (R/W
    memory), 441
Reballing method, 425–426
Rebooting, 134
Recovering data, 4
"Recovery" process, 29
regexp. *See* Regular expression
    (regex)
Regular expression (regex), 450
    RegEx (GREP) tab, 450
    searching, 450–451
        domain only expressions,
        452–453
        Email regular expressions,
        452–454
        fraud-related regular
        expressions, 453–454
        GPS devices, 454
        GREP, 451
        internet and miscellaneous
        related regular expressions,
        454
        working examples, 451
Relay Nodes (RN), 59
Removable storage, 99
Replay Protected Memory Block
    (RPMB), 439–440
Report process, 107, 171